JERUSALEM
UNBOUND

GEOGRAPHY, HISTORY, AND THE FUTURE OF THE HOLY CITY

MICHAEL DUMPER

Columbia University Press
New York

Columbia University Press
Publishers Since 1893
New York   Chichester, West Sussex
cup.columbia.edu
Copyright © 2014 Columbia University Press
All rights reserved

Library of Congress Cataloging-in-Publication Data
Dumper, Michael, author.
Geography, history, and the future of the holy city / Michael Dumper.
p. cm.
Includes bibliographical references and index.
ISBN 978-0-231-16196-1 (cloth: alk. paper)—ISBN 978-0-231-53735-3 (e-book)
1. Jerusalem—History.   2. Jerusalem—International status.
3. Jerusalem—Boundaries.   4. Jerusalem—Ethnic relations.   5. Israeli West
Bank Barrier.   6. Arab-Israeli conflict—1993—Peace.   7. Arab-Israeli
conflict—1993—Territorial questions.   8. Diplomatic negotiations
in international disputes.   I. Title.
DS109.15.D86 2014
956.94′42—dc23
2013039550

Columbia University Press books are printed on
permanent and durable acid-free paper.

This book is printed on paper with recycled content.
Printed in the United States of America
c 10 9 8 7 6 5 4 3 2 1
Cover Design: Jordan Wannemacher
Cover Image: © AP Images

To my brother and sister, Nicholas and Hildegard

CONTENTS

Acknowledgments ix
Abbreviations xiii

INTRODUCTION 1

1. THE HARD BORDERS OF THE CITY 19

2. THE "SOFTER" BORDERS OF THE CITY 54

3. THE SCATTERED BORDERS OF HOLINESS 97

4. THE INTERNATIONAL COMMUNITY
AND THE LIMITS OF SOVEREIGNTY 146

5. JERUSALEM IN THE TWENTY-FIRST CENTURY:
WHAT PROSPECT OF PEACE? 186

Appendix: Web Site and Facebook Surveys 237
Notes 265
Bibliography 307
Index 325

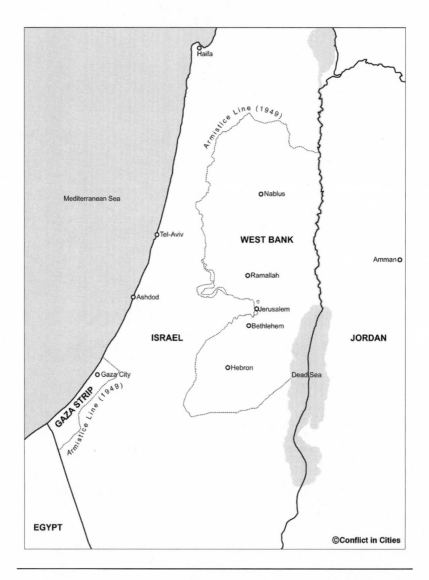

MAP 0.1. Jerusalem and Region

ACKNOWLEDGMENTS

T HERE ARE SCORES of people who have helped in writing this book. Some did so directly by agreeing to be interviewed or by providing feedback, advice, and introductions to others. Others did so indirectly through informal conversations, though mealtimes at their homes with their friends and families, and by letting me share a part of their lives. I offer them all my deepest and most humble thanks for their time and effort, which they gave freely and graciously. This whole endeavor would have been much poorer without their support and interest. In particular, I would like to thank my colleagues who worked closely with me on the Conflict in Cities and the Contested State project—Wendy Pullan, Liam O'Dowd, James Anderson, Max Sternberg, Britt Baillie, Rami Nasrallah, and Haim Yaacobi. Of this excellent team I would like especially to mention three people: Craig Larkin, my research associate for the five-year duration of the project—our collaborative study of the city was a highlight of the project for me; Lefkos Kyriacou, the cartographer of the project, who put many hours into developing the maps used in this book and also supplied some of the photographs; and Razan Makhlouf, my fieldwork research assistant and photographer whose photographs are also included in this book. Much appreciation must also go to Adam Whittock for helping in the preparation of the manuscript for publication.

In Jerusalem and the region there are almost too many people to mention but in particular I would like to thank Amneh Badran, Azem Bishara, Hillel Cohen, Ray Dolphin, Fouad Hallak, Mahmoud Hawari, Kevork Hintlian, Hiba Husseini, Adnan Husseini, Huda Iman, Nazmi al-Ju'beh, Haifa Khalidi, Israel Kimhi, Menachem Klein, Ruth Lapidoth, Awad Mansour, Meir Margalit, Yusuf Natshe, Mazen Qupti, Amnon Ramon, Yitzhak Rieter, Bernard Sabella, Maha Samaan, Patricia Sellick, Danny Seideman, and Salim Tamari. Their encouragement often went beyond the call of duty, and I am grateful for their time and insights, in some cases, their friendship and hospitality. Others not resident in Jerusalem were also of great help. These include Trond Bakkevig, Marshall Breger, John Bell, Michael Bell, Rosemary Hollis, and Mike Molloy. All the aforementioned people may have contributed to my understanding of the dynamics of the city, but they are in no way responsible for any mistakes or inaccuracies. Finally I would like to thank by wife, best friend, and partner, Ann, and my two boys, Rowan and Declan, for their forbearance during the course of writing this book. When I was physically at home, I was often either locked in my study or mentally and emotionally in Jerusalem.

I would also like to thank the Economic and Social Research Council for providing the funds to conduct the research on this book. The full title of the project is Conflict in Cities and the Contested State: Everyday Life and the Possibilities for Transformation in Belfast, Jerusalem and Other Divided Cities (Research Grant No: RES-060–25–0015).

◊ ◊ ◊

A note on the transliteration of Arabic and Hebrew words and names into English is required. One of the main problems in arriving at a consistent transliteration system has been the crossover of Arabic and Hebrew names. Many English transliterations of Arabic names are actually transliterations of Hebrew transliterations of Arabic. A good example is the way in many English texts al-Azariyya (transliteration from the Arabic) is spelt Eizariya (English transliteration of the Hebrew transliteration of the Arabic).[1] Tracking down the actual Hebrew or Arabic spelling to transliterate is not always easy, and some inconsistencies have crept in for which I apologize. In the main this book uses the transliteration system followed by the *International Journal of Middle East Studies* except where English names a better known; for example, I use Bethlehem, not Bayt Lahm (Arabic), Temple Mount, not Har Habayit (Hebrew). However, I do use Haram al-Sharif rather than its English translation, the Noble Enclosure, which is not so well used and I find to be an ugly translation.

ABBREVIATIONS

ACRI	Association for Civil Rights in Israel
CEC	Central Elections Commission
EU	European Union
IDRC	International Development Research Centre
OPTs	Occupied Palestinian Territories
PLC	Palestinian Legislative Council
PLO	Palestinian Liberation Organization
PA	Palestinian Authority
PNA	Palestinian National Authority
NGO	Nongovernmental Organization
UN	United Nations
UNCC	UN Conciliation Commission on Palestine
UNCTAD	UN Conference on Trade and Development
UNDOF	UN Disengagement Observer Force
UNDP	UN Development Program
UNEF	UN Emergency Force
UNESCO	UN Educational, Scientific and Cultural Organization
UNGA	UN General Assembly
UN GAOR	UN General Assembly Official Records
UNHCR	UN High Commissioner for Refugees

UNICEF	UN Children's Fund
UNIFIL	UN Interim Force in Lebanon
UNISPAL	UN Information System on the Question of Palestine
UNOCHA	UN Office for the Coordination of Humanitarian Assistance
UNOGIL	UN Observation Group in Lebanon
UNRWA	UN Relief and Works Agency for Palestine Refugees in the Near East
UNSC	UN Security Council
UNSCOP	UN Special Committee on Palestine
UNSCMEPP	UN Special Coordinator for the Middle East Peace Process
UNTSO	UN Truce Supervision Organization

JERUSALEM UNBOUND

INTRODUCTION

Only when borders disappear does the need arise to construct walls.

—RÉGIS DEBRAY, *ÉLOGE DES FRONTIÈRES*

TANDING ON THE Mount of Olives that looks down over the historic centre of Jerusalem, an observer would be struck by several contradictory
impressions. At first sight, she would notice the many and varied architectural styles that are scattered throughout the valleys and ridges below
and even inside the walled Old City itself. From Chalcedonian shrines to
Byzantine basilicas, from Mamluk domes and minarets to Ottoman forti-
fications, from British colonial facades to Israeli modernist high-rises and
hotels, these all reflect the consecutive conquests and occupations that the
city has been subjected to. Also from this vantage point, a long-sighted
observer would notice, despite its prominence in the world's media and corridors of power, how small the city is. Comprising less than 1 million inhabitants, on a clear day one can see the outer limits of the city in all directions.[1]
Indeed, when traffic is light you can drive from north to south or from
east to west in less than ten minutes. The astute observer would also surely
notice a revealing absence in the landscape—no chimney stacks and smoke
polluting the air—both telltale signs of the lack of heavy industry, of manufacturing, and of mining industries. This would lead our observer to register the barrenness of the surrounding hills, the paucity of the agricultural
hinterland especially in the dry summer months, and the absence of large
stretches of parkland and trees—all indicating a scarcity of water. A reflec-
tive observer would then ponder as to why such a small city with so little

obvious economic attributes and assets could be the focus of so much political interest and military strife. Thus at the heart of the study of Jerusalem lays the peculiar conundrum of the city—it has had little military or strategic value but, at the same time, it is sought after and contested by many. It is no coincidence, for example, that during his occupation of the region at the turn of the nineteenth century, Napoleon Bonaparte, the secularist from revolutionary France, ignored Jerusalem and focused his attentions on the coastal cities of Jaffa and Acre. Others, however, have expended vast resources in wealth and lives attempting to seize control over the city. Why?

The answer to this conundrum and the set of contradictory images I have just described really lies closer to the foreground of the observer's gaze— almost at her feet. Looking down the hill, one can see the ancient Jewish cemetery stretching down to the Garden of Gethsemane, which in turn borders the Muslim cemetery abutting the walls of the Old City. The Old City of Jerusalem!—the walled core of the city which is both the key to the kingdom of a peaceful agreement between Israelis and Palestinians and also the eye of its never-ending storm. For Jerusalem is a city that is uniquely sacred: it contains the holiest sites of Judaism, Christianity, and Islam—the dual Muslim-Jewish site of the Temple Mount and the Haram al-Sharif and the Church of the Holy Sepulchre. These are all to be found in the Old City, which, on one hand, has profound eschatological significance as the site of "the end of days" and, on the other, is deemed holy in toto—not just specific sites, but the whole city, and not just to one religion but to all three. Furthermore, as it is clear from our vantage point on the Mount of Olives, the holy sites of these religions are not only close beside each other but also on top of each other, are reluctantly shared by each other and, alas, at the same time, deeply contested. The ramifications of this enduring fact are the core of the study of this book.

This will be my third book on Jerusalem and the need for another to accompany my first two requires some explanation.[2] In the early 1990s, when I first started researching and writing on Jerusalem, there was a dearth of both primary and secondary sources to work from. The study by the former Israeli deputy mayor of Jerusalem, Meron Benvenisti, *The Torn City*, was the only book of much value to a researcher.[3] There were a number of microstudies carried out by the Israeli research center, the Jerusalem Institute for Israel Studies, and an anthropological study by Michael Roman and Alex Weingrod, but apart from these very little else.[4] However, since the Oslo Accord in 1993—and the opening up of the possibility of some sort of political reconfiguration of the city to allow for a formal Palestinian political presence in the city—there has been a plethora of books on the city's past, present, and future.[5] Menachem Klein's *Jerusalem: The Contested City* is an excellent in-depth study and complemented my first book on the city, *The Politics of Jerusalem Since 1967*, very well.[6] Then, due to the large number of discussion fora and conferences on the topic of the city, there emerged in the late 1990s and early 2000s several compilations that have added a great deal to our understanding of the dynamics in the city. Marshall Breger and Ora Ahimeir's *Jerusalem: A City and Its Future* and Philipp Misselwitz and Tim Rieniets's *City of Collision* are particularly noteworthy.[7] These studies, which take a broader and more encompassing approach to the study of the city, have also been supplemented by narrower and more focused studies. In the same category one should mention Yitzhak Rieter's study of the role of the Islamic movement in Jerusalem, Sami Musallem's Palestinian perspective of the struggle over Jerusalem, and the controversy over the reconstruction of the Jewish Quarter in the Old City by Simone Ricca.[8] In addition, Jerusalem has become the subject of numerous reports by governmental and nongovernmental bodies, international agencies such as the UN, and research institutes, almost too many to absorb and process.[9] Finally, there have been a large number of excellent journal articles that have stood the test of time and are worthy of repeat readings. Perhaps the most influential on my own understanding of the political dynamics unfolding in the city have been two (no less) by Ian Lustick, the first entitled "Has Israel Annexed Jerusalem?" and the second, "Reinventing Jerusalem."[10]

WHY ANOTHER BOOK ON JERUSALEM?

In the light of all this research and publications why is there a need for another tome on the city. I have three reasons for wishing to write another study of the city. First, events in Jerusalem move rapidly and it is already ten years since Klein brought out his book—the last significant and sole-authored overall study of the contemporary city. The study of the city is in urgent need of an update, particularly in the light of the impasse in the negotiations between the two sides. What would be useful to policy makers, researchers, students, the media, and activists is a kind of stocktaking exercise which incorporates the research of the past decade and outlines the main directions of travel in the emerging social, economic, and political trends. A second reason for undertaking this work is that for the past five years I have been part of a project entitled Conflict in Cities and the Contested State.[11] Funded by the UK Economic and Social Research Council, the project focuses on both Belfast and Jerusalem as primary targets of research, and, with my colleague from Cambridge University's School of Architecture, Dr. Wendy Pullan, I have been responsible for much of the Jerusalem research, supervising a research fellow and a research assistant on three discrete research modules. The result has been a series of working papers, journal articles, conference papers, seminar presentations, and huge quantities of fieldwork notes, site observations, and interview notes. This material is original and is crying out for a synthesis and deeper analysis.

A particular feature of the Conflict in Cities project is that it is interdisciplinary, involving sociologists, urban planners, political geographers, anthropologists, architects, and architectural historians. Their insights, drawn from theoretical frameworks and methodologies that are quite different from mine as a political scientist, have opened my eyes to new approaches to and new relationships between the sets of empirical data. For example, my analysis of the separation barrier bisecting Jerusalem (or the Wall, as it is sometimes referred to) was quite conventional. But, after listening to my architectural and geography colleagues, I was able to see how the physical erection of the barrier itself, intimidating as it is, grotesquely rupturing communities and neighborhoods and destroying businesses, is, nevertheless, not the whole story. As my project colleague Wendy Pullan has noted, in construction terms it has no foundations. The Wall simply rests on a wide concrete base, but is not secured into the ground and thus could be easily removed (or tipped over in an earthquake!).[12] I now realize that, in studying the barrier, what is also important to focus on is the enforced reorientation of the daily life of the inhabitants in the vicinity of the barrier away from it. This can be most obviously seen in the network of new roads and new services and amenities that have been built as a result of its construction. The barrier or wall may be temporary, but the roads and new institutions will lead to lasting changes as people build their lives around them. This kind of insight comes from interacting with those who have knowledge of engineering, structural design, urban planning, and sociology. As a political scientist focusing on power and political groupings, I would have missed this broader picture. There are many other insights that debates with my colleagues from the Conflict in Cities team have stimulated. It has changed by perspective on Jerusalem and has enriched my understanding of the complex dynamics in the city. In writing this book, it is from this well of inspiration that I intend to draw.

The third reason for writing a third book on the city is that I wish to develop and explore a new argument, which I believe will contribute to the rational debate over the city's future. The main argument of this book will be that as a consequence of its rich, complex history and the intersecting religious and political interests in the city, Jerusalem is what can be termed *a many-bordered city*. Before I explain this idea further, I should make sure that the reader is familiar with the various geographic areas included in the designation Jerusalem. The Palestinian Arab name for Jerusalem is al-Quds (or "the holy") and refers to a range of different areas. These can at different times include the walled Old City of Jerusalem, the Jerusalem of the British mandate, which comprises both the new city to the West and the older parts to the east, the six square kilometers of the area of the Arab municipality that existed during the Jordanian period between 1949 and 1967, and the wider East Jerusalem area of seventy square kilometres added after the Israeli occupation in 1967. More recently, the Palestinian designated Jerusalem governorate has comprised a Jerusalem 1 and a Jerusalem 2 sector with the former being an electoral district almost congruent with the borders of East Jerusalem (see the maps in chapter 1) For Israelis, Jerusalem is called Yerushalayim (the "abode of peace") which comprises, like the Palestinians, different delineations of the city over different periods. In this way it includes the walled Old City, the new city of the British Mandate period, West Jerusalem of the partition period, and now the wider post-1967 area. More recently, the notion of Greater Jerusalem encompasses satellite suburbs such as Mevaseret Zion in the west and at least three Israeli settlements built since 1967 in the eastern edges of the city: Maale Adumim, Givat Ze'ev, and Gush Etzion.[13]

My contention in this book is that examination of these areas and formal political borders will not reveal the full dynamics of power and control in the city and that a more nuanced approach of disaggregating the functional, political, and social borders is required. This has had a profound impact on its current development and politics, the planning of its future, and on how residents of the city work, play, shop, and pray. For example, the Israeli checkpoints, which used to ring the entry and exit points to the city and which are now supplemented or replaced by the separation barrier, constitute a security border as impermeable as any international frontier. However, what is very important to understand is that they are not congruent with the political border declared by Israel in 1967—the Israeli municipal border within which certain civic services are provided and throughout which Israel has sought to impose its legal jurisdiction. This lack of congruity leaves many areas of occupied East Jerusalem in a twilight zone where citizenship, property rights, and the enforcement of the rule of law are ambiguous. At the same time, it also suggests areas of greater flexibility over a negotiated agreement on the city. Another example of the many-bordered phenomenon is what can be termed the education borders, that is, the distinct areas where either the Jordanian-Palestinian or the Israeli curriculum is taught in schools, which reveal a pattern of ongoing segregation despite over forty years of Israeli domination in East Jerusalem. In many areas there is no difference between the urban areas of the West Bank (under Palestinian jurisdiction) and East Jerusalem (under Israeli jurisdiction) as the Palestinian curriculum is taught right up to the Armistice Lines of 1949 (the Green Line) and does not stop further east, as most other Israeli laws do, at the Israeli municipal borders created in 1967. In this sense one can say that there is a separate Palestinian education border that ignores the political and security borders and remains at the Green Line. These overlapping functional and political borders indicate that there needs to be a highly complex and multilayered division of responsibilities in any peace agreement. A study of the recently constructed security barrier or wall will be analyzed in this broader context.

FOUR THEMES

Within this overall argument, four main themes will be explored which are both derived from the many-bordered character of the city and, at the same time, contribute to the emergence of such overlapping and diverging borders. The first theme draws attention to the paradox at the heart of the Jerusalem question. Whereas Israelis and Palestinians both aspire for the city to be their national capital, thus to assert their national sovereignties over the city, the religious and highly internationalized nature of the city places extensive limitations on state sovereignty. Even with complete military control, Israel has not been free to act with impunity in the city and is obliged to accommodate historical precedents and international law while exercising its sovereignty. The book will explore this paradoxical theme through the notion of the many-bordered city, an argument that runs through all the chapters of the book.

The second theme is the pattern of resacralization of the city. Perhaps a more accurate term is the *religious reclamation* of the city, since the city has always been religious and holy. However, there is a contemporary tenor to religious contestation in the city which needs to be distinguished from that which preceded it. Here the start and end point of the theme may be the management and development of the Jewish, Christian, and Muslim holy places, but it also encompasses the penetration of the Israeli settler movement, with its messianic agenda, into the different agencies of the Israeli state concerned with Jerusalem. Not only have they acquired Jewish heritage sites as bridgeheads for further expansion in Palestinian residential areas, but their supporters have attained important positions in the Israeli Jerusalem Municipality and National Parks Authority, the Jewish National Fund, and the Israeli Antiquities Authority. A mirroring dynamic has been the growing importance of Muslim holy sites in the mobilization of Palestinian nationalist sentiment and the emergence of Palestinian Islamists from inside Israel as a significant political force as defenders of the al-Aqsa Mosque. The prominence given to religious claims in the city will increase what conflict resolution theorists refer to as the "problem of indivisibility"— that is, how does one negotiate or trade goods that are so deeply associated with identity and values?[14] I intend to draw on my personal involvement in interreligious dialogue fora and with off-the-record discussions between Israeli and Palestinian policy makers and their advisers (known as Track 2 discussions) on the holy sites to examine these issues in greater detail.

The third theme places Jerusalem as both a divided city and a partially occupied city in comparative perspective. Cities divided along ethnic, religious, and linguistic lines are not so uncommon. Johannesburg, Montreal, Bradford, and Baghdad are frequently cited examples.[15] But cities which are both divided and are also located in states whose presence in the city is contested and whose borders are disputed are a subcategory of divided cities of special significance. These are cities where a national or ethnopolitical conflict is manifested in their urban space. Such cities include Belfast, Mostar, Kirkuk, and Nicosia, possibly Beirut and Brussels. How these cities are affected by conflict, and how, in turn, the divisions in these cities have an impact on a conflict, present some useful and interesting comparisons with Jerusalem. For example, Mostar, a city that suffered terribly in the civil war of former Yugoslavia between 1992–95, continues to be divided residentially, religiously, economically, educationally, and electorally—despite the formation of the Croat-Serb-Bosniak federation of Bosnia-Herzegovina. Muslim Bosniaks fear their role in the city is being constrained by the desire of the Bosniak Sarajevo political elite to offer their Croat partners a regional capital in the same way that the Bosnians Serbs have Banja Luka and the Bosniaks have Sarajevo. Thus the reconstruction and reconciliation processes are hampered at city level by the compromises being delivered at the national level. The relationship between the divided city and the contested state is highly volatile and can spin into either virtuous or vicious spirals. The role played by external regional and international actors, by religious leaders, by the policies of residential segregation and the discriminatory use of public shared space are all important factors such cities hold in common. Yet what are as interesting and revealing are the differences, rather than the similarities, within this subcategory. This perspective will be used to delineate those features in Jerusalem which are shared by other similar cities and those which may remain unique to the city.

A final theme has already been touched upon and that is the role of external actors in the history and the future plans for Jerusalem. Much attention has been given to the role of the U.S. and the EU and their attempts to keep alive the Palestinian-Israeli negotiations over the city. What has received less scrutiny has been the involvement of less overtly political actors such as the Islamic Development Bank and Christian and Jewish diaspora organizations and NGOs. These have all had a significant impact upon alleviating poverty conditions, providing training and education, and indirectly contributing to the resilience of both of the main ethnic communities in the city. An important role has also been played by intergovernmental organizations such as UNESCO; its controversial inscription of the Old City on its World Heritage List has drawn the UN agency into the minutiae of the excavation, restoration, and planning issues in the city, bringing upon it the criticism and opprobrium of both parties to the conflict who feel their interests are not being protected sufficiently. Nevertheless, as holder of the global and universal benchmarks for preservation and the management of cultural sites, it is well placed to have an important monitoring and supervisory role. Examining the role of these external actors at their different levels of operation will both contextualize their engagement but also allow us to evaluate their impact and effectiveness in conflict resolution.

CHAPTER OUTLINES

These four themes and the main argument that Jerusalem is a city of many and shifting borders weave in and out of the five chapters of this book. Although focusing largely on the post-1967 period, and in particular the period after the collapse of the last significant political negotiations, the Camp David summit of 2000, it will also make reference to earlier periods. The different chapters will each highlight examples of the many borders of Jerusalem, examining the range of factors that impinge upon the urban and political fabric of the city and the fluidity of the situation on the ground. They will also explore in greater detail the four themes I have described: the constraints on secular power, the resacralization of the city, comparative perspectives on its divided and occupied nature, and the role of external actors. Chapter 1, for example, will concentrate on the visible or "hard" borders of the city, taking as its starting point the separation barrier under construction around parts of the city since 2003.[16] It will examine the debates around the barrier, its impact on the hinterland, and the positive and negative results that have flowed from its construction in both urban and political terms. In order to explain the construction of the barrier, the chapter will then proceed to examine the question of the city's political and security borders more deeply. It will examine the expansion of the city's borders from 1948, and its establishment of the national capital of the Israeli state, through to the dramatic growth of the city after 1967. The main focus will be the tension between the attempt by the Israeli government to assert its political control over the new borders and its inability to consolidate a hegemonic presence in the eastern part of the city. All four themes play an important in our understanding of these dynamics.

Chapter 2 will turn the reader's attention to the more subtle phenomenon of the porosity of these borders on other levels. To be more specific, the chapter will focus on a range of subnational, functional, and residential borders which are to most people invisible. By examining the "lived-in" city and how patterns of residence, of employment, of commerce have evolved and changed, one can delineate the impact this has had on the way the city is governed. The lack of congruence between political and military borders, on the one hand, and these social and functional borders, on the other, plays an important part in understanding how and why Jerusalem is a "many-bordered city." It also points to the likelihood of complex structures of coordination between Israelis and Palestinians in any future political agreement.[17] While clearly echoing the experience of other divided cities, the main themes that emerge from this chapter are the constraints of secular power and the role of external actors, particularly in the form of international law.

Chapter 3 explores the impact of the presence of the holy sites on the politics and urban development of the city. It is a chapter where all the four themes outlined here have an important role to play. The chapter also forms a discrete case study of the many-borders thesis in that it highlights how the religious sites of the city have created an archipelago of semiautonomous enclaves in the city that, in turn, have placed restrictions on the exercise of state sovereignty. While it is an argument that has been explored in my second book on Jerusalem, *The Politics of Sacred Space*, this chapter will present new research focusing on how such restrictions on state power have opened up a highly contested political space in which religious groups are competing for control. The chapter will explore the exploitation of these religious enclaves for political ends by focusing on the role of Israeli settlers, the use of archaeology and conservation, and the growing involvement of radical Islamist groups in direct action in an attempt to reverse the encroachments by the settlers. The response of the Israeli government in the form of heightened security presence, the contracting out of some security services to private companies, and the domination of settler groups in key state institutions concerned with land use in Jerusalem will also be examined, which will suggest revealing parallels with the situation in Hebron—a similarly divided city with internal security and political borders.

Chapter 4 further develops the argument of Jerusalem being a city of many borders by turning to the last theme in more detail. The reader's attention is drawn to the critical role played by the international community in supporting or undermining specific developments in the city. There are few other cities in the world where the international community, especially the U.S., UN, EU, and the Arab and Islamic world, has demonstrated such an interest in how a city is governed. While ostensibly playing the role of facilitators, these important actors are in many ways both competing with each other and with the main protagonists, the Israeli government and the PLO, in attempting to frame the agenda for discussing the city's future and its borders. The focus of this chapter will be on the diplomatic maneuvering that has taken place since 2000, with an emphasis on discussion concerning the relevance of previously internationally agreed borders and armistice lines. Debates concerning the controversial recommendations of the EU

Heads of Mission Reports on Jerusalem, the relocating of the U.S. embassy, the work of UN bodies, such as UNESCO's "reinforced monitoring mechanism," and the role of the donor communities all reveal the engagement of these actors in the minutiae of the configurations of the city.

The fifth and concluding chapter will examine developments in political negotiations between Israelis and Palestinians since 1993 in light of the research presented in this book. It will include a dissection of the various proposals mooted at both the formal peace negotiations—Camp David, Taba, Annapolis, the Mitchell process, etc.—but also those put forward by civil society organizations such as the Geneva Initiative and the Jerusalem Old City Initiative. Borders are at the heart of their discussions. The intention will be to link these political discussions to a detailed knowledge of the impact they will have on the ground. A section of the chapter will suggest a possible formulation for bridging the different concerns and aspirations of the two parties. The chapter closes by attempting to identify the key trends that are emerging both on the ground in the city but also in the corridors of power. The primary aim of such a task will be to peer over the horizon, so to speak, in order to sketch out the likely contours of, on one hand, a durable political agreement over the city and, on the other, the likely consequences if such an agreement is not reached.

This book is entitled *Jerusalem Unbound: Geography, History, and the Future of the Holy City*. The focus on Jerusalem should be explained more fully. In essence, I in common with many others are convinced that without a peace agreement on Jerusalem there will not be a peace agreement between Israel and the Palestinians, nor between Israel and the rest of the Arab world. In fact, the absence of an agreement will not just mean the absence of peace and the continuation of the current stasis. It will mean more than that. It will mean ongoing conflict in and around the city, year after year of low-level violence with spasms of conflagration and high-intensity conflict breaking out. The situation in the city is not stable, and its links to the wider conflict draw both outside forces and the conflict in the region into the city. But, by elevating Jerusalem to this status as "deal breaker," I am not overlooking the other issues, such as borders, security, water, Israeli settlements, etc. (known in the Middle East peace process as the permanent status issues) that have yet to be resolved. In particular, I am aware of the huge chasm that separates the two sides over the Palestinian refugee issue and the inconceivable probability that Israel will allow even a small fraction of the refugees languishing in camps in Jordan, Syria, Lebanon, Sinai, the West Bank, and Gaza Strip to return to their ancestral homes.[18] However, it is much likelier that those problems will be finessed and resolved if the conflict over Jerusalem issue is resolved, and the converse is not true. If those problems are resolved, their resolution will not impinge on the resolution of the Jerusalem issue in the same way. Jerusalem is, in effect, sui generis, and, in the jargon of the conflict resolution discipline, *nontradeable* or *non-fungible*. A nonagreement or a poor agreement on Jerusalem cannot be exchanged for a resolution of the other outstanding permanent status issues.

For the fact of the matter is that Jerusalem has an existential dimension in the national state-building project of each side. Its role over the past several decades in religious, cultural, and national identity of both Israelis and Palestinians has led to a situation of a zero-sum game, where if one side gains the other side loses, thus making compromise almost impossible. Despite the hours of discussion, despite the reams of paper, the miles of travel, and the millions of dollars spent on meetings and workshops, the prospect of a resolution is still very distant. No doubt, compared to the period before the Oslo Accord in 1993, considerable progress has been made. There is, for example, grudging recognition by the Palestinians of Israeli security concerns, of the permanence of some of the Israeli settlements, and of the attachment of Israeli Jews to the Jewish holy places in the city. For their part, the Israelis are no longer quite as insistent on incorporating all the peripheral Palestinian suburbs and villages into an Israeli Jerusalem; they understand how an enlarged Israeli Jerusalem will bisect the West Bank and disrupt the integrity of a future Palestinian state and they mostly accept that Palestinians should be custodians of their own shrines. Nevertheless, the question of sovereignty in the heart of the city, particularly over the Old City, and the impact of the passage of time in reordering the lived-in borders of the city, with possibly irreversible shifts in the population distribution, has made an Israeli withdrawal from key areas and Palestinian concessions over sovereignty more and more improbable. Hence the importance of trying to understand and explain the changes and shifting dynamics of the city, and hence, ultimately, the purpose of this book.

My main argument in this book centers on the notion of "a many-bordered city," and, clearly, the meaning of borders needs to be explored in this introduction. In the book I use terms such as *hard, soft, visible, invisible,* and *scattered* borders. These are all rather inadequate stumblings toward a definition that tries to encompass both fluidity and a range of specificities. Before I attempt to explain further, I should briefly introduce to the general reader some of the difficulties that academics have in coming to a clear and robust set of definitions regarding the meaning of borders and boundaries. In the disciplines of political geography and political science, in particular, there is quite a subdiscipline concerned with walls and borders. There is a pretty wide consensus that such demarcations are a post-seventeenth-century phenomenon that emerged with the concept of state sovereignty.[19] As Paul Hirst argues: "Borders existed before the modern state, but they were mainly zones of control, like the Roman *limes*, or shifting lines of conquest and colonisation between rival civilisations."[20] As states consolidated their institutions and were able to project power and control territory in a sustained fashion through standing armies, roads, and the subjection of population, so too did the borders between one polity and another become clearer and more defined. In modern times the border between two states is transformed from a disputed area or a zone of control into a line. In turn, by differentiating the "us" from the "other," borders became vital instruments in the construction of a supratribal and supraregional national identities.[21]

In urban areas and in divided cities, this clarity loses some force and is more complex. A line through a city, if it is a hard impermeable line like a wall, divides the city into two or more parts. It is no longer one city but at least two. In order for there to be a minimum level of what is called urban functionality, cities require a degree of porosity and what the scholar of urban planning in divided cities, Scott Bollens, refers to as a "flexibility of urban form."[22] Thus in divided, conflicted, and contested cities a wide range of demarcations between ethnic, religious, and national groups and areas can be found which, at the same time, still preserve the integrity of the urban form of the city. These range from highly visible prisonlike walls to more imperceptible signs of division such as the language and script of street names. In fact, Peter Marcuse has pulled together a typology of urban "walls" consisting of five categories.

- Prison walls are designed to preserve a group's identity through segregation
- Barricade walls have the same function but comprise symbols such as street signs and colours of a national flag.
- Walls of aggression express military domination through fences, barriers, checkpoints and patrols.
- Sheltering walls are the classic gated communities for the rich and privileged where entry but not exit is denied.
- Castle walls are usually for government compounds and the homes and offices of the premier politician.[23]

While these categories are not sacrosanct, and many will find them too imprecise for the city or group of cities they are studying, nevertheless, the virtue of this typology is more to draw attention to the fact that cities are criss-crossed with different kinds of borders and demarcations that can take on national and political significance in certain instances. There is also, for example, the way community and neighborhood identities are demarcated by acts of violence and the emergence of "no-go" areas.[24] This is particularly relevant in the case of many of the cities studied in the Conflict in Cities project where the presence and legitimacy of the state is contested and where the borders have yet to be finalized in the sense of an agreement being arrived at.

To add to the complexity in coming to an understanding of the meaning of borders is the impact of globalization, not just upon the post-Westphalian state but also upon cities themselves. Across the world we are seeing overlapping and multilayered frameworks being constructed which regulate economic unions, cross-border and pan-continental security cooperation, and environmental agreements. The chief result of this for our argument is the way in which, through globalization and international cooperation, functional borders diverge from national-territorial and political borders.

The European Union as a whole is a good example of this, and the Schengen Agreement security zone within the EU demonstrates this point even more clearly.[25] This disaggregation of borders into political and a range of other functional borders is central to our understanding of the dynamics taking place in Jerusalem today.

The many-bordered city thesis of this book was first mentioned, almost in passing, in my first book on Jerusalem in 1996.[26] In 2005 Menachem Klein developed the idea of the internal walls of the city further in an article entitled "Old and New Walls in Jerusalem." Here he used the idea to demonstrate the different forms of control that Israel exerts over the Palestinian population and how it would preempt Palestinian aspirations for the city.[27] My thesis in this book differs slightly from his in that the emphasis is not so much to illustrate the different forms of control but more how the fluidity and imprecision of the borders in Jerusalem create opportunities for political agreement over the future of the city. Earlier I referred to how, in chapter 2, I will look at a number of functional borders or demarcations such as residential segregation and the parallel education system. These I have characterized as enclaves and "soft" borders in contrast to the "hard" borders of walls, armistice agreements, and military checkpoints, and these terms need some justification.

First, with regard to enclaves, my contention is that the Israeli occupation of East Jerusalem since 1967 and the alteration of the city, as a result of its infrastructural development and demographic changes, have led to the "enclaving" of the eastern part of the city. East Jerusalem is not simply occupied militarily, with the population and layout of that part of the city left intact under military supervision. It has been transformed into virtually an Israeli Jewish city with small islands of Palestinian residency, commerce, and culture. The implantation of Israeli colonies or settlements in East Jerusalem has been accompanied by all the infrastructural paraphernalia of connecting roads, services, and security systems that have sliced up East Jerusalem into pieces and surrounded the Palestinians areas. The resilience of these Palestinians enclaves in the face of this onslaught is the focus of chapter 2, and I will not expand on this aspect at this point. However, the use of the term *enclave* is deliberate, as it conveys a sense being encircled, of being detached, and of belonging to something else. It is not meant to also convey the erroneous impression that these enclaves are surrounded by walls like large prisons. There are prisonlike features to these enclaves, in the form of continual Israeli surveillance and monitoring, but for most of the time there is freedom of movement to adjacent areas. There is a porosity to the borders of the enclaves that keeps them part of the city and contributes to its urban functionality in a limited way.

I also refer in this book to the city as having *soft* borders. As illustrations of this I look at the differentiated application of Israeli law to East Jerusalem, which has created a number of important anomalies in the way Israeli jurisdiction operates, the separate educational systems and curricula, the parallel processes of political representation for Israelis and Palestinians in the city, and the degree of autonomy experienced by the religious hierarchies in the city, and how they together create a series of overlapping and overlaying borders in the city. But by soft I do not mean that these functional borders are in themselves accessed by both Israelis and Palestinians

FIGURE 0.1. View of Old City from the Mount of Olives with participants of a Conflict in Cities project workshop in the foreground (2010).

and hence do not constitute a hard division between them. Israelis do not use the Palestinian educational system in the city or vote in Palestinian presidential elections and vice versa. So in this sense the examples are as *hard* as the municipal borders or the separation barrier, but I use the term *soft* here in the sense that cumulatively these subnational and functional borders "soften" the hard political and military borders. Israeli sovereignty in East Jerusalem is softened at the edges in that it is not applied to East Jerusalem as it is applied to other parts of Israel.

The following chapters explore these issues and draw out their ramifications for the political future of the city. I began writing this book in November 2011 and completed it in November 2012, making some revisions in early 2013. During this period the conflict over the city continued unabated and the prospects for a peaceful and negotiated agreement looked ever more unattainable. Nevertheless, the situation remains dynamic, and regional changes suggest that some new and transforming possibilities may be appearing. We need to remember good things do happen: the Berlin Wall was dismantled, almost literally, by the people it sought to contain and Nelson Mandela walked free from jail and became president of the state that imprisoned him. I recall a New Year's Eve party I attended in the early 1990s. It was at a friend's house in the foothills of the Picos Europas, Spain, where I fell into conversation with the Spanish harpist Xavier Sainz. As the midnight hour passed, and we were sharing our concerns on the year to come, he memorably remarked, "I am an optimist; things could be worse." Yes, things could be worse in Jerusalem, and herein lies a kernel of hope.

1

THE HARD BORDERS OF THE CITY

UST AFTER LUNCH on August 9, 2001, a young Palestinian carrying a
guitar case walked into Sbarro Pizzeria on the corner of King George
and Jaffa Streets, in the heart of Israeli West Jerusalem. The small café
and shop was milling with families, schoolchildren, teenagers, and passing tourists. When the guitar case exploded—packed as it was with nails,
screws, and bolts—it ripped the place apart, killing fifteen people, including
four children under the age of ten, and wounding ninety. It caused may-
hem in the surrounding area as streets were blocked off, traffic halted, shop-
pers and office workers left for home frantically telephoning and texting
in an attempt to track down loved ones, checkpoints ringed the city. Palestinian workers caught in the melee around the central business district
were rounded up by Israeli border police and interrogated. King George
Street was cleared except for emergency vehicles and ambulances with their
sirens wailing and blue lights flashing; Orthodox Jewish medics began their
gruesome task of identifying and scraping together the scattered lumps of
charred flesh into plastic bags so that the victims could be given a decent
burial.[1]

The Israeli intelligence services had been braced for such an attack. The
week before they had carried out the assassination of two senior political
leaders of the radical Palestinian Islamic movement, Hamas, in Nablus, so

it was no surprise that the perpetrator of the Sbarro bombing, Izzidine al-Masri, from the Jenin area of the West Bank, was identified as a member of Hamas. Israel's initial response was a knee-jerk reaction. Holding the PLO leader, Yasser Arafat ultimately responsible, it closed Orient House, the PLO-affiliated office in East Jerusalem, and Israeli jets bombed the main Palestinian National Authority (PNA) police station in Ramallah.[2] But the then Israeli prime minister, Ariel Sharon, also knew that such tit-for-tat responses would not be sufficient to counter the wave of bombings that Hamas and other radical Palestinian groups were carrying out against Israeli targets. According to a report by the Jerusalem Center for Public Affairs, between 2000, the beginning of the second Palestinian uprising, and November 2004, there were 600 different kinds of attacks by Palestinians on Israeli Jews in Jerusalem, killing 210 people and wounding many more See Note 3.[3] One hundred and seventy-four people were killed by suicide bomb attacks on buses, cafes, and in the streets of the city, 14 were killed by gunfire.[4] Another comparative study highlighted the enormity of the overall situation in Jerusalem. During the period 1989–2003, Jerusalem experienced what it defined as 73 terrorist attacks with a total of 2,350 casualties (283 dead and 2,067 wounded). Transposed onto London, with its far greater population, this would be the equivalent of over 23,000 casualties, or roughly 1,500 a year.[5]

Whatever one's views about the legitimacy of Palestinian resistance to the ongoing Israeli occupation and colonization of the West Bank and Gaza Strip, or the confrontational and short-sightedness of the Israeli policies that engendered such attacks, the result of this bombing campaign by Palestinian militants was a national crisis for Israel. Their capital was sliding into a city of fear and danger, recreating the militarized frontier zone it had been during the period between 1948 and 1967. Cafés and shops were heavily securitized, checkpoints were scattered throughout the city, and the mobility of residents and goods was severely curtailed. The dream of the former Israeli mayor of Jerusalem, Teddy Kollek, that Jerusalem would be a mosaic of communities living together was turning into a nightmarish "dead zone" encompassing the heart of the city.[6] On top of this was the impact on property prices and the economy, estimated for the first four years of the uprising to be approximately $1.4 billion.[7] A similar impact can also be detected in other parts of Israel, as tourism declined and the uprising impacted upon inward investment nationally.

It was at the height of this crisis that the Israeli political elite turned to the idea of constructing a barrier to separate the Israeli Jewish population from the Palestinian Arab population of the West Bank. This was to be constructed ostensibly along the 1949 Armistice Lines that marked the de facto borders of the state of Israel.[8] A previously mooted idea, it had been set aside as both impractical and expensive and also preempting the evolution of security understandings with the PNA. The Oslo Accords in 1993 between Israel and the PLO were premised on the idea of two political entities—Israel on land acquired by Jewish communities and Zionist settlers in 1948 and a Palestine on the remnant of mandatory Palestine that had subsequently been occupied by Israel in 1967—the West Bank, Gaza Strip, and East Jerusalem. The accords were an attempt to manage a transition process to this goal of two states. It established, on one hand, a framework for administrative and security cooperation for an interim phase, and, on the other, a timeline for negotiations on what was termed final status issues—borders and security between the two states, the division of water sources and supplies, the future of the Palestinian refugees, the future of the Israeli settlements in the Occupied Palestinian Territories (OPTs), and, finally, the future of the city of Jerusalem. Powers were to be gradually transferred to a body set up for the interim phase, the Palestinian National Authority. In addition, the accords set in train an Israeli withdrawal of its armed forces from the main Palestinian urban areas, known as Area A, but kept its forces in Areas B (designated areas of joint Israeli and Palestinian security responsibilities) and C (Israeli only) until a full withdrawal was agreed upon.

The accords were vehemently opposed by the Israeli right wing and nationalist camp which saw them as selling out the maximalist Zionist dream and surrendering to implacable enemies both the geographical and biblical heart of Judaism. It was equally opposed by many Palestinians who considered the accords a betrayal of the rights of refugees to return to their original homes in what is now the state of Israel and who saw the PNA itself as a stooge of the Israeli state and a puppet of the U.S. government.[9]

Despite this opposition, and despite the mutual suspicion borne out of years of conflict, the implementation of the accords began, haltingly but promisingly. However, Palestinian support for the accords waned rapidly when it became clear that Israeli colonization of the OPTs would continue during the interim phase with Israeli settlements expanding in numbers and size. Throughout the interim phase, new Palestinian land was being appropriated and new settler roads were being rammed through farmland and grazing pastures. By 2002, Israeli settlements and Israeli armed forces had expropriated 59 percent of the West Bank and 20 percent of the Gaza Strip.[10] What made the accords increasingly unpalatable was the realization that the Israeli conception of a future Palestinian state was one that would be heavily circumscribed by Israeli security concerns. Israeli negotiators made it clear that Israel would control the borders of the Palestinian state and the movement of people and goods through them. In addition, the airspace and electromagnetic field (for mobile phones, Internet and satellite signals) of the new state would also be under Israeli jurisdiction, and the Palestinian army limited to small arms. Finally, the Palestinian economy, imports and exports, would be entirely dependent on Israeli grace and favor.[11]

Hamas was able to capitalize upon the growing Palestinian dismay at what was being offered and its attacks against Israeli targets, alongside other groups, increased. Israel, in turn, accused the PLO leader, Arafat, and the PNA security forces of not doing enough to restrain Hamas and, indeed, of being covertly complicit in the support for the anti-Oslo camp. Further bombings in the late 1990s and the opening of a subterranean passage in Jerusalem's Old City in 1996, during which riots Palestinian police forces turned their guns on Israeli soldiers, confirmed Israeli fears over the unreliability of Palestinians. As a result, Israel increasingly acted unilaterally in detaining Palestinian activists, assassinating Palestinian opposition leaders, and carrying out raids and patrols in the Palestinian-controlled Area A. The final nail in the coffin of a cooperative security arrangement came after the collapse of peace negotiations in 2000 between the Israeli prime minister, Ehud Barak, and the Palestinian president, Yasser Arafat, hosted by the U.S. president, Bill Clinton, at Camp David. These negotiations revealed the deep divisions still remaining between the two sides and how their opposing visions of a peace agreement made security cooperation well-nigh impossible. Even before Izzidine al-Masri picked up his guitar case and headed for Jerusalem, the seeds of the idea of a separation barrier had taken root in Israeli security planning. The Sbarro bombing merely added to the momentum moving in that direction.

THE SEPARATION BARRIER

The construction of the separation barrier is regarded as one of the largest infrastructural projects in Israeli history. The original idea was discussed during the period of Yitzhak Rabin's premiership in the 1990s, but was shelved because of the expense and the difficulties in identifying a suitable route that would both provide protection to the Israeli settlements in the West Bank and not deviate too much from the 1949 Armistice Lines. However, when, as we have seen, the political, economic, and social costs of Palestinian infiltration increased, the proposals were reexamined, and in 2003 construction began. The barrier is comprised to a large extent of fencing, ditches, razor wire, combed sandy paths, an electronic monitoring system, patrol roads, and a buffer zone. As such, the barrier can stretch up to 70 meters in width and shows itself as a huge gash in the countryside, cutting through farmland, gardens, olive groves, and pasture. Land for the barrier is requisitioned by the Israeli Ministry of Defense from Palestinian landowners.[12] In urban areas, such as Jerusalem, Bethlehem, Tulkarm, and Qalqiliya, the barrier takes the form of a 28-foot-high concrete wall made up of connected segmented slabs. The height and opaqueness is partly to prevent snipers shooting at Israeli vehicles and houses, but also because space was not available for the fencing, paths, and roads in densely populated urban areas. In 2004 the estimated costs of construction were between $1.5 billion and $2.1 billion. For the Jerusalem section alone, it was $145 million.[13]

Legally, the most controversial element of the construction of the barrier has been its route, which has sliced off parts of the West Bank and placed them on the western side of the barrier. The length of the Armistice Lines of 1949 (or Green Line), is 320 kilometers, but the route taken by the barrier is approximately 708 kilometers, that is, over twice the length.[14] In fact, it is estimated by UNOCHA that when the barrier is completed only 15 percent of it will be along the Green Line while 85 percent will be inside the West Bank, that is, to the east of the Green Line.[15] Not only will this detach approximately 9.5 percent of the West Bank land from the West Bank, but it suggests a preemption by the Israeli government of the discussion on what the borders of the future Palestinian state will be. It is also significant to note that the route of the barrier was revised on a number of occasions to comply with international and legal pressure. Responding to several petitions to the Israeli High Court of Justice and the Israeli Supreme Court by Palestinians farmers and residents that they were going to be cut off from their livelihoods by the barrier, the Court conceded that changes were necessary to minimize damage to people's lives.[16] The implementation of these rulings has been subject to delay and further debate by the Israeli government.

The construction of the barrier in the Jerusalem area constitutes the single most important change to the city since 1967, particularly for the Palestinian residents of East Jerusalem. Already in the early 1990s it was increasingly difficult for West Bankers to gain access to East Jerusalem through the ever-tightening noose of Israeli checkpoints, but the construction of the separation barrier has been a step-change. Affecting mostly West Bank and East Jerusalemite Palestinians, the barrier has also had a deleterious impact on Israelis from the settlements and West Jerusalem. In the Jerusalem area the barrier will be approximately 142 kilometers in length. The significance of this is that only four kilometers of this route will be along the Green Line, less than 3 percent of its length in the Jerusalem area. The rest will loop round to include large Israeli settlements which serve as dormitory townships for Jerusalem and Tel Aviv. In fact, all the settlements in the Jerusalem area and virtually all of East Jerusalem will be placed on the western side, or "Israeli" side of the barrier. Thus, in the northwest of the city, the barrier diverges over 10 kilometers from the Green Line to incorporate the Giv'at Ze'ev settlement bloc, in the east, another 14 kilometers from the Green Line to include the huge settlement of Maale Adumim (comprising some 50,000 residents), and in the southwest, another 10 kilometers to include part of the Gush Etzion settlement bloc.[17]

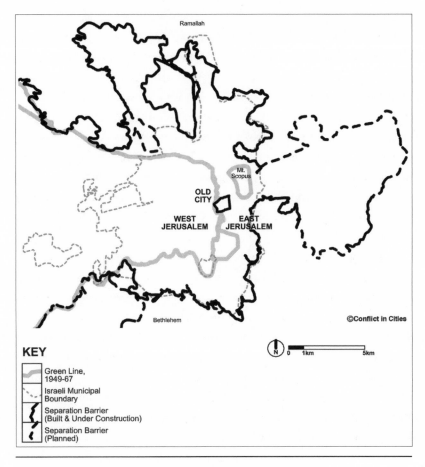

MAP 1.1. Map of separation barrier (2013).

The implications of these deviations from the Green Line, which is the internationally recognized border of Israel and the basis of numerous UN resolutions as well as the premise upon which a two-state agreement is based, are profound and far-reaching. However, before exploring these broader political issues we need to consider the impact of the barrier in more concrete and specific terms.

The disruption the barrier has caused Palestinians has been well documented in numerous reports and studies, and only a few examples will be given in the notes here.[18] One of the main effects of the barrier is the threat

THE HARD BORDERS OF THE CITY

it has on the residency rights of East Jerusalem Palestinians. Palestinians residing in East Jerusalem after the Israeli occupation in 1967 were granted the status of "permanent residency" and not citizenship following a census in 1968.[19] As carriers of a blue identity card, rather than the green one issued to Palestinians in the West Bank, they were allowed to move and work in East Jerusalem, West Jerusalem, and the rest of Israel. One of the main values of a blue ID is that, while it made them mandatory contributors to the Israeli National Insurance Institute, East Jerusalem Palestinians could also be recipients of various benefits such as retirement, disability, unemployment, poverty, and child allowances.[20] In the absence of a functioning state in the OPTs, these benefits were highly prized and the blue ID card a much-sought-after asset.

It is estimated that the barrier will leave approximately one hundred thousand Jerusalemites who have residency permits to live in the municipal borders of Jerusalem on the West Bank side of the barrier, depriving them of access to families, schools, hospitals, religious sites, and commercial networks. Eight out of twelve access roads from the West Bank to Jerusalem have been closed to Palestinians, severely affecting commerce, trade, and social networks.[21] The Palestinian economy in the communities adjacent to the barrier has received a severe battering. In the Palestinian suburbs of Ar-Ram and Abu Dis, for example, some estimates suggest that rentals and house prices have fallen between 45–50 percent.[22] Because the rents are so low, some landlords are choosing to leave their properties empty as they cannot cover the cost of maintaining a rented property.[23] In the areas to the east of the barrier, commerce has also been badly affected by the declining population as residents either relocate to the western side of the barrier in order to preserve Jerusalem residency status or return to their villages because their access to employment in Jerusalem has been blocked. Neither having so many local customers nor being accessible to the rest of Jerusalem residents on the other side of the barrier, shops have shut in the hundreds. In the Palestinian suburb of Shaykh Sa'ad, for example, of the more than forty shops that existed before the construction of the barrier only eight remain, and it has been estimated that approximately half the houses are empty.[24] In A-Ram there has been a 45 percent drop in retail outlets since 2003. Similar declines are also occurring in Bir Nabala and Abu Dis.[25]

There are three categories of areas of the West Bank and Jerusalem particularly affected by the barrier. The first is what is known as the "Seam Zone," that is, the area between the barrier and the Green Line, usually caused by a divergence of the barrier from the Green Line to include an Israeli settlement further to the east of it. Palestinians residing in the Seam Zone are required to apply to the Israeli government for permits (to live in their own homes!) and have to pass through checkpoints to have access to services and employment and to maintain their family connections. If you are a Palestinian farmer who has land in the Seam Zone but live to the east of the barrier you also have to apply for permits to work your land and only have access through certain gates which are open for limited periods of time.[26] Once the barrier is complete, UNOCHA estimates that approximately twenty-five thousand West Bank Palestinians will reside between the barrier and the Green Line. The relevance of the Seam Zone to our examination of Jerusalem is, once the barrier has been completed, that most of East Jerusalem falls into this category, since it lies between the barrier and the Green Line. As holders of Jerusalem residency permits, Palestinian East Jerusalemites are in a better position than those West Bank Palestinians who have recently been cast into this new category of Seam Zone residents, but, nevertheless, it reinforces the ambiguity of their status as Jerusalem residents living in a legal gray area—neither Israeli citizens nor able to be fully integrated into Palestinian life and politics and being dependent on permits for their everyday needs.

The second area category can be termed "west of the wall West Bankers"; those communities of Palestinians in the West Bank that as a result of the deviation of the barrier from the Green Line are now located on the western side of the barrier on the Jerusalem side. Their situation is particularly difficult. Residents in these communities, numbering approximately twenty-five hundred people, do not have Jerusalem residency permits and do not have the right to live in the municipal boundaries of Jerusalem. They are frequently stopped at army road blocks and by random police checks in the streets of Jerusalem and detained for long periods until their position is clarified. As a result, they are deterred from finding work or taking advantage of the services available in the city. At the same time, their access to the West Bank is severely curtailed by the barrier and the checkpoints that they have to pass through. The degree of disruption and intrusion into their lives is shocking, damaging their customary family life to the extent that, as an UNOCHA report indicates, some communities report that they are only allowed to bring in sufficient food for personal consumption.[27]

The third area category of particular note affected by the barrier is the reverse of the "west of the wall West Bankers." These are communities and suburbs located within the municipal boundaries of Jerusalem but find themselves on the West Bank side of the barrier. These communities, comprising approximately fifty-five thousand people, are mostly in the north of the city around Kufr 'Aqab and the large Palestinian refugee camp of Shu'fat. Residents of these areas have Jerusalem residency permits but are obliged to go through the daily ordeal of crossing the barrier checkpoints in order to get to their work, schools, hospitals, and other services. In addition, despite paying the *arnona*, or Israeli municipal tax, and despite some cosmetic municipal oversight operated remotely from offices located at the checkpoints, these areas receive little or no services with waste disposal and sewage treatment dependent upon local volunteers.[28] To all intents and purposes, they have been abandoned by the Israeli state and the residents live in a growing security vacuum.[29] In Kufr Aqab, for example, there are no police stations or uniformed police. The closest police presence for the Palestinian suburb is at the former border between the Israeli municipality of Jerusalem and the West Bank.[30] However, these are Palestinian police who are not allowed to operate in Kufr Aqab. Palestinian police can arrest offenders, but they have to release Palestinians with Jerusalem IDs because it is not within their jurisdiction. They cannot charge people with Jerusalem ID cards.[31] A common perception is that the Palestinian intelligence services can sometimes assist in cases of theft and robbery, but in informal ways. When traffic is congested at the adjacent Qalandya check point, traffic "organizers" appear on the Palestinian side. These are presumably Palestinian traffic police, but they operate in civilian clothes. In Shu'fat, clan-based protection groups have emerged to fill the vacuum and to both control and cooperate with criminals acting with growing impunity.[32] In addition, residents fear that they are caught in a trap: if, as it is likely, Israel declares the barrier as the new municipal boundary or some other form of quasi-official delineation, their use of municipal services at the checkpoints will prove that they have been residing outside the wall and they will therefore be denied their Jerusalem identity card status and lose their entitlements.[33]

These bare facts do little to convey the personal misery caused by the construction of the barrier to the Palestinians caught on either one side or the other. Some of the case studies on the impact of the barrier collected by the UNOCHA team make one want to weep with frustration at how their talents, goodwill, and prospects have been squandered by petty restrictions. Fuad Jado, for example, lives with his family of seven between Jerusalem and Bethlehem. He has a West Bank identity card but is on the Jerusalem side of the barrier. In 2005 his mother had a heart attack, but the Palestinian Red Crescent Society based in Bethlehem was unable to reach them because of the barrier. He attempted to contact the Israeli equivalent, the Magen David Adom, but was told that they were not allowed access to what was designated a military area. He was obliged to physically carry his mother across fields to an uncompleted stretch of the barrier, but once through found that she had died in his arms on the way.[34] Another example is seventy-one-year-old Abu Zahriya living with his family in Dahyat al-Barid to the north of Jerusalem. All his family have West Bank identity cards but found the barrier had placed them on the Jerusalem side. His son of thirty-one dares not look for work in case he is caught in the city without a permit and his wife, who is originally from Bir Nabala, on the other side of the barrier, has not been able to visit her family to show her parents their two grandchildren. Abu Dahriya himself has only a six-month permit that is restricted to the immediate vicinity in which he lives.[35] There are many other stories that could be cited; cumulatively they all show how the barrier exacts a great personal cost on the affected communities and these in turn are not without costs for Israelis. The balance sheet of the barrier is still being compiled and the increased security it has ostensibly brought to Israeli communities is not the complete picture.

Probably the most striking of the unintended consequences of the construction of the barrier around Jerusalem has been the increase in the Palestinian population in the city. Fearful of losing their access to medical and educational services, to employment, to their entitlements as Jerusalem ID card holders, and also to the freer and less intrusive Israeli military presence in Jerusalem, Palestinians who had moved out to the periphery of Jerusalem have quickly reversed their decisions and are relocating back into the more central areas on the western side of the barrier. At one point Israeli army officers at checkpoints to the city reported an average of fifteen trucks a day entering the city laden with household furniture and personal effects.[36]

This increase is both in absolute terms and also as a proportion of the total. Since the year of the barrier's first construction, 2003, until the present day, official Israeli statistics show that the Palestinian population has increased by approximately thirty thousand and is in excess of the natural increase of the population.[37] Official Palestinian figures suggest the figure may be at least twenty thousand higher. (This discrepancy is partially explained by the numbers of Palestinians who do not have Jerusalem identity cards but still reside in the city and are unlikely to reply to Israeli censuses.)[38] Preliminary studies suggest that approximately one-third of those returning to Jerusalem make their way to the Old City where the density and congestion has never been so great, while the rest have spread throughout East Jerusalem.[39] Largely as a result of this recent influx, the proportion of Palestinians to Israeli Jews in the city has shifted from 33 percent in 2003 to 35.7 percent in 2009. It is still too early to say that the policy of separating Palestinian communities from Israeli Jewish ones through the construction of the barrier is backfiring, but it is certainly posing some additional challenges to the Israeli state as it seeks to consolidate Jewish dominance in the city.

This sense of a dynamic shifting population working against Israel's favor is accentuated when one considers that a new trend of Palestinians moving into Israeli settlements in East Jerusalem is emerging. This is a direct result of housing shortages brought about by Israeli policies to curtail Palestinian development, which will be discussed in greater detail in a later chapter. Such shortages have increased rapidly since 2003, and, in contrast to the situation on the other side of the barrier, rental and house prices have risen sharply. In 2006, prices in Beit Hanina, a wealthy Palestinian suburb in northern Jerusalem, rose an estimated 15–35 percent, while in Ras al-'Amud, to the east of the city, sale prices are said to have increased 45 percent.[40] Palestinian tenants faced with a rise from $500 to $650 a month are being priced out of these areas to cheaper and already more densely populated neighborhoods. At the same time, those who are confronted with these prices are able to consider renting an apartment in the more expensive Israeli settlements, particularly Neve Ya'akov, Pisgat Ze'ev, and latterly the salubrious French Hill, where the urban environment, services, and transport links are far superior to the Palestinian areas. At present there are no reliable figures on this demographic shift, but fieldwork carried out in the 2005–6 suggest a pattern of initially some floors then whole apartment blocks being taken over as Israeli Jewish residents leave. Moreover, the deterioration of urban conditions, lawlessness, and isolation of the Shu'fat refugee camp is acting as a major push factor for Palestinians to seek flats in Pisgat Ze'ev, literally a stone's throw away from the camp, but on the Jerusalem side of the barrier.[41] It is too strong to characterize this development as a gradual "Palestinianization" of some of the settlements, but when taken together with a steady migration of professional Palestinians from inside Israel, especially from Galilee, into places like French Hill, it has, nevertheless, begun to cause distinct unease in political circles.[42]

A further unintended consequence of the construction of the barrier is an acceleration of the emigration of the Israeli Jewish population from Jerusalem. This is a trend that started many years ago, particularly with younger and more secular Israeli Jews, as a result of poor employment opportunities and an increasingly conservative cultural environment resulting from the rise in the Orthodox Jewish population. For example, between 1982–89 approximately fourteen hundred and eighteen hundred Israeli Jews left the city annually, amounting to some six thousand departures.[43] One estimate is that over the last twenty years approximately one hundred thousand Israeli Jews have left the city.[44] In 1992 the Israeli deputy mayor of Jerusalem, Amos Mar-Haim, was quoted as saying, "the figures are worrisome. The population of Jerusalem has been growing, on the one hand, but on the other, year after year we are losing the best of our young people."[45] One should be clear that many of these departures were to Israeli settlements ringing the city and in the long-term they may yet be regarded as Jerusalemites. Nevertheless, the drift to the coastal plain, approximately 22 percent of the total, where employment, housing, and cultural opportunities are much greater, is a phenomenon that has for many years already been altering the demographic balance in the city and the political composition of its leadership. The bombing campaign carried out by Palestinian groups prior to the construction of the barrier helped continue this trend, while, since its construction, there is evidence that, despite efforts to consolidate the Israeli Jewish population, the rate of emigration has continued. The only reason that the Israeli Jewish population of the city continues to grow is natural increase, mostly from the Orthodox Jewish community, which in turn acts as a catalyst for the non-Orthodox Jewish population to leave.[46]

In addition to these demographic and economic issues triggered by the construction of the barrier, one also has to recognize the impact of its construction on other elements of urban life in Jerusalem. As my colleagues on the Conflict in Cities project have argued, it is not just the barrier that causes the profound rupture in the urban integrity of the city and of the Palestinian suburbs. The barrier through the city is in itself temporary; it is built as a high wall on a broad concrete base, manufactured in segmented slabs that can be hoisted away by crane.[47] Instead, it is the road system and the reorientation of life away from the networks that existed prior to the construction of the barrier that cause the most lasting damage. They write: "over time, Road 1 [Jerusalem's central north-south road which connects Israeli settlements to the city] may be more damaging than a wall. After all, in a few short years, the Berlin wall was obliterated and its path lost in many parts of the city; but road alignments are perhaps the most enduring or urban interventions."[48] New roads and bypasses have been built for Israeli Jews to ameliorate the inconvenience of the barrier and the various checkpoints. For Palestinians there has been no such investment, but former tracks and lanes have been spontaneously commandeered by those seeking new ways to work, schools, hospitals, and other services.

During 2005–6, in the period leading up to the final stages of construction of the barrier when it was still possible to find alternative routes through its gaps, I recall several chaotic *serviis* (shared taxi) trips between Ramallah and Jerusalem when, in order to avoid Israeli checkpoints, Palestinian drivers would dramatically leave Road 1, taking off through unpaved narrow lanes between apartment blocks and along dirt tracks through small olive groves, climbing mounds of earth and builders rubble, sliding down slippery slopes, snaking between cars and lorries coming in the other direction, all the time the horn blaring and invocations to the Almighty forthcoming. Hair-raising as it was, the experience would also have been comical if it had not been for the several narrow misses of hapless pedestrians and the danger of being crushed by a bouncing articulated lorry precariously attempting to circumnavigate its way through what amounted to an urban savannah. At one point in 2005–6 all the daily traffic that ran between Ramallah and Jerusalem—cars, buses, vans, trucks—was obliged to leave the main artery and fan out across the suburbs and fields to find a route that avoided the steady closing of the barrier. Most of these cowboy routes are now closed as a result of the barrier's completion but their sudden emergence demonstrates the haphazard and unplanned process by which some of the new roads in the Palestinian areas on both sides of the barrier have been created. Former backwaters have become through routes, irrespective of their suitability for traffic and potential danger. On top of this, the new roads mark a reorientation of life away from the barrier. Unable to access schools, hospitals, shops, mosques and churches, graveyards and places of leisure because of the barrier, Palestinians have been obliged to find alternatives on the side of the barrier they are residing. Over time these access routes will become embedded in the urban topography of the city and create new networks and patterns of movement.

In the education sphere alone, when the barrier is complete it is estimated that it will cut off some eighteen thousand pupils and eight hundred teachers from their schools.[49] As a result of Palestinians moving back to the central areas of the city, registrations in Palestinian schools in East Jerusalem have dramatically increased, leading to severe classroom shortages. One result has been a rate of absenteeism estimated by an Israeli NGO to be approximately nine thousand pupils.[50] Corresponding sharp falls in numbers for preschool education has taken place in communities on the east of the barrier, also marking the population shift taking place.[51] A similar story can be seen in the medical field. As Ray Dolphin has explained, one of the chief benefits of retaining a Jerusalem identity card has been access to higher standards of health care available from Israeli health facilities as well as largely Palestinian-staffed institutions such St. John's Ophthalmic Hospital, Augusta Victoria, and al-Muqassed Hospital. Seventy-five percent of the staff of the latter institutions lived on the eastern side of the barrier and they, in turn, as private institutions depend upon West Bank Palestinians to balance their books.[52] Thus the restrictions to the former centers of education and medical services created a crisis in these sectors in East Jerusalem, but also has reinforced the new patterns of linkage and mobility created by the barrier, which will divide communities on either side of it for decades to come.

The political impact of the barrier has been immense. In the first place it has become a global iconic image of the Israeli occupation and of the oppression of the Palestinians. The walled sections of the barrier have become the site and object of artistic works ranging from popular graffiti artists such as Banksy, comedians such as Mark Thomas, and musicians such as Roger Waters.[53] Numerous international protests against it have forced images of the walled sections onto our television screens, and there are now few pictures of Jerusalem in news reports that do not also present the wall and barrier in some form. Images of the walled sections of the barrier have virtually replaced those of Che Guevara as the symbol of resistance by young and progressive movements against colonial exploitation. In public relations terms it is a cataclysmic disaster for the Israeli Ministry of Foreign Affairs, invoking as it does images of apartheid, of the inhuman treatment of the Roma in Hungary, and, indeed, of the Nazi-controlled Jewish ghetto in Warsaw during the 1939–1945 war.

Coinciding and possibly causing the impasse in political negotiations between Israel and the PLO, another direct impact of the barrier is the increasing isolation for Israel in the international community. In a later chapter we will examine in greater detail the role Jerusalem plays in diplomatic acrobatics around the peace negotiations. Here we just need to highlight the serious setback Israel received as a result of the construction of the barrier to its attempt to designate East Jerusalem, the West Bank, and the Gaza Strip as "disputed territories," rather than occupied territories, and therefore that it was not obliged to withdraw from all areas it had occupied. In 2004, in response to a UN General Assembly request, the International Court of Justice (ICJ) was asked to give its opinion on "the Legal Consequences arising from the Construction of the Wall (sic) being built by Israel."[54] The ruling, which became known as the Wall Opinion,[55] confirmed that the areas occupied in 1967 were indeed occupied territory as well as the fact that the barrier was not a bilateral matter between Israel and the PLO but also one of UN responsibility.[56] This was a crushing blow to decades of diplomatic work by Israel to nudge the international community toward accepting the incremental and de facto Israeli annexation of East Jerusalem and parts of the West Bank. By the same measure, despite the erosion of their presence in the city on the ground, Palestinians were able to revive support for their position that East Jerusalem would be the capital of a future Palestinian state.

The benefits of the barrier for Israel also received greater scrutiny. There is no doubt that one can correlate a decline in suicide and other attacks

FIGURE 1.1. The Israeli Separation Barrier as an iconic monument.

on Israelis with the completion of the barrier. Nevertheless, correlation is not causation, and one can argue that the decline in attacks has as much to do with the truce announced by Hamas and Islamic Jihad and better Palestinian-Israeli cooperation as it has to do with any Israeli security measures such as the barrier.[57] The coffee shops of Ramallah, Bethlehem, Qalqilya, Tulkarm, and East Jerusalem abound with stories of how Palestinians have managed to cross the barrier by covert means—over it by climbing ropes or with the assistance of a friendly crane operator (possibly the same ones that put the segmented slabs in place), under it through sewage outlets and water tunnels, and through it by deceiving the checkpoint guards. If my personal experience is anything to go by, despite the proclaimed security justification for the barrier, circumventing Israeli security along the barrier is neither difficult nor dangerous. Returning by bus to Jerusalem from Ramallah via the Qalandia checkpoint, I have been turned back several times by Israeli soldiers. It is a simple procedure to walk back through the milling crowd to find a driver with a Jerusalem number plate waiting around just for this eventuality, offer him (usually a him) thirty to forty shekels and be driven to another vehicle-only checkpoint, such as Hizma near Pisgat Ze'ev, and to be waved through by Israeli security with nary a glance, let alone a baggage search.

In the face of this anecdotal evidence and the general impression of the barrier being a very leaky seal, the jury is still very much out on its security benefits. Indeed, a prominent Israeli lawyer in Jerusalem, Danny Seideman, has frequently highlighted the perverse effects of the wall in radicalizing the Palestinians of East Jerusalem. Since 1967, Palestinian East Jerusalemites have been noted for their relative quiescence and docility in nationalistic acts of resistance. However, since the construction of the barrier, despite the effective neutralization by the Israeli intelligence services of radical groups such as Hamas in the city, "homegrown" acts of resistance by Palestinians with Jerusalem IDs have increased.[58]

A further impact of the barrier has been to recreate for Israelis the atmosphere of Jerusalem as a frontier zone. While this can be minimized by building fast roads between the city center and outlying Israeli Jewish settlements that bypass Palestinian suburbs and villages, the hostility the barrier

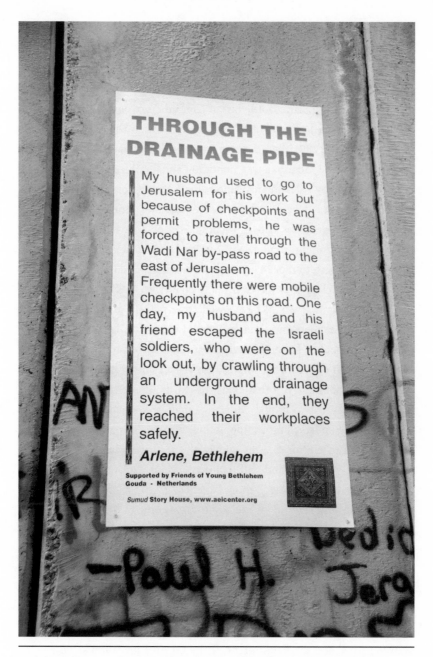

FIGURE 1.2. Separation Barrier Mural: "Through the Drainage Pipe."

has created in the Palestinian hinterland, the arresting and intimidating visual impact on the landscape, the heightened presence of Israeli security services and the military in and around the city all combine to create an impression of a dangerous and closed area. Herein lies the weakness of this great act of unilateralism. Borne out of contradictory policies of wishing to consolidate Israeli Jewish control over the city but at the same time being obliged to include nearly a quarter of a million Palestinians has resulted, on one hand, in a chaotic urban fragmentation and, on the other, rejection and noncooperation by Palestinians. All this for little tangible return for Israel.

Like the Gaza debacle, where Israel withdrew from the Gaza Strip without prior agreement with any Palestinian body, it is leaving behind a political and planning vacuum. And Gaza is not a precedent that Israeli leaders would wish to repeat: The unilateral withdrawal from there in 2005 left a hostile enclave that was eventually taken over by Hamas with no set of arrangements that would have eased Israel's troubled relationship with that area and, at the same time, no concessions given by the Palestinians in their back pocket. In the Jerusalem case the extension of areas of Israeli control without either formal annexation or Palestinian agreement, and the de facto abandonment of other areas, also without any clear arrangements with the Palestinian National Authority, may be a swaggering exercise in demonstrating an Israeli projection of force and may bring some short-term benefits both in electoral terms and in the security sphere. Nevertheless, it is inherently unstable and will require constant vigilance and additional expense. Just think how much more beneficial it would have been for Israel and the long-term stability of the city to have come to a set of agreements with the Palestinians over security, over transit issues within the city and between the city and its hinterland, over development, and over infrastructure.

Indeed, the barrier, which is the result of a lack of agreement with the Palestinians over the future of the city, is for Israel a policy disaster of long-term strategic consequences as well. By deviating from the Green Line, the barrier has undermined that de facto border as the basis of negotiations between Israel and the Palestinians. If the Green Line is not sacrosanct to Israel, why should it, in turn, remain sacrosanct to the Palestinians? If the Israelis wish to include in the future borders of Israel the settlement blocs of Gush Etzion and Ariel, which bite great chunks out of the West Bank, then surely the Palestinians can put on the table too areas in Israel that have Palestinian demographic superiority, such as the Triangle and the Galilee. Thus, by privileging Israeli settlements and settlers over an agreement with the Palestinians, Israel may be risking the long-term interests of the state. In Jerusalem, if the Green Line is not to be the foundation upon which a shared Palestinian-Israeli capital is built, then, in the same way as Israelis seeking to consolidate their position to the east of the that line, what is to prevent Palestinians from seeking to do the same to the west of it, in areas that were formerly Palestinian owned? The construction of the barrier has opened a Pandora's box that may not ultimately be to Israel's advantage. I will examine these questions in more detail in the final chapter.

THE BORDERS OF JERUSALEM

This brings us to the central underlying questions in any discussion of Jerusalem: what are in reality the borders of the city over which there is so much discussion and contest? How have these borders changed over time and do those changes reflect the internal developments of the city? Indeed, to understand the full significance of the enormous changes wrought by the barrier and the impact of recent events upon the future of the city, we need to appreciate the evolution of the borders of the city and its rich and dark history. The focus of the rest of this chapter, therefore, will be on the changing nature of the borders of the city, the separation barrier being only the latest episode in a series of shifts and modifications that have taken place since 1948. While the focus of the remaining sections of this chapter will be on these shifts since that date, nevertheless, in order to fully understand the significance of what happened in 1948–1949, when the city was partitioned, and then again in 1967 when Israel occupied the eastern part, we need, briefly, to go a little further back, to the late Ottoman period when Jerusalem first entered the modern period.[59] In doing so I shall avoid repeating a potted history of the Israel-Palestine conflict and of Jerusalem, as this has been well covered in numerous other books. In this overview I wish merely to draw out some of the key developments and patterns that contribute to understanding the contested nature of the city.

For many centuries the size and borders of Jerusalem were defined by the huge walls constructed by Suleiman the Lawgiver in sixteenth century. The walls encompassed two of the holiest shrines in Islam, al-Aqsa Mosque and the Dome of the Rock, both situated on a large plaza abutting the northeastern parts of the walls. Also within their surrounds was the Church of the Holy Sepulchre, designated as the site of Jesus Christ's crucifixion, and the holiest site in Judaism—a small exposed section of what is held to be Herod's Temple, known as the Wailing Wall. The rest of the walled city, comprising only approximately one kilometer square, was made up of marketplaces, large monumental buildings housing tombs, seminaries, and hostels, as well as churches, mosques, and synagogues. Narrow streets and alleyways led to densely constructed houses and rooms usually centered around an inner courtyard. Surprisingly in such a small space, there was also considerable open land within the walls, which indicates both the small permanent population that made up the city, although this would swell with pilgrims to several times its size on important religious occasions.

Despite the prominence of the walls in the topography and history of the city, we should not conclude that the city was an isolated enclave far from the fertile coastal plain and the main trading routes. Although the gates the of the city had to be closed at dusk until well into the twentieth century to deter raids by Bedouin bands living in the hills nearby, the hinterland was nevertheless well populated. Jerusalem was surrounded by a ring of villages which later became suburbs in the modern city. During the later part of the nineteenth century as security in the hinterland was improved, summer houses and mansions were constructed by wealthy Palestinian families which spawned ancillary housing to serve them.[60] In addition, as the first signs of Jewish settlement appeared, large housing estates were constructed to the west of the city which also saw the establishment of large ecclesiastical building to house the increasing number of pilgrims.[61] In this way, while the walled city of Suleiman remained the core until the mid twentieth century, the environs became increasingly important and heralded the future lines of growth.

In political terms, Jerusalem was relatively precocious. As early as 1840 the Ottoman authorities in Istanbul had established the city as the capital of a new province of Jerusalem. This was in response to two countervailing pressures the Ottoman regime was experiencing. On the one hand, in order to reenergize the empire and to stimulate greater wealth and productivity the Ottomans had embarked upon a program of decentralization. Greater administrative responsibilities were allocated to the regional elites based in the large cities in Greater Syria, including the area of Palestine. On the other, the Ottoman authorities were aware of the international interest (mainly European and Russian) in Jerusalem in particular and the attempts to circumvent their jurisdiction there, so they wanted to ensure slightly more control over the city's affairs to preempt such encroachments.[62] In addition, in 1863 Jerusalem was one of the first cities in the Ottoman Empire to be granted a *majlis*, or local council, to administer services in the city, and their responsibilities extended to the growing urban space outside the walls. One should recall that Ottoman urban administration was relatively advanced, in contrast to popular images of oriental squalor and decline. There is no doubt that in the mid to late nineteenth century Jerusalem suffered from major health and sanitation problems in common with many cities of that period, but, at the same time, we should not overlook the comparable squalor of major cities in Europe as depicted by Charles Dickens and Victor Hugo and that street lighting, for example, was not available to the inhabitants of Birmingham until the turn of the nineteenth century, some thirty years after that provided for in Jerusalem.

During the closing years of the Ottoman Empire, congestion and unsanitary conditions inside the walls led to a rapid increase in the population outside the walls and the spread of urban areas. During the British Mandate period, from 1922–1948, this extramural expansion was recognized and new borders were designated to include a larger area of the walled city's environs. What was controversial in these British changes is a pattern that has been followed to this day, which perhaps is also common to other contested cities—the designation of borders to defend or promote the interests of a particular ethnic or religious group in the city. The British borders swung in a wide arc west of the city to incorporate the new housing estates established

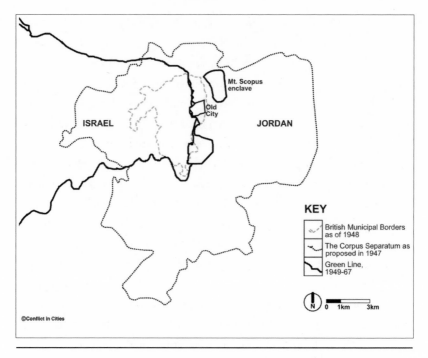

MAP 1.2. The changing borders of Jerusalem 1922–1949. Municipal borders of Jerusalem at the start of the British Mandate, the proposed UN International Zone in 1947, and the 1949 Armistice Line.

by Jewish and Zionist settlers. In contrast, while large numbers of new settlers were being incorporated into the city limits, in the east the municipal borders slid between the walls of the city and the Palestinian villages virtually abutting the walls in order to exclude them. The prime intention of this blatant gerrymandering of the borders was to ensure an electoral advantage of the Jewish community of the city over its Palestinian residents.

Acknowledging this manipulation is not to assert that there were no significant demographic changes taking place in the city during this period. Jerusalem under the British Mandate was flourishing. Its economy was expanding, roads were opening up new markets. Employment opportunities in the city were booming due mainly to the locating of all the Mandate government offices in the city. The population of the city increased from 1922 to 1946 from 62,000 to 164,000 with approximately 55–60 percent being Jewish.[63] Elsewhere I have argued that these figures and the proportions within them of Palestinian Arabs and Jews are misleading.[64] There was, for example, an overcounting of new Jewish immigrants who first came to Jerusalem then moved to Tel Aviv and an undercounting of Palestinians whose villages were excluded from the population count as a result of falling outside the municipal borders. Taking these factors into consideration, one can estimate that, by the time of the last British census, there were approximately 69,000 Palestinians Arabs and 97,000 Jews in the city. A Jewish numerical dominance in the city is not in doubt, but the extent has been frequently overstated.

What is also of interest is the segregated distribution of the population. Most Jews lived in the new northern and western parts of the city, in what became known as the New City. By 1947 it was estimated that only 2 percent of the Jews of the city lived in the walled Old City.[65] Palestinians also spread into other parts of the city. The wealthier classes and mostly Christian Palestinians built suburbs in the southwest of the New City, while the Muslim community dominated the eastern and northern suburbs.

Of even greater significance is that the demographic spread did not correspond exactly to the land ownership patterns in the city. While comprising the largest proportion of the population, Jews owned much less property. Figures are difficult to accurately compute, but extrapolating from the figures supplied by a former senior tax official in the British Mandate government, Sami Hadawi, it is possible to estimate that no more than 35 percent of the municipal area was owned by Jews or Jewish philanthropic societies and companies.[66] Indeed, as the indigenous land-owning community, the land area occupied by Palestinian Arabs was by the same token also much greater than that of Jews.

Implicit in discussing the relative demographic, geographic, and ownership strengths and weaknesses of the population groups in Jerusalem is the assumption that dominance in one or all of these areas confers greater rights over the city to that group. Israeli Jews will tend to emphasize their demographic superiority in the city as sign of their stronger claim to the city. Palestinians will point to their ownership and longevity of tenure and also to their demographic preponderance in the hinterland that is not enumerated

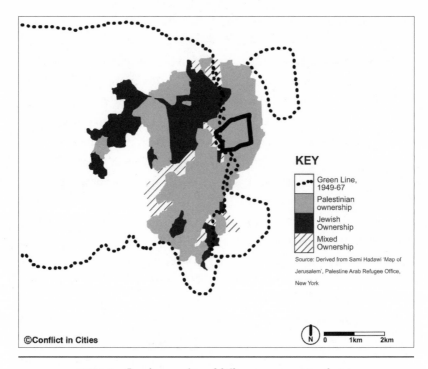

MAP 1.3. Land ownership of different communities during
the Mandate period (1922–1948).

in the statistics as proof of their greater claim. These are valid data sets which
help construct an overall argument but still leave the observer and analyst
with the issue of what is the city that is being discussed. How can we come
to a judgment as to the rights of each group when the city keeps moving, so
to speak, with borders that keep changing and the human profile and urban
character is constantly metamorphosing? These questions are important because it is during the British Mandate period, standing on the brink of the
creation of the state of Israel and the dispossession of the Palestinians, that
the contest between Jews and Palestinians over the city becomes nationalist
and ideological.

Following the decision by the British government to turn its Mandate
for Palestine over to the United Nations and to evacuate the country, Jerusalem is struck by two momentous political events in quick succession. The

first is the UN Partition Plan in 1947 which not only proposed the enlargement of Jerusalem by five or six times but also its detachment from the
proposed Arab and Jewish states to form an international enclave or *corpus
separatum*.

Under this plan Jerusalem would be demilitarized and under the jurisdiction of a UN Trusteeship Council which would draft a statute for Jerusalem and administer the city for ten years after which there would be a
referendum.[67] The plan was never implemented due to the inability of the
international community to enforce it in face of the ongoing fighting between Jews and Palestinians. Jerusalem, which during the months preced-
ing the Partition Plan being adopted by the General Assembly in 1947, had
been sliding into a deeply segregated city with checkpoints and barbed wire
separating the different communities. With the defeat of the Arab armies
that entered the conflict to assist the Palestinians, the second major political
event took place: Jerusalem was partitioned into an Israeli-controlled West
Jerusalem and a Jordanian-controlled East Jerusalem.

The lead-up to the division of the city was bitter and tragic. As a result of terrorist attacks, approximately sixty thousand Palestinians from the
New City and from villages in the western hinterland of Jerusalem fled
to the east. At the same time, the remaining Jews in the Old City and in
scattered blocks of the eastern part of the city fled to the west.[68] The worst
fighting between the Jewish and Palestinian militias took place between
November 1947, after UN adoption of the Partition Plan, and May 1948
when the Jewish community in Palestine declared the creation of the state
of Israel and the Arab states joined in the war. Following the Jordanian
entry into Jerusalem in mid-May 1948, the divisions in the city hardened
and the front line between the protagonists was ultimately formalized by
the armistice agreements signed in April 1949 between Jordan and Israel.
The Armistice Lines run from north to south through Jerusalem with a
band of no-man's land separating the two sides. Beside the walls of the
Old City, the no-man's land narrowed to a very slender strip, to the extent
that properties on either side could be subjected to sniper fire. A number of
incidents took place which required the mediation of the UN Truce Supervisory Organization.[69]

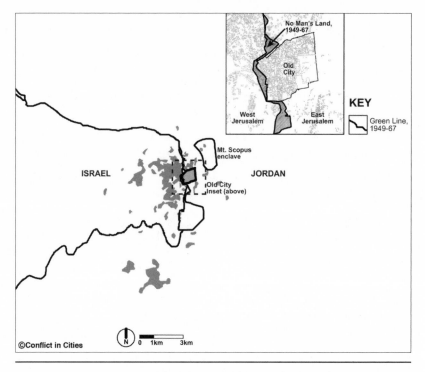

MAP 1.4. No Man's Land and Old City (1949–1967).

As a result of the armistice agreements, Jordan retained control over the Old City and the main holy places of the city in the east. Israel, however, controlled approximately 84 percent of the former municipal area of Jerusalem.[70] Israel also held onto a small enclave in the northeast of the city on the Jordanian side of the Armistice Lines enclosing the Hebrew University on Mount Scopus. Despite this advantage of controlling a greater land area of Jerusalem, the Jewish population of the city actually fell by between 30–40 percent.[71] It was not until the mid-1950s that an increase was achieved, mainly through the immigration of Arab Jews from North African and Asian countries. The same pattern occurred in Jordanian-controlled East Jerusalem. Meron Benvenisti estimates that half the Palestinian population of approximately 60,000 left the city.[72] A Jordanian census carried out in 1952 shows that the population of East Jerusalem was 46,700.[73] Despite the fact that this total included a municipal area slightly enlarged by the Jordanian government, as well as the village of Silwan just below the city walls, it still points to a significant drop.

From these two momentous political events we can see how the city was buffeted by the national struggles taking place around it and by the concerns of regional and international actors. The first event was an international response to the growing tensions in the city during the Mandate period, taking the form of its enlargement, its detachment from the intercommunal rivalry, and proposals for its internationalization in the form of a *corpus separatum*. However, this approach was swept aside by the contest between the Jewish settlers and the Arab world over control of the city.

Yet the borders of the city continued to shift even after these momentous events. During the period between 1949 and 1967, both Israel and Jordan initiated border changes to their sides of the city. In 1950, West Jerusalem, which, as already mentioned, comprised the greater part of the British Mandate municipality, was extended to include the now empty Palestinian village of 'Ayn Karim and the new Hadassah hospital that was being built nearby. By 1967, however, the Israeli municipality, which was estimated to be approximately thirty-six square kilometers, was running out of space for the housing and utilities required and poised for a further expansion to the west. Despite the fall in population in the eastern part of the city, Jordan also expanded the municipal borders of "Arab East Jerusalem," as it was subsequently called, to include the surrounding villages of Silwan, Ras al-'Amud, Aqabat al-Suwana, 'Ard al-Samar, and parts of Shu'fat which had been increasingly surburbanized during the British Mandate period. Nevertheless, in contrast to Israeli West Jerusalem, the area still remained small at only six square kilometers

In both parts of the city, the ongoing conflict between Israelis, Palestinians, and Jordanians and the partition continued to have an impact on the development of the city. In West Jerusalem the pressures for enlargement in the west were largely due to the fact that the area along the Armistice Line was deemed dangerous and not attractive for habitation. The result was that the population density in those areas was low as Israelis sought safer parts of the city in which to reside. This applied to long-time residents and new immigrants alike. In East Jerusalem the expansion was almost entirely due to the displacement of Palestinians from the former New City, now on the Israeli side of the Armistice Lines. Refugees from these areas crammed into the Old City and surrounding areas, leading to rapid infilling in the low-density villages and resulting in their transformation into suburbanized communities requiring municipal services.

Contact between the two sides of the city during this period was minimal. Despite clauses in the armistice agreements that would allow Israelis access to the religious sites in East Jerusalem, this access did not take place. Jordan took the view that the refusal of Israel to allow the return of Palestinians to their homes in the former New City now in West Jerusalem voided that clause in the agreement. Nevertheless, Israeli convoys, escorted by the UN, were allowed to resupply the Israeli enclave on Mount Scopus and Christian clergy were given special permits to cross the border at a designated control point just north of the Old City between Shaykh Jarrah in East Jerusalem and Mea She'arim in West Jerusalem, known as the Mandelbaum Gate.[74]

In June 1967 another momentous change in the city and its borders occurred when the Israeli army occupied the west bank of Jordan and the eastern part of Jerusalem. The occupation set a new pattern of development for the city and border changes that lasted until the construction of the barrier in 2003. During this thirty-six year spell, the city was transformed almost beyond recognition. A long-time resident or visitor would still be able to identify the Old City and the surrounding basin, the main religious and cultural features, and the overall topography of the city. But the enormous wide boulevards and shops, fast roads swirling through tunnels and across bridges, housing stretching star-shaped into the hills and valleys around the city, and the dominance of the motor vehicle are all disorienting. In part this can be attributed to the 1967–2003 period coinciding also with the postwar unraveling of command economies, the rise of neoliberal capitalism, and the new advances in architecture, construction, and civil engineering. In this way, the changes in the city are very similar to those occurring elsewhere. The transformation of Amman, for example, is just as dramatic and a rupture with the past as that of Jerusalem. Nevertheless, the main driver of these changes upon the city has been the determination by the Israeli government

to consolidate the Israeli Jewish presence in the city and to constrain that of
the Palestinians—in all fields—housing, population growth, economy, and
cultural expression. This policy objective, which manifests itself in differentiated service provision, in planning and zoning, and in security regimes,
will be covered in the following chapters of the book. Here I wish to focus
on the way the city was defined and bordered as a result of such objectives.

The first step the Israeli government took in this regard was to amend
an existing Israeli law that allowed it to extend its jurisdiction to any area of
"Eretz Israel [*sic*] designated by the Government by order."[75] This was then
followed by an order designating East Jerusalem and adjacent parts of the
West Bank as areas to be covered by the amendment, which in turn was
followed by another amendment extending the Israeli municipality of West
Jerusalem into those new areas.[76] The former deputy mayor of the Israeli
municipality, Meron Benvenisti, recounts how the actual borders of the municipality were subject to intense debate between those who wanted to have
a cohesive and smaller municipal area and those who had broader strategic
and security concerns in mind. The final line, which bore little reference to
cultural associations or natural affinities between certain areas, was drawn
up with a mix of economic, demographic, and military considerations. The
phrase that has circulated in media and activist circles that Israel wanted
the land without the people has become almost a cliché in describing the
outcome of this process, nevertheless, it continues to hold a great deal of
truth. The new borders of the city, stretched north to include the airport
strip, but snaked southward in a way that avoids the densely populated villages of Abu Dis, Al-Azariyya, Beit Hanina, and A-Ram in the east and
northeast. Another consideration was to secure the strategic heights around
Jerusalem to prevent, in the event of a later withdrawal from the West Bank,
the possibility of Jordanian shelling onto the city or any other military advantage. In this way the new municipal borders also incorporated hilltops
and defensible valleys near al-Birah, Neve Ya'acov (which had been a Jewish
settlement during the Mandate period) in the north, and those overlooking
Bayt Jallah and Bethlehem in the south.[77]

An important point to note is that these new municipal borders were
identical to the area designated by Israel as under its legal jurisdiction. Thus

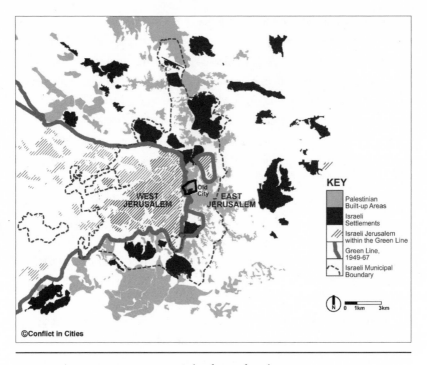

MAP 1.5. 1967 borders and settlements.

Israel was able to claim that it was merely initiating an "integration of Jerusalem in the administrative and municipal spheres," not implementing a unilateral annexation that would have, at that time, caused it difficulties in the UN and with its main allies.[78] While in practice these legislative acts amounted to an annexation by the back door, it is also clear that it was a different kind of annexation. As Ian Lustick has pointed out, the terminology in the Israeli legislation avoided any hint of annexation and that among the criteria of annexation is the imposition of citizenship. Israel did impose citizenship on the Palestinians in areas it acquired in 1948 that had not been allocated to Israel by the Partition Plan, such as in Galilee and the area known as the Triangle. However, it refrained from doing so in 1967 when it extended its jurisdiction in exactly the same way to East Jerusalem and adjacent areas of the West Bank.[79] This ambiguity has many implications and opens up many questions. To what extent is East Jerusalem part of Israel? How does the formal and proclaimed position put forward by Israel actually map out on the ground? Does the international community, and hence the force of international law, confirm the validity of these legislative acts? Some of the answers to these questions are addressed in the next chapter. At this point I wish to focus on the extent to which international law contributes to our definition of the city. In essence, what are the borders of the city enshrined in the various debates and resolutions in the UN and its related agencies?

Most debates concerning Jerusalem and international law have focused on the relative strengths and weaknesses of the claims by the different parties over the city.[80] Much less is written or prescribed in the official UN documents on the actual borders of the city.[81] As we have seen, the UN Partition Plan of 1947 demarcated an international zone of Jerusalem, and this remained the desired position of the international community until 1967. Neither Israeli control over West Jerusalem nor Jordanian control over East Jerusalem was recognized by the international community.[82] However, it is possible to argue that this position has been superseded both in terms of UN resolutions and in practice by the longevity of the UN armistice agreements and the Israeli occupation in 1967. In response to the occupation, the UN Security Council passed Resolution 242 which, in calling for the withdrawal of Israeli forces from territories it occupied in 1967, neither mentioned the city of Jerusalem nor demarcated any borders. Clearly, East Jerusalem was occupied in 1967 and should be withdrawn from, but, nevertheless, the resolution does not call for a return to the borders of the Jewish and Arab states recommended by the UN Partition Plan. By inference it calls for a withdrawal to those of the Armistice Lines of 1949. Ever since then it has not been clear whether, therefore, UN Resolution 242 is an endorsement of the armistice agreements and the partition of Jerusalem, which at their signing in 1949 were seen as temporary. In this sense, there has been an incremental and grudging acceptance by the international community that the Armistice Lines of 1949 constitute the borders of Israel, leaving the remaining areas of Palestine—the West Bank, Gaza Strip, and East Jerusalem as the location of the putative Palestinian state.

In fact, UN Resolution 242 provided the basis of the Oslo Agreements signed by Israel and the PLO. Although the Oslo Agreements made the drawing up of agreed borders subject to further negotiations, the subsequent phases of negotiations have gradually confirmed the view that the Armistice Lines would be the base of any territorial exchanges.[83] Furthermore, the International Court of Justice Advisory Opinion in 2004 explicitly and emphatically confirmed that East Jerusalem is part of the occupied Palestinian territories from which Israel should withdraw, suggesting in this way the renewed partition of the city.[84] Finally, a recent UN report on the barrier stresses the role of the ICJ Advisory Opinion in determining that the barrier in East Jerusalem should be dismantled and rerouted along the Armistice Lines.[85]

Taken all together, it is clear that the extension of the municipal boundaries in 1967 and more recently the delimitation of the city by the barrier are not acceptable to the international community. While the international community has refrained from forcefully challenging Israeli policies and, as a consequence, Israel has been given a free rein in implementing programs to consolidate its presence on both sides of the city, nevertheless, without international recognition and acceptance this can only go so far. The absence of international legitimacy not only undermines its prospects of securing a peace agreement with the Palestinians, it also hampers the development of the city and its integration into the global economy. In the face of contested land title and the lack of clarity over state jurisdiction, few major companies, or the commercial insurers who underwrite major public and private development, will invest in the city.

The main conclusion that can be drawn from this exploration of the borders of the city is their evolutionary and dynamic nature. As in all cities that have grown in the modern period, the borders of Jerusalem needed to be adjusted to accommodate its burgeoning population. However, we should bear in mind that cities function and flourish through interaction, exchange, and the movement of people and goods. In this sense ethnically mixed cities are an anathema to a militant ethnically based ideology as, short of ethnic cleansing, the dominant group is obliged to accommodate the subordinate groups. As we have seen, unlike 1948, which led to the mass displacement of Palestinians from the western parts of the city, in 1967 Palestinians did not leave in such large numbers. This presented a very different challenge to

Israel and, more fundamentally, to Zionism. The approach adopted by the Israeli political elite has been both the gerrymandering of borders to contrive a demographic dominance and the colonization of land and property to channel Israeli Jewish settlers into Palestinian areas. This book seeks to understand why despite over forty years of occupation this challenge still remains. In chapter 2 I explore how the hard borders of the city are "softened" by layers of residential segregation, cultural praxis, and functional operations that constitute alternative borders in the city to the ones discussed in this chapter.

2

THE "SOFTER" BORDERS OF THE CITY

WAS BORN and brought up in West Malaysia, and in the 1960s as a family we spent our annual holidays exploring the upper reaches of the Pahang River. Our favorite spot was the National Park headquarters where the wide, muddy, and sluggish Tembeling River met the dark and swift-flowing waters of the Tahan. I recall playing frequently in the confluence of the two rivers and sometimes swimming across from one bank to the other. Once, after heavy rains, I was swept away by faster than usual currents and had to be rescued by my elder brother and a party of Malaysian Boy Scouts who happened to be canoeing by. As dangerous as that had been, I also recall, in the midst of panic and fear, my marveling at the quick, repeated, and unexpected changes from hot to cold water as the two rivers met and gradually merged. The Tembeling, oozing out of the densely forested lower hills, was warm and slower moving, while the Tahan, snaking its way through the green jungle-clad mountains further upstream, carried a nip of the peaks of the Gunung Tahan range, the highest mountains in West Malaysia. Even while tumbling too fast down the river out of my brother's reach, I remember registering my movement across the confluence by the temperature and color of the water around me.

Walking around Jerusalem, I often recall my Malaysian escapade. Several times an hour, let alone a day, you can suddenly be aware of "temperature" changes as you move from one part of the city to another—even from one street corner to the next. There is no obvious visible border being crossed, but you sense a transition, an unexpected change in atmosphere and pace. Sometimes it may be the sudden disappearance of pavement, and when you look around you notice the rows of apartment blocks and their neat gardens have ended. It then registers that you have moved from an Israeli Jewish area to a Palestinian one and, further along the road, you can see that it becomes pitted and eventually perhaps unpaved and, unlike the Jewish area, surrounded by houses that are largely unfinished and have lost their regular gridlike arrangement. Sometimes, perhaps, the difference is signaled by the particular kind of bustle on the street, the dress of the passersby, the appearance of bi- and trilingual shop signs, the graffitiesque paintings of the Kaaba in Mecca or the Dome of the Rock on front doorways, or the remnants of homemade plastic kites caught kicking in the electric cables overhead. At other times it might be the different cooking smells wafting out of kitchens, subtle changes in music being played on the radio, or the greetings being called out as neighbors enter each other's houses. The transitions are not only just between East and West Jerusalem but also within those areas. The absence of women in certain public spaces at certain times is not necessarily the sign of a conservative Palestinian suburb, but rather perhaps that you are leaving the realm of short skirts and bare arms along Ben Yehuda Street in West Jerusalem and are entering Mea She'arim, an Orthodox Jewish stronghold also in West Jerusalem but as forbidding to outsiders as parts of Qom in Iran.[1]

And the transition from "hot" to "cold" is also more accurate as an analogy than it first might seem. At times of political friction the city may be going along with its usual staccato and busy rhythms and you may be window shopping or walking to a café to meet an interviewee when, suddenly, you can sense a tension in the air. There are fewer cars, buses have stopped running, the air feels thinner, your feet more echoey on the street. You register that there is a low growl of chanting in the distance and shopkeepers are standing outside their front doors, keys at the ready to pull down the shutters. A dull thud and a few muffled crumps signal teargas being fired and you hesitate to carry on. Then, turning a few streets to your left, you find café tables on the pavement are crowded with people, schoolchildren are standing in line at bus stops, families are peering into shopwindows. You could be in a different city altogether. One part of the city seems to be experiencing strife and conflict while the other parts carry on with everyday life. When out and about in these circumstances, as a rough indicator of safety, I use what I call "the Dumper pram-quotient": the more baby carriages in sight, the safer the street. I certainly do not use the presence of police or uniformed security forces as a good indicator; in fact they are, more often than not, a sign not to venture out.

As many readers will know, these changes in temperatures within a city are not necessarily unique to Jerusalem. I, like others, will have experienced similar transitions in other divided cities such as Belfast, Beirut, and Mostar and indeed in less contested cities such as Paris and Singapore. The provision of municipal services and the manifestations of civic pride are never uniformly distributed throughout a city, and such differentiation is often accentuated by class and ethnicity. Cities are a mosaic of interlocking, overlapping, and contrasting enclaves. In 2000 I walked, for over three hours, the whole length of Manhattan, New York, mostly along Broadway, and was astonished at the cultural diversity from one block to another. You could move from swanky shops to a Colombian street market to bohemian bistros within a hundred paces. What, however, is different in a divided city like Jerusalem or Belfast or Mostar to the expected mosaics of a less politically contested city is that the division is more than just class and ethnicity, so that the transitions are more than just moving from a working-class or a North African suburb, say, in Paris, to a more up-market or more Caucasian one. In a divided or an occupied city, the legitimacy of the state, its agents and organs, are denied and resented by a significant section of the population. This provides an undercurrent of tension, a bass thrumming below the surface sounds that gives the transitions from neighborhood to neighborhood a different character. In any city one can still feel the transition from hot to cold as one moves from a run-down or low-life area to that of bijou shops or detached houses with walled gardens. Some areas feel safer than others. But that sense one can get in all cities of being on the margins of the state's authority, together with the associated hint of criminality, is, in a divided city, compounded by a greater sense of trespass and of being "out of place." The sinews that run through a city and unite it, those of waste collection, of lighting and water provision, of roads that are ordered and purposeful, of public transport and public spaces that are shared, are, in a divided city such as Jerusalem, both provisional and contingent. Their implementation and acceptance is related to the conflicting political identities and allegiances operating within wider political processes.

One should also remember that if, as a visitor, one notices the unevenness of these transitions that resonate with the political tensions one may have seen on the television the night before, how much more do members of one or other of the city's ethnopolitical groups feel them when they move from one part of the city to the other. As a visitor your perception or understanding of the transition is partially shaped by interaction with people who see you or you pass by. Usually some allowance is given to you as being a temporary presence or perhaps being lost or a sightseer. The glances, stares, greetings, and the kinds of deference you encounter when, say, crossing a street, can be hostile, but, more often than not, they are either indifferent or positively friendly. As a member of the opposing group or the ethnic "other," however, your presence will be more threatening. Why are you here? What does your presence mean? Are you an inspector looking for unofficially built houses? Are you a sign of some new encroachment in the offing? Are you carrying a weapon or a bomb? The sense of trespass is palpable and thus the transition is much greater.

In this way the mosaic of enclaves within an ethnically diverse city becomes the foundations for the construction of informal borders within it. In times of heightened political tensions, the enclaves become "no-go" areas for your ordinary resident of the opposing ethnopolitical group. They become areas where only state officials go if they have to or areas where the police are always armed and in highly mobile units. In times of political impasse and violence, the borders move from being permeable to impermeable, from "soft" to "hard" as streets are ripped up, barricades and walls erected, and checkpoints sprout beside key access points.[2] The ebb and flow of tensions in Belfast saw exactly this pattern as Protestant Unionist and Catholic Republican enclaves detached themselves from neighboring enclaves to form a patchwork of no-go areas across the city. Walls, fences, and barricades made access to them subject to close surveillance, and the role of the local police was replaced on the one hand by internal militia and vigilantes and on the other by the British armed forces.[3] Mostar is less an example of the subtlety of these transitions and patterns of enclaving as both a wide boulevard and a river running through the city forms part of the dividing line between the two dominant communal groups—Croatian Christians and Bosniak Muslims. However, since its reconstruction, there has been a deliberate blurring of the edges where such transitions can be observed.[4] The hardening of previously porous and loosely demarcated borders in time of strife can also be seen in recent years in Beirut. The previous divide between Christian East Beirut and Muslim West Beirut has been gradually replaced by new enclaves controlled by Sunni groups supporting the March 14 political bloc and Shi'a groups supporting the March 8 bloc.[5]

In Jerusalem we certainly can see this pattern occurring during the latter part of the British Mandate period where Palestinian and Jewish areas consolidated themselves as exclusive zones. The only area for communal interaction became the central business district in the streets around Jaffa Road in the New City which was controlled by the British and known as Bevingrad, after the British foreign minister.

As we saw in chapter 1, the end result of the war between the two sides in 1948 was the division of Jerusalem and the evacuation of Palestinians from western districts of the city and of Jews from the east. The city was completely divided with a very hard border (see map 1.2). In 1967 the Israeli conquest of the eastern part of the city reunited it, but this time under Israeli authority.[6] Since that date, the establishment of Israeli settler colonies in the eastern side has reintroduced an enclaving of such complex proportions that a redivision without their accompanying evacuation is difficult to conceive of. That this was a deliberate objective by the Israeli political elite will be explored further in this and other chapters of this book. At this point I want to connect this pattern of enclaving and soft borders with the change and transitions visitors and residents alike experience.

My contention is that while this experience may be subjective it is also based upon substance and hard facts. The sense of transition from one area to the next, mainly between West and East Jerusalem, is not just cosmetic and a result of shop signage and kitchen smells reflecting the cultural diversity of the city. The erosion of the Green Line or Armistice Lines through Jerusalem by the colonization by Israelis settlers in Palestinian areas may have eradicated the stark divisions between the two sides of the city to a large extent.[7] However, the establishment of colonies throughout East Jerusalem over the past fifty years has transformed Jerusalem from a divided city and partially occupied city into a city of Israeli and Palestinian enclaves. But these Palestinian enclaves in an Israeli-dominated city are not yet just washed-up pockets of the remnants of Palestinian culture. They are grounded in political realities that are, on the one hand, residues from the pre-1967 period but, more importantly, on the other hand, are structural, long-standing, and current. They are, indeed, more pervasive, more extensive, and stronger than it may first appear to the visitor or to the uninformed resident. The Palestinian position in the various rounds of peace negotiations has always been that the basis of any negotiations over the future of the city should be recognition of Palestinian sovereignty over all of East Jerusalem, that is, everything east of the Armistice Lines (see map 1.2). The Israeli argument that this position is based on fantasy, and therefore not a credible starting point for negotiations, is effectively countered by the persistence, resilience, and ongoing threat of these enclaves to Israeli hegemony in the city.

This chapter will explore the hidden components that support these enclaves and how, as a result, the city, particularly in East Jerusalem, is crisscrossed by subnational, residential, and functional borders that have political implications of some importance behind them. My argument is that spatial usage, social traditions, economic practices, dress, and religion, etc., are rooted and buttressed by structural and legal elements that explain their continuous presence and resilience. I start by first explaining how the Israeli policy of annexation in East Jerusalem was partial and incomplete, leaving important Palestinian jurisdictions intact. I then look at two categories of activities where Palestinian autonomy can be seen to continue and which question Israeli presumption of sovereignty in East Jerusalem. The first category concerns identity and cultural issues and comprises two case studies—the electoral and education systems in East Jerusalem. The second category is more structural and legal and comprises control over land and housing, residential segregation and the provision of municipal services. A final section will draw together the ramifications of these enclave "supports" and conclude with some observations as to their impact on the future of the city.

HOW ANNEXED IS EAST JERUSALEM?

As we saw in chapter 1, the Israeli incorporation of East Jerusalem and adjacent parts of the West Bank into Israel was a unilateral act flowing from its occupation of those areas in 1967. This needs no more reiteration here. However, what is most important to emphasize, as it continues to have ongoing reverberations and is relevant to the formation of enclaves and their soft borders, is that this act of incorporation was not recognized by a single other country in the world and its activities there continue to be deemed illegal by the whole international community,[8] a position that was confirmed by the ICJ Opinion in 2004.[9] This renders all Israeli activities in East Jerusalem illegal and is the main impediment for Israel in absorbing East Jerusalem into the western part of the city. Without international recognition, every visit by foreign dignitaries, every cultural festival, all investment and construction in East Jerusalem is surrounded with controversy and difficulties.[10] There is constantly a question mark over everything that Israel does in East Jerusalem. Despite its dominance on the ground, despite Israeli protestations and legal arguments, and despite Israeli attempts to cast a cloak of normality over its policies, the international community has barely moved an inch from this position and has thus rendered Israel quite weak in terms of establishing its acquisition of East Jerusalem as an incontrovertible fact. More fundamentally, the continued illegality of Israeli activities as the occupying power supplies the Palestinians with moral and political support for their formal position that East Jerusalem will be the capital of the new Palestinian state and that this political objective is feasible and resting on international legitimacy and sure foundations. Ultimately, the international community's refusal to accept the Israeli occupation forms the bedrock of Palestinian resistance and mobilization against its policies in East Jerusalem and the persistence of enclaves there.

Within this overall context of illegality of Israeli status, some ambiguity has undoubtedly crept in.[11] This is partly due to the longevity of the Israeli presence in East Jerusalem, which has created a new status quo and arguably some rights as a result.[12] There has also been what Palestinians see as a lack of backbone in the stands taken by the Security Council and the reluctance of the United States to enforce UN resolutions.[13] At the same time, an ambiguity has also always been there from the start—in 1967—largely due, paradoxically, to Israeli policies themselves, which have been ambivalent about incorporating not the land but the residents of East Jerusalem. There are two elements to this Israeli ambiguity. One is ideological and concerns the role of Zionism as a driver in Israeli expansion. The other arguably flows from this in the way the annexation of East Jerusalem was only partially implemented.

One of the fundamental challenges to Zionism as a result of its engagement with Palestinian nationalism is its inability to resolve the problem of how to incorporate into the state those Palestinians who are located within the borders of Israel. If the land of historic Palestine had, indeed, been as empty as the Zionist ideologues proclaimed, then there would have been no problem. Israel would have been established on a tabula rasa, and Jewish-only institutions could have been established without fear of accusations of racism and exclusivity. The fact that after the fighting in 1948 some Palestinians remained on their land, in the cities, towns, and villages and now, in 2013, constitute 20 percent of the population of Israel has posed the most enduring problem for Israel since its inception.[14] Nevertheless, as non-Jews they are not permitted to participate in the life of the Israeli nation in the same way as Jews. While having Israeli citizenship and the right to vote, their status is circumscribed in a myriad of ways which renders them second-class citizens—exclusion from certain employment, confiscation of their land and property, continuing forcible exile of family members, designation of Jewish-only residential zones such as *kibbutzim, moshavim, mitzpayim*, inferior infrastructure and public services, and greater police surveillance. The paradox of this policy of exclusion is that it leads a situation where Palestinians feel marginalized from mainstream Israeli Jewish society and thus turn to alternative sources for identity construction and political support. Instead of being included and given the shared identity of Israeli, irrespective of being a Jew or a Palestinian Arab, Zionism places them in a separate category. As the ideology dedicated to the development of a Jewish state, driving and undergirding the Israeli state-building project for Jews, it can find no place for the Palestinians inside its borders. The result has been the reinvigorating of Palestinian identity, of ties with the Palestinian diaspora, and of greater anti-Zionism. Like other ethnonationalist ideologies, one of the fundamental contradictions in Zionism, therefore, is that its essential exclusivity generates a reaction that threatens the success of its very objectives.

This is very clearly the case in Jerusalem and goes a long way to explaining the resilience of the Palestinian enclaves. The creation of Jewish-only enclaves in East Jerusalem on confiscated Palestinian land, the discrimination in favor of Jews in zoning, planning, and provision of services, the curtailment of political and cultural freedoms, the overt and covert state support for the intimidating, racist, and illegal behavior of some settler groups have all combined to antagonize Palestinians who might have considered some sort of accommodation with Israeli interests and aspirations in Jerusalem.[15] The early ideas of the former Israeli mayor of Jerusalem, Teddy Kollek, of creating a mosaic of religious and ethnic communities under a benign and protective Israeli authority, naive and superficial as they were, have been brushed aside by a more muscular and fundamentalist Jewish nationalism that sees the Palestinian only in terms of threat and not as partners sharing a site of common reverence. The result is a reiteration of Palestinian nationalist claims to the city and a search by Palestinian residents for sources of political and financial support other than that from the Israeli state to fund basic municipal services and infrastructural developments which, in turn, has drawn in external international forces in the Muslim and Christian world.[16] In this way Zionism in Jerusalem has helped consolidate the very enclaves in Jerusalem that jeopardize Israeli hegemony over the city.

Compounding this ideological superstructure has been the way in which Israeli law has been introduced in East Jerusalem. The incremental, discretionary, and arbitrary manner of its implementation also served to create a separate set of localities in the city and thus reinforced the strength and distinctiveness of the Palestinian enclaves. As I mentioned in the introduction, Ian Lustick has argued in a pair of complementary and controversial articles that Israel has never formally annexed East Jerusalem.[17] His argument is that Jerusalem, in contrast to other areas Israel has annexed, has received special treatment. For example, in areas such the Galilee and the Triangle which were outside the borders allocated to the Jewish state in the 1947 UN Partition Plan but were acquired by conquest in 1948 or ceded and annexed to Israel in the armistice agreements with Jordan in 1949, citizenship was imposed upon the Palestinian residents of those areas whether they liked it or not. By contrast, citizenship was made optional for the Palestinian residents of East Jerusalem. They were made "permanent residents" and entitled to vote in municipal elections, but were neither made citizens of Israel nor given the right to vote in national elections. In addition, Lustick points out that the term *annexation* was not used in any of the legislation concerning the incorporation of East Jerusalem into Israel, while it did not hesitate to do so elsewhere.

Critics of Lustick have rejected these arguments on the grounds that they are merely semantics and that to all intents and purposes Israel has annexed Jerusalem. It has full military control and is effective in imposing its jurisdiction over both sides of the city. In the early 1990s I was a participant in a series of off-the-record workshops organized by the American Academy of Arts and Sciences on the future of Jerusalem. Comprising both Israeli and Palestinian academics and policy makers, I recall in one session an intense and heated discussion between Professor Lustick, himself a former soldier in the Israeli army during the 1973 war, and a high-ranking Israeli diplomat and a left-wing Member of Knesset on just this issue. The diplomat and politician were vehement in their denunciation of Lustick's argument since it undermined the foundations of Israeli policies in East Jerusalem. We were meeting in the Notre Dame Hotel in Jerusalem, and, as the discussion heated up and slipped into Hebrew and as it also clearly became an internal Israeli and Jewish debate, I remember the Palestinian participants saw this as an opportunity for a cigarette break on the balcony overlooking Musrara and the Old City. As they got up to leave their seats, they raised their eyebrows at each other, fully aware of the irony of Israelis and Jews disagreeing among themselves over the nature of their occupation of East Jerusalem. The reasons that Lustick's interlocutors gave for the absence of the imposition of citizenship and of the term *annexation* was that, in the early legislation after 1967, Israel did not wish either to pre-empt some kind of agreement with Jordan over the future of the West Bank and East Jerusalem or to alienate Western support for its actions in1967. The absence of the term *annexation* or the imposition of citizenship was simply a question of realpolitik and that Israeli formal sovereignty had indeed been applied and subsequently reaffirmed in the Basic Law on Jerusalem in 1980. Lustick's response was that in playing the realpolitik card they were actually confirming the overall thrust of his argument—the absence of explicit annexation—and that, moreover, the Basic Law of 1980 did not use the term *annexation* either. Why?[18]

While both sides are able to present valid arguments to back up their views, what is significant in this debate for our exploration of the soft borders and enclaves in Jerusalem is Lustick's fundamental point that East Jerusalem has been treated differently from other parts of Israel for whatever reason. In this way the very foundations of the Israeli legal and political edifice in East Jerusalem are unstable. In conjunction with the denial of recognition by the international community, this confers upon East Jerusalem a unique status that sets it apart from the rest of Israel. As a result, the whole of East Jerusalem, and particularly the Palestinian enclaves, are infused with a sense of difference based on political and legal realities.

We can see this more clearly if we turn to specific aspects of the application of Israeli jurisdiction over East Jerusalem. In chapter 1 we saw how the delineation of the borders of East Jerusalem in 1967 themselves were the result of debate and compromise by different Israeli interests.[19] As important as this has also been the way in which, over the whole panoply of Israeli legislation, East Jerusalem has been subject to wide exemptions. As we have already seen, one of the first laws Israel passed after its occupation of East Jerusalem in 1967 was to extend the borders and responsibilities of the West Jerusalem municipality to encompass the Jordanian Arab Jerusalem municipality and areas adjacent to it. On the same day, it passed the Law and Administration Ordinance Law, ostensibly designed to integrate East Jerusalem into the Israeli legal system, but the significant part of this law was actually the exemptions it contained. These exemptions were included to make the Israeli presence less intrusive in East Jerusalem, but over time have served to buttress the enclaves that emerged.[20] For example, East Jerusalem was exempted from many health and safety regulations that would have impinged upon the operations of its markets and wholesale trade. In the same way, Israeli labor laws were not applied fully so as to permit the continuation of small family businesses, and there were also exemptions to Israeli practice in the registration of businesses where Palestinian businesses that had registered with the Jordanian government were not obliged to apply for registration with the Israeli government but were granted automatic registration, even if they did not seek it as part of their refusal to recognize Israeli authority in East Jerusalem. Money changers are not allowed in Israel, but those in Salah Ed-Din Street in the central business district of East Jerusalem and in the Old City were allowed to ply their traditional trade.[21] As a result, the Palestinian Arab commercial system was allowed to continue to follow practices of the Jordanian era.

Indeed, what is truly remarkable were two further exemptions. First, it was made illegal to take cognizance of the fact that East Jerusalem Palestinians were Jordanian citizens and therefore in Israeli law regarded as an "enemy."[22] This was to prevent the wholesale disruption of social and economic life in East Jerusalem. Second, the draconian Israeli Absentee Property Law of 1950 was amended to exempt the residents of East Jerusalem who as Jordanian, and therefore technically an "enemy," would be liable to have their property confiscated by its provisions.[23]

In the sections below I shall examine how this early legislation, together with the position of the international community and the legal ambiguity over annexation, has provided a platform for the continuing Palestinian physical, political, and cultural presence in the city and how the experience of transition from one area to another, from hot to cold zones, is real and substantiated. In the meantime, a graphic example of what this graduated and differentiated application of Israeli legislation meant could be seen when one entered the Old City in the period after 1967. I clearly recall on my first visit to Jerusalem in 1977 how as a young backpacker I was looking for cheap accommodations in one of the Palestinian hostels in the Old City. Walking from the West Jerusalem bus station and passing by the very Westernized grocery stores and supermarkets along Jaffa Road, I was struck and initially repelled on entry into the *suq* in the heart of the Old City by the rows of uncovered and unrefrigerated carcasses—sheep, goats, cattle, and camels—skinned but complete, with heads and dead staring eyes, hanging up in the front of Palestinian butcher shops. The narrow pavement between them was spattered with blood, offal, bits of horn, hoof, and bone, clumps of hair and fatty off-cuts, like the remains of some medieval battle scene. I now know that this was the Suq al-Lahamiin, or Butcher's Row, in the Old City and one of the best places to get a good but cheap cut of meat. Yet it remains a vivid illustration of the ways in which Israeli food safety legislation was not applied to East Jerusalem, which in turn affirmed the Palestinian nature of the quarter.

IDENTITY AND CULTURE

In this section and the next I want to demonstrate how the Palestinian en-claves are not merely the residues of a pre-1967 demography, similar to the Palestinian communities in Jaffa, Ramle, Lydda, and Acre inside Israel who cling on desperately to the remnants of their culture, property, and public space. Indeed, the argument I have made is that these enclaves are con-firmed and to some extent consolidated by international community, by Israeli legislation, and by the ongoing vibrancy of the Palestinian political and cultural life in them despite the deprivations they experience. To under-stand this more, I wish to describe how both de jure and de facto the iden-tity and culture of the Palestinian residents is delineated in two fields: that of electoral politics and that of education. Clearly a fundamental compo-nent of identity and culture is also religion. However, because religion is so central to the history, politics, and everyday life of Jerusalem and therefore needs examining in some depth, I will not include it in this section. Instead chapter 3 is devoted to its discussing its role, impact, and ramifications for the future of the city.[24]

ELECTIONS IN EAST JERUSALEM

Not many Israelis or internationals are aware that Palestinian residents of East Jerusalem are blessed with the entitlement to vote in elections for two different polities—the Jerusalem municipal elections in Israel and the Palestinian national elections in the OPTs. Indeed, it is a quite remarkable and often overlooked fact that in the heart of the Israeli capital one-third of the population vote for representatives in another national system. If we turn to the Israeli municipal elections first, we can see a consistent pattern of non-participation. In the first Israeli municipal elections after the occupation, in 1969, 7,150 of the 25,000 eligible East Jerusalem Palestinians voted, roughly 28 percent of eligible voters. This was the high point of Palestinian participation. Anecdotal evidence suggests that most of the Palestinian voters were municipality employees anxious to retain their posts. Since then there has been both a decline in voting as well as much debate in Palestinian circles over the extent to which participation would serve Palestinian interests or simply provide Israel with a propaganda coup by suggesting that Palestinians were accepting its control over the city. In the face of a PLO-inspired boycott of the elections, the percentage in Palestinian participation has steadily declined, rarely reaching more than 20 percent.[25] Nevertheless, notable individuals have argued that Palestinian interests would be better served if they were able to represent Palestinian views on the Israeli Municipal Council and, more importantly, if Palestinians were able to have greater influence over the zoning of land and of the discriminatory allocation of municipal budgets. In 1989 an attempt was made when Hanna Siniora, a prominent Palestinian businessman and newspaper editor, tried to form a list, but was dissuaded by PLO admonishments and arson attacks on his property.[26] In 1993, discussions between Israelis and Palestinians in Jerusalem over the possibility of forming a joint list were well advanced before the PLO leadership intervened to squash the initiative.[27] In 1998 another Palestinian sought to push the idea of participation on pure pragmatic grounds and planned to stand as an independent, but was persuaded to withdraw.[28] Those that made the case for participation have argued that, in addition to the need to influence planning decisions and the allocation of resources, the Israeli vote was deeply split between secular and Orthodox Jews and that if Palestinians voted *en bloc* they would be a dominant force in the Municipal Council or at least be able to exert considerable leverage through judicious alliances. Palestinian enclaves would benefit from better roads, paving, sanitation, planning, education, health provision, and cultural facilities without the future status of East Jerusalem being predetermined.

Critics point out that participation would legitimize the Israeli occupation and convey a Palestinian acceptance of Israeli sovereignty over the city in a highly symbolic way. Imagine the diplomatic coup for Israel, they say, if an East Jerusalem Palestinian deputy mayor of the Israeli Municipal Council was on hand, beneath an Israeli flag, no less, to meet, for example, foreign VIPs such as the high representative of the EU. Indeed, one can also see how the daily routine of negotiating agendas, of compromises, of making alliances, of public appearances, of hosting festivals and sporting activities would both cast a mantle of normality over the occupation of East Jerusalem and also loosen the ties that connect East Jerusalem to the West Bank and Gaza even further. In addition, one could argue that supporters of participation are naive to think that Palestinians in East Jerusalem would be allowed to exert much influence over municipal provision. Putting aside the difficulty of ensuring a united Palestinian voting strategy and the likelihood of several competing lists splitting the Palestinian vote, the possibility that the Israeli state will leave important strategic decisions concerning the use of land and changes in residency to a council potentially dominated by Palestinians and their Israeli left-wing and peacenik allies is very remote.[29] A quick glance at the powerlessness and ineffectiveness of Palestinian communities and municipalities in Israel illustrates the determination with which the Israeli state will confront that challenge.[30] Furthermore, a Palestinian grouping in the Israeli Municipal Council will very quickly come under pressure from its supporters (and critics) to raise the explosive issue of the restitution of Palestinian property in West Jerusalem or to lose credibility. How, they would legitimately ask, can a Jerusalem city council with Palestinians sitting on it ignore the fact that half the city is built on confiscated Palestinian land. If a Palestinian list ran in the municipal elections, before one could say Nebuchadnezzar national issues would raise their head and cause crises and political impasse.[31]

Nevertheless, the overarching point I wish to make in this discussion is this: despite the pressures on Palestinian enclaves which participation in municipal elections may alleviate even slightly, despite the internal debate on the issue of participation, the national Palestinian consensus on a electoral boycott has held, both in terms of low turnouts and in terms of the fact that not a single major Palestinian political grouping or sectional interest in the city has broken ranks to align themselves with sympathetic Israeli parties. In light of the vibrant cross-city trade, employment, and retail patterns, this is quite a remarkable phenomenon and one that undergirds the enclave nature of East Jerusalem. Without representation in the major political institution in the city, the Palestinians of East Jerusalem simultaneously look elsewhere for leadership and set themselves apart. This distinctiveness is reinforced by their very contrasting activity of participation in the elections for the Palestinian Legislative Council.

The PLC was established under the 1993 Oslo Accords, and, while voter turnout in Jerusalem has been much lower than the national average, the controversy surrounding the elections, the obstacles placed in the way of voters by the Israeli state, the attention of the international community through election monitors and media have all highlighted a critical anomaly of the Israeli occupation—that one-third of the population of the capital of the Israeli state is eligible to vote in the quasi-parliament of a neighboring country. The Declaration of Principles, or Oslo Accords, states that "Palestinians of Jerusalem who live there will have the right to participate in the election process."[32] Nevertheless, this concession by Israel was surrounded with qualifications and restrictions in a desperate attempt not to signal, prior to a final status agreement, any erosion of Israeli sovereignty over the city. While Israel also accepted the definition contained in the Palestinian Election Law of 1995 of who a Palestinian was, Palestinians, in turn,

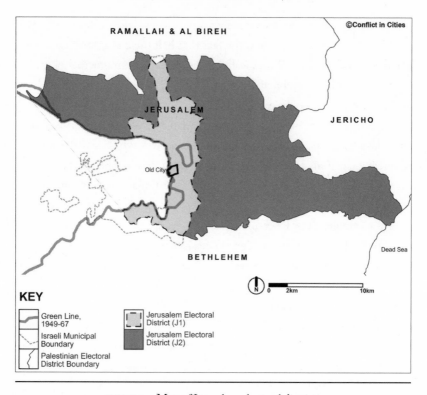

MAP 2.1. Map of Jerusalem electoral district.

were obliged to accept for the purposes of the PLC and Palestinian presidential elections a Jerusalem electoral district that encompassed the existing Israeli-defined municipal borders.[33]

While the Palestinian Central Electoral Commission (CEC) was permitted by its agreements with Israel to establish an electoral role in the parts of the Jerusalem district outside the municipal borders, it was not allowed to do so inside. Instead, Israel agreed that a Palestinian educational institution in East Jerusalem, the Ibrahimiya College, was allowed to carry out a canvass of voters, provided no Palestinian emblems were displayed on the materials that would undermine Israeli sovereignty. In the same way, Israel was concerned over the presence of polling booths in East Jerusalem. It feared that this would signal an introduction of the Palestinian Authority's role in the city and set a precedent for future activities and thus undermine its negotiating position. After much discussion and pressure from the U.S., it was finally agreed between the PLO and Israel that polling booths would be set up outside the Israeli municipal borders to which East Jerusalem Palestinians would go to vote. Only a limited number of voters (between 6,000 and 7,500) would be allowed to vote in the city itself, and they would do so at post offices designated by Israel and not at polling stations.[34] This was to ensure that the act of voting was seen as an Israeli-controlled activity within an Israeli government–run agency. A polling station in a recognized Palestinian institution such as Orient House would be transformed, Israel rightly feared, into a celebration of Palestinian nationalism. At the same time, placing them in Israeli post offices also served as a deterrent for those Palestinians who had fears over their residency status. However, the controversy did not stop there. Frantically attempting to minimize any hint of Palestinianism in the electoral process, Israel insisted the ballots be placed in envelopes tha would then be mailed to the CEC for counting. Indeed, it refused to call them ballot boxes, and the Palestinians had to agree on the term *receptacles*. The shape and design of the ballot boxes then became crucial. Israel wanted the boxes to have the entry slit on the side to resemble a mailbox, while the Palestinians insisted that they be on the top like normal ballot boxes. A compromise was reached where a slit was placed at one of the edges on top of the box so it neither resembles a mailbox nor a ballot box![35] Finally, any election campaigning would require a permit from Israel.[36] In all these ways Israel sought to emphasize that East Jerusalem was not under the jurisdiction of the Palestinian CEC, the PLC, and the PNA and sought to empty the voting process of any Palestinian nationalist content.

There have been three national elections so far: the 1996 and 2006 PLC elections and the 2005 presidential elections. For Palestinian nationalists, voter turnout in the Jerusalem district in all three will have been a great disappointment. In 1996 approximately 30 percent of the Palestinian electorate in the Jerusalem district voted, while in 2005 only 20 percent voted. In the PLC elections of 2006 the number rose to 50 percent. In all three cases the number was considerably below the Palestinian national average. Voter turnout for Palestinian residents in those areas within the Israeli municipality, as opposed to the wider Jerusalem electoral district, was even lower—10 percent in 1996, 6 percent in 2005, and 16 percent in 2006. For those who wish to stress the Palestinian connection to Jerusalem and its important role in the national consciousness and state-building narrative, the results are worrying. Surely, as a city under occupation, demonstrating the engagement of Palestinian Jerusalemites in Palestinian political life is critical. Surely it should be seen by Palestinian residents as part of their resistance and rejection to Israeli rule in the city? Surely the turnout should be higher than the national average?

There are a number explanations for this low turnout. Many observers have highlighted the fears Palestinian voters had as to whether their participation would jeopardize their residency permit and the restrictions placed on Palestinian voters in accessing polling booths. Only a few (six thousand) were allowed to vote inside the municipal borders; all other voters had to find the right polling station in the suburbs on the other side of checkpoints and the separation barrier. Crossing over on the day of the elections was not made easy, and there were long queues at the checkpoints overseen by a heavily armed Israeli security presence. As the Israeli police adviser on Arab affairs in the municipality, Reuven Berko, admitted after the 1996 elections, "we did not threaten people to dissuade them from voting, but we did influence them."[37] In addition, the Palestinian political elite were inexperienced and disorganized in electoral politics, so that, in addition to the obstacles placed in the way of Jerusalemite Palestinians by Israel, information as to where to go and how to get there, which was a Palestinian responsibility, was sparse. The election campaign planning required to get one's supporters to the polling stations was not there. It is significant that voting nearly doubled between 1996 and 2006. Much of this difference is due to the Hamas boycott of the elections in 1996 and its participation in 2006. At the same time, the increase was also due to the fact that mobilization in general was much more evident: leaflets were printed and busses to the polling stations were laid on.

More complex issues concerning East Jerusalem's status can also be identified as reasons for a low voter turnout. As a result of the Israeli policy of preventing West Bank and Gazan Palestinians from entering the city and the closure of most of the PLO-affiliated organizations in the city, the

PNA and PLC were not effective or salient in East Jerusalem. In these circumstances, many Palestinian residents asked themselves why they should risk their residency status or give up a day's livelihood trying to get to distant polling stations or be stuck in lines outside a post office where Israeli soldiers, police, militant settlers, and anti-Palestinian Israeli activists can intimidate them. As a seasoned Israeli analyst of Palestinian politics, Professor Menachem Klein, noted of the 1996 elections:

> Jerusalem's distance, as a frontier city, from the political center [Ramallah] was expressed in the elections not only by the low level of registration and low number of participants, but also by a lack of order, bad organisation, and no information on the election procedures. Even in Silwan, which became part of the front line against annexation in the 1980s, when Israeli settlers bought houses there and moved in, only 40 per cent of eligible voters registered. The elections emphasized Jerusalem's remoteness from the political center rather than the front line of confrontation with Israel.[38]

While this observation should be somewhat qualified by the general Palestinian recognition that the city still remains a key to peace and a stumbling block in the progress of negotiations between Israel and the PLO, it does highlight the fact that not only is East Jerusalem different from other Israeli cities, it is also increasingly different from other Palestinian cities as well.[39] This is a point I will develop in my last chapter.

How does this analysis of the electoral politics of East Jerusalem fit into our argument about the enclaving of East Jerusalem and how these subnational and functional borders diverge from the hard political borders? At first sight they seem to undermine the earlier illustrations presented on the tenacity and depth of those enclaves. The irregular election cycle, limited participation, and accompanying media and international attention does not seem to offer strong support for enclaves under siege by other Israeli policies. To grasp the significance of the electoral politics in this argument, one has to combine both the boycott of Israeli municipal elections and the low participation in Palestinian national elections together. What we have is a crisis of representation and leadership leading to a political vacuum, but, at the same time, a high sensitivity to what political direction the Palestinian population of the city will take. The political leadership on both sides is constantly asking the same questions about the intentions of Palestinian Jerusalemites. Will they boycott or will they vote for the municipality elections, will they be persuaded to take risks to vote in the Palestinian national elections? Or will they keep their heads down in the face of hostile Israeli scrutiny? The Palestinian voter in East Jerusalem remains, after all, potentially one-third of the electorate of the city and rising. This creates a political atmosphere and culture of distinctiveness which in turn is reinforced by the illegality of the Israeli presence in international law and the ambiguity in Israeli jurisdictions. No doubt each time an election takes place, whether it be Israeli municipal or Palestinian national, the sight of posters on lampposts and walls sporting smiling portraits, the fresh appearance of different-colored graffiti slogans and logos, all in Arabic, are a highly indicative territorial marker. At election time you definitely know when you are moving from an Israeli area to a Palestinian area (even if, during the Israeli municipal elections, the posters have been placed by Hebrew-speaking Israelis, they are, all the same, in Arabic—why would they try and get Palestinian voters out by using Hebrew?). Nevertheless, it is the lack of representation that is the greater territorial marker and leads to the myriad ways in which Palestinian enclaves can be identified and seek to survive.

EDUCATION

A second way in which Palestinian identity and culture is consolidated in East Jerusalem and undergirds the enclaves there is through the education system.[40] Here an equally remarkable phenomenon is taking place, often undetected by non-Jerusalem residents and foreigners: a Palestinian education is being taught in East Jerusalem and, what is more, the Israeli Ministry of Education and Israeli municipality is picking up the tab! In addition, in terms of the central argument of this book on the multiple borders of Jerusalem, we can see another anomalous delineation. The educational "border" for Palestinians is not the municpality border, not the separation barrier, but the Armistice Line of 1949 running through the center of the city.

With respect to the crucial issue of curriculum content, Palestinian education inside Jerusalem is almost identical to that being taught in the West Bank and Gaza Strip. In this field, therefore, the state borders of Israel are not congruent with the Israeli state and municipal borders of the city, but are in reality those that existed in prior to June 1967.

In the field of education in Jerusalem we have another example of what I described earlier in this chapter as the strategic confusion of the Israeli political elite that flows from policies driven by a Zionist ideology. The Zionist objective of securing East Jerusalem as an integral part of the Israeli state is being undermined by the Zionist policy of privileging Israeli Jews and thus neglecting the needs of non-Jews. This strategic confusion leads to a contradiction between objective and policy in the field of education and gives support to Palestinian enclaves in two ways: first, Palestinian identity and culture is maintained through the school curriculum and, second, the neglect and underfunding of the educational infrastructure leads to Palestinians in East Jerusalem to seek alternative sources of support to the Israeli state and municipality.

The role of education in divided cities inside contested states is a widely studied field. While we do not have space to enter into this study at any great length here, the main point to note is that to whom and by whom education is provided is crucial in exacerbating or ameliorating conflict between ethnonational groups living side by side.[41] It is broadly accepted that segregated schools lead to poor cross-communal communication and encourage sectarian divisions. Children growing up without ever playing or interacting with ethnic groups from different parts of the city are less likely to understand their political demands in later life. In cities where the curriculum is also based on different narratives and national myths, the chances of a harmonious convergence on the allocation of resources and the use of shared space are minimal. In the light of these observations, the failure to establish an equitable and integrated educational system in Jerusalem after over fifty years of occupation is a spectacular blunder by the Israeli political establishment with long-term implications for Israel's hold on the city. An opportunity for two generations of the most sophisticated and metropolitan Palestinians under Israeli occupation to be drawn into the Israeli worldview has been squandered. This could have been done, not necessarily by Juda-izing or de-Palestinianizing the Palestinian of East Jerusalem, but by re-spect being shown to their culture and their aspirations at the same time as showcasing the best of Israeli and Jewish culture. Indeed, not only has this opportunity been carelessly squandered, but the opposite result has taken its place. Despite the incompetence and ineptitude of the PNA, and while they may not be at the forefront of Palestinian nationalism, Palestinians from East Jerusalem have become much more disenchanted with the Israeli state. If they are ever, in the future, to be a bridge between the two communities, as they are sometimes characterized, then it will be by default and in spite of Israel's educational policies in Jerusalem.

This remarkable achievement by Palestinians to maintain educational continuity was not achieved without considerable struggle. Aware of the importance of the role of education in the integration of the city under Is-raeli rule, Israel initially tackled the issue head-on. From the outset of the occupation in 1967, Israel introduced the curriculum it used in Palestinian schools inside Israel itself to replace the Jordanian curriculum. This included the study of Hebrew, but also Zionist Israeli narratives of history and geog-raphy.[42] More contentious was the relative attention given in the curriculum to religious aspects. For example, under the Israeli curriculum 156 annual school hours would be devoted to Jewish texts as opposed to only 30 hours to the study of Islam. Under the Jordanian system, 360 hours was devoted to the study of Islamic literature.[43] Palestinians regarded this as an attempt to detach their children from the cultural roots and separate them from their compatriots in the West Bank and the Gaza Strip. On a more practical side, the attempt to replace the Jordanian matriculation, the *tawjiihi*, with the Israeli *bagrut*, was particularly worrying for Palestinian parents. The Israeli *bagrut* was not recognized in any of the higher education institutes in the West Bank, Gaza Strip, or the Arab world and their children would there-fore not be eligible to apply. In effect, what the Israeli policy was offering them was a ticket to nowhere—no further education and no jobs.

It is no wonder that they left the municipal-controlled schools in droves. Between 1967 and 1972 there was a 65 percent drop in enrollment in the municipal secondary schools! In the three most important and prestigious municipal-run secondary schools in East Jerusalem—the Ma'muniyyeh,

Abdullah bin Hussein, and Rashidiyyeh schools—there was an 85 percent drop, from about eighteen hundred pupils to only three hundred pupils.[44] This was despite the fact that the municipal schools were free. Palestinian parents instead enrolled their children in either fee-paying private schools, mostly run by Christian organizations and churches that tended to follow European or U.S. curricula, or in schools run by the Waqf Administration, or looked for schools outside the Israeli Jerusalem municipality in Ramallah and Bethlehem. Some even dusted off their refugee antecedents and tried to enroll in the eight well-regarded UNRWA schools that catered to refugee families both in Shu'fat camp as well as in Palestinian suburbs such Silwan and Abu Dis.

As a result of this boycott, Israel relented and allowed the Jordanian curriculum to be taught in municipal schools, subject to a review of textbooks and maps and the requirement that Hebrew was also taught. Israel even allowed inspectors from the Jordanian education ministry to visit Palestinian schools to monitor the *tawjiihi* examinations.[45] As Hillel Cohen points out, this climbdown would have significant repercussions for the Palestinian enclaves in East Jerusalem in the future: "This was a rare accomplishment for the nationalist circles (which was achieved by both pro-Jordanian and Palestinian factions) and one that also had ramifications for the future: as a result of the schools' adherence to the Jordanian curriculum, it was easier for the PA [PNA], after its establishment, to replace the Jordanian curriculum with the Palestinian one."[46]

In the mid-1990s this is exactly what happened. By that time approximately half the Palestinian schoolchildren of the city were enrolled in Israeli municipal schools. The rest were in private, Waqf Administration and UNRWA schools. In 1994 the PNA established the Palestinian Ministry of Education, which took over responsibility for determining the curriculum content from its Jordanian counterpart. Very few changes were made, as any incitement against Israel or the Oslo Accords in the course material had already been removed. In effect, the PNA simply replaced the seal of the Hashemite Kingdom of Jordan on the covers of the textbooks with the Palestinian seal. This was a step too far for the Israeli municipality, and it felt obliged to cover the Palestinian seal with stickers of the emblem of the city of Jerusalem.[47] While it prevented PNA inspectors from operating in municipality schools, it was obliged to permit the PNA oversight of examinations. Papers (without a PNA seal) were handed over at Israeli checkpoints on the borders of the city and were returned after examinations to be marked by PNA teachers.[48] The actual examination in all Palestinian schools is administered by the Waqf Directorate of Education.[49]

As a result of this reversal in policy, by 2011 73 percent of Palestinian pupils were enrolled in municipal schools or schools recognized by the municipality.[50]

In 2011–2012, as a result of pressure from nationalist Israeli legislators, a new attempt was made to alter the curriculum.[51] These were mainly limited to history and literature and included the removal of any Palestinian flag; reference to the Palestinian Nakba (the expulsion in 1948) and right of return; and mention of Acre and some references to Jerusalem, the Israeli occupation, and Palestinian resistance. Again, there was a mobilization of the Palestinian population, with parent-teacher associations featuring strongly in the resistance to these proposals and the PNA giving the issue an international profile. Ultimately, some of the proposals were mostly reversed by the Municipal Council and only references to highly symbolic issues were censored.[52] This may have defused an explosive issue for the time being, but Palestinians are still aggrieved and wary of further Israeli attempts at censorship when the political opportunity arises.

Nevertheless, few politicians and teachers on both sides of the divide failed to note the rich irony in the fact that the sector of the Palestinian education system in East Jerusalem that had the most students learning the PNA curriculum was the one funded and managed by the Israeli municipality. Furthermore, the fact that in schools across East Jerusalem the same subjects and perspectives are being taught as in Palestinian schools in Jericho, Nablus, and Tulkarm is a major brake on the erosion of the connections between East Jerusalem and the OPts. Not only will they share a similar schooling experience and thus many assumptions and points of contact, but they also have access to universities and places of employment that would otherwise have been closed to them. In addition, probably more than any other factor, save the question of the color of one's ID card, the segregated educational system gives East Jerusalem Palestinians a separate identity and culture which consolidates the territorial divisions between their places of residences and those of Israeli Jews.

While the curriculum issue is clearly of immense importance, the other dimension to Israeli policy toward the educational system in East Jerusalem that appears to support Palestinian enclaves is, paradoxically, its neglect in provision and infrastructure. Two Israeli NGOs, Ir Amim and the Association for Civil Rights, have been active in holding the Israeli municipality to account on this matter. They point to the shortfall of over one thousand classrooms required to accommodate not only the natural increase in Palestinian students but also new arrivals as a result of the erection of the separation barrier. Promised new construction will only cover 27 percent of the required classrooms, despite categorical promises made by the Israeli municipality to the Israeli High Court to address the shortfall.[53] In addition, more than a quarter of all classrooms have been judged by the Israeli municipality itself to be below standard, and provision of training and quality assurance is well below that being provided for in Israeli schools.[54] The NGOs also argue that as well as Israel being in breach of international conventions to which it is a signatory, the Israeli government is also breaching its own laws to provide a free education up to the end of the secondary level.[55] The main result of such poor provision is the emergence of "recognised but unofficial" schools run by private companies "under contract" by the municipality.[56] Nearly one-quarter of Palestinian schools in East Jerusalem fall into this category. A final result of this neglect and refusal to allocate sufficient resources has been the difficulties that parent have in enrolling their children in any school. Without enough classrooms, municipality schools are obliged to turn pupils away, and poorer families cannot afford to send them to fee-paying schools. Ir Amim and ACRI reveal that there is now a growing population of Palestinian children, 5–6 percent, who are not in school at all. Combined, these policies reveal the limits of the Israeli state in safeguarding the education of Palestinian children. An important result is both a dependence on nonmunicipal schools and the increase in inferior educational standards compared to Israeli Jewish pupils. Attempts to rectify this situation are being carried out by both the Faisal Husseini Foundation and the Hashemite Madrasati Initiative. Funds are being directed toward

FIGURE 2.1. History textbook used in Palestinian schools in East Jerusalem with the seal of the Palestinian National Authority in the top right-hand corner.

upgrading both the facilities and equipment in private and Waqf Administration schools in East Jerusalem.[57] These projects also highlight the way in which, because of discrimination and neglect, Palestinian teachers and parents look to non-Israeli sources of support, thus separating the education system further from the Israeli state.

Finally, the system of higher education in East Jerusalem has also provided support to the Palestinian enclaves there. With approximately seven thousand students, al-Quds University is not only the leading higher education institute in East Jerusalem but possibly also the largest Palestinian institution in any sector. It is therefore of considerable importance both culturally and politically. As important is the fact that the university is not registered with the Israeli Council of Higher Education, but rather with the Palestinian Ministry of Higher Education, which accredits and approves its courses and programs and recognizes its diplomas and degrees.[58] Here there is a further irony in that while al-Quds University may not be recognized by the Israeli Council of Higher Education, the same council does recognize Palestinian universities and higher education institutions in the OPTs. The denial of recognition is a deliberate attempt to undermine Palestinian institutions and organization in East Jerusalem. There is, however, a converse impact.

The structure and organization of al-Quds University reflect very closely the difficulties of institution building in East Jerusalem, as most of its departments and affiliated colleges are located outside both the Israeli municipal borders and the separation barrier. Only the small Institute of Islamic Archaeology, the Centre for Jerusalem Studies, the Women's College, and the School of Humanities are located within the central areas, that is, west of the separation barrier and on the Israeli side.[59] The main administrative offices and offices of its senior staff are based west of the barrier on the Palestinian side. This gives the university a weblike quality, with buildings dotted around the city, straddling both the barrier and the municipal borders yet serving to accentuate the Jerusalem-wide nature of the institution. Staff members and students I have spoken to often lament the great inconvenience that the barrier poses to their free movement across the university and their ability to meet, since some staff and students do not have permits to enter the areas west of the barrier. It does not, however, seem to undermine their sense of belonging to the university, mainly because its disparate geographical spread can absorb such intrusions. The physical impact, therefore, of the university on the enclaves is not so conspicuous in terms of students milling around, attending classes, going to meetings, cafés, and shops catering to a Palestinian student clientele, or the housing market in the vicinity adapting to student accommodation needs. Rather the impact of the university can be seen in the independence of its operations, the engagement of the student body in the wider politics of Palestine, and the framework it provides for Jerusalem-centered Palestinian activity.

One should note that, with regard to educational policy in East Jerusalem, Israel is in a bind. As Israeli proponents of imposing an Israeli curriculum in East Jerusalem must be aware, while it is ideologically attractive to have Israeli writ running throughout the areas incorporated in 1967, it will also produce problematic consequences in the educational sphere. An

Israeli curriculum will generate many thousands of Palestinians with Israeli qualifications who have nowhere else to go but Israel for employment and further education. I doubt that this is what they want. Already there are concerns in Israeli nationalist circles at the number Palestinian undergraduates in Israeli higher education institutions, creating not only a significant non-Zionist minority at the center of Israel intellectual life but also sharp tensions in a sector of the population that tends toward radicalism and militancy. An influx of Palestinians from East Jerusalem would undoubtedly raise the stakes even further. Moreover, once graduating either after high school or university, where will these Palestinians go for employment? Indeed, who will employ them when there are already many Palestinians from inside Israel looking for work that may also be available to Palestinian Jerusalemites? What advantages can a Palestinian Jerusalemite, without citizenship and only a permanent residency status, offer Israeli employers over a Palestinian from inside Israel who has citizenship and fluent Hebrew? The international job market would be equally problematic. Why should Microsoft or Reuters or DHL employ a Palestinian without a proper passport and with an Israeli educational qualification over either an Israeli or an Arab from the Middle East? The niche in the jobs market will be very narrow indeed. The likely result of such nationalistic educational policies is a pool of Palestinian Jerusalemites who will have very restricted employment opportunities and who will hold the Israeli state responsible for their lamentable position. Be careful what you wish for! would seem to be the appropriate riposte to such ideologues. The task of managing a growing population of underemployed and overqualified high school students and graduates, simultaneously marginalized politically and culturally, must be a daunting prospect to the Israeli security establishment.

STRUCTURE AND INFRASTRUCTURE

In addition to the support that the electoral status and the education system give to the maintenance of Palestinian enclaves in East Jerusalem, there are more tangible ways in which the Palestinian presence is defended and consolidated. It is neither possible nor necessary to cover all these ways in the same depth, and this section shall focus primarily on three clusters of issues: a) planning, property ownership, and housing segregation; b) the provision of services; and c) economic questions such as trade and employment. Other issues such as the road system and residency status have been touched upon earlier in our discussion on the impact of the barrier and will not be tackled further here.

All cities are obliged to address the critical issue of population growth and movement either from natural increase or from immigration or from the expansion of the city's borders into the suburban and rural hinterland. As a result, new population groups are absorbed into the city, which changes its demographic structure and even the balance of power between the constituent population groups. Managing this ongoing change is a key challenge for governments, municipalities, and the local urban elites. In ethnically diverse cities an important objective in containing tensions arising from such changes is achieving a mix between heterogeneous and homogeneous residential and retail areas so that residents can feel their cultural norms are allowed to flourish but that differences do not become so sharp that the interaction between them is conflicted. The equitable distribution of land, housing stock, and infrastructure becomes the key mechanism by which this objective is obtained and, consequently, the arena of intense political activity. In most cities, failure to achieve this balanced mix is, in fact, the norm—which is why they are the sites of so much tension and conflict. But the constant attempt by governments, municipalities, and civic groups to rectify this failure and to improve the situation provides sufficient goodwill and cross-community mobilization to head off complete collapse and the descent into anarchy. Viewers of the U.S. television serial drama *The Wire* will recall nightmarish scenes in the city of Baltimore of racial conflict, social breakdown, corrupt politicians, union leaders and businesspeople, and the emergence of no-go areas controlled by drug barons. The city seemed nightly to be on the brink of disaster. Yet there was enough determination, whether because of cynicism and the thirst for power or due to idealism and the triumph of personal relations, to make the city function as a whole. Most cities repeatedly slip, slide, and stumble, but they do not quite fall.

In cities that are divided and inside contested states, such Jerusalem, Kirkuk, Belfast, and Mostar, the issue of housing is even more critical. Residential segregation not only points to the possibility of further divisions and of hard borders emerging in times of tension and political breakdown, but it is also acts as a territorial marker and a vehicle for more territorial acquisition. The expansion of the Catholic, largely Republican population of Belfast during the 1950s and 1960s was the main driver in the emerging civil rights movement calling not only for equality in employment and representation but also for more and better housing. Their expansion into North and East Belfast was a catalyst for the Protestant and largely Unionist reaction, which led to the sectarian conflict in the Irish Troubles. Developing one side's housing stock at the expanse of the other side, or constructing residential enclaves on land inside areas inhabited by the other side, are, in such divided cities, acts of territorial expansion as emphatic as any invading army. Indeed, if one accepts the axiom that armies can invade but cannot hold onto land indefinitely, segregated housing projects in divided cities can be seen as the second wave of conquest where land is both conquered and held. In Jerusalem this is clearly the case.

The acquisition of West Jerusalem was one of the prime aims of the Zionist settler forces in 1948. What is often overlooked is that Jerusalem could not have been the capital of Israel if that conquest was not also accompanied by wholesale expulsion of the Palestinian residents. While Jews may have comprised the greater part of the population of the city prior to 1948, certainly in the New City, at the same time, they only owned about 30 percent of the property and land in the New City and Palestinians and Christian institutions owned over 50 percent.[60] If Palestinians had not fled or been evicted, the sense of a Jewish Jerusalem would have been difficult to maintain. As we saw in chapter 1, only a handful of Palestinians remained in the western part of the city, so the new state of Israel was able channel new Jewish immigrants and others into the houses and areas vacated by Palestinians. In terms of a generic Jewish identity, at least, a homogenous and exclusively Jewish West Jerusalem was created.

However, Israel was obliged to confront the converse difficulty in 1967. Although some Palestinians fled after the Israeli conquest, by far the greater proportion remained. Comprising partly refugees from former Palestinian areas in West Jerusalem with nowhere else to go, partly economic migrants from the Hebron area, partly the residents of ancient villages whose land and houses had been absorbed into the urban growth of the city, and partly long-standing Jerusalemites who could trace their roots in the city over hundreds of years, barnacle-like, they have proved hard to dislodge. Indeed, as we saw in chapter 1, the population of Palestinian Jerusalemites has nearly quadrupled, and their proportion of the total population of the city steadily has increased. This has been despite huge efforts by successive Israeli governments to fragment and encircle Palestinian residential areas with exclusively Jewish zones of residence—the settlements.

Israeli colonization policy in and around Jerusalem is well documented in UN, NGO, and press reports, and I do not wish to tread a well-trodden path here.[61] The bald facts are that approximately 35 percent of the territory that the Israeli government incorporated into Jerusalem in 1967 was confiscated, mainly from Palestinian owners, to form part of a framework of three consecutive rings of settlements: a metropolitan, a municipal, and an inner ring (see map 1.5).

The metropolitan ring lies outside the municipal borders, but through a network of roads and tunnels bypassing Palestinian areas and Israeli checkpoints and offering fast and easy access to the center of the city, they are linked closely to the city. They not only serve to disconnect Palestinian areas in Jerusalem from the West Bank hinterland and but also have utilized Palestinian land on the outskirts of the city that was available for Palestinian growth and development. The separation barrier, diverted to encircle these metropolitan settlements, has left the Palestinians within it even more tightly enclosed and divided from the West Bank. The second ring of settlements—the municipal ring—comprises twelve large settlements with approximately two hundred thousand Israeli Jewish residents, all of which lie within the barrier walls. These settlements fragment East Jerusalem even further and break up, in particular, the north-south contiguity in the remnants of Palestinian-owned land in the city. The final ring of settlements is the inner ring located in the densely populated central areas of East Jerusalem including the Old City, Silwan, Sheikh Jarrah, the Mount of Olives

(At-Tur), Wadi Joz, Ras al-'Amud, and Jabal al-Mukabbir. While much smaller in size and comprising only two thousand residents, they are led by militant Zionist groups and designed to prevent any Israeli withdrawal from these areas as a result of a peace agreement.[62]

In addition to these constructions, the planning and zoning policies by the Israeli government over the past forty-five years have led to the removal of other areas from Palestinian use. In addition to the 35 percent confiscated for settlement construction, another 22 percent has been allocated as green areas for parks and other public infrastructure. A further 30 percent of mostly Palestinian land is designated "unplanned," therefore all construction is deemed illegal under Israeli law and potentially subject to demolition.[63] In these ways the physical structure of the Israeli occupation is less in a military presence on street corners, but more in the expropriation of land and the encircling of Palestinian areas by Israeli Jewish residences—a conquest by enclaving.

There are two additional dimensions to the impact of this policy which are relevant to the way in which Israeli policies heightens the enclave nature

FIGURE 2.2.   The Israeli settlement of Har Homa as seen from the neighboring Palestinian village of Sur Bahir.

FIGURE 2.3. The Israeli settlement of Har Homa—internal view.

of East Jerusalem. The first concerns the physical appearance of the settle-ments. These are generally built on high ground, overlooking Palestinian areas, often surrounded by a high fence, wall, or buttressed and enclosed roadways that act as an internal barrier between the two communities. In addition, the apartments and houses tend to be inward-facing, often ex-posing only an outer wall with smaller windows than those on the inner wall and laid out in a way that either deters or confuses the nonresident.[64] A classic example of this kind of defensive yet intimidating architecture is Har Homa, the settlement built upon the former lands of the Palestinian village of Sur Bahir. The village is characterized by multiple points of access that blur its separation from the surrounding olive groves and fields upon which it traditionally relied for generating wealth. In contrast, like some medieval fortress, Har Homa has only one main entrance and another small side entrance. The approach to the main entrance is along a road that rises up from open land around it so that visibility of all that travel upon it is unimpeded.[65]

The value of this kind of construction was seen during the Palestinian Intifada in 2000. A settlement like Gilo in the south of Jerusalem, facing the towns of Beit Jalah and Bethlehem across a valley floor, was subject to

FIGURE 2.4. Contrasting internal borders in Beirut, Belfast and Mostar: posters of Ayatollahs Khomeini and Fadlallah (*top*) signify Hizbollah territory in Beirut; a mural disguises a "peace wall" separating Protestant loyalist housing from Roman Catholic nationalist housing in Belfast; a broad boulevard divided Christian Croatian areas from Muslim Bosniak areas in Mostar (2009–2012).

mortar and gunfire attacks by Palestinian militants. Some Israeli residents were harmed and there was extensive damage along the southern stretches of the settlement, but it served its purpose of providing a defensive shield for the residents of the settlement. But here in this defensive function also lies the fundamentally anti-urban, divisive, and dystopic vision as the underlying characteristic of Israeli housing policy in East Jerusalem—the settlements are primed for war. A city needs to be designed for peace with mobility, openness, and sites for interactions placed at the fore, but the Israeli settlements double up as pillar boxes and little fortresses. Many cities have areas that are "semidetached" either through the privatization of public space such as shopping malls or through the creation of gated communities, but the settlements are extreme expressions of this drift toward securitization.

In effect, the architecture of the Israeli settlements has reversed the order in which cities unravel during ethnopolitical tensions. As we have seen in other cities, instead of a series of phases where polarized communities retreat into their core areas as the political tension increases until, ultimately, in a situation of breakdown, we have barricades thrown up across the street excluding all nonresidents. In contrast, the settlements in Jerusalem start from the premise that the breakdown has already occurred, which indeed it already has, by virtue of the occupation and the design of their enclaves. In this way the Israeli Jewish enclaves in East Jerusalem are a reification of the occupation and an acknowledgment that once the coercive apparatus that supports them is removed they will be exposed and vulnerable. By the nature of their introduction into East Jerusalem—the confiscation of Palestinian land, their ethnic exclusivity, their use as a site of surveillance and control—Israeli settlements separate themselves completely and delineate nonsettlement areas as "the other" and inherently hostile. It is not a way to design a city comprising such ethnopolitical cleavages and cultural and religious sensitivities and it reinforces physically and visually the Palestinian enclaves in East Jerusalem.

One result of this intrusion of Israeli settlements into East Jerusalem is the sharper delineation of the Palestinian enclaves, heightening their homogeneity and separateness from the Israeli state and municipality. In addition, the zoning and planning regime established since 1967 has created a sense in the Palestinian enclaves of being under siege. Not only are the lands around them being expropriated and put out of use, the residents are also being subjected to two other related threats to their livelihood and existence—house demolitions and the loss of residency status. Only 13 percent of East Jerusalem is zoned as land available for Palestinian construction. But even in these areas, which are already very densely populated, obtaining permits is expensive, complicated, and fails to meet anything like the demand of a burgeoning population. As a result, Palestinians have erected houses without permits, both in the zones allocated for construction and in other areas. These are often done overnight or during Israeli holidays when Israeli municipal and Housing Ministry inspectors are not touring the area. Since 2000 more than eight hundred Palestinian-owned structures have been demolished, which amounts to just over one a week over the past twelve to thirteen years.[66] The personal tragedies, the loss of income and livelihood, such measures bring reverberate constantly throughout the Palestinian areas in East Jerusalem.

Adding to this steady drumbeat of fear and insecurity for Palestinian East Jerusalemites is the threat of losing their residency status. As we have seen, Palestinian East Jerusalemites were not offered citizenship in the state of Israel but given permanent residency in the city. This entitled them to travel freely within the city and, as municipal and income taxpayers, to also receive health, social security benefits, and pensions. Permanent residency was restricted to those who had been present in East Jerusalem at the census in 1968 and their descendants. It did not include Jerusalemites who fled abroad during the fighting or those who were out of the country for study or on business. It also conferred upon Palestinian East Jerusalemites a status akin to complete foreigners who reside in Israel. As the Israeli NGOs HaMoked and B'Tselem explain: "Permanent residency is the same status granted to foreign citizens who have freely chosen to come to Israel and want to live in the country. Because Israel treats Palestinians like immigrants, they, too, live in their homes at the beneficence of the authorities, and not by right. The authorities maintain this policy although these Palestinians were born in Jerusalem, lived in the city, and have no other home."[67]

As the Palestinian population increased and successive Israeli governments became concerned that they were "running to stand still" in their efforts to change the demographic balance in Jerusalem in favor of Israeli Jews, they tightened the criteria for permanent residency. From the mid-1990s the Israeli Ministry of Interior began to revoke the residency permits of Palestinians who could not prove continual residency within the city borders. Between 1967 and 2008 over thirteen thousand Palestinians have had their residency status revoked. Nearly half this number has been revoked during the past six years, amounting to almost one thousand per year or over three people a day. You can imagine the anxiety this can cause. Daily life becomes permeated with the fear of the knock on the door, of the casual interrogation at a random Israeli checkpoint, of the arrival of an official-looking letter, and of the loyalty of one's neighbors.

What is clear is that the accumulation of these policies amounts to a kind of "warehousing" of the Palestinians of East Jerusalem. *Warehousing* is a term adopted by scholars in the field of refugee studies to highlight the plight of refugees who are located in huge camps in the host country, usually formally under the legal protection of UNHCR. Warehoused refugees can wait in their camps endlessly while their political leaders, regional powerbrokers, and the international community struggle to find a solution to their situation. Sometimes refugees can eke out a reasonable existence, but more often than not they are dependent upon aid and the informal or black economy to survive. Their status as noncitizens gives them little formal and institutional leverage in the politics of the host country and they are reliant upon international agencies such as UNHCR and other NGOs to protect their interests. In some cases they turn to refugee militias to advance their cause. The huge camps of Dadaab in Kenya, numbering over four hundred thousand refugees, are often cited as examples of refugees who have been housed, fed, and watered by the international community in the absence of any political arrangements to enable them to return, to be resettled or integrated into the host country.[68] It has also been applied to Palestinian refugees in Lebanon where their ability to work outside the camps is severely restricted by the Lebanese government.[69] Economically, Palestinians in East Jerusalem are not in such a poverty-stricken and dependent situation, but in a legal sense they are in a worse situation, since at least refugees have some form of internationally legal protection while Palestinian East Jerusalemites have neither Israeli nor Palestinian citizenship but are in this legal void called permanent residency.[70] Furthermore, they have been corralled into ever smaller and smaller areas by the panoply of restrictions I have delineated to the extent that their enclaves are becoming controlled zones. The continual deferring of their future status adds the dimension of time and brings their situation very close to that of the warehousing of refugees.

The final area where the hard borders of the city are softened by a series of subnational and functional borders that reinforce the enclave nature of the eastern part of the city is in the provision of services. I have written elsewhere on the issue of power supply to the city and how Palestinian areas were able to maintain an electricity distribution network that was independent to some degree of the Israeli state. In the same way I have written on sewage and solid waste disposal and the water supply to Palestinian East Jerusalem and how these issues both revealed the extent to which Palestinians areas were neglected with serious implications for the environmental health of the city and also how Palestinian areas were able to find alternative sources.[71] In addition, health provision is clearly an important factor in people's lives and its differentiated provision in Jerusalem has an impact upon the life within the various enclaves.[72] However, rather than systematically, and possibly tediously, go through each and every way in which the Israeli occupation discriminates against Palestinians, the focus of this chapter is more on those aspects of service provision that reinforce the enclave nature of the city and undergird Palestinian identification with and rootedness to the enclaves. To that end I wish to close with one further example of how Israeli policies have heightened the differences between Israeli and Palestinian enclaves—the imbalance in the municipal budget in allocations to Palestinian and non-Palestinian areas. From this we can see how through short-term and myopic responses to the Palestinian presence in the city Israel has strengthened the Palestinian detachment from the Israeli state and inadvertently reinforced its connections to the OPts and beyond.

When I first started researching on Jerusalem in the mid 1980s, it was apparent to all but the most zealous supporter of the Israeli occupation that the Palestinian areas of East Jerusalem were grossly neglected. However, to highlight and draw attention to this discrimination was almost taboo. The Israeli occupation was seen as benign, bending over backward to incorporate

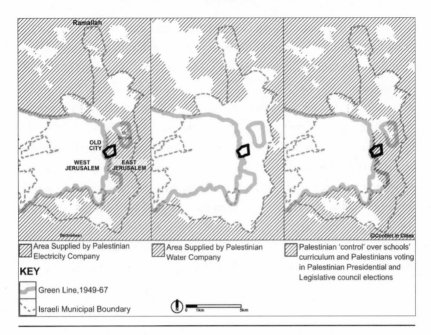

MAP 2.2. The "functional" borders of Jerusalem (2005).

all the communities of the city in a culturally sensitive way. Teddy Kollek was a minor global celebrity in this respect, and no picture of him was complete without a background of dignitaries in colorful and exotic headgear. Only a few Israeli activists, researchers, and journalists challenged this consensus, and were designated naive leftists, while the few Palestinian studies that existed were dismissed as being simply pro-PLO.[73] Over the past twenty years the situation has been almost completely reversed. The publications of the former Israeli advisor on Arab affairs to the mayor of Jerusalem, Amir Cheshin, and Moshe Amirav, former chairman of the Likud party, with some journalist associates such as Bill Hutman and Avraham Rabinowitch, broke the mold with their revelations of official quotas and targets that discriminated against the Palestinian population.[74] Coming from such an establishment figures as Cheshin, who was, in addition, a resident of an Israeli settlement himself, and Amirav, a senior Likudnik, and in the context of political negotiations where East Jerusalem was being discussed, several Israeli NGOs were emboldened to highlight how such discrimination was neither legal under Israeli law nor advancing the interests of Israel in the peace negotiations.[75] The groundbreaking work of Meir Margalit, an Israeli Jerusalem Municipal Council member, saw the detailed analysis of budgets that revealed the extent to which Palestinians were excluded from provision.[76] In very simple terms, while Palestinian East Jerusalemites comprise approximately 33 percent of the city's residents, only 12 percent of the municipal budget is allocated to services in Palestinian enclaves. Indeed, the figure is probably much lower.[77] As Cheshin points out, costs for the construction of Road 1, running through the center of the city, and the football stadium in West Jerusalem were taken out of the budget allocated to Palestinian areas, presumably on the assumption that Palestinians would also use these facilities.[78] In reality it was a way of redirecting funds from a constituency that had no advocates in the Israeli Municipal Council deliberations.

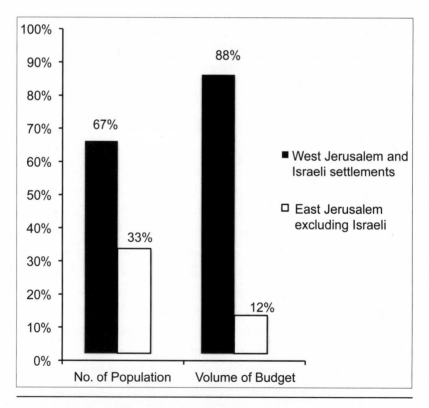

GRAPH 2.1. Municipal budget allocations in relation to population.

Exasperated at the continual sniping at him from both left and right, in a famous interview Kollek declared:

> We said again and again that we would make the Arabs' rights equal to the rights of the Jews in the city. Empty talk. They were and remain second and third class citizens. For Jewish Jerusalem, I did something in the past twenty-five years. For East Jerusalem? Nothing. What did I do? Schools? Nothing. Sidewalks, nothing. Old age homes, nothing! Yes, we did install a sewage system and improve the water supply. You know what? Do you think that was for their benefit? For their welfare? Think again! There were a few cases of cholera there and the Jews were afraid it would reach them so a sewage system and water network was put in.[79]

As Amirav points out, it was Kollek's successor as Israeli mayor of the city, Ehud Olmert, who realized the danger for the Zionist project of controlling the city if services to East Jerusalem were not brought up to the standards of West Jerusalem.[80] Commissioning a detailed report, which revealed that double the number of Palestinians in East Jerusalem lived below the poverty line than Israeli Jews, that the Palestinian housing sector was twice as overcrowded as the Israeli Jewish housing sector, and that Palestinian East Jerusalem lagged behind in the provision of roads, water, sewage systems, pavements, street lighting, sanitation, fire stations, postal services, and social services.[81] Armed with this data and with the argument that it would serve the strategic interests of the Israeli state, Olmert persuaded the Israeli government to intervene with additional financial support to reduce the inequalities between the two sides of the city. Nevertheless, as Amirav details in his book, commitments were continually revised downward to the extent that it is now broadly accepted that in reality only 5 percent of the municipal budget is allocated to East Jerusalem.[82]

In many ways this chapter "deconstructs" the previous one. In chapter 1 I focussed on the hard borders of Jerusalem and how they evolved to meet the changing political circumstances of the Arab-Israeli conflict that affected and were played out in the city. In chapter 2 I have built on the fact that the borders frequently changed over time: there has been little that was eternal or sacred about their exact configurations. The borders of Jerusalem are not only mutable but they can be disaggregated into many levels—political and legal, security, electoral, educational, residential, and allocative. It is this disaggregation that softens the hard political and national borders, makes them permeable, and at the same time gives substance and weight to the Palestinian enclaves that have persisted in East Jerusalem. The chapter has also highlighted the paradox of an ethnonationalist ideology such as Zionism in a city of mixed ethnicity. In attempting to dominate the subordinate groups within the city through marginalization and neglect, it has engendered a Palestinian resistance through population growth and housing expansion. And here we see how the religious nature of the city plays a crucial part in these dynamics of competition and conflict. The presence of deep-rooted religious communities, of long-standing religious hierarchies, and of religious sites of international renown add to the tension and the disputes around how the city should be governed and what its future should look like. Chapter 3 examines this contribution to the argument of the many borders of Jerusalem in greater detail.

3

THE SCATTERED BORDERS
OF HOLINESS

F OR ALL ITS swirling tensions and frequent eruptions of violence, Jerusalem can still have its moments of pure magic. Occasionally you are captured by a sense of peace and tranquillity which can almost take your breath away. Paradoxically, one of the places you can most strongly feel this is in the eye of the storm—the Haram al-Sharif. Early on a crisp spring morning, when the sun is bright but has not yet reached its midday heat, and the colors are still rich and velvety with shadows, you can sit on the steps leading up to the Dome of the Rock and feel time slow right down. There are a few cleaners and guards quietly going about their duties, and a handful of worshippers whisper as if in awe of where they have found themselves, but even they are swallowed up in the wide tree-lined spaces between the Dome and the al-Aqsa Mosque. Before the bustle of schoolchildren taking shortcuts through the Haram enclosure and before the arrival of shuffling clusters of tourists, a peace reigns over the Haram that seems to place a gentle hand over your busy thoughts and lets your mind center down as if slowly entering a cool pool of water. Here is a time and place when you can reflect on the beauty of the architecture, the nobility of the faith that produced it, and what it means to be human amidst so much strife.

Another place where the wonder of Jerusalem has struck me is more prosaic. You can walk along the Ottoman walls of the Old City, and on the southeast corner there is a vantage point that on one side overlooks the

Armenian and Jewish Quarters and, on the other side, the Palestinian village or suburb of Silwan. I first came across this spot when a Swedish colleague and I were walking along the wall late one Friday afternoon. The sun had not yet quite gone down, and groups of black-coated Orthodox Jews, sidelocks swinging to and fro, were hurrying with short determined strides to get to their homes or seminaries or the Wailing Wall before the start of the Sabbath. As the setting sun lit up the ivory stone of the city with a dark and fiery pink, edging into crimson, you could feel a sense of anticipation, akin to that moment in a forest at twilight when the birds fuss and fiddle before they finally settle down for the night. The city seemed poised and expectant. My colleague felt it first, and she stopped me, with a silent touch on my arm, and we waited, looking at the village beneath us, the Mount of Olives in the near distance and the Jewish Quarter to our left. Then a quiet stillness gradually spread, softly, like a blanket around us. The distant growl of the traffic seemed more muted, the clink of cutlery and crockery from the houses nearby faded, and the cries of playing children tailed off. The stillness lasted less than a minute, but it was the deep silence of the moment before prayer. As nightfall swelled up from the shadows in the dark alleys of the Old City, a clear tuneful call to prayer burst from the al-Aqsa Mosque, rolling across the rooftops, the domes, steeples, and cupolas, which was echoed by the mosques from Silwan in the valley below. Almost simultaneously you could hear the low rumble of chanting from the synagogues of the Jewish Quarter, songs being sung down by the plaza in front of the Wailing Wall, prayers being delivered by a crowd of nodding heads at the huge stones at its base. The city seemed alive with prayer and praise for the Almighty. At least for this short moment, one could put aside the cynicism about how religious beliefs have been manipulated in the conflict and see and feel the beauty of the city stripped down to its prayerful core. It would have been too much to ask for the ringing of church bells as well and perhaps a bit too cheesy. But there have been many times when there has been such a conjunction of religious celebrations and you are reminded forcefully that religion and faith is ultimately the purpose and raison-d'être of the city.

More than any amount of reading, these kinds of experiences bring home to you that, for all its similarities with other cities, Jerusalem is also very different. It is a holy city, chockablock with religious sites: synagogues, churches, mosques, prayer rooms, seminaries, monasteries, convents, hostels for pilgrims, mausoleums, and cemeteries. The Old City alone, an area of not more than 1 kilometer square, is reputed to have between 225 and over 300 holy sites—an incredible 1 holy site for every 3 to 4 square meters![1] In fact, Jerusalem must be the holy city per se. Residents and frequent visitors or long-stayers like myself frequently overlook a blindingly obvious fact: Jerusalem is not just holy to one religion, but is holy to three. And it is not just holy to any three, but holy to one of the oldest religions in existence— Judaism—and holy to two of the largest religions in the world—Christianity and Islam. And it is holy to these three religions which are not only the main monotheistic religions of the world but are also closely intertwined with each other, having emerged from each other's traditions and cultures. Layer upon layer of faith and belief has been deposited upon the city. When you live in or have known Jerusalem for any length of time, you become so accustomed to the plurality of faiths and variety of rituals on the streets around you that you often fail to recognize the utter uniqueness of this rare phenomenon and the total remoteness of the possibility of this occurring again in any part of the world.

We need to pause here to understand more clearly what is meant by a holy city. There is little dispute that "holy cities" exist as a separate category of cities and have their own dynamics and problems. Apart from Jerusalem, we can see examples where religion plays a dominant role in urban settlement in such cities as Varanasi, Lourdes, Mecca, and Kyoto. However, what makes up a holy city and what its attributes are is rarely explored. Is it just the number of holy sites themselves? If so, how many sites make up a holy city—five, twenty, two hundred? And what proportion of holy sites to land area or population defines its holiness? A very large city is bound to have hundreds, perhaps thousands, of holy sites by dint of its large population, but does that make it holy in the sense that Jerusalem and Mecca are uncontroversially and consensually regarded as holy? In addition, the holiness of a city can change over time. Some cities were holy from their inception due to the location of a spring or well. Others became holy as a result of being the burial place of a revered personage, such as the tomb of Imam 'Ali in

Najaf, Iraq.[2] Holiness in a city seems to depend on variables ranging from the natural to the human.

On top of this, surely it is the activities that are carried out in and around the holy sites that are the real indicator of holiness. Prayer, pilgrimage, preaching, and the rituals of daily life all confer a meaningful patina on the physical structures of the holy sites and the surrounding urban area. Conversely, empty unused holy sites would be closer to a cemetery than a city. In Islamic and Middle East studies there has been empirical research on popular and religiously based urban networks, such as the Sufi orders or militant Islamic groups, or on the role of traditional religious elites, the *ulama*', and the pan-Islamic nature of certain religious sites.[3] Indeed, much of the theoretical debate on the nature of holy cities has actually focused upon defining an "Islamic city" rather than holy cities in general.[4] At the same time, scholars have found that identifying specific Islamic features in the wide regions where Islam is practiced has proved to be very elusive.[5] For example, a seminal work on the subject argued that the concept of an Islamic city itself was intrinsically flawed since a Buddhist city or a Christian city is not discussed in the same terms.[6]

One useful way of defining a holy city is to compile a typology, or a list of its attributes. Professor Francis Peters, who has studied both Mecca and Jerusalem in some depth, has highlighted what he regarded as the four main attributes of a holy city. These are an institutional hierarchy comprising senior clergy and priests, an administrative apparatus owning land and property such as glebe land or waqf endowments a source of revenue independent from the regime or state authorities within which the city is located, and, finally, an international network of allies and supporters that has evolved through and is maintained by pilgrimage and educational activities.[7] This typology conveys the importance of structures and the political economy undergirding the prayer and ritual which give holy cities their distinctive character. Nevertheless, useful as this is as a starting point, it is based upon the presupposition that, if Mecca and Jerusalem are holy cities and have these attributes, then these attributes are the ones that define a holy city. Perhaps there are other more compelling attributes which have nothing to do with institutional hierarchies of clergy or waqf endowments, such as a city's role in religious literature, ritual, and eschatology. Methodologically, there is much more to explore and discuss.

In this book I do not wish to continue at any length into the debate over what is a holy city. Interesting as it is, it will detract from the main focus of the book which is the way in which the many borders of Jerusalem have been formed and play a part in the future politics of the city. However, I raise these issues in order to show the reader that the simple designation of a city as holy does not encompass its complexity or the religious and political sensitivities that can be attached to the term. In many ways also, the debate on holy cities is, for Jerusalem, beside the point. Despite the methodological caveats I have raised, it is still true that any definition of a holy city that does not include Jerusalem will be a nonsense. As I have already said, Jerusalem, by virtue of its role in the three monotheistic faiths of the world, has to be the holy city per se. And it is this multifaith plurality that leads to the second major difference to note between Jerusalem and other cities. Jerusalem is "doubly unique" in that not only is it a holy city, it is also a holy city that is divided. It is true that in all the cities that have been categorized as divided, and are located in contested states, religion plays a significant role. This clearly applies to Nicosia, which is divided between the "Muslim" Turkish Republic of Northern Cyprus and the "Christian and Greek Orthodox" Republic of Cyprus in the south. It similarly played a part in Mostar between Catholic Croats, Muslim Bosniaks, and Serbian Orthodox Serbs and between Muslims and Christian Arabs in Beirut. I could go on. But none of these cities would be regarded as holy, and it is in this sense that Jerusalem, having many other things in common with other cities, is again a special case.

The reason this is so crucial in understanding the conflict in Jerusalem is that a religious conflict, no more vicious perhaps than an ethnic or linguistic or class-based conflict, has several features that make it much, much more intractable. And in Jerusalem we have intractability by the shed load. As a city that is not just inhabited by people of three faiths but is actually holy to all three, the very air you breathe is part of the conflict. Since the early 1990s, I have been involved in numerous off-the-record discussions over ways in which a political agreement between Israelis and Palestinians can be constructed to accommodate the control and management of the holy places of Jerusalem. I shall draw on this experience more later in this chapter and the next. Here I just want to recount the astonishing fact that when these discussions drilled down to the mechanics and logistics of the control and security of the holy places, there were often members of all three faiths and of both ethnopolitical groupings who would declare that if we wanted a resolution of the conflict we would need to keep the priests out of the negotiations. Sometimes this was declared aloud to the group to great and ironic laughter, sometimes it was whispered to me in a conspiratorial undertone. On one occasion one of my interlocutors was actually a bishop, conscious that any compromise over the Christian holy places would play badly with his peers.

There are attempts by religious leaders in Jerusalem to cooperate. A Council of Religious Institutions of the Holy Land comprising the religious leaders of the main denominations of each faith meet irregularly to liaise over issues of common interest such as restraining extremism and to ensure the smooth running of their religious services.[8] But their progress toward making a definitive contribution to the political stalemate of the holy places in Jerusalem is painfully slow. There have been so many years of mutual suspicion that dialogue and negotiations are a zero-sum game for religious communities. The fear is that any concession by one community will only result in a gain for another. However, the main reason for the stalemate is that the communities are, with some notable exceptions, umbilically and quite naturally connected to their lay congregations who in turn look to their political representatives for leadership in the negotiations and not, in the main, to their clergy. Thus despite the aspiration to be proactive, the chief activity of the council is reactive, issuing press releases, for example, condemning arson attacks on religious property.[9]

The reason for such intractability is complex and the subject of much debate in academic circles. It is tied up with the fact that holy places are much more than mere edifices for a certain kinds of religious activity. They become tied up with a community's sense of identity, its values and its principles. Their presence is internalized, and the attachment to them pervades all sectors and classes, having resonance beyond the sphere of personal piety and touching on the very basis and integrity of the community. In this way a population will go to much greater length to protect their holy places.[10] In a groundbreaking article, Ron Hassner also points to two further characteristics of holy places that make compromise and negotiations over them almost impossible. The first is their indivisibility. Unlike other territorial assets in an armed conflict, holy places cannot be divided, partitioned, or separated into their component parts without their integrity being impaired and a desecration incurred. You cannot easily partition and share the use of a mosque, church, or synagogue without the community who has had this arrangement forced upon them resenting it and striving to reverse the situation.[11] The use of spaces for ritual and their function as commemorative sites are often integral to the faith and religious practice so that the loss of a part renders the remainder diminished. In conflicted cities where borders change and insecurity is greater, such an occurrence has an added intensity as it strikes at the heart of the existential faith of the affected communities.

A second characteristic impeding compromise is what Hassner has termed the "non-fungibility" of holy places, that is, holy places cannot be exchanged for other goods or assets. In negotiations, fungibility is a critical part of their success. One side may be able to trade a flourishing port, for example, in exchange for a strip of land with valuable minerals. With holy places, there is absolutely no alternative site and no substitution for them.[12] Their loss or dismemberment would hollow out part of the faith. Hassner writes: "The more central the space in the religious landscape of the community, the greater the divine power vested in the place and the greater the obligation of the community to defend the sanctity of the space. This obligation is owed, not only to all members of the community, but to future generations, deceased ancestors and the gods themselves, leaving the community with no ability or desire to bargain over the space with rivals."[13]

One result of this indivisibility and nonfungibility is the protracted nature of disputes involving religion. In an article analyzing different forms of armed conflict, Isak Svensson explored the argument that the religious dimension in conflicts make such conflict less likely to be settled through negotiations. One of the main reasons that supported this argument is very pertinent to the Jerusalem case: religious groups have a long time horizon and are prepared to absorb huge costs in order to preserve their claim and use of a holy place.[14]

An additional complication that flows from both the multifaith nature of the city and from the intractability of disputes over holy places is the way they impact upon the territorial integrity of the city. As I will show, histori- cal precedent and the close geographic proximity of clusters of religious sites have created an archipelago of semi-autonomous religious enclaves, mostly centered in the Old City, but spreading out across the city. This phenom- enon is yet another illustration of the many-bordered thesis that the borders of Jerusalem are not only subject to change, to contradictory and parallel jurisdictions and to varying degrees of legitimacy and recognition, but also that the city itself is criss-crossed with soft and permeable borders that rep- resent both demographically and functionally differentiated enclaves.

In the next section I shall explore the genesis of such enclaves by look- ing briefly at the key sites, locations, and organizational structures of the three faiths. The following two sections will then examine how the national conflict over control of religious spaces is affecting the religious tensions in the city, which in turn is fueling the intractability of the conflict. I do this by taking as case studies, first, the activities of the Israeli settler movement in Jerusalem, whose expansion is incrementally changing the borders of the ex- isting religious enclaves as they reposition themselves from the fringe of Is- raeli politics toward the center. Second, I explore how the Palestinian fight- back and the revival of radical Islamic politics in the city has come from an unexpected quarter with the entry of Palestinian Islamists from Israel. The final section will argue that a new political order is being imposed on the management of the holy places in Jerusalem similar to that in existence in Hebron, which is both unraveling much of the modus vivendi that emerged after the Israeli occupation of East Jerusalem in 1967 and redrawing the soft borders of the religious communities in a politically dangerous way.

RELIGIOUS ENCLAVES AND THE ISRAELI STATE

As any student of political science will know, the first and perhaps most im- portant attribute of a state is its ability to impose its power and jurisdiction over every part of its territory. The possible reasons for the ebb and flow of state power within a given territory and over time have provided the main corpus of literature for the discipline. Yet states rarely have full sovereignty and control over their territory. There have always been vested interests (such as the City of London Corporation in London), marginal areas and autonomous zones (for example, the self-governing tribal areas in Pakistan), federal arrangements where states have devolved their authority, and treaty agreements where states have either shared or suspended their sovereignty.[15] The notion that a state controls every inch of its territory is idealized and illusory. This is not just a phenomenon in what are known as weak, fragile, or failed states but also in relatively strong ones. Strong states also enter into arrangements where their sovereignty is curtailed, sometimes willingly, as in the European Union, or sometimes because they are obliged to. As we saw in chapter 2, this is certainly the case with the exercise of Israeli authority in East Jerusalem, partially by design and partially due to historic precedent. The history of the religious communities of Jerusalem and their holy places in the city bring the curtailment on state sovereignty home quite clearly, and I will look at each in turn.

JEWISH COMMUNITIES IN JERUSALEM

One of the most interesting borders in Jerusalem is the *eruv* border. Despite being approximately one hundred kilometers long, most people do not see it. It comprises a thin wire stretched between poles located on top of fences, walls, houses, and along a railway line. It is what Eyal Weizman, the radical Israeli architect, has called a "mobile frontier" that transforms, according to Talmudic law, all within its confines into a private domain. This means that during the Jewish Shabbat restrictions on movement and other activities such as carrying objects (even house keys) or pushing wheelchairs and baby carriages are relaxed inside the *eruv* as it is not a public domain.[16] The border defines a religious area.[17] For much of the 1980s and 1990s it stretched from Mea She'arim in the center of the city to its western entrance and from the Rambam Road in the south to the ultra-Orthodox areas in the settlement of Ramot just across the Armistice Line.[18] More recently it has been extended from the eastern wall of the Old City; up onto Mount Scopus, it follows the new settlement road to encircle the northern settlements of Pisgat Ze'ev and Ramot, then down to the Tel Aviv Road to encompass the former Arab village of 'Ayn Karim and the Hadassah Hospital, then across the southern borders of the city between Gilo and Malha to the edge of Har Homa, turning sharp left and north, skirting the edge of the Palestinian neighborhood of Abu Tor, back to the Old City.

The eruv is, therefore, a border that signifies the Jewish part of the city and facilitates within it a special set of religious laws, for a brief time once a week, that does not apply to other parts. The eruv wire also has to be maintained vigilantly, as any break in the wire will revert the enclosed area to the public domain where Talmudic restrictions on the Shabbat would once again apply. In itself, however, it has little impact on the functioning of the city—the fluttering red ribbons used to mark its presence—and the stray kites caught in the wire—usually raising as much remark as a telephone cable overhead. Nonetheless, it has symbolic significance, and its extension

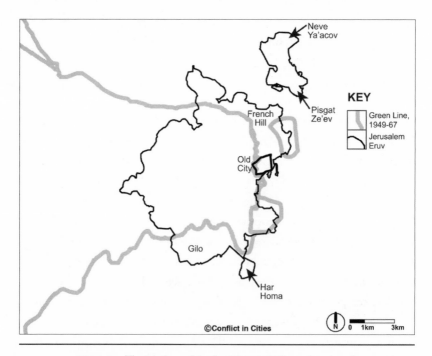

MAP 3.1. The borders of the Jewish eruv in Jerusalem (2013).

FIGURE 3.1. Wire stretched between two lampposts near the Israeli settlement of Pisgat Ze'ev demarcating Jewish eruv area (2012).

during the period of the Israeli occupation of East Jerusalem is a source of controversy.[19] Encroachments of the eruv into Palestinian areas are viewed both as a symbol of the expansion of Israeli hegemony and as harbingers of more invasive incursions. At the same time, the eruv border is not congruent with the Israeli municipal and state borders of the city, and this, in itself, tells us a great deal about which areas are defined as Jewish by an important constituency in Israeli politics. These are clearly the areas which will be defended robustly by Israel in political negotiations over the future of the city. They are in effect the Israeli interpretation of the Clinton parameters that have been deemed the starting point of any future negotiations.

Nevertheless, the eruv also has much to say about the internal conflict within the Jewish community in Jerusalem. Disliked and opposed by Palestinians, its gradual extension has also not been welcomed by the predominantly secular Israeli majority who also see it as a sign of the growing influence of the ultra-Orthodox over the politics and cultural life in the city.[20] Indeed one of the main challenges facing politicians and administrators in Jerusalem is how to accommodate the growing power of the ultra-Orthodox Jewish communities who for much of the early years of the state of Israel remained outside key government ministries and institutions but are now knocking on the doors to have a seat in its inner sanctum.

The Israeli Jewish community in Jerusalem is made up of a myriad of population groups. Ethnically there are Ashkenazi, Sephardi, and Mizrahi Jews, and these in turn can be divided into smaller subgroups. Mizrahi Jews, for example, can hail from Yemen, Iraq, and Egypt; Sephardi Jews are traditionally Ladino speaking and trace their origins to pre-*Reconquista* Iberia; the origins of Ashkenazi Jews range from Russia and East Europe to North America, and quite a few speak Yiddish as their first language. But the cleavage that cuts through all these subgroupings which has become increasingly acrimonious and politically significant is the secular-religious divide. This separation has emerged as the main political division in the Jewish community in the city. Definitions of what is an "observant," "religious," "Orthodox," or "ultra-Orthodox" Jew, as opposed to a "secular" Jew, vary, so ascertaining numbers in the city is difficult.[21] In the mid-1980s, estimates of "ultra-Orthodox" Jews comprised between 20 percent and 38 percent of the Israeli Jewish population.[22] In 2011 the figures for the "observant" and "ultra-Orthodox" were approximately 50 percent.[23] The chief result of this growth in population has been twofold. First has been the outflow of Orthodox Jews from their main areas of settlement in northwest Jerusalem in Mea She'arim, Geula, and the Bukharin quarter to adjacent areas as well as to new areas including settlements in the vicinity of Jerusalem such as Ramot, Rekhes Shu'fat in the north and Beitar Illit in the southwest.

This expansion is not without its knock-on effects on the city. Orthodox Jewish sects have very strict rules concerning behavior and the observance of a religious life. In Orthodox areas, roads are blocked on the Sabbath, mixed gender leisure activities are prevented, restaurants, cafés, and cinemas cannot open on Friday nights, and dress codes are imposed even on those who are not religiously observant. An Orthodox Jewish influx into a secular area is usually a concerted and systematic communal effort. For example, funds are directed to acquire first one street or apartment then another. Seminaries, surprisingly noisy affairs, are established in residential areas, which disturb the occupants. Orthodox families set up Orthodox schools, which lead to a decline of numbers in non-Orthodox schools and their eventual closure, driving even more secular families toward other areas.[24]

The cumulative impact of these activities leads to our second result: the decamping of the more secular Israeli Jews to other areas of the city and further afield, mostly to Tel Aviv. For them it is not just that the expansion of the religiously observant is penetrating into other areas of the city but that they are imposing their puritanical lifestyle on the rest of the neighborhood. For years, due to ultra-Orthodox opposition, Jerusalem was left without a soccer stadium, despite its team being one of the leading clubs in the country. There is similar opposition to mixed gender swimming pools, to archaeological excavations, and to advertising portraying exposed bodies or women singing. Secular protestors in the West Jerusalem suburb of Kiryat Yovel, for example, have been carrying out acts of vandalism on eruv fence posts in an attempt to stem the spread of haredi influence and settlement in the area.[25] Fed up with the growing influence of the Orthodox in the city, the young, the educated, and the professional classes are heading for the coast where the employment prospects are better and a more modern lifestyle can be espoused without comment or fear of harassment. Even more sensitively, this trend has also had an impact on the Jewish Quarter in the Old City. The tensions brought about by the political situation, the growing sense of being cut off from Israeli West Jerusalem, and the changing nature of the Old City have all combined to encourage a flight of the secular middle classes from the Jewish Quarter and their replacement by Jewish Orthodox and ultra-Orthodox families and absentee time-share tenancies.[26]

Municipal planners have long been concerned that it is not only the proportion of Orthodox Jews to secular Jews which is changing, but that the absolute numbers of seculars are declining.[27] Huge efforts have been put in trying to persuade the Israeli government to prioritize investment in Jerusalem away from settlement building into light and high-technology industries as a way of holding onto this sector of the Israeli Jewish population, but without much success. The election of a religious mayor, Uri Lupiansky in the early 2000s marked a significant shift in power away from the seculars who had hitherto dominated the municipal politics of the city to the Orthodox Jewish community. While in the 2008 elections the mayoralty has reverted once again to a non-Orthodox Jew, Nir Barkan, it was only possible by seculars forging a united front against the Orthodox. This may have secured them power in the Municipal Council, but it further polarized the Israeli Jewish communities in the city.

Although these cleavages do not amount to the same depth and intensity as that which can be seen in between Israeli and Palestinian areas in East Jerusalem, and the transition between secular and Orthodox areas in West Jerusalem is less dramatic and more blurred, they do create a tense and fragmented cultural community held together, it often seems, by a common opposition to the Palestinians. Further, there is a significant similarity between Palestinian and Orthodox Jewish populations. They both question the legitimacy of the Israeli state and its objectives in the city. An accommodation of sorts has been reached between the Orthodox sects and the Israeli state in the form of financial support for educational activities, exemption from military service (until very recently), and a degree of tax discounting. Indeed, Orthodox Jews are no great advocates of Palestinian rights, and their main political parties are equally opposed to any concessions over Jerusalem in the peace negotiations. Nevertheless, their opposition to the Zionist nature of the state and to many of the municipal policies in the cultural field does make governance and the rule of law increasingly problematic.

This focus on the ultra-Orthodox should not give the impression that it is only the ultras who are religiously observant. Other strands of Judaism are well represented in Jerusalem and play an important in the political, economic, and cultural life of the city. The main point I wish to make is that one of the main challenges to the Israeli state and successive Israeli governments is not only from the Palestinians in East Jerusalem but from a section of its own citizenship. To say that this challenge has curtailed the exercise of Israel's sovereignty is perhaps to go too far. Nevertheless, the accommodation the Israeli state and municipality has been obliged to make with the interests of this important constituency does illustrate the constraints under which the Israeli state operates in the turbo-charged religious environment of Jerusalem. The eruv border is not a hard border in that it is neither physical nor permanent and it only applies once a week. But, as powerfully as a minaret or a steeple, it does bring the religiosity of the city to the fore and touches on the question of whose city Jerusalem is, who is in control thus territorializing religious claims to the city.

CHRISTIAN COMMUNITIES IN JERUSALEM

In contrast to the ultra-Orthodox Jewish community in Jerusalem, the Christian community is in steep decline as a proportion of the total city population. In 1946 Christian Palestinians constituted over 19 percent of the population of the city and were dominant in British government service, in education, and in commerce. However, since 1967, while the Christian Palestinian population may have climbed slowly from about 11,000 to approximately 14,600 in 2010, in light of the total population growth of the city this has meant, proportionally, a drop to just under 2 percent![28] Much of this can be explained by the effects of the 1948 war when the majority of the Christian Palestinian population who lived in the New City were expelled and set up new lives, mostly in Amman but also further afield. In addition, since 1967 the proportional decline can be also attributed to a lack of Christian Palestinian immigration in contrast to the Jewish and Muslim communities and the low birthrate that usually accompanies higher income and better-educated sectors of the population.[29]

One of the chief characteristics of the Christian population is the multiplicity of denominations or sects. In addition to the "Big Three"—that is, the Greek Orthodox, the Armenian Orthodox, and the Roman Catholic Churches, who comprise approximately 80 percent of the Christian community in Jerusalem, there are twelve other sects, such as the Armenian Catholics, Syrian Orthodox, and Syrian Catholics; Coptic Orthodox and Coptic Catholics and Ethiopian Copts; Maronites, Greek Catholics, Lutherans, Anglicans, and a number of smaller Protestant and evangelical sects.[30] Relations between the sects has not all been Christian sweetness and light. There are frequent disputes between the churches and their leadership concerning precedence and responsibilities in some of the shared holy places, such as the Church of the Holy Sepulchre.[31] Over the centuries, right down to today, fights and tussles have broken out between clergy over the right to clean or repair sections of the building, as such tasks would confer responsibility and consequently strengthen their claims to the ownership of those sections. Such was the animosity between the sects on this issue that the British mandate government was obliged to examine the existing practices to ensure that it had a reference guide to arbitrate in such disputes. This guide, Cust's *The Status Quo in the Holy Places*, became a kind of bible for the churches with regard to practices in the shared holy places in Palestine and continues to serve as the key reference in any disagreement.[32] As a result, it is not an uncommon sight to see clergy of the different sects accompanying the processions or participating from a distance in the services of another sect. This is not only ecumenism in practice but also a form of ecclesiastical surveillance to ensure that established and agreed practices are adhered to and no advantage has been surreptitiously gained by the celebrating sect.

In essence the disputes between the churches in Jerusalem reflect the shifts and changes in power relations on the international level. The Greek Orthodox Patriarchate has been wary that its historically preeminent position is being gradually undermined by the power and international influence of the Vatican and that it will eventually be eclipsed by the Roman Catholic

Church. The Armenian Orthodox Patriarchate also has a long-established position in the city and is one of the largest and most cohesive communities with significant land holdings. It is wary that its concerns will be overlooked by the "Greeks" and the "Romans." Around the Big Three cluster the smaller churches who have built up a web of personal relations and alliances with the senior clergy in dealing with each other and with the Israeli and Palestinian authorities. One contributing factor in the tensions between the sects has been the predominance of foreign or expatriate clergy in the upper reaches of the clerical hierarchies. Their presence, often not speaking Arabic, and more closely attached to the societies from whence they came, has led to a disjuncture between the Palestinian lay community and the clergy.[33] Palestinian nationalism as a unifying ideology has not penetrated into the senior positions where more particularistic and foreign agendas are pursued. These divisions have been a great cause of weakness for the Christian community in the city, and there is an argument that this has allowed the Israeli government and municipality, and also at times, the PNA, to play sects off against each other in order to gain some advantage over them.[34]

Nevertheless, despite these divisions, and despite the decline in relative numbers, the churches in Jerusalem remain a formidable force in a number of areas. Acting semiautonomously, their presence adds to the panoply of constraints placed upon the Israeli state in asserting its jurisdiction and sovereignty in the city. The main source of their strength in this regard comes from three factors. First the traditions and activities of the churches have a long historical precedence which has been recognized by state authorities over the centuries. The Status Quo of the Holy Places agreed between the churches received official support from the Ottoman sultans, the British mandate government, the Jordanian government, and, since 1948 and 1967, the Israeli government.[35] Their freedom to appoint clergy, to have their property exempt from taxation, to maintain and develop their properties are all prerogatives of the churches that states were reluctant to tamper with. Furthermore, Christian communities have their own religious courts to regulate issues of personal status, such as marriages, wills, and endowments, which add to the sense of being a separate parallel society to that run by the Israeli state.

Second, the churches have extensive property holdings. A recent study by the Jerusalem Institute for Israel Studies estimates that they own land in Jerusalem comprising approximately 1,200 acres (5000 dunams). In 1967 they owned almost 10 percent of the land area of the city.[36] What is significant about this land is that it is concentrated in key areas of the city, those that will be subject to intense negotiations during any peace talks— the Old City, the Mount of Olives, the Garden of Gethsemane, Silwan, Ras al-ʿAmud, the land around the Mar Elias monastery near the Har Homa settlement, and the Valley of the Cross upon which the Israeli Knesset stands. As a consequence, despite the low numbers of Christian Palestinians currently in the city, the landscape, both east and west, is dotted with churches. One estimate is that there are over 160 churches in Jerusalem and 20 educational institutions.[37] A survey from the early 2000s indicates that in the Old City and Mount Zion area alone there are approximately 117 Christian institutions and holy sites.[38] Thus, as we can see, the social and demographic hinterland of the churches may be declining, but their institutional and physical presence in the city still remains strong.

In connection to this is the critical role Christian churches and institutions play in the single most important sector of the city's economy— tourism. The Church of the Holy Sepulchre, the Mount of Olives, and the Garden of Gethsemane are all key sites in the itinerary of a pilgrim and its twenty-first-century incarnation, the tourist. The participation of overseas visitors in the Celebration of the Holy Fire at Easter or at the various Ascension and Christmas services is high. Ramon notes that in 2010 66 percent of tourists to Israel and Jerusalem were "Christian" and that, due to the volatility of the region, the potential for even higher numbers remains.[39] While many of these visitors may gravitate towards pilgrim hostels and hotels run by churches, their sheer numbers and the limited capacity of the Christian institutions to accommodate them all means that there is a significant overspill into commercial hotels, thus benefiting a wider range of Jerusalemites. Not wishing to disturb the goose that lays this particular golden egg is a consideration that Israeli and Palestinian politicians of all stripes have taken on board and confers upon the Christian churches some latitude over the use of their properties.

A third factor that safeguards the Christian presence in the city is the churches' connections to their diasporic communities, their parent churches, and the states that have historically supported them. The very presence of pilgrims and tourists visiting the holy sites and interacting with local Christians confers on those areas a degree of immunity. These are people with cameras, phones, Internet connections, and access to media outlets in their home countries. Any form of reprehensible behavior by the Israeli authorities in the vicinity of the holy places and other institutions will be observed. In addition, politicians from countries with Christian traditions visiting Jerusalem will be invited, as a matter of course, to different churches to meet and hear of their experiences. They can and do make representations to either Israel or the PNA on behalf of that community. Each time a Russian diplomat visits Israel, for example, the issue of the property the Israeli state has acquired from the Russian Orthodox Church in West Jerusalem is raised.[40] Roman Catholic countries in the United Nations, when often voting en bloc, can be influential in key UN forums.[41] Visits by politicians from such countries are not to be ignored. In this way, each and every action by Israel and the PNA that may have an impact upon the churches and their congregations is subject to constant clerical scrutiny and can be rapidly channeled to the diplomatic level or to the world media. The prospect of incessant interventions from this quarter and the lack of capacity in both Israeli and PNA administrations to deal with such scrutiny has been a sure incentive for Israeli state agencies and the municipality to avoid ruffling the feathers of the churches' Western supporters.

This is not to imply that therefore the churches can act with impunity in the city. Far from it. There have been many incidents where the position of the Christian leadership has been eroded, where church land has be confiscated, and where the laity have found their rights of access to the holy places denied.[42] A significant watershed took place in 1990 when Israeli settler groups took over a Greek Orthodox Patriarchate property in the Old City—the St. John's Hospice. In the midst of a tussle between the settlers and Greek Orthodox priests and laity outside the entrance of the hospice, the patriarch was pushed to the floor. The clear lines of complicity between the settlers and Israeli state agencies and the humiliation meted out to the patriarch by the settlers indicated a significant shift in the relations between the Israeli state and the Christian community. Already severely strained by the brutal Israeli response to the first Palestinian intifada, what we saw in this incident was the transformation of a set of arrangements in which the Christian communities were being gradually co-opted by the Israeli state to one in which the acquisition of land was given much greater priority.[43] Since then (1990), relations between the traditional Christian community of the city and the Israeli state and its ministries has deteriorated sharply. Israeli attempts to influence the appointments of senior clergy have largely backfired, culminating in a standoff between the Greek Orthodox Church and Israel over the appointment of the new patriarch in 2005, with Israel refusing to recognize Patriarch Theophilus, who in turn is recognized by the Palestinian National Authority.[44] Continuing disputes over land sales and appointments have had a deleterious impact upon the conduct of Christian festivities which require some cooperation with the Israeli authorities. For example, in 2010 local Christian Palestinians found that their traditional Easter processions leading up to the sharing of the Holy Fire were severely curtailed by the Israeli security services, despite strong representations from senior clergy and diplomats.[45] At the same time, it remains the case that, in many parts of the city, Christian enclaves continue to provide a space where their activities are relatively free from interference and scrutiny and where the Israeli state refrains from entering for fear of the wider political costs it will incur.

THE MUSLIM COMMUNITY IN JERUSALEM

Earlier in this chapter when describing the tranquillity you can find in the Haram al-Sharif, I also characterized it as the eye of the storm in the Palestinian-Israeli conflict. The golden tiles of the Dome of the Rock in the Haram enclosure dominate the skyline of central Jerusalem like no other building in the city. From virtually every raised point in the city, wherever you can find a clear view, your gaze is drawn down toward it. And like no other building in the city its very presence casts a long and dark shadow over the Israeli claim to the city. Here in the heart of the capital of the

Jewish state, Israel, lies a monument of global import whose very existence calls into question the Judaic foundations of that claim. The Dome of the Rock and the al-Aqsa Mosque in the Haram al-Sharif lie in the center of a powerful web of social, political, and religious relations that keep it, and the Muslim community that reveres it, both separate from and in opposition to the Israeli state. As a symbol of the limits to Israeli sovereignty in the city, it must be galling to nationalistic and expansionist Israeli politicians that they can see it from most places in the city, and they can see it every day!

The Dome of the Rock is also the foundation stone upon which the borders of the Muslim community, as a religiously observant community, rest. In relation to the permeable borders of the Jewish and Christian communities, those of the Muslim community are toward the harder end of the border spectrum. There is just so much more land and property, more administrative responsibilities, and more unbroken historical practice involved that in certain parts of the city, the Old City in particular, the sense of being in a parallel world or of entering a state within a state is much more palpable. The Israeli occupation of the city in 1967 wrested political and military control from the Jordanians and Palestinians, but it did not sever the connection of the Muslim community either to the heart of the city or its dominant position in key institutions and buildings.

One of the first steps carried out by the occupying Israeli forces in 1967 was to raise the Israeli flag over the Dome of the Rock.[46] As soldiers lined up to be photographed in front of it, orders to remove the flag were immediately issued by the Israeli defense minister, General Moshe Dayan. Not wishing to unnecessarily antagonize the Palestinians, the Jordanians, and the wider Muslim world, in removing the Israeli flag he was also signaling that Israel was not seeking to take over the Haram itself, which would be left to the Muslim leadership to administer. This was a decision that many Israeli politicians have subsequently regretted. A similar retreat also was made over the extension of Israeli jurisdiction over the Waqf Administration and shari'a court system in East Jerusalem. The Israeli Ministry for Religious Affairs was initially given responsibility for the affairs of the Palestinian Muslim community, including the maintenance and administration of its holy places, associated religious buildings and the shari'a law courts.

However, as we saw in chapter 1, this simple extension of Israeli rule came up against the unique status of Jerusalem. The Muslim clergy who ran the Waqf Administration and law courts were not pushovers. As the then director general of the Waqf Admininstration, the late Shaykh Hassan Tahbub, said to me in an interview, "I do not want to go down in history as the one who allowed the Israelis to take over the holy places of Jerusalem."[47] He and his colleagues resisted strongly and refused to accept any Israeli involvement. Fearing a diplomatic crisis that would erode its claim to be providing freedom of worship in the city, the Israeli government backed down, and responsibility for dealing with the Muslim leadership was returned to the Israeli Ministry of Defense who took a more pragmatic and noninterventionist view of how to best proceed. Ultimately, these shifts in policy made it clear that the Israeli state accepted that Israeli civilian rule over the Muslim religious sites of Jerusalem was not possible under the circumstances.[48] If the Israeli annexation of East Jerusalem had been carried out to the letter of the law, the Israeli Ministry of the Interior would have been given jurisdiction over the upkeep and administration of Islamic monuments and archaeological remains and the Waqf Administration would have been subordinated to the Israeli Ministry of Religious Affairs, as are similar Waqf Administrations in Jaffa, Acre, and Haifa.

In reality, the Jerusalem Waqf Administration has continued to fulfill this role and take on quasi-state functions. Thus, when taken together with the exemptions and anomalies in the application of Israeli law to East Jerusalem that we outlined in previous chapters, the property of the Muslim community, particularly in the Old City, is in effect a semiautonomous enclave within areas of Israeli military control. With regard to the extensive Waqf uncapped holdings of the Muslim community, the extension of Israel sovereignty was suspended and parallel Israeli and Palestinian legal and moral frameworks operated. Due to the long-established and deeply embedded institutional bureaucracies and the extent of endowed property in the city, the Muslim community (and, by a proxy identity, Palestinians) is thus able to maintain a formidable presence in the city. One of the main buttresses of this presence is the extent of Waqf uncapped land holdings in the city. Exact figures are difficult to obtain, but we can estimate that more than two-thirds of the Old City is waqf. Estimates for East Jerusalem outside the Old City are even more difficult to arrive at, but figures suggest that nearly 30 percent of East Jerusalem is Islamic waqf and therefore administered by the Waqf Administration.[49]

Nevertheless, these figures do not start to suggest the wide and varied role the Waqf Administration has in Jerusalem. The offices of the Waqf Administration are located in the Madrasa Manjakiyya, an elegant and spacious Mamluk building abutting the Haram enclosure. From early morning, it is usually buzzing with activity and crowded with tenants seeking assistance. Leading steeply up to a wide corridor lined with high vaulted offices, the cool marble steps provide a welcome resting place for those queuing in the growing heat of the day. Once inside, through the wide open windows you can catch stunning glimpses of the Dome of the Rock, which seems to calm even the most ill-tempered dispute between tenant and waqf engineer. The offices are busy because the Waqf Administration reaches down to so many parts of people's lives. For example, all public waqf properties are registered at the Waqf Administration Finance Offices, which must be notified of all changes of tenancy or of use. Changes of use must also be carried out in consultation with its Engineering and Maintenance Department. The Engineering and Maintenance Department is responsible for the repair and upkeep of outside and inside walls, roofs and floors, windows, and doors: interior and exterior decoration are the responsibility of the tenants. However, because of the low rent levels, the department is not able to fulfill its management responsibilities as it should, and intense negotiations often take place between the tenants, the Engineering and Maintenance Department and the Finance Office. Due to the overcrowding in many of the properties of the Old City, the Engineering and Maintenance Department also finds itself heavily committed to resolving problems of access and of partitioning, over and above its regular maintenance and repair work.

There are other functions. In the absence of a Jordanian presence and of a Palestinian state, and as part of its refusal to surrender any of its responsibilities to the Israeli state agencies, the Waqf Administration also found itself taking on additional roles concerning the preservation of its waqf real estate, often when these roles would normally have been carried out by an national agency such as an antiquities department or housing ministry. It set up a Department of Islamic Archaeology which also became involved in management-tenancy relations—since many of the Islamic monuments in the city have been converted into residences and careful negotiations had to be entered into before any restoration work could proceed. However, its prime task was an ambitious restoration programme designed to improve the quality of living conditions in many of the properties under its control. It also continued the al-Aqsa mosque restoration project in the Haram ash-Sharif to international acclaim in the form of winning in 1983 the prestigious Aga Khan Award for Islamic Architecture.[50] As a result of this work, by 1982, it employed almost 500 people.[51]

In the late 1990s I witnessed long convoluted and sometimes heated debate between tenants of the Madrasa al-Muzhuriyya and waqf engineers and architects which gives an insight into the complexity of the Waqf Administration's task in Jerusalem. The Madrasa comprises a high arched portal opening into beautifully a proportioned courtyard with spacious, deep, and arched diwans on three sides. Stone steps in the corner led up to small rooms behind a stone balustrade. A meticulously executed program of restoration had just been completed by the Waqf Administration's Department of Archaeology, save for one more phase. During the earlier phases, the tenants had agreed to move out temporarily while the work was underway, and the last phase of the project was the removal of the toilet and the washhouse. Roughly constructed out of cinder blocks and corrugated metal, it sat in the center of the courtyard, obscuring the lovely moldings, carvings, and cleaned stone faces of the restored work. But the tenants wanted it to stay, preferring convenience over art. The alternative suggested by the architects and engineers were not acceptable to them, and a heated debate continued for weeks. Some tenants threatened to go over the heads of the Waqf Administration to enlist the support of the PLO or even the Israeli Antiquities Authority, which would have offered the Israeli state a useful point of entry into the Waqf Administration restoration program. Finally, much to the disgust of the architects, the chief engineer relented and decided that the toilet block could stay. In an interview, he explained his long view. The property had been restored and was now safe. In the context of

Israeli encroachments elsewhere in the Old City, it was important to keep the tenants happy and *in situ,* and if that meant sacrificing a view of a classic Mamluk courtyard and diwan, so be it.[52]

Another way in which the Waqf Administration has bolstered it semi-autonomous activities is through a systematic engagement in education. As we saw in chapter 2, education was a problematic issue at the interface between Palestinian national identity and Israeli attempts to secure its control over the city. In the late eighties, it ran twenty-two primary and secondary schools in Jerusalem. By 2011, in conjunction with the Palestinian Ministry of Education and Higher Education, the Waqf Administration was responsible for thirty-eight schools, providing an education to over twelve thousand primary and secondary schoolchildren.[53] The Waqf Administration also established a Shari'a College and several seminaries known as *dur al-qur'an* and *dur al-hadith.* Many of the leading Islamists in the Palestinian community are alumni of these institutions.[54] Similarly, it set up a Department of the Revival of Tradition and the Islamic Sciences which collected and published copies of ancient manuscripts, archival material, and commentaries. A huge UNESCO grant also allowed it to undertake the expensive task of restoring and preserving the al-Aqsa library, training and employing several Palestinian specialists.[55] For over a decade, a journal on contemporary Islamic issues, *Hoda al-Islam*, was published once a month and provided a forum for discussion and debate. Although not necessarily of a standard to rival other major seats of Islamic learning in the Muslim world, the result of this emphasis on education was to generate, at least in the Haram enclosure, a visible atmosphere of study and discussion. It is not unusual to see separate clusters of young men, of women, and of retired people sitting on chairs in the shade of the olive trees between the dome of the Rock and al-Aqsa Mosque, open books on their laps, discussing the finer points of Islam. As a prominent leader of the Palestinians in Jerusalem, the late Faisal Husseini, explained to me: while he was an observant Muslim and not a fundamentalist, he supported these religious-based activities in the city. In his view they attracted significant numbers of young men to the Old City and the Haram enclosure, and their very physical presence served as an added deterrent against attempts by militant Israeli settlers in their activities to take over Palestinian land and property. In all these ways Islam has offered what can be seen as a protective mantle for the Palestinian presence in East Jerusalem.

Nevertheless this enclave status is subject to strict constraints and constant attempts to encroach upon Palestinian community affairs, and the autonomy I have suggested should not be overstated. For example, despite the degree of sensitivity shown to the Muslim religious establishment by the Israeli government immediately after the occupation, at the same time it did not hesitate from razing 135 homes and two mosques and evicting 650 people from the Magharib quarter in order to build a plaza in front of the Wailing Wall for Jewish worshippers. Similarly, a year later, in 1968, it expropriated 29 acres of mostly Palestinian and Islamic property in the Old City for the purpose of extending the traditional Jewish Quarter.[56] Since this period there has been a steady stream of small acquisitions by the Israeli state of Palestinian property. From the 1980s there has been covert and increasingly overt Israeli state support for the activities of radical Israeli settlers who are engaged in the acquisition of property in the Old City in order to provide a platform for establishing some kind of Israeli foothold in the Haram courtyard itself. It is to this development in the changing territorial configurations of the religious and ethnopolitical groups in the city that I will now turn.

ISRAELI SETTLERS AND THE HOLY PLACES

Since 2000 the population of the Old City has grown to approximately fifty thousand residents, of which approximately five thousand are Israeli, the overwhelming majority of whom live in the expanded Jewish Quarter. Given this preponderance of Palestinians, it takes one by surprise the extent to which the few Israeli residents living in other parts of the Old City have made themselves felt. This came home to me a few years ago during the early hours of the morning whilst staying in a friend's flat on the Tariq Bab al-Silsilah (the Street of Chains). The Tariq Bab al-Silsilah is the main pedestrian route from Jaffa Gate to the Bab al-Silsilah (Chain Gate), a magnificently grand Mamluk double entrance to the Haram enclosure, but almost tucked away in the tall ramshackle apartments and houses that have grown up around it. When you emerge from one of the deep and broad arches over the street and are confronted with this huge larger-than-life gate, there is a whiff of Orientalist decaying splendor, as if you have just stepped into a David Roberts painting. Children are playing on the steps to their houses abutting the gate, washing is hanging from the windows, and a small doorway shop selling cigarettes and soft drinks spills out into the courtyard in front of it. Opposite the gate is a dormant fountain and dry water basin collecting rubbish and rubble and beside it is the impressive Mamluk frontage of the Madras Tankiziyya, the former seat of the Palestinian Supreme Muslim Council and now, sequestered by Israel, used as an Israeli police station. Lying half awake perspiring in the heat in a spacious bedroom built on top of an arch over the street, my gloaming-dreaming was constantly interrupted by walkie-talkie exchanges in Hebrew, punctuated by static, then more Hebrew. This went on for several hours until the Old City stirred and woke in the dawn and the radio sounds were subsumed by a cacophony of domestic noises as families and people in the houses around made their ablutions, their breakfasts, and their preparations to leave for school or work. But each night thereafter I heard the radio chatter in Hebrew and through the open windows observed how much night traffic of groups of young Israeli men there was, not just to the police station beside the gate, which was very quiet most of the time, but from different points along and around the Tariq Bab al-Silsilah. I have been tracking the growth of the Israeli settler groups from the early 1980s, when they were a new phenomenon, and so was very well aware of the number of properties they had acquired in the Muslim Quarter of the Old City.[57] But it was not until that night when I then realized the extent to which they not only had permeated all areas of the Old City but also lived a kind of parallel shadow life there—one that you could only perceive clearly when the daily lives of the Palestinians around them retreated for the night.

Israeli settler groups in the Old City began their activities in the early 1980s. The election of the right-wing Likud party in 1977 had given a fillip to the settler movement in the West Bank and Gaza Strip. But it was the Israeli withdrawal from the Sinai and the demolition of the settlements there as a result of the 1979 peace agreement with Egypt that acted as the driving catalyst for expansion. The negotiations over Palestinian autonomy and further possible withdrawals in the West Bank also during this period led to a heightened determination in Israeli nationalist circles to ensure that there was a strong Israeli presence in all parts of East Jerusalem. While there may have been a national debate in Israel over the relative advantages and disadvantages of retaining all of the West Bank and Gaza Strip, there was a nigh national consensus that all Jerusalem (however delineated) should be retained.

Nevertheless, during the early 1980s and the years leading up to the Oslo Accords of 1993, the collection of settlers groups active in the Old City of Jerusalem could be easily differentiated from the state-supported settlement activity that had taken place and continued outside the walls in East Jerusalem. I described the construction of huge state-financed housing complexes on the high ground and the edges of the city in chapter 3. The settler groups that began working in the Old City in the 1980s were not initially state supported and saw themselves as the cutting edge of the radical fringe of the settlement movement.[58] While maintaining a number of different foci, they were united in two ways. The inspiration for their work was derived from the teachings of Hafetz Chaim who argued that when the Jewish Temple was finally "rebuilt" on the Haram enclosure or Temple Mount it would require priests, or *cohanim,* to carry out the services and the animal sacrifices. It was therefore incumbent on them to prepare for this eventuality by studying Temple lore and initiating trained adepts. The second goal the groups had in common was that in order to create the conditions in which the Temple could be rebuilt, Jews should settle in areas close to the Haram to create a Jewish city, and this was to be done by appropriating former Jewish-owned properties in the Old City and where possible other suitable properties.[59]

By the end of this period, between the election of the Likud party in 1977 and the 1993 Oslo Accords, nearly one hundred properties had been acquired in the Old City. Some of these were formerly Jewish owned, but the large majority were not and had been acquired by such nefarious means that the government was obliged to set up a commission of inquiry to investigate their behavior and that of government agencies dealing with them, and many so-called purchases were beset by court cases.[60] Initially, official state support had either been lacking or covert and indirect, but by the mid-eighties some of the groups began receiving state support for educational activities and by the time of the Oslo Accords public funds for house purchases and renovations were being openly directed to the Old City settlers. Indeed, cooperation between settler groups and state agencies increased with, for example, the Israeli land registry office (the Israel Lands Administration) and the Jewish National Fund passing on information on vacant properties and land to settler groups. From the nineties onward, this cooperation became overt and publicly acclaimed, with successive governments and municipal administrations vying to brandish their nationalist credentials by supporting the expansion of these groups' activities.

Following these beginnings, the settler movement also began to direct their energies to areas outside the city walls. There are many reasons for this. Despite the rhetoric proclaiming their progress in their fund-raising brochures and despite the relative success in acquiring properties, the actual numbers of Jews residing in these sites was low. Estimates range between 500 and 750 Jewish residents in the Christian and Muslim Quarters of the Old City. [61] I have been struck frequently on my more recent visits to the Old City how little activity actually emanates from these acquired properties during the daytime. Many of the residential properties, whose doors are armor plated, whose windows are heavily barred and shuttered, and where there is often a small unit of soldiers or a private security team standing close by, appear unused, standing like concrete bunkers jutting into a busy river estuary. In the mid-eighties, when I first conducted research on them, I had received the opposite impression—extensive renovation and construction works, clusters of young armed men moving from one collection of properties from the Tariq al-Wad to the Aqabat Khalidi, processions of small schoolchildren snaking their way under armed escort from their fortified homes to the Jewish Quarter schools. It is true in 2011 I witnessed an impressive and provocative demonstration of settler power when they virtually closed down all the Old City to conduct a celebratory series of rallies and marches along the Tariq al-Wad and Via Dolorosa in the heart of the Muslim Quarter, virtually taunting the Palestinian residents behind a shield of soldiers and police.

Nevertheless, it does appear that their main target for recruitment— young families with an ideological commitment to Jewish settlement in the Old City—has not been a success in the long-term.[62] Despite sophisticated electronic monitoring and security systems through which guards are radioed to accompany settlers from the Jewish Quarter or Jaffa Gate or Damascus Gate to their homes, or schoolchildren from their schools, and despite saturation surveillance in the form of, at last count, over seventy closed-circuit television cameras (CCTV) along virtually every stretch, corner, alleyway in the Old City, the conditions and the critical mass to establish Jewish family residences do not yet exist.[63] The fallback position of relying on young male seminarians, especially in those areas in the Old City more remote from the Jewish Quarter, was evident for several years, but my impression is that this too has not been as successful as was hoped. The transient nature of such groups of young men, and the probable high financial and labor costs of maintaining a sufficient through-put has, I suspect, reduced the attractiveness of this option.

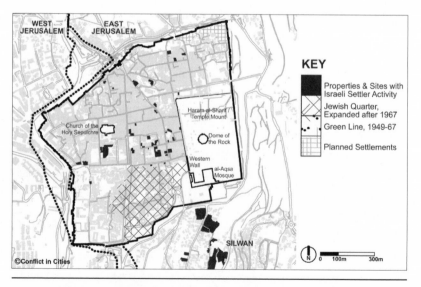

MAP 3.2. Israeli settlers in the Old City and adjacent areas (2013).

FIGURE 3.2. Securitized Israeli settler accommodations in the Old City (2011).

Contributing to this lack of clear success in recruiting and holding onto young settler families has been the influx of Palestinians into the Old City since the construction of the separation barrier in 2003. Already in the mid-1990s, despite the emigration of Palestinians from the Old City recorded by a detailed survey by the Palestinian Welfare Association, the Palestinian population of the Old City was 13.5 percent of the total Palestinian population in the whole of the city. This has created a population density of approximately fifty people per dunam (or quarter of an acre) in the Muslim Quarter.[64] One can imagine that in this crush of humanity the challenge of carving out a sufficiently comfortable Israeli Jewish enclave for aspiring middle-class families, despite the huge investment in protection and security by the state, is beset with difficulties that are experienced incessantly and daily. After 2003 and the construction of the barrier, population density has increased dramatically in all the non-Jewish quarters of the city. The Welfare Association reports many rooms in apartments containing families of ten or more persons.[65]

Three other reasons why Jewish residential settlement in the Old City may have lost its momentum are worth mentioning. One is the impact of the St. John's Hospice incident mentioned earlier in this chapter. This was an event where not only did the Old City settlers publicly humiliate the patriarch of the Greek Orthodox Church, but they also drew much unwelcome international attention to themselves. Consequently, the incident alerted both local residents and a wide range of national and international organizations and political actors to their activities. This in turn had the effect of coalescing disparate and ad hoc resistance by Palestinians. It is also quite likely that, in taking the long view, a strategic decision was made by settler leaders to revert to their earlier "softly-softly" approach to property acquisitions in the hope that Palestinian hostility to the introduction of actual Israeli residents as neighbors would be blunted if it were not accompanied by a huge security and media presence carrying national political significance. I would also surmise that, given the growing ties between the settler movement and Israeli state agencies and government ministries that the Klugman Commission uncovered, they did not wish to prejudice further government assistance by embarrassing it with controversial public property grabs. A second reason has already been alluded to—that of a more coherent Palestinian resistance to settler encroachments in the Old City being embarked upon. The most effective and firmly grounded approach has been that initiated by the Welfare Association which invested not only huge sums and expertise in property renovation but also in community capacity building. Their work will be examined in more detail in the next section.

A final reason has to do with the broader political discussion taking place over the future of Jerusalem and which parts of the city may be ceded to the future Palestinian state. In the final chapter we shall explore how the growing awareness of the many-bordered nature of Jerusalem has helped erode the taboo in Israeli politics around contemplating withdrawing from those parts of East Jerusalem that are clearly difficult for the Israeli state to absorb. Indeed the Clinton parameters in 2000, accepted by the then Israeli government (with reservations), laid out a vision of a city divided along the existing residential divisions. Part and parcel of these discussions was the exploration of some sort of shared Israeli-Palestinian authority over the area known as the Holy Basin.[66]

As a result, radical Israeli settler groups became concerned with the possibility that, even if they were successful in expanding areas of Jewish residence in the Old City, the immediate hinterland might be lost to them if it was either subjected to shared Palestinian administration or, even worse, full Palestinian sovereignty. They therefore began to find ways in which a Jewish presence could be increased in these areas.

Taken together, these reasons led to a significant change in strategy of the radical settler groups. The new strategy was multileveled, physically and politically. Physically they began to broaden out their efforts to encompass not only a wider geographical area, broadly concomitant with the Holy Basin borders on the eastern part of the city, but also to go underground, exploring and excavating ancient tunnels, cisterns, and caves. The streets of the Old City became only one part of their activities, with equal efforts being put into the tunnels along the western wall of the Haram, as with Silwan, Ras al-'Amud, Sheikh Jarrah, the Mount of Olives, and Palestinian Musrara. Their biggest success has been, significantly, in the creation of the biblical theme park, City of David, just below the walls of the Haram itself. This is

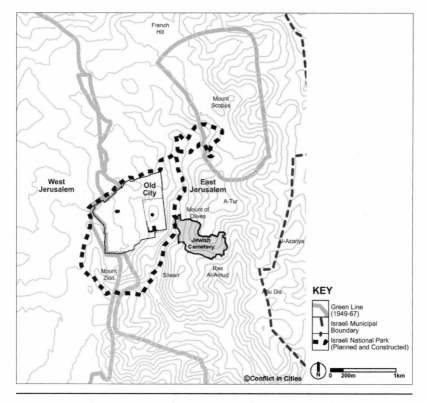

MAP 3.3. The area often referred to as the "Holy Basin" (2012).

run by El-Ad, a settler group founded in 1986 that emerged out of the radical West Bank and Gaza Strip settler group Gush Emunim. Having been granted the contract to develop this archaeological site by the Israel Nature and Public Parks Protection Authority, the City of David park is now one of the most visited sites in Israel and Jerusalem and a prominent fixture on the tourist itinerary.[67] It also marks progress toward the more subtle strategic goal of encircling the Haram inside and outside the Old City with Jewish sites that are imbued with religious and national meanings. Thus the City of David is connected by a series of tunnels to the network of tunnels running alongside the western wall underneath the Muslim quarters.[68]

Politically, we can see how settlers and their sympathizers have found positions in key government agencies such as the Office of the Custodian of Absentee Property, which has responsibility for Palestinian refugee property; the Israel Lands Administration, which owns the legal title of all state land; the Israel Antiquities Authorities, which has jurisdiction over the heritage sites and archaeological excavations; and, finally, the Israel Parks Authority.[69] Over the past decade we have witnessed the emergence of a network linking government funds to settler properties and key state offices and agencies. The main result of these activities has been to transform the settler movement in Jerusalem from being the outrider of radical Zionism to the vanguard of the Israeli establishment. The settlers' chauvinistic and exclusivist visions of the city have become mainstream politics.

In concluding this section, we should note that that through these activities the Israeli government is creating new areas of potential flashpoints between Israeli Jews and Palestinians. Israeli colonization is not only taking place in densely populated areas in the heart of the Old City and Palestinian East Jerusalem but also in the highly religiously sensitive areas that are close to Muslim and Christian holy sites as well. The insertion of settlers into these areas is not simply the arrival of new residents into the neighborhood or street as in any other city. It has much more impact than that. The acquisition of property by the settler groups in these areas brings with it not only new neighbors—individuals, students, families, etc.—but also a whole panoply of security systems including Israeli armed soldiers, police outposts and checkpoints, Israeli private security firms, settler militia, patrols, and electronic surveillance. Semienclosed and private spaces beside a circle of houses have become zones of conflict where children fear to play and surveillance cameras and armored doors create an atmosphere of oppression and suspicion. It is the equivalent of a military occupation, and the lives of the neighboring Palestinians are totally blighted. Though their numbers, especially in the Old City, are not large, the settler groups have gradually shifted the contours of the religious and ethnic enclaves in Jerusalem and are poised to achieve a hegemonic shift whereby some of the sites they have acquired have become increasingly imbued with national and religious significance so that any withdrawal from them through peace negotiations will bring high political costs to the incumbent Israeli government. I will explore the implications of this more in the last section

PALESTINIAN AND ISLAMIC RESISTANCE

Palestinians, both Christian and Muslim, have not been entirely passive in the face of this erosion of their presence in and around the holy sites of the city. As we saw in an earlier section, the traditional Islamic institution in the city, the Waqf Administration, was subject to strong pressures regarding its independent existence and for many years after the Israeli occupation it resisted the undermining of its role and activities. In the mid-eighties the combination of generous funds from the Islamic world and the accelerated colonizing activities of a Likud government acted as a catalyst for the Waqf Administration. It embarked upon an extensive program of renovation and refurbishment of its properties in East Jerusalem, including shops, residencies, marketplaces, mosques, monuments, hostels, schools, and public baths.[70] The crowning glory of this phase was the renovation of the al-Aqsa Mosque, for which it received the Aga Khan Foundation Award in 1986.[71] Following the Oslo Accords in 1993, much of this renovation work fell into abeyance, partly due to the lack of funds and partly due to rivalry between the PLO and Jordan over their respective claims in Jerusalem. In addition, in the light of partial Israeli withdrawal from the West Bank under the terms of the accords and the setting up of the Palestinian National Administration there, the Israeli government to attempted to consolidate its hold over the city by placing restrictions and stepping up of the surveillance of the activities of the Waqf Administration. One result of this was that the Waqf Administration began to focus more on monumental restoration work in the Haram enclosure itself, leaving the more politically fraught renovation work outside the Haram to be carried out by Palestinian NGOs such as the Welfare Association.

To a large extent, the same pattern can be seen in the intramural activities of the Christian churches. An early phase of passivity was followed by institutional growth, renovation, and a reinvigorated community activity, although, in the Christian case, much of this was directed at the Christian communities that had moved outside the walls, with new schools and churches being built in the Al-Azariyya and Beit Hanina suburbs. One manifestation of this extramural drift can be seen in the controversial closure of the Austrian Hospice Hospital on Tariq al-Wad and Via Dolorosa junction in the Old City during the mid-eighties, thus removing a key communal facility for Old City residents, who were obliged to turn to medical facilities outside the walls.[72] In addition, amid concerns of the steep decline in the Christian population in the Old City, the mid-nineties also saw attempts to bring employment to and enhance facilities for the Christian residents. Housing was improved in the Christian and Armenian quarters, seminaries established, cafeterias were opened in hostels, and a concerted effort made to resolve denominational differences over the restoration and upkeep of the Stations of the Cross and the Holy Sepulchre.[73]

It is also important to remember the role of the PNA in the immediate aftermath of the Oslo Accords. Despite the fact that they were not permitted by the Israeli government to operate openly in East Jerusalem, it emerged as a significant actor for a short period. Through a satellite office in East Jerusalem, known as the Orient House, they were able to coordinate a large number of activities, often presented as research or data collection in preparation for the final phase of the negotiations outlined in the Oslo Accords, ranging from policing to representation and the provision of some services. In 2005 Orient House was closed by the Israeli prime minister, Benjamin Netanyahu, and the PNA was barred by the Israeli government from working in the Jerusalem. Nevertheless, informally and through the cooperation between Palestinian institutions and PNA ministries, a residual influence has been retained. In the previous chapter we saw how this was achieved in the electoral and educational fields, but also could also be seen in the health and medical fields outside the Old City.[74]

However, it is in the religious sphere that one can see the ebb and flow of PNA influence in the city most clearly. In the mid-nineties the minister of religious affairs of the PNA (ostensibly wearing the hat of a functionary in an advisory council in order to avoid Israeli restrictions) maintained an office in a former Mamluk madrasa along the Tariq Bab al-Silsilah in the Old City. An agreement with Jordan in 1997 transferred the responsibility of the Waqf Administration to the PNA, and the Jordanian-appointed mufti of Jerusalem saw his authority eventually being replaced by that of the PNA-appointed mufti.[75] Through its control over appointments and the budget of the Waqf Administration, the PNA was able to exert a remote-control influence in Jerusalem, especially over the holy sites, in the face of Israeli policies designed to undercut its role there. Ultimately, this influence waned, and the PNA's role has been replaced more recently by a weak and tentative Jordanian-backed administration. This transition is discussed more fully in the next section.

Palestinian resistance to the encroachments of the Israeli state and the settlers was also evident in the growing mobilization of the community and the emergence of civil society organizations that sought to retake the initiative. It is important to recognize the context. With an Israeli state committed to a Zionist ideology, which results in the neglect of the welfare of non-Jewish residents of the city, and with the absence of formal and recognized Palestinian institutions being allowed to provide services, Palestinian NGOs offer a critical minimum level of welfare provision. While we should note that these NGOs are not formally linked to the PNA, nor do they take orders from PNA ministries, they nevertheless work within a Palestinian consensus on the Palestinian claim to the Old City. As such, they coordinate their activities with PNA agencies and work broadly within legal parameters concerning the relationship between the PNA and Palestinian NGOs and have senior personnel on their staff and boards who act as advisers to the PNA on Jerusalem. One of the most important of these NGOs, by virtue of the size of its budget and the ambitious scope of its work, we have already referred to: the Palestinian Welfare Association.

An important and controversial example of its work lies in the field of housing and renovation in the Old City of Jerusalem. As we have seen, the combination of the Israeli closure policy and the separation barrier has led to huge pressures on housing in the Old City. In the last ten years the population in the Muslim quarters of the Old City has increased by at least 50 percent. Much of the housing available is substandard, and, according to survey carried out by the Welfare Association in 2004, 20.5 percent in the Palestinian areas are unfit for habitation.[76] The reasons for this developmental blight in the Old City are numerous and largely connected to municipal neglect, ambiguities over the rule of law, and the lack of enforcement of

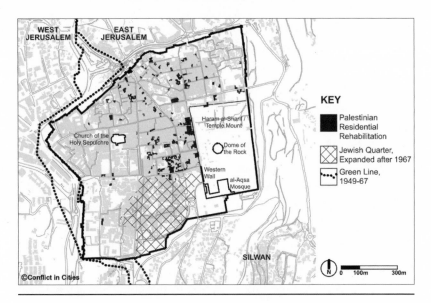

MAP 3.4. Welfare Association projects in the Old City (2010).

tenancy contracts.[77] In an attempt to reverse this decline, the Welfare Association embarked upon an ambitious program of surveying, restoration, and renovation. Through its Old City of Jerusalem Revitalisation Programme , it identified a number of key properties and areas within the Old City for priority renovation, mostly around the Haram compound and adjacent to the Jewish Quarter. While focusing on property renovation and restoration, the OCJRP has also sought to use the program to foster community development and preempt the activities of the Israeli settler groups in those areas.[78]

The professionalism of it work and its engagement with stakeholders and local residents in the planning and execution of its projects has won the projects plaudits internationally and it too received the Aga Khan Foundation Award for Architecture in 1996.[79]

A final actor to be considered in the mobilization of Palestinian resistance to Israeli state and settler encroachments in Jerusalem is the role of the Islamic movement in Israel. Since 2000 Palestinian Muslims in Israel have emerged as a significant player in Palestinian politics in the city. The most active and prominent is the northern branch of the movement, led by Shaykh Ra'id Salah, a lawyer and former mayor of Umm al-Fahm, a large Palestinian town in the area of Israel known as the Triangle.[80] Initially coming to the fore during the excavation of the Marwani prayer halls under the Haram enclosure, during which they supplied both the funds and the voluntary labor, the Islamic movement has increasingly been seen as the key defender of the Palestinian presence in the city. In the post–Second Intifada period after 2001, Palestinian politics in East Jerusalem was characterized by fragmentation and lack of direction. Following the deaths of the charismatic Fatah leader Faisal Husseini and the respected Shaykh Hassan Tahbuub, the former director general of the Waqf Administration and former minister of religious affairs for the PNA, the PNA failed to develop a coherent strategy on Jerusalem. At the same time, Israel was able to reverse the PNA's influence in the religious sphere by preventing the appointment of nationalists to positions in the Haram.[81] It also succeeded in neutralizing the influence of Hamas through arrests, detentions, and expulsions.[82] While to some extent Jordan was able to reassert its position in the Waqf Administration, its ability to be proactive was circumscribed by a shortage of funds and a reluctance to provoke the Israeli government. As a result, Palestinian leadership in the city has been notable by its almost complete absence. It is into this political vacuum that the Islamic movement was able to enter with significant results.

The Islamic movement's activities in Jerusalem have been directed toward three main areas: heritage, property, and Islamization. Following its success in restoring and opening up the Marwani prayer halls in the Haram enclosure, the movement took the lead in resisting Israeli attempts to encroach on other areas of Islamic heritage in the city.[83] A particularly confrontational and ongoing campaign has been around the collapse of the ramp leading up to the Maghrabi Gate in 2007. Israeli plans to rebuild the ramp were denounced as further encroachments on the Palestinian heritage in the area and provided an opportunity to highlight the destruction of the Palestinian Maghrabi quarter that took place at the beginning of the Israeli occupation in 1967. The Israeli plans for a replacement ramp to the gate were portrayed as having military functions to allow armored cars to enter the

Haram enclosure. In protest, the Islamic movement held demonstrations in Palestinian towns and villages up and down Israel as well in East Jerusalem, and Ra'id Salah himself was barred by the Israeli government from entering the Old City. The movement notched up another success when Israel was forced to accept UNESCO involvement and put its plans on hold. In essence UNESCO introduced a "reinforced monitoring mechanism" which would furnish bimonthly (!) reports to the World Heritage Center.[84]

In the area of resisting property acquisitions by Israeli settlers in East Jerusalem, the Islamic movement has had less immediate success. Despite regular demonstrations, the initiating of court cases, and the establishment of protest tents, few properties seized by the settlers have been returned to their Palestinian occupants. Nevertheless, the mobilization of East Jerusalemites and the personal sacrifices shown by the Islamic movement supporters, the use of the Internet and social media to draw in a global audience has catapulted the movement to the forefront of the Palestinian groups in Jerusalem, earning Ra'id Salah the epithet of Shaykh of al-Aqsa.[85] It is in the area of Islamicization, or reassertion of the Islamic identity of the city, that the Islamic movement may have the most impact over the long term. Any long-standing visitor to Jerusalem will have noticed the changes over the past decade. If you take a short walk through Damascus Gate and down Tariq al-Wad, which is the route to the Haram, you cannot help but be struck by the proliferation of new shops that no longer cater only to Western tourists. On either side you will see stalls selling Islamic paraphernalia such as prayer beads, prayer rugs, digital Qur'ans, *azan* (call-to-prayer) alarm clocks; toy shops with veiled (*muhajibba*) Barbie dolls, and jihadi computer games; the beat of hip-hop or techno music is being eclipsed by shops filled with the slow, entrancing sound of seriously mellifluous Qur'anic singers; women's clothing shops still sport modish fashions, but are also accompanied by banks of colorful scarfs and retro-Islamic hijabs; the always exotic perfume shops front the alcohol-free perfumes that are permitted. This is very different from the 1980s when the rage was either T-shirts emblazoned with "Israel is Real" or outrageously priced Bedouin camel panniers. No doubt the commodification of Islam in this way is not peculiar to Jerusalem and is also a global trend. Nevertheless, the market for these goods has been deliberately created and supported by the Islamic movement by bussing in Palestinians from all over Israel to Jerusalem. Between 2001 and 2004 the number of busses chartered for these Jerusalem trips doubled from 3,000 to over 7,000 and from 150,000 passengers to over 350,000.[86] This bussing campaign is not just confined to a kind of "retailing as resistance." It is also supplemented by the sponsorship of popular festivals such as the children's March of Flags of al-Aqsa Mosque, volunteering projects like tree planting in the Haram and social welfare events such as providing the *sahour* and *iftaar* meals during Ramadan to approximately 1,000 pilgrims. The aim is explicit: "The Revival of the Old City (within the walls of Jerusalem) through the renewal of the communal spirit and the commercial life of the market, so that there is no need for the sale of property to settlers, who lie in wait, day and night, looking to pounce on any store or house. Our people in Jerusalem are the interface and the first gate and defence of the blessed al-Aqsa Mosque."[87]

In these and many other ways, Palestinians have sought to hold back the drip-drip-drip of Israeli encroachments in, over, and around their religious sites. Restoring property, injecting communal activities into deprived and blighted areas, creating coalitions of resistance have all, to some extent, failed to reverse the gains made by Israel in these areas. The most one can say is that they have raised the political costs to Israel and the settler groups of the encroachments. In the concluding section I want to look how these dynamics may unfold in the short to medium term by examining the way in which the pattern of Israeli encroachments in Hebron may be replicating itself in Jerusalem.

THE "HEBRONIZATION" OF JERUSALEM?

This chapter has described and discussed the ways in which the traditional religious communities, through their historical attachment to numerous religious sites have also carved out areas of control that have to some extent been incorporated into the ethnonational conflict between Israelis and Palestinians. It also then sought to show how these scattered borders have undergone further shifts and alterations as the dominant Israeli Jewish community is able to make use of the coercive power of the state to encroach on the roles and responsibilities of the other communities, thus extending its sphere of influence and areas of control. What is of concern is that this shift constitutes the first steps to what I call the Hebronization of Jerusalem, that is, the process by which the protection and development of Jewish holy sites also becomes the vehicle or bridgehead for further encroachments on Muslim property in Jerusalem by the Israeli state.[88] In this process, these sites are first securitized by the army and then become a platform for Israeli settlement activity in the vicinity. This is the pattern that has emerged in the West Bank town of Hebron. Is it beginning to occur now in Jerusalem?

The Jewish population in the Old City of Hebron is only approximately 400 people, in contrast to the over 20,000 Palestinians living there. Nevertheless they are protected by 2,000 Israeli soldiers who also patrol the routes between the Old City and the Israeli settlement of Kiryat Arba where approximately 6,650 Israeli settlers live. Palestinians in the rest of Hebron number in the region of 110,000. Since the Oslo Accords, and more specifically the Hebron Protocol signed by Israel and the PLO in 1997, the city has been divided into two parts. H1 is part of the municipal area that was transferred to PNA jurisdiction and H2 remained under Israeli rule. Although geographically much smaller than H1, H2 comprises most of the Old City (including the al-Ibrahimi Mosque), the sites of Israeli settler activity, and also 40,000 Palestinian inhabitants. In this tense maelstrom the al-Ibrahimi Mosque, or the Cave of the Patriarchs, plays a significant role. As the traditionally held resting place of both the biblical and Qur'anic prophets Abraham, Isaac, and Jacob and their wives, Sarah, Rebecca, and Leah, it is a shared holy site that has attracted the attention of Muslim and Jewish worshippers and pilgrims down the centuries. Indeed, during the whole of the post-1967 period in Hebron we can see a a symbiotic relationship between the holy site and Israeli settlement activity and how the presence of the tombs of the prophets was the key driver for Israeli settlement.

After 1967 and the occupation of the city by the Israel army, the Israeli Ministry of Defense imposed a set of arrangements for worship in the al-Ibrahimi Mosque. The Israeli scholar Yitzhak Reiter has described them as

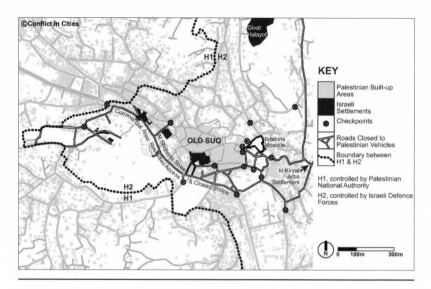

MAP 3.5. Hebron Old City and adjacent area (2012).

a division between the two religions both temporally and spatially.[89] In essence, the arrangements meant that Muslims retained use of the main hall, the Isaac Hall, as a mosque for their daily prayers, while Jews were allocated the remainder of the building and the enclosure. Jews were also allowed to pray in Isaac Hall at certain times and on certain days. Muslims were able to stipulate the rules of behavior on the site and were responsible for all maintenance and renovation. Despite the initial cooperation of the Waqf Administration, these arrangements broke down amid violent confrontations culminating in 1994 in the mass killing of 29 Muslim worshippers, with 125 wounded by the settler-soldier Baruch Goldstein. An Israeli commission of inquiry was set up, which recommended a new model that attempted to constrain the activities of the settlers and put the Israeli army firmly back in charge.[90]

In the post-1994 commission period, basic security for worshippers on this site has improved, with the Israeli army monitoring both the Israelis settlers and Palestinian Muslims more closely. Nevertheless, the contrast with the period before 1967 is, from the Palestinian point of view, quite dramatic. From untrammeled access, use, and responsibility for the entire al-

Ibrahimi Mosque, they are now obliged to pass through formidable Israeli checkpoints with scanners, revolving gates inside cages, and body searches. From my more recent visits, it is clear that some attempt has been made to improve the training of the soldiers who carry out the searches. More respect is shown and some attempt is made to maintain the dignity of the Palestinian Muslim worshippers. But the process is inherently intrusive and the respect grudgingly displayed. The whole experience of entry into the mosque is confrontational and as far from an uplifting or spiritual experience as you can imagine: Once you have passed through the security gates and entered the enclosure, the atmosphere is tense and fraught, with mosque attendants anxiously looking round at strangers, CCTV cameras silently recording all those who enter, the crackling sound of Israeli army walkie-talkies punctuating the air and disturbing the peace of the Isaac Hall, and altercations between soldiers and those wishing to enter bounce along the walls of the passageway. At the same time, areas of the mosque are cordoned off and closed, breaking up the unity of the structure and the holiness it once conveyed. There are only men present. It is a far cry from the casual use of mosques by women and children in the Islamic world. From Istanbul to Jakarta, you often see groups of women meeting in a corner praying and chatting, children lolling about leafing through prayer books. Not anymore, it seems, in the al-Ibrahimi Mosque in Hebron.

But, more important, in terms of the model that the Hebron situation presents for Jerusalem, is that, currently, Palestinians are confined to certain areas of the mosque only. They are closely monitored and have access to other parts for only ten days of the year. Thus during the post-1967 period we can see how the growing presence of the Israeli settlers in Hebron and their use of the mosque has been at the expense of the Palestinian Muslim access to the mosque. In addition, the model is seen by the Palestinian community as an imposed one, one that they have not agreed to and is neither satisfactory nor durable but contingent solely upon the current Israeli military dominance. It is not a model of coexistence but of incremental penetration leading to a full takeover. The question, then, to ask is whether this the dynamic that can be seen taking shape in Jerusalem.

FIGURE 3.3. Israeli army checkpoints outside al-Ibrahimi Mosque in Hebron (2011).

FIGURE 3.4. Israeli settlers praying inside al-Ibrahimi Mosque, Hebron (2011).

There are many parallels and, of course, many differences that are crucial. East Jerusalem has a much stronger Israeli presence in terms of numbers. In 2009, while the Palestinian population was estimated to be 275,900, the Israeli settler population of East Jerusalem was approximately 198,000.[91] Israeli also has much more control over land use, infrastructure, and mobility in East Jerusalem, which makes it more akin to a Palestinian area in Israel, such as Acre, Nazareth, or Jaffa, rather than to Ramallah, Nablus, or Hebron in the West Bank. And it is in the context of this powerful, broader dynamic of demographic presence and control that the changes initiated by the radical Israeli settler movement around the Haram al-Sharif are critical. As we have seen, the Palestinian demographic predominance in and around the Old City is not under immediate threat. Palestinians in the Old City and in the suburbs around the walls still vastly exceed the numbers of Israeli settlers. Nevertheless, the increase of settlers in the Old City, the steady increase of settler enclaves in an inner ring of settlements around the Old City, buttressed by a ring of larger settlements separating East Jerusalem from the West Bank and, of course, the erection of the Israeli separation barrier, have all succeeded in breaking up the contiguity of the Palestinian areas and providing space for both increased settler and mainstream Israeli development activity in the areas close to the Haram.

As in Hebron, a rampant settler movement in Jerusalem is increasingly accompanied by a culture of impunity. Seeking to avoid a confrontation with the settlers, who are able to portray themselves as defenders of Jewish heritage and Jewish rights in the city, the Israeli state leaves illegal property acquisitions unchallenged. Palestinians have recognized that any recourse to the Israeli courts serves merely to slow the process of acquisition down, but will not stop it. There has also been an increased focus on the Haram al-Sharif/Temple Mount area itself by Israeli religious groups and the settler movement, which has seeped into the Israeli national politics. The official Israeli Rabbinate injunction that Jews should not enter the Haram al-Sharif to pray, in case they accidently step onto the site of the former Holy of Holies—the inner sanctum of the historic biblical tabernacle and Temple—is being eroded.[92] Radical settler groups and other Jewish groups look instead to other rabbinical teachers for guidance on entry into the Haram enclosure.[93] These teachers are less concerned with the broader political sensitivities that such a course of action may provoke. One group has claimed to have delineated the exact dimensions and coordinates of the Holy of the Holies and consequently identified areas where Jewish prayer can take place on the Haram. Over the past decade the activities of the settlers and their supporters in government agencies have managed to draw into mainstream Zionist discourse the possibility of some sort of construction of a synagogue on the Haram.[94] One reason given for the collapse of the Camp David peace talks between the PLO and Israel in 2000 was the proposal by the then Israeli prime minister, Ehud Barak, that Israel be allowed to construct a synagogue in one section of the Haram enclosure. The fact that such a controversial proposal was even submitted is an indication of the extent to which such ideas were no longer espoused by the radical fringe of Israeli politics. In 2011 Palestinians witnessed small groups of Israeli Jews, ostensibly presenting themselves at the gates of the Haram as tourists, gathering near the southern corner of the Haram enclosure, near the al-Aqsa Museum, praying in small groups and on occasion rolling about on the paved floor in a trance.[95] In a further twist and ratcheting up of the tension, two members of the Israeli Knesset, Arieh Eldad and Ben Michael Ari, proposed a bill to allow Jews to pray on the Haram al-Sharif according to set times in the same way as Jews are given access to the Cave of the Patriarchs at the al-Ibrahimi Mosque in Hebron. One can see how such activities herald both further Israeli protection against Palestinian protestors and demands for regular access and the accompaniment of prayer books and other religious paraphernalia.

As a result, one can anticipate the scene being set for further encroachments by settlers and their supporters on the Palestinian and Muslim use of space in and around the Haram al-Sharif. By virtue of the sheer number of sites acquired, the physical contiguity and overlapping of settler enclaves with Muslim religious sites, it is obvious that the number of potential flashpoints has increased. And the settlers are no shrinking violets either—they make their presence felt. The number of religious occasions where the observances of the two religious communities overlap may not have increased, but the numbers participating has. The likelihood of a confrontation leading to serious rupture in public order has been ratcheted up. While we need to bear in mind that such confrontations have taken place in the past and have been contained either by the religious authorities or the Israeli security forces, what is different now is the mainstreaming of the settler ideology and the increased centrality of the sites they have obtained. The Western Wall Foundation operates from the Israeli Prime Minister's Office, while the City of David has become a prime tourist site in the city. The political context has significantly changed in the past twenty years since the signing of the Oslo Accords. These scattered borders of the religious sites are undergoing critical shifts and are likely to provoke reactions in a way that makes it more likely that the Israeli army will be asked to intervene in any confrontation. The result of such an intervention will be the consolidation and extension of the gains made by the settlers. It is in this way that we see parallels with Hebron. Left to their own devices, it is quite probable that the settler movement and its supporters in an ultranationalist Israeli government would seek to exploit the current balance of power in its favor. It is arguably only the fear of international opprobrium that constrains Israeli actions in this area. To this crucial area we now turn.

4

THE INTERNATIONAL COMMUNITY AND THE LIMITS OF SOVEREIGNTY

JERUSALEM LIES ON the cusp of two environmental climates—the Mediterranean and the Arabian Desert. The climatic division almost follows the Green Line through the city, with the greener forested areas to the west falling down the valleys of the Judean and Samarian hills toward the coast and, in the east, the drier, more barren rocky ridges plummeting sharply down to the Jordan valley and the warm tepid waters of the Dead Sea.[1] At approximately 2,500 feet high, the altitude of the city can take you by surprise. In winter it can be both very cold and foggy and also very wet. On some visits to the city, I have often wished I had brought a pair of Wellington boots with me. But the weather is also very changeable, and, a few days after a cold spell, you can sometimes feel the warm wet winds blowing off the sea. In summer the sun bakes down relentlessly; it dries out your skin like it does the land around you, and you tend to carry out your business and your errands in the cooler early mornings and the late afternoons.

Far from Jerusalem, in a quiet, lush, and very green corner of Britain, close to the English-Welsh border, stands a ninth-century cathedral rising from the low-lying countryside and catching the morning sun on its two tall towers. As you enter its hushed, shaded, but cavernous interior and shuffle nervously around the huge Gothic pillars, you almost accidentally come across, in the north choir, one of the most marvelous maps of the medieval world—the Hereford Mappa Mundi. Drawn by a cleric in the 1300s, the map is a schematic representation of the known world, and Jerusalem is right in the center. Miles away from the Mediterranean and desert climate of the Holy Land, Hereford was part of a world where Jerusalem was the central focus, a point of reference for geography as well as theology. The Hereford Mappa Mundi is not unique. There is a genre of medieval maps focusing on Europe, North Africa, and Asia and were primarily intended for "edification and improvement" and not designed as guides for travelers.[2] They were used to convey both the harmonious ordering of the world, the beneficence of the Almighty, the wonders of creation, and they all had Jerusalem as the center of the world.

How true is that still today? Does the Holy City still play that central role in the world, acting as a magnet not only for prayers and pilgrims but also for armies and adventurers? One way of having a rough sense of its contemporary role in the popular imagination is to look at its presence on the World Wide Web. I carried out a survey of the number of Web sites for Jerusalem on four different search engines then compared these figures with figures from a number of categories of cities: major cities of the world, other holy cities, and other divided cities in the Conflict in Cities project.[3] The results were not quite as I expected. From the tables ap1.1 and ap1.2 in the appendix, you can see that the number of Jerusalem Web sites to those of the ten largest cities of the world, according to the Global City Index, Jerusalem comes in as a distant tenth, just above Seoul and below Hong Kong, and some hundreds of millions below London and New York, which have over five times as many Web sites. Comparing Jerusalem to other holy cities, Jerusalem comes third after Rome and Lourdes, although it has nearly three times as many sites as Mecca (see table ap1.4).[4] In the final category, the other divided cities that are part of the Conflict in Cities project, table ap1.3 shows that Jerusalem comes in a creditable second after Berlin and with three times as many Web sites as Belfast and Brussels.[5]

These results require further consideration. Immersed as I have been in the study of Jerusalem for so many years, I had assumed that Jerusalem would be far and away the city with the most Web sites, certainly, at least in the holy cities category. A city that is so important to the three main monotheistic faiths of the world would surely have millions more Web sites than Rome or Lourdes. Similarly, in the category on divided cities, I was less surprised that Jerusalem was not in the number one position than struck by the fact that Belfast was in the third position after Jerusalem. However, it was the huge gap between the number of Web sites on Berlin and that of Jerusalem that made me realize that these figures need further analysis and contextualization. Of course, Berlin would have many more Web sites. It is a huge city with four and a half times the population of Jerusalem;[6] it is also the seat of government of a much larger territory than Israel and Palestine put together and has an economic capacity that utterly dwarfs the economy of Jerusalem. A simple comparison of numbers of Web sites as I carried out will not reflect any of these factors. Clearly there will be a correlation between the size of a city's population and the number of Web sites. More than that, the numbers of Web sites will also increase exponentially for each unit of population increase: particularly in industrialised countries with an advanced technological infrastructure, every business, every civil society organization, every government or council department will have a Web site that will include a reference to the city's name. And it is probably possible to compute a formula that can predict the numbers of Web sites for any given unit of population. Nevertheless what will be interesting and relevant to gaining an understanding of the role of Jerusalem in the world today is the extent to which Jerusalem exceeds that predicted correlation. To this end I took the figures for Google in the Any Language category and divided them with the population of the city to get a Web sites per capita figure. From graph 4.1. we can see that Jerusalem has a middling position behind Sydney, which is first (!), Chicago, Los Angeles, London, Singapore, and Paris. In relation to other holy cities (graph 4.3), we should put the overwhelming dominance of Lourdes aside, since the population of the city is so small while the number of Any Language Web sites is relatively large (33 million less than Jerusalem) that the per capita figure goes through the top of the table. In this scenario, Jerusalem is by far and away the dominant city, with nearly three times as many Web sites per capita as Kyoto and seven times as many as either Rome or Mecca. With regard to other divided cities, Jerusalem comes in a surprising fifth behind Belfast, Berlin, Mostar (unexpected), and narrowly behind Beirut (graph 4.2).

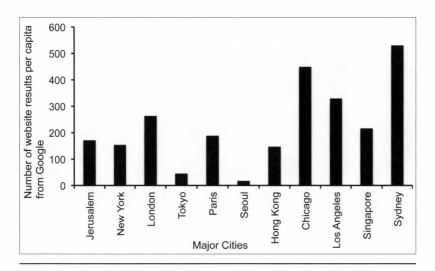

GRAPH 4.1. Comparison of numbers of Web sites per capita: Jerusalem and major cities of the world.

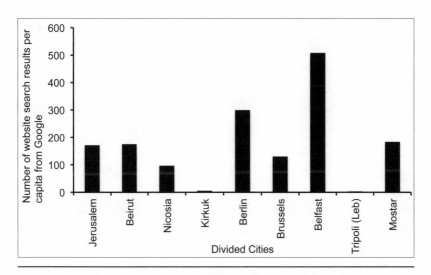

GRAPH 4.2. Comparison of numbers of Web sites per capita: Jerusalem and other selected divided cities (Google. Language: Any. 2012).

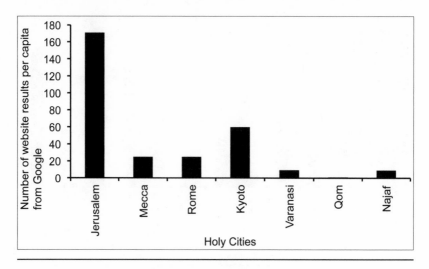

GRAPH 4.3. Comparison of numbers of Web sites per capita: Jerusalem and other selected holy cities (Google. Language: Any. 2012).

These tables and graphs paint a broad picture of the prominence of Jerusalem in the modern world and have to remain purely illustrative. There are too many caveats regarding the Web sites themselves and the uneven degree on Internet connectivity across the world for them to demonstrate anything conclusively. While going some way to showing the role of Jerusalem in the contemporary popular imagination, they do not quite capture it, since Web sites are focused on institutions and businesses. One way to discovering the extent of discourse around the city is again to turn to the Internet and consider its salience on Facebook. The three charts that follow take the Likes comment from Facebook sites of the same three categories of cities as above. From graph 4.4 you can see how in the Major Cities category Jerusalem almost disappears, having ten times as few Likes posted as New York, and comes at the bottom of the chart after Singapore and Sydney. In the category of divided cities (graph 4.5), it drops to fourth behind Berlin, Beirut, and Brussels, when in the Web sites chart it came second and in the Web site per capita chart it came fifth. In the final Holy Cities category (graph 4.6), it lags behind Rome and Lourdes and is about equal to Mecca. Clearly there are also caveats to be attached to this overview. Facebook is still confined to technologically savvy sectors of the popula-

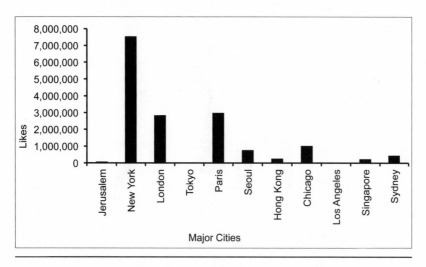

GRAPH 4.4. Comparison of Facebook "likes for major cities.

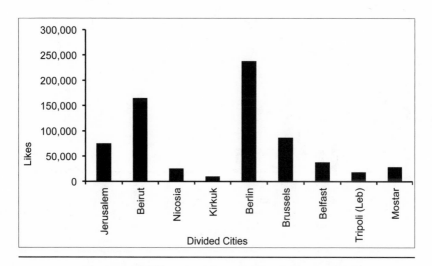

GRAPH 4.5. Comparison of Facebook "likes" of divided cities.

tion and to countries with the Internet infrastructure that can cope with these social networks. This probably explains the very high scores for New York. Nevertheless, they do tell story. Still largely the domain of the young, the Likes charts suggest possible future trends and also a snapshot of what these sectors of the population are concerned with. Jerusalem has clearly

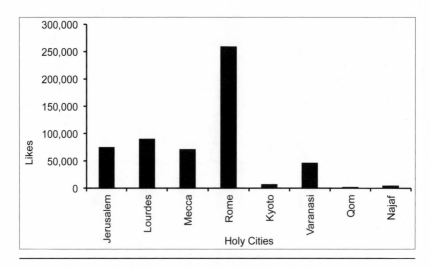

GRAPH 4.6. Comparison of Facebook "likes" of holy cities.

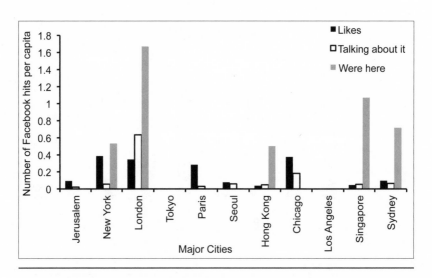

GRAPH 4.7. Comparison of Facebook "hits" per capita for major cities.

virtually no Facebook profile in comparison with the other major cities of the world, which may be expected. What is much less expected is the Holy Cities category. The fact that it is level-pegging with Lourdes and Mecca and a long way behind Rome is surely indicative how its centrality, if not yet diminished, is on the way to being so. Graphs 4.7, 4.8 and 4.9 compare

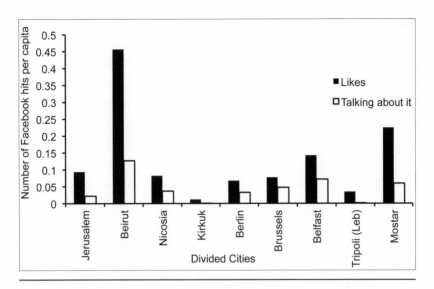

GRAPH 4.8. Comparison of Facebook "hits" per capita for divided cities.

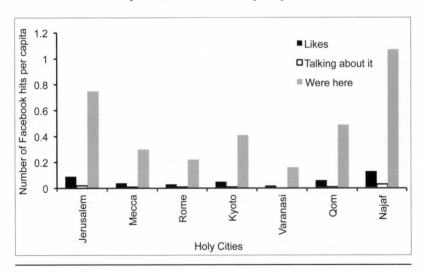

GRAPH 4.9. Comparison of Facebook "hits" per capita for holy cities.

Jerusalem by Facebook hits per capita and produce some puzzling results. In the major cities category (graph 4.7), it falls way behind London, Singapore, Sydney, and New York, but surprisingly ahead on Tokyo and Los Angeles, which do not even figure statistically. In the divided city category (graph 4.8), it is behind Beirut (by about a factor of 5), Mostar, and Belfast, but ahead of Brussels, Nicosia, and Berlin on the Likes button, but, significantly, behind them for the "Talking about it" button. In the holy cities category, it is second to Najaf on all the three buttons: Likes, "Talking about it," and "Were here." Clearly, these graphs are purely illustrative and do not present a conclusive picture of Jerusalem's fall from preeminence in the modern era, but they do give an impression of the direction of travel. Nevertheless, at the same time, while it is beyond the scope of this book to quantify, we should not forget that Jerusalem will still be figuring in the daily prayers, in the liturgy and rituals of worship, and in the sermons of religious clergy that will not be recorded in a Like or Talking About It button.

If this is an interesting but, nonetheless, a less than satisfactory depiction of the important role Jerusalem plays in the global public discourse, another measure would be the huge press corps and media presence in the city. Exact figures for comparison are hard to come by, but it is generally believed by the journalist community that the size of the press corps in Jerusalem is second to Washington, DC, and almost on a par with London, which is used as a media hub for Europe and North Africa. Indeed since the collapse of Beirut as a feasible Middle East base in the 1980s, and the increasing difficulty in operating and moving about in other Arab capitals, Jerusalem is seen by Western media as the most stable base from which to cover the Middle East.[7] For example, the three main world news agencies, Reuters, Agence France Presse, and Associated Press all have large bureaus stationed in Jerusalem; every main British, French, American, and German newspaper has at least one staff member and, more often than not, one backup correspondent, plus most probably a local fixer or translator or office manager; the main newspapers and weeklies of Italy, Spain, the Netherlands, and the four main Scandinavian countries would also be represented, either by staffers or a well-paid contract stringer, either imported or local. The smaller daily papers in the U.S. will also have accredited correspondents in Jerusalem or Tel Aviv as well, although these may not be permanent staff but on contracts.

Turning to the electronic media, the BBC has at least three full-time staff correspondents and sometimes up to half a dozen more contract "stringers." Indeed, while its bureau in Jerusalem is not as large as the main news agencies, it is, nevertheless, one of only 3 places in the world where the

BBC also has a bureau chief to supervise and determine coverage. The main TV news networks, that is, CNN, Sky, ITN, Channel Four, the two main French channels, most other European channels, including Euronews, the full contingent of U.S. channels such as ABC, CBS, NBC, Fox, PBS, and NPR, as well as the two main Canadian channels and ABC Australia have permanent representatives and almost certainly local support staff. Finally, there are now also journalists from the former Soviet bloc, particularly Russia and Poland, and the other members of the BRICS, that is, the larger developing or recently developed nations like Brazil, India, and China (the last especially) also have staff teams there or contracted nationals hired locally or sent there on contract from home bases. From this fairly anecdotal count alone, one can see that we are talking about hundreds of people.[8] Recent exchanges with journalists in Jerusalem also suggest that it is one of the few cities in the world that has not felt too seriously the recession that has affected most of the foreign desks in the media.

Clearly this prominence in both the Internet and in the media is connected and a reflection of the part it plays in the politics of the region. The symbiotic relationship between the issue of sovereignty over Jerusalem and the long conflict between Israel and the Arab world ensures that developments in the city play out through various information platforms across the world. The sad truth is that cities in conflict are cities of extra-ordinary attention. To this we need also to add the additional significance of Jerusalem to major religious faiths who are spread across the world, whose adherents play an active part in the politics of their countries, including its foreign policies. Joseph Stalin may have scoffed at the pope's lack of tank divisions in the aftermath of the Second World War, but would not have been so dismissive if he had lived to the postcolonial period in which large number of Catholic states were admitted to the United Nations and often cast their votes as a bloc.[9] In the same way, the post–oil boom of the 1970s saw the rise in influence of the Organization of Islamic Conferences (OIC), which also voted en bloc in the whole panoply of world fora, particularly over the issue of Jerusalem.[10] And we see how Jerusalem emerges as a feature in European and, more remarkably, in U.S. domestic politics in the strident debates on recognition over Israeli occupation.

This chapter will explore these issues in some depth, not only because they are important in themselves and in advancing our understanding of the conflicts that permeate and penetrate the city, but also because they add a crucial contextual framework to our thesis of the many borders of Jerusalem. In highly significant ways, the international interest and involvement in Jerusalem both constrains the assertion of sovereignty, whether it be Israeli or Palestinian, and consolidates the ambiguity over the current borders. In previous chapters we have discussed the impact of the lack of international recognition accorded to Israel over its claims to both parts of Jerusalem as its capital city. In this chapter we unpack this dimension in more detail. The main thrust of my argument is that the international position on Jerusalem, whether it be the UN and its sister agencies, the U.S. or EU, the OIC or the World Council of Churches, support for the Israeli claim over Jerusalem is either entirely lacking or ambiguous at best. In turn, the lack of international support undermines the foundations of Israel's policies in East Jerusalem and increases the political costs of states that may be sympathetic to its policies, such as the United States. The first section of the chapter will describe the historical background and antecedents to such external interventions. The second section will examine the part played in the city by the UN both in terms of the size of its interventions and the range by discussing the role of UNRWA and UNESCO. The third section looks at two critical actors, the European Union and the United States, and attempts to show how the combination of their positions, whether it be on recognition of the PLO or the location of their embassies, provide the international political and legal architecture that ultimately subverts the Israeli position in the city. The final section assesses the extent to which interventions from the Arab and Islamic world in the form of project funding contribute to the undermining of Israeli positions in the city.

ANTECEDENTS OF INTERNATIONAL INTEREST IN THE CITY

A key point to note at this stage is that such international interest in the city is not new. It is not a spin-off of greater access to the city through new faster modes of transport, of new technologies, and of globalization. The history of Jerusalem is a history of a successive series of invasions by both neighboring and more far-flung powers. Apart from a brief period during the Solomonic and Hasmonean eras, it is not as if Jerusalem itself has been a metropolitan hub controlling peripheral provinces, a motherland from which conquests were sprung. More often than not it has been victim rather than aggressor. As a religious city without great natural resources, its main source of external income has always been donations, endowments, and pilgrimage. But even the ostensibly benign activity of visiting the city on pilgrimage could be overlaid with geopolitical nuances, and sometimes not so subtle ones. Muslim pilgrimage to Jerusalem was frequently used and encouraged to counter whichever faction or dynasty controlled Mecca.[11] In addition, the importance of a pilgrimage to Jerusalem was enhanced by the proliferation of a genre of writings and prayers known as the *fada'il al-quds*, or "merits of Jerusalem," that spoke of its beauty and the blessings which would accrue to its visitors and residents alike. In the sixteenth century, Volney describes how Christian pilgrimages during the medieval period took on the form of such large gatherings that they eclipsed the local population, possibly crossing the not-so-fine line between welcome guests and an invading army.[12]

On top of these influxes of pilgrims was the investment that steadily fed into the city from external sources, primarily through religious institutions such as the waqf system.[13] These religious endowments, and the construction of mosques, seminaries, pilgrim hostels, schools, and public water fountains they engendered, established much of the urban fabric of the city.[14] The antecedents of today's external involvement can clearly be seen in the period after 1187 c.e. when Salah ed-Din captured Jerusalem from the Crusaders. It was one of the most prolific phases in the channeling of external funds into Jerusalem. As a result of the genocidal slaughter of the Muslim population by the Crusaders, Salah ed-Din sought to attract new Muslim immigration into the city by creating numerous waqfs as a form of state investment in services such as schools, fountains, hostelries, and khans.[15] His initiative was followed by successive Muslim dynasties, reaching its peak during the Mamluk period when the *amir*s became patrons of architects and craftsmen and blessed the city with many monumental buildings of great beauty and magnificence.[16] The direction of funds into Jerusalem continued also during the Ottoman period when the great walls surrounding the Old City were built between 1537 c.e. and 1541 c.e. and an aqueduct supplying essential water to a growing Jerusalem population from pools as far away as in the Bethlehem area was constructed.[17] External funds entering the city were not restricted to just the Muslim community. A similar pattern can also be seen in the way churches and synagogues and pilgrim hostels were built by the Christian and Jewish communities with spin-offs for the city's economy. In fact, during much of the medieval and Ottoman period, the poverty of the Jewish community was mostly alleviated by the *halukka* system of funding prayer and study in the city. These were funds collected for the purpose of maintaining a Jewish presence in Palestine and became part of ritualistic giving in the Jewish diasporic communities.[18] Thus revenue from the pilgrim industry, from endowments, and from bequests to the Christian and Jewish communities sustained a city that, we might recall, was some distance from ports and the trade routes of the coastal plain and lacking in natural extractable resources or a manufacturing base.

The pattern of the international community's interest in the city is not all conquests à la Crusades, but also encompasses a more removed involvement through proxies and the co-optation of local leaders. This can particularly be seen from the mid-Ottoman period onward in the growing power of the European and Christian Great Powers and their manipulation of religious denominations to extend and protect their influence in the city. A significant milestone of this process was the signing of the first "capitulation" treaty in 1535 between the Ottomans and the French. Following capitulation treaties gave other European countries various powers over the administration of the Christian holy places, such as the Church of the Holy Sepulchre in Jerusalem and the Church of the Nativity in Bethlehem. These powers and responsibilities were exercised either through the churches under their patronage or through their consuls. Here we see the first building block in the construction of the semi-autonomous religious administrations we referred to in chapter 2. By the late nineteenth century, the French and British consuls in particular had amassed considerable influence over political developments in Jerusalem. The main vehicle for European penetration in the city was often through the privileges held by the different denominations and recognised by the Ottoman authorities. For example, the Greek Orthodox and Russian Orthodox religious hierarchies were supported by Russia, the Roman Catholic and Armenian Orthodox by the French, and the Jewish and latterly the Protestant hierarchies by the British.[19] They all struggled against each other for control over the various Christian holy places and for the prestige such control would render their interpretation of the faith. Violent clashes periodically erupted to the extent that the Ottomans were obliged to codify the arrangements concerning the management of the holy places. In 1757, Sultan 'Uthman III issued an edict which became known as the "Status Quo" that established a crude "pecking order" for the different denominations and their access to and management of the sites.[20] This hierarchy of privileges and responsibilities in turn reflected the balance of power between the different European states on one hand and between them collectively and the Ottomans on the other.

International interest in Jerusalem increased steadily in the nineteenth century. The economic and military decline of the Ottoman Empire and the growing strategic importance of the Levant to Europe following the construction of the Suez Canal in 1869 all combined to enhance the value of the city. In attempt to curtail European influence in the city, the Ottomans made Jerusalem the administrative capital of the new province of Jerusalem. At the same time, the growing weakness of the Ottoman state structures allowed European influence in the city to increase dramatically, both in terms of the powers of the consuls and demographically, as a European-style "New City" emerged along the western ridges outside the Old City walls.[21] It was also during this period, from 1839, that the British took the Jewish community of Palestine under their wing, which meant that increased Jewish immigration to Jerusalem received British protection. By the 1870s, Jewish building societies were established, and the Mea She'arim quarter was built to the northwest of the walls. By the 1890s, at the dawn of Zionism, immigration and construction for the burgeoning Jewish population provoked the protests of leading Jerusalem Muslim families.

INTERNATIONAL SUPPORT FOR JOINT SOVEREIGNTY

A new visitor to Jerusalem will be struck by the number of white cars with a large "UN" written in tall black letters along their sides, some occasionally with a light blue flag fluttering on the bonnet. Weaving in and out of the traffic, they move with the same pace and urgency that is allowed all other vehicles, stopping at lights, driving into restaurant car parking bays, dropping children off at school, and collecting groceries from supermarkets. The sheer banality of their activity jars with the portentous nature of the symbol, one you usually associate with environmental emergencies, violence, war, forced migration. The normality and the embeddedness of the UN in the urban rhythms of the city are unexpected. And it is not just one UN agency—there is a megasized bowl of alphabet soup of them: UNRWA, UNOCHA, UNTSO, UNSCOP, UNDP, UNCC, UNICEF, UNESCO, and UNSCMEPP are just the ones that have or have had specific activities in the city. But there are also employees of UNIFIL, UNOGIL, and UNDOF having short breaks from their duties in the northern borders of Israel or UNEF who patrolled the southern borders before the 1967 War. And we should not forget the overarching presence of UNSC and UNGA whose resolutions, as we have seen in previous chapters, sprinkle a kind of international angel dust over the city, backed up by UNCTAD for the economists and the archives of UNISPAL for academics and researchers.[22]

Modern Jerusalem is a city incubated, born, and brought up amidst a welter of UN resolutions and agencies. In a collection of UN documents from between 1947 and 1996, there are no less than sixty-six Security Council, General Assembly Council, and UNESCO resolutions on Jerusalem.[23] The number vastly increased after 1967 when the Israeli occupation received particular attention from the UN. In chapter 1 I described the adoption of the UN Partition Plan by the UN General Assembly in 1947 which proposed a *corpus separatum* for the city and direct UN administration for ten years.[24] This has become a key international legal reference point for policy makers and negotiators. Likewise, the UN Truce Supervisory Organization was responsible in 1949 for the General Armistice Agreements between Israel, Lebanon, Syria, Jordan, and Egypt that led to the de facto partition of the city along the Green Line. And Security Council Resolution 242, adopted in 1967, calling for the Israeli withdrawal from territory occupied is now the key starting point for most of the contemporary negotiations over Jerusalem.[25] In addition to this overarching and formative framework, the operational arm of the UNSC and UNGA, the agencies of the UN have played an important role. There can be no doubt that such a plethora of UN agencies in the city will an impact. The impact is not only in terms of their designated activities but collectively, as they impose a pattern of work practices and norms derived from and framed by a matrix of protocols, conventions, and codes based on international law and good practice.

One of the major UN agencies that has worked in Jerusalem has been UNRWA.[26] Immediately following the Armistice Agreements, UNRWA took over from the International Committee of the Red Cross the responsibility of Palestinian refugees, mostly fleeing from West Jerusalem, who had sought shelter in the abandoned Jewish homes in the Old City in 1948.[27] These homes had been placed under the control of the Jordanian Custodian of Enemy Property who then rented them out to UNRWA.[28] At this early stage it has been estimated that there were approximately 7000 refugees rising to some 12,000 by the early 1960s.[29] After the Israeli occupation in 1967, these and other refugees in the Old City were transferred to Shu'fat refugee camp on the outskirts of Jerusalem but within the new Israeli municipal borders, which became one of the largest camps in the West Bank.[30] Another refugee camp in Qalandia was also included in the new Israeli borders of 1967. Salman Abu Sitta estimated that in 1998 there were approximately 152,000 Jerusalemites registered as refugees with UNRWA, of which 54,000 resided in camps in the West Bank but mostly in and around Jerusalem.[31]

These camps are not merely residential areas. UNRWA provides health and education facilities and social welfare in the form of income for hardship cases and microfinance to encourage small-scale enterprise. This entails the construction of schools, clinics, ration centers, and offices and the employment of staff, teachers, and their training. In addition to these activities, the main field office of the West Bank and many of the major departments of the headquarters are located at a prime site in Jerusalem. What takes you by surprise is the location and size of these central offices. The address is Sheikh Jarrah, a wealthy Palestinian enclave north of the city where many of the consulates to the Palestinian Authority can be found. However, if one takes the main road No. 1 from the Old City north toward Ramallah, instead of turning right to Sheikh Jarrah, you actually have to turn left into an area of Israeli Jewish housing estates. The UNRWA complex, tucked behind high fences, trees, and multi-colored clouds of bougainvillea, is an extensive low-level range of buildings laid out almost like a school with a large open assembly area. You feel you are in a kind of humanitarian "Green Zone," an international enclave inside a foreign country. The grounds are well-maintained, security is quite tight, and you are not allowed to enter until clearance is received by the Palestinian doormen and guards. Once inside the compound, you become aware that this is not just a site for offices and office workers. In one corner there are large warehouses containing supplies for emergency rations and for "hardship" cases. Forklifts buzz around ferrying huge cases onto white UN lettered trucks. In another corner there is what appears to be a car pound or depot with garages carrying out repairs. The offices themselves may be housed in fifties-style minimalist blocks, but inside they have all the equipment and communications of the twenty-first century. All around you can hear Arabic and good English spoken and notices on the corridor boards are in either of these two languages. Occasionally you catch the waft of both Arabic and Italian coffee. A glance through the open window reminds you that while this is legally on the Palestinian side of the Green Line, nevertheless all around it have been built Israeli settlements giving it the feel of being in West Jerusalem, a feeling that is compounded by the construction of Route No. 1 which cuts it off from the rest of Palestinian Sheikh Jarrah. Apart from a few isolated Palestinian houses, the UNRWA complex is a de facto Palestinian outpost in what has become a de facto part of West Jerusalem.

Another UN agency which is less hands-on than UNRWA but nonetheless plays a critical role in curbing the competing assertions of national sovereignties in Jerusalem is UNESCO. The remit of UNESCO is very broad and its global activities encompass scientific development, education, folklore, and wildlife.[32] In Jerusalem the main focus of its work had been on heritage and urban conservation, largely carried out through its World Heritage Center. The significance of this is what the World Heritage Center has constructed over the years, through a series of conventions and protocols and a set of international benchmarks for archaeological excavation and conservation by which it assesses projects and confers recognition.[33] In some cases specific procedures are laid out and manuals devised. Funding for UNESCO-supported projects is contingent upon adherence to these procedures. But their impact goes further: professionals working in these fields are under peer group and moral pressure to follow UNESCO and other respected agency benchmarks.[34] In this way many projects, even if not funded by UNESCO, follow or are framed by UNESCO guidelines, and their work is both subject to international scrutiny. In addition, the states sponsoring or approving archaeological and conservation projects find their activities and approaches subject and constrained by UNESCO-based guidelines.

Unlike other UN agencies, UNESCO has no offices in Jerusalem, and its physical presence is slight, but its reports, resolutions, and recommendations have been controversial and cumulatively compelling, obliging both Israelis and Palestinians to consider the response of UNESCO and other international professional bodies to their work. One way to examine the role of UNESCO in Jerusalem is to disentangle its work into three main strands: the establishment of international benchmarks as a way of addressing conflicting claims over heritage conservation, the range of projects funded by UNESCO and by its in-house or networks of expertise, and, finally, its engagement in dialogue and mediation work over particularly contentious issues.

In Jerusalem, UNESCO walks through a minefield. Treading inevitably on the competing national narratives of Palestinians and Israelis has stymied its work and frequently blown if off course.[35] I observed one very illuminating example of the obstacles facing its work in 2007 at an off-the-record workshop in Istanbul between Israelis and Palestinians. The gathering was convened by a group of former Canadian diplomats to discuss ways in which a peace agreement could encompass the Old City of Jerusalem and comprised approximately twenty people split equally between Israelis,

Palestinians, and internationals drawn from the academic, policy, and advocacy communities. Almost at the start of the very first session of the workshop, an Israeli lawyer, well-known for his sympathy and tireless work for the Palestinian population in Jerusalem, lamented what he perceived to be the denial of Jewish claims to their religious and cultural heritage in the city by the Palestinian interlocutors. In particular, he objected to the characterization by Palestinians of what he termed the First and Second Temple periods as Iron Age and Roman. The use of these terms rather than the Israeli terms highlighted what he thought was a pattern of deliberate and hurtful erasure of the Jewish historical presence in Jerusalem. His main Palestinian respondent was a historian and a colleague of the Israeli lawyer in many Israeli-Palestinian joint activities. He was outraged. The criticism both implied a lack of professionalism on his part and impugned underhand motives to his use of certain terms. He insisted that the Iron Age and Roman periods were the internationally recognized periodization that applied to the whole Mediterranean region under which particular national narratives could be subsumed, but in no way constituted denial of a Jewish presence in the city at that time. Accusations and counteraccusations flew across the table. The heat generated by this discussion nearly caused the collapse of the meeting, and you could see the hackles rise even amongst those participants who were not aware of the subtleties of the debate.

Ultimately the issue was grudgingly resolved and the meeting proceeded to other issues, but what it highlighted was not only the sensitivity around the use of terminology but also how it reflected the more profound and deeper clash between a universal and a national perspective on heritage. There is an inherent tension between the inclusive values represented by the conventions and protocols of UNESCO and the nationalist agendas of the states in which contested sites are located.[36] UNESCO is at the forefront of this clash, and Jerusalem is often where this clash is played out not only most often—due to the close proximity of different sites and the deep layers of history beneath the ground—but also in the full glare of the national and, as we have seen, the international media. For UNESCO, supporting projects in Jerusalem is like placing your head into a lion's mouth. Nevertheless, its work in establishing international benchmarks in the city, while not being able to resolve the fundamental differences between Palestinians and Israelis, has to some extent prevented the situation from being much worse.

In terms of practical projects carried out in the city by UNESCO and its World Heritage Center, it is possible to locate them in three main phases.[37] The first phase, between to 1967 and 1999, is characterized by years of poor cooperation between Israel and UNESCO, if not outright hostility over Israeli policies in Jerusalem and specifically the Old City. It was during this period that numerous resolutions were passed condemning Israeli actions and when the Old City was added to the World Heritage List (1980) and List of World Heritage Sites in Danger (1982). The Israeli government was incensed because UNESCO accepted Jordan as the nominating party when Israel which had de facto control over the city.[38] The second phase, between 2000 and 2011, was when UNESCO and Israel attempted to put aside their differences and work on projects that would preserve the Old City without prejudicing the outcome of negotiations. For Israelis, this was an overdue recognition of Israel's role as the responsible power in the city.[39] For Palestinians it was evidence that UNESCO had been co-opted into the "normalization" of the occupation process and could not be relied upon to defend Palestinian patrimony. The final phase could be said to have started in October 2010 when UNESCO recognized the sites of al-Haram al-Ibrahim/ Tomb of the Patriarchs in Hebron and the Bilal ibn Rabah Mosque/ Rachel's Tomb in Bethlehem as Palestinian. The recognition of Palestinian authority over these sites was less a rebuttal of the Jewish connection to them but more a rejection of Israel's attempt to assert its sovereignty in the occupied West Bank.[40] It led to a renewed deterioration in the relationship between Israel and UNESCO that was given added impetus by the acceptance of the Palestinian Authority as a full voting member of UNESCO, despite a loss of 25 percent of its funding when the United States and Israel withdrew as a result. Nevertheless, despite these fluctuations in UNESCO's relationship with the Palestinians and Israelis, the discussions, negotiations, reports, and resolutions all constituted a kind of surveillance of the activities carried out by Israel and by Palestinians. Israel did unilaterally erase the Magharib quarter in front of the Wailing Wall to create a plaza for Jewish prayer, civic and military ceremonies; it did renovate an extended version of the Jewish Quarter, guided by spurious pseudo historicism; it did excavate the Umayyah palaces south of al-Aqsa without the agreement or consultation of Palestinian or Jordanian specialists; it did create tunnels along the western wall of the Haram al-Sharif and renovate properties in the Muslim quarters irrespective of the needs and concerns of Palestinian residents. Yet, at the same time, it was obliged to constantly justify its work to UNESCO and, in this way, subject its methodologies and principles to scrutiny by an international network of archaeologists, conservation architects, and historians. For their part, Palestinians have been much more cooperative with UNESCO, welcoming its expertise, its funds, and the overt and tacit support. In the face of Israeli encroachments in and around the Old City and the lack of Palestinian leverage to prevent them, the backing of UNESCO has provided important political cover. But, in the same way, soliciting UNESCO support has obliged Palestinians to meet the standards and benchmarks laid down by UNESCO for excavation and conservation.

Funding for projects in the city come from both UNESCO's own regular program and a mix of other sources. The common denominator being UNESCO's involvement in pulling together the project, providing much of the expertise and identifying funders. For example, the establishment of a Center for Restoration of Islamic Manuscripts, located in the Madrasa Al Ashrayfiyyah within the Haram al-Sharif, was followed up in 2010 with $190,000 from UNESCO to provide training to new and existing staff in the fields of paper restoration and electronic inventorying.[41] Another project, the development of an Architectural Heritage Preservation Institute, was funded in 2011 by the European Commission to the tune of €700,000 and implemented in collaboration with the Welfare Association, the leading Palestinian NGO in this field, already mentioned in chapter 3. In 2009 a project to refurbish and revitalize the Islamic Museum of the Haram al-Sharif was funded by Saudi Arabia ($1,130,000).[42] Its most ambitious project began in 2005 with the launching of an "Action Plan" for the Old City. This comprised two phases: First, the compilation of a conservation database and an Old City inventory, which provided an essential baseline reference point for future work in the Old City. The second phase was an ambitious Action Plan that has been more problematic. In addition to the devising of

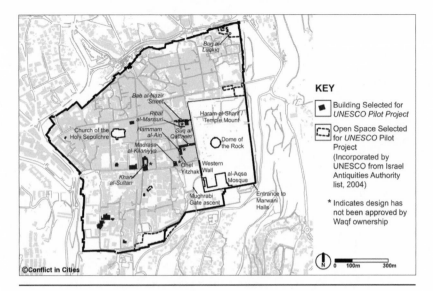

MAP 4.1. Map of UNESCO projects in the Old City (2010).

rehabilitation manuals for residential housing and proposals for the training of local craftspeople, for microfinancing schemes, and for cultural activities, it also included nine conservation projects, involving churches (St. John the Baptist), yeshivas (Etz Hayim), Islamic schools (Madrasa al-Kilaniyya), and souks (Suq al-Qattanin; see map 4.2).[43] As of 2012, two of the proposals have received funding, one from the Italian government and the other from the Greek Leventis Foundation.[44]

The Action Plan eloquently displays the strength and weaknesses of UNESCOs role in the city. On one hand, it is able to summon the international expertise required and collate the data to provide an overarching plan for safeguarding the city's cultural heritage. On the other hand, the plan exists almost in a bubble as it sidesteps the critical existential, political, and administrative issues of who has the authority to implement such plans. For example, the Manual for Housing Maintenance and Rehabilitation has 153 pages, entering into precise details of the "pathologies of structures, roofing, facades, joinery, ironworks, installations," but makes no reference to the political context of the Israeli occupation which has resulted in disputed legal ownerships and the denial of building permits that is rife in the Old City.[45] Another example is the plan for the rehabilitation of the Suq al-Qattanin, a famous Mamluk market in the heart of the Old City. The Action Plan has impressive designs and a program of works, but, at the same time, it completely ignores the reality of Israeli security checkpoints at its entrance, the closure of the Haram al-Sharif entrance by Israeli security which provides the passing pedestrian traffic to make the market viable, and the restrictive laws governing commercial licenses.[46]

The final area in which UNESCO exerts some influence in the city and constrains the actions of both Israeli and Palestinians is its attempts to mediate over contentious disputes. To a large extent, given the disputed nature of the Israeli occupation of East Jerusalem, this is a never-ending task and covers virtually every aspect of heritage preservation, and it is also one where UNESCO has had little direct effect. At the same time, there are a number of flashpoints over which UNESCO has played an important role in bringing together the Jordanians, the Israelis, and the Palestinians, the Waqf Administration and the Israel Antiquities Authority. Notable failures in these attempts to mediate include the Israeli excavations of Umayyad palaces to the southeast of al-Aqsa Mosque and the long tunnel running beside the western wall of the Haram al-Sharif and the Palestinian excavations under the Haram enclosure to construct the subterranean al-Marwani prayer rooms and, finally, the clearing of the Mamilla Muslim cemetery and its replacement by an Israeli-sponsored Museum of Tolerance.[47]

It has had, however, more success in some recent disputes such as the possible collapse of a portion of the southern wall of the Haram al-Sharif where it was able to facilitate repair work by the Jordanian government without provoking an Israeli intervention.[48] But it is its engagement with the dispute over the Mughrabi Gate Ascent where the complexity, effectiveness, and future potential of the role played by UNESCO in Jerusalem can be seen. Following the collapse in 2007 of the pathway (technically referred to as an "ascent") to the Mughrabi Gate, one of the main entrances to the Haram al-Sharif, Israel presented plans to build a larger ramplike structure.[49] The proposals were rejected by Palestinians, Jordanians, and also some Israeli experts and became a cause celebre of the Islamic Movement inside Israel, which denounced them as a preparatory step for an Israeli bridgehead in the Haram al-Sharif.[50] UNESCO also objected to the proposals, but took active steps to find a consensual solution. In February 2007 it commissioned a technical team to assess and report on the work carried out by the Israelis and suggested a more modest plan for the restoration of the ascent after consultation with the Waqf Administration and the Jordanian government.[51] More significantly, it also recommended that excavations should only resume under the supervision of international experts coordinated by UNESCO. In addition, UNESCO initiated a two-track approach to manage the controversy. First, it instituted a new procedure known as the Reinforced Monitoring Mechanism. This introduced a system of reports being compiled on a bimonthly basis and sent directly to the director of the World Heritage Center and was designed to ensure that international scrutiny of developments regarding the ascent remained prominent.[52] As intended, this resulted in Israel proceeding with great caution over the implementation of its proposals. Second, it facilitated a number of professional encounters "at the technical level between Israeli, Jordanian, and Waqf experts to discuss the detailed proposals for the proposed final design of the Mughrabi ascent, prior to any final decision."[53] Several of these have taken place, and, notwithstanding the lack of results, a degree of transparency and consultation has been injected into the renovation and redevelopment process.

The dispute over the Mughrabi Gate ascent has not been resolved and is ongoing, but it conveys both the opportunities and limitations of UNESCO's presence in Jerusalem. Palestinian frustration at the lack of leverage being exerted over Israel by UNESCO is palpable and demonstrates the fact that, despite UNESCO's attempts to cooperate closely with Israel, UNESCO has limited powers of enforcement. The World Heritage List may provide an international platform for "naming and shaming" states who fail to fulfill their responsibilities, but it cannot compel compliance or prevent the deliberate destruction of cultural heritage.[54] At the same time, the Mughrabi Gate ascent dispute and other disputes also highlight UNESCO's potential role as an international and independent mediator in issues of heritage preservation. Given the polarisation of views between the two parties over the future of the city and how they have enlisted conservation and heritage issues as vehicles to promote their respective claims, the need is ever greater. Indeed the very fact that both parties resort to UNESCO's mediating offices and refer to its conventions and protocols in evaluating the projects of the other side reveals the extent to which their freedom of maneuver is constrained and their ability to act unilaterally diminished. By its continuous presence in the city and the international reputation of its experts and advisers, UNESCO has been able to instill a culture of restraint. The accession of Palestine as a member state of UNESCO and the lack of U.S. leverage over the organization may result in UNESCO taking a stronger line over Israeli encroachments on international law.[55] A recent indication is a public statement reiterating UNESCO's position that East Jerusalem is an inseparable part of occupied Palestinian territory.[56]

OTHER EXTERNAL ACTORS: THE EUROPEAN UNION AND THE UNITED STATES

THE EUROPEAN UNION

The involvement of the European Union in the Jerusalem issue is based upon its long-standing and extensive links with the Middle East and North Africa (MENA) region.[57] From the classical period of ancient Greece and Rome to the Crusades, the Renaissance, the Ottoman Empire, and the colonial period of British and French League of Nation Mandates, a history of exchange and fusion has been in existence. Earlier on in this chapter we saw how the European Great Powers took under their protection Christian and Jewish communities as vehicles for furthering their strategic interests in Jerusalem and the Eastern Mediterranean region known as the Mashriq. In the post-1945 period, economic interdependence between the two regions has increased with, on the one hand, European dependency on the region's hydrocarbons (80 percent of its energy supplies come from the Middle East) and, on the other, the EU being the main trading partner of virtually every state in the region, including Israel. Yet for many years the EU and its predecessor, the European Community (EC), was excluded from the political negotiations between Israel, the Palestinians, and the Arab states for two main reasons. First, the cold war dynamics in the region, particularly since the Suez crisis of 1956, meant that the U.S.-USSR rivalry over influence in the region during the fifties and sixties left little space for a collective "European" policy.[58] But, second and perhaps more important, was the absence of EU institutions that could express a European foreign policy. As a result, there was little EU policy in the region as such, but instead there an aggregate of separate bilateral relations carried out by individual states. In this way, initiatives such as the EC Venice Declaration of 1980, which controversially called for the inclusion of the PLO in peace negotiations, were often successfully opposed by the United States. Similarly, it was not without significance that the cosponsors of the Madrid conference that launched the Arab-Israeli peace process in 1991 were the U.S. and the Soviet Union/Russia, with the EU sidelined along with the United Nations. It was given no role in any of the bilateral negotiating tracks between Israel and its neighbors and was relegated to chairing the Regional Economic Development Working Group.[59] This can be contrasted with its current inclusion as a member of the Quartet (U.S., Russia, the UN, and the EU), which has been delegated by the international community as overseers of the peace negotiations.

This change was brought about by two developments which occurred in the 1990s and transformed the pattern of European involvement in the region. First, the collapse of the Soviet Union led initially to the emergence of a unipolar international system characterized by a hegemonic U.S. control over the Middle East region. This was gradually replaced by a more multipolar international system where other key actors such as Russia and China and of course the EU vied for influence. Second, in 1994 members of the EC signed the Maastricht Treaty, which established institutions for a collective EU foreign policy and provided it with an opportunity to intervene more forcefully in the region.[60] From the perspective of the Europeans, the impetus toward a negotiated solution between Palestinians and Israelis following the Gulf War in 1990 was being squandered by the United States. Although the Oslo Accords between the PLO and the Israeli government in 1993 was brokered in 1993 by a non-EU state, Norway, it was nevertheless seen as a European initiative and a European attempt to inject life into the peace negotiations that had become moribund under U.S. direction of the Madrid conference framework.

Thus, during the 1990s, EU pressure to be more closely involved appeared to be bearing fruit. Europe's expertise in economic development issues in the region came to the fore in the other multilateral fora and put the EU in a strong position to have a significant input into the outcome of the future negotiations. Also a little earlier, in 1991, the creation of the post of European Union Special Envoy to the Middle East Peace Process gave the EU a greater ability to respond to events and a greater visibility in the peace process.[61]

Part of the impetus in the EU's efforts to strengthen movement toward the establishment of the Palestinian state was derived from a multilateral forum initiated by the EU. This was the Euro-Mediterranean Partnership (EMP), launched at the Barcelona conference in November 1995 and since 2008 renamed the Union for the Mediterranean (UfM).[62] The process launched a series of Mediterranean regional conferences and meetings at the foreign minister level, with the EU providing the secretariat. Despite being seen as a separate from the Madrid and Oslo frameworks, the EMP/UfM process nevertheless required progress on the Arab-Israeli conflict and on the Jerusalem issue in order to attain its objectives. In this way, the EU became structurally involved in the progress of the peace negotiations in the region.[63] The significant element in the EMP was that, being a regional organization, it was a framework which did not include the U.S., the UN or Russia or any other emerging actors. Thus we can see how over the past three decades the EU position on the peace process and consequently its approach to the Jerusalem issue was built on three pillars: first, the body of UN Security Council Resolutions (particularly 242 and 338) and UN General Assembly resolution and also other articles of international law regarding military occupation (namely, the Geneva Conventions) second, the political frameworks established by the Madrid conference and the Oslo Accords, and, finally, on its own institutional approaches: the European Security and Defence Policy and EMP process.[64]

In the early 1990s the EC/EU established an office in East Jerusalem to coordinate its funding policies in the Palestinian territories. Together with the appointment of a special envoy to the Middle East Peace process these actions have ensured that the EU can play an active role in discussions concerning the city's future. Despite making inroads into what had previously been U.S. and USSR/Russia diplomatic preserve, it was and is still the case that EC and EU policy toward the Jerusalem issue has been marked by a lack of coordination between the member states and a failure to follow up the various positions the EC and EU have articulated. In part, this is caused by the traditional deference to the U.S. sensitivities over putting pressure on Israel, but there has also been a discrepancy between the policies of the EC/EU and those of its member states. Domestic considerations often oblige EU member states to pursue narrower more opportunistic policies in their bilateral relations while simultaneously espousing more principled and universalistic policies at the EU level without fear of domestic political reactions. This inconsistency, however, does not obscure the fact that most EC/EU policies have been broadly sympathetic to Palestinian and Arab perspectives on Jerusalem while avoiding an open confrontation with the United States or Israel.

Despite its subservience to U.S. policies, and despite its failure to coordinate the policies of its own members states consistently and despite the criticism of its funding policies as being a form of financing the Israeli occupation and buying-off of Palestinian militancy, there is an important element in EU praxis which is often overlooked but which is, nonetheless, crucial in the unfolding politics of Jerusalem: the EU is inherently and structurally constrained by the rule of law. Indeed, I would argue that for all the failings of the EU, the most important and overarching factor in the relationship between the European Union and the Palestinian-Israel conflict is the grounding of its foreign policy in the rule of law and its adherence to international legal principles. The European Union is a voluntary union, not a coercive one in which one dominant state has absorbed subordinate neighbours. It is based upon a complex network of treaties, negotiated over decades and comprising a comprehensive range of issues. All these are firmly based on agreed legal principles and frameworks. Despite many examples of political expediency over-riding certain agreements, particularly over setting the EU budget, the main result is that the European Union is nothing if it is not based on the rule of law.

This has several important effects on the conduct of foreign policy. The coordination of 27 member states can only work if it is based on legal agreements and procedures and on international law. While this creates a slow, ponderous and reactive foreign policy, it is nevertheless, a powerful force which provides strong backing for the international community's legal position on Jerusalem. Thus, because European Union's policy on Jerusalem is based both on UN Security Council Resolution 242 and UN General Assembly Resolution 181, it has never accepted the Israeli annexation of East Jerusalem or the validity of the 1980 Israeli Basic Law on Jerusalem.[65] Moreover, all European Union member states have all located their embassies to Israeli in Tel Aviv, rather than in Jerusalem, indicating that the status of Jerusalem as a whole is yet to be resolved.[66] In addition, the EU has accepted the advisory opinion of the International Court of Justice regarding the Barrier as being illegal and made representations to Israel to that effect. Both these actions provide powerful support for the Palestinian argument that East Jerusalem is occupied and should be returned to the Palestinians and that the question of sovereignty over West Jerusalem is still subject to negotiation.

A useful way of understanding the position of the European Union on Jerusalem is to examine the reports of the European Union Heads of Mission in East Jerusalem. Ostensibly secret, but usually leaked to the media, the reports do not have the status of a declaration or any prescriptive force. They are merely noted in European Commission meetings in Brussels. Nevertheless, they are very revealing on the thinking in the European policy community and have a significant impact beyond their lowly status as an internal document. In fact, in contrast to many other diplomatic documents on the Middle East which are either completely anodyne or have been fudged into vacuity, the notoriety of the reports as documents punching above their weight can be inferred from the number of people who wish to be associated with them! I have often been struck over conversations in the Ambassador Hotel or the American Colony Hotel, where much of the diplomatic community, international advocacy groups and the media gather to gossip and plot, how many diplomatic missions claim authorship or some sort of contribution to the reports, how many people claim to have supplied the information and how many believe they are responsible for the leaks to the press.

The reports are compiled annually by European Union diplomatic staff in Jerusalem and comprise two main parts. The first describes the situation on the ground and assesses the prospects of a possible resolution. What is quite remarkable about this part of the report is not only the depth and quality of research but the unsparing and flinty depiction of Israeli policies in East Jerusalem, covering the whole litany of discrimination from the unequal provision of services, application of law, of house demolitions, ID confiscations and the like. Couched in measured tones, the impact is more powerful than a dozen reports from the very competent and professional advocacy NGOs operating in the city. In addition to the reliability of the data presented, however, the reports have another important impact. Like the use of Webster's or the Oxford Dictionaries in a contentious game of Scrabble, they have become the baseline reference point on the situation in East Jerusalem. Constituting a kind of "annual report" they determine the terminology used in the discourse and the measurements by which Israeli and Palestinian actions are judged. Set at the same time in the context of a clear and detailed re-iteration of the European Union's ongoing support for UN resolutions on Jerusalem, unlike in other policy declarations of the European Union on the Middle East, there is little hint of backsliding or obfuscation.

The second part of the reports is no less significant. This part, or Annex 2, comprises recommendations of actions that can be taken by member states in the conduct of their diplomacy in and around Jerusalem. The specificity and far-reaching nature of some of these recommendations is quite jaw-dropping. For example, one section on "East Jerusalem as the future Palestinian capital" recommends amongst other things that member states should "Promote the establishment of a PLO focal point/representative in East Jerusalem" and that EU missions with offices or residences in East Jerusalem should regularly host Palestinian officials when visited by senior

EU officials. Furthermore, EU diplomats should "avoid having Israeli security and/or protocol accompanying high ranking officials from Member States when visiting the Old City/East Jerusalem."[67] The European Union has been particularly concerned that given its opposition to Israeli settlements in the occupied Palestinian territories that products from these settlements should not benefit from the trade agreements it has established with Israel. The Heads of Mission reports pay specific attention to the possibility of this occurring with the settlements in and around Jerusalem. The 2012 report states that member states should "prevent/discourage financial transactions from EU MS [member states] actors supporting settlement activity in East Jerusalem, by adopting appropriate EU legislation." They should also "compile non-binding guidelines for EU tour operators to prevent support for settlement business in East Jerusalem (e.g., hotels, bus operators, archaeological sites controlled by pro-settler organizations, etc.) and "ensure that the EU-Israel Association Agreement is not used to allow the export to the EU of products manufactured in settlements in East Jerusalem."[68] As Israel's largest trading partner, with approximately 30 percent of Israeli exports directed to the European Union, these guidelines have a significant impact on the market available to settlement products and are designed to disincentivize international investment in the settlements in and around Jerusalem and the OPts. Indeed, there is evidence to suggest that the European Union position exacerbated the legal, financial, and technical problems encountered by the Jerusalem Light Rail Train project—a multimillion dollar project to construct a light railway to connect Israeli settlements in the north of the city to the center of West Jerusalem. Not only was the railway the focus of an international divestment campaign, but it was also condemned in the UN Human Rights Council.[69] As a result, the two main international contractors for the project, Alstrom and Veolia, are reported to have lost more than ten billion dollars worth of contracts elsewhere.[70]

THE UNITED STATES

The other main actor whose position on Jerusalem has an important impact on Israeli and Palestinian policies in the city is the United States. I have written in some depth on this topic in my previous book, *The Politics of Jerusalem Since 1967*, and do not wish to recycle the same material here.[71] However, the main point to grasp is that despite U.S. passivity and to some extent complicity in the face of Israeli attempts to consolidate its position in East Jerusalem, its formal position remains that East Jerusalem is occupied territory and that the status of the whole of Jerusalem is undetermined and subject to the outcome of negotiations between Israelis and Palestinians. The fact that over the past three or four decades it has been reluctant to exert any meaningful pressure on Israel to conform to UN resolutions demanding the cessation of Israeli policies in the city does not diminish the impact of the U.S.'s refusal to recognize Jerusalem as the capital of Israel or the annexation of territories after 1967.

One of the major indications of U.S. consistency that subverts the Israeli claim to the city is the refusal to move the U.S. embassy from Tel Aviv to Jerusalem. In concert with every other nation on the planet, all embassies are located in Tel Aviv as a sign of the international community's refusal to accept the Israeli incorporation of East Jerusalem into Israel. This is quite a remarkable fact, and I am not aware of any other total and comprehensive diplomatic boycott of a fellow member state in the UN in this way. And it is a boycott which is largely overlooked in popular and media representations of the symbiotic relationship between the U.S. and Israel.[72] Despite huge pressures from different political constituencies in the U.S., and despite Congress legislating to enforce relocation of the U.S. embassy to Jerusalem, and despite successive presidential candidates and elected presidents professing an intention to implement this law, the embassy still remains in Tel Aviv. The relocation of U.S. embassy to Jerusalem would be hugely symbolic both to Israel and to U.S. allies and foes in the region, and the ongoing resistance to do so clearly needs further examination.

Initially, in 1948, the location of the embassy was not a problem. Immediately after the Declaration of Israeli Independence, all Israeli government offices were located in Tel Aviv, even though the declaration included the announcement that Jerusalem was the capital of the new state, It was only when the Israeli leadership decided the international zone for Jerusalem—the *corpus separatum*—was no longer feasible and that the UN was not going to enforce its implementation that the president of Israel's official residence and the Ministry of Foreign Affairs moved to Jerusalem in 1952, and the issue of the location of diplomatic missions surfaced. In the context of ongoing stalemate between Israel and the Arab states, and in the context of support for the UN *corpus separatum* still being the official positions of many of the key players in the international community, the U.S. was reluctant to jeopardize the possibility of a negotiated settlement between Israel and the Arab states by recognizing Jerusalem as the capital of Israel. As a result, embassy engagements in Jerusalem were severely restricted, and the U.S. Consulate in Jerusalem was not permitted to deal with Israeli officials on any issue at the national level but confined to representing U.S. interests in the designated international zone.[73] In 1967, when Israel occupied and expanded the city to the east, this position by the U.S. was maintained, if not strengthened and reiterated. Again, in 1980, after the Israeli Knesset passed the Basic Law: Jerusalem, which claimed that both sides of Jerusalem were the "eternal" capital of Israel, the U.S. position remained the same and, indeed, joined in the international pressure on states who had over the previous years moved their embassies to Jerusalem to remove them, which they did.[74]

Nevertheless, the goal of relocating the U.S. embassy to Jerusalem became a focal point for pro-Israel groups across the political spectrum in the U.S.. Their efforts culminated in a series of Congressional measures that sought to tie the hands of any U.S. administration and force it to relocate the embassy. In 1988, the so-called Helms Amendment provided for the simultaneous establishment of two "diplomatic facilities" in Tel Aviv and Jerusalem. This was followed, on the last day of the Reagan presidency, by the 1989 Lease Agreement, signed between Israel and the U.S., which provided for a plot of land for the building of a "diplomatic facility."[75] The next step that upped the ante for the U.S. administration was in 1995 when both the Senate and the House of Representatives passed, by huge margins, U.S. Public Law 104–105, otherwise known as the Jerusalem Embassy Act.[76] This act allocated $100 million for construction of an embassy in Jerusalem and, unbelievably, included a punitive clause that reduced the State Department's housing and maintenance budget by half until the embassy was opened! To avoid a presidential veto yet, at the same time, make sure it was clear to the various political groups lobbying for embassy relocation that the failure to open an embassy in Jerusalem was entirely the fault of the president, the act also included a clause that gave the president a waiver over this clause if he found it in the security interests of the United States to do so.[77] Since the passage of the act, the presidential waiver has been exercised over twenty-two times, and while the waiver has often been accompanied by sweet words assuring the act's proponents that the intention to relocate the embassy is still active pending an opportune moment, the fact remains that the U.S. State Department still is of the view that such a move would be both inflammatory in the region and extinguish the last flickering embers of the moribund peace process.[78] To compound the complexity of the issue, Palestinian owners of the land allocated for the embassy have marshalled legal arguments based upon the confiscation of their land by Israel.[79] This will put the U.S. in a very difficult legal bind, for to recognize the validity of these arguments will open up a Pandora's box of other claims to Palestinian property both in Jerusalem and in other parts of Israel and former Palestine. To ignore them will only exacerbate the controversy around the relocation of the embassy. Further attempts are currently being made to remove the presidential waiver, but it is unlikely that the administration will allow its hand to be forced in this way.[80]

We can see how the refusal of Israel's closest ally to recognize both its declared capital and its acquisition of East Jerusalem is a serious blow to Israeli attempts to obtain recognition and legitimacy internationally for its claim that Jerusalem is the capital of the Israeli state. Without the U.S. leading the way on this issue, few other states will take the initiative, as the political costs in terms of a concerted international reaction, and not just from the Arab and Islamic worlds, would outweigh any marginal benefits accruing to them. And it is here that the overall context in which the European Union plays a very important part is highly significant: By putting the full force of twenty-seven member states behind UN resolutions, many of whom are key actors in world politics and who as a collective are the largest economic bloc in the world, it is the position of the European Union, for all its faults and dysfunctional decision-making processes, that is to a large extent holding the line on Jerusalem. The fact that East Jerusalem has not been absorbed into West Jerusalem like Jaffa has been into Tel Aviv, and the fact that Jerusalem as a whole is not as Israeli as Tel Aviv is Israeli, can be partially attributed to the EU's adherence to the corpus of international law on Jerusalem. In addition, by providing the ballast or the backbone for the support of international law, it makes it politically more costly for states like the U.S. to succumb to pressures to support Israel over Jerusalem. In light of this overarching position in the international community, exemplified by the policies of the European Union and the United States, the role of international civil society is illuminating. The last section of this chapter will examine, albeit briefly, the various interventions of international nongovernmental actors.

OTHER ACTORS

In previous chapters I drew attention to a paradox in the implementation of the militant form of Zionism that has dominated the Israeli political scene as a policy of state building.[81] By privileging Jewish citizens of the Israeli state, militant Zionism pushes non-Jews to the margins of the state and encourages them to look toward other states and movements for sources of funding and support. The focus on Jewish development and aspirations thus creates a representational and funding vacuum in state support for its minorities that is filled by others. The main result of this is to reinforce opposition and resistance to the imposition of Zionist state-building policies. With regard to Jerusalem, this ideological intervention cannot be exactly characterized as an impediment or constraint on the exercise of Israeli sovereignty in Jerusalem in the fashion of the interventions of the other international actors we have just looked at. Yet, it does encourage an external engagement by non-Zionist elements that both step into the vacuum and subvert Israeli attempts to consolidate its hegemonic presence throughout the city. As such, this is a lesser intervention, but it still acts as a kind of brake on the exercise of sovereignty. In the first section of this chapter I described the ways in which this kind of intervention is long-standing, usually taking the form of donations, endowments, and pilgrimages that supported the livelihoods of different religious and ethnic communities in Jerusalem. In this last section I will examine some of the interventions by the Arab and Islamic world in the city, focusing particularly on the financing of projects in East Jerusalem. My argument is that cumulatively they provide a significant source of alternative financial, legal, political, and moral support that undermines Israeli attempts to consolidate its position in Jerusalem. There are also other interventions of this nature, particularly the role of U.S. Christian fundamentalist churches and U.S. Jewish citizens and sympathetic corporations who contribute significant amounts of money to enhance the Israeli and Jewish presence in the city.[82] This chapter will not analyze these contributions as they not part of my argument that the exclusivity of Zionism has unintended consequences in an ethnically mixed city such as Jerusalem and contributes to the erosion of Israeli hegemony there. They are part of another dynamic underlying the importance of Israeli-Jewish diaspora links in maintaining the prosperity and vibrancy of the city.

Clearly the most important source of external funding is from the Palestinian National Authority. Its establishment on the very borders of East Jerusalem as defined by Israel and its refusal to either accept those borders politically or permit them to interrupt its engagement in the development of Palestinian communities in East Jerusalem has resulted in a porosity between PNA-controlled areas and East Jerusalem that Israel has only partially attempted to control. There are many examples in the field of security and the provision of some infrastructure where cooperation, both covert and tacit, between Israel and the PNA has taken place.[83] At the same time, a consistent and credible Palestinian national strategy on how to consolidate its position in Jerusalem is manifestly lacking. Indeed, the PNA's efforts can be characterized by poor coordination, overlapping and duplication, an inconsistent stop-start implementation of programs, all dressed up with empty rhetoric full of sound and fury. The death in 2001 of the leading Jerusalemite, Faisal Husseini, who was both the scion of an ancient aristocratic family of the city, the son of a Palestinian commander and war hero in the 1948 War, and a prominent Fatah figure in the city dealt a severe blow to Palestinian efforts in East Jerusalem. A fluent speaker of Hebrew from spells in

Israeli jails, he was committed both to dialogue with Israelis and to a vision of Jerusalem as capital for the states of Palestine and Israel.[84] His strategy was to build up a network of Palestinian institutions in East Jerusalem, with a view that their coordination would ultimately provide a shadow municipal structure running parallel to the formal Israeli municipality and eventually make it redundant.[85] Following his early demise, the strategy of the PNA has shifted. Since a similarly charismatic and organizationally competent leader has not emerged in East Jerusalem, the main result has been that more and more direction and control has been provided, or usurped, depending upon one's perspective, by the PNA, particularly the Office of the Presidency, based in Ramallah.

The PNA established a cabinet-level ministry for Jerusalem to coordinate and provide strategic direction to the PNA activities in the field of health, education, social welfare, planning, and security that could also apply also to East Jerusalem. But without a budget beyond its own running costs, and without a strong commanding figure to override the bureaucratic turf wars, the ministry is often sidelined and the minister's position regarded somewhat as a sinecure.[86] Nevertheless, the PNA is active in East Jerusalem, and there is a modicum of coordination derived from two key documents: the Palestinian Strategic Multi-Sector Development Plan for East Jerusalem and the Palestinian National Development Plan for 2011–2013.[87] The funds directed into East Jerusalem are quite substantial. I have not been able to complete a comprehensive survey of all subventions from the PNA to Palestinian projects and institutions in East Jerusalem, and we should recall that some figures on expenditure also include the Palestinian administrative district of the Jerusalem governorate, known as J2, and lies outside the Israeli Jerusalem municipality and stretches down to include Jericho. However, a relatively superficial Web survey in 2012 suggested that at least $25 million was allocated between 2010 and 2011 directly from the PNA to East Jerusalem. The greater proportion of this has been in three areas: health, education, and housing. For example, al Makassed Hospital, one of the largest Palestinian hospitals in East Jerusalem, received between $2 and £3 million per year.[88] In the field of education, the Palestinian Ministry of Education and Higher Education supplements the low wages of Palestinian teachers working in non-Israeli Jerusalem municipality schools to the tune of 1,500 new Israeli shekels a month per teacher (approximately $30).[89]

While the PNA is unable to directly intervene in terms of housing provision in East Jerusalem, which, as we saw in chapter 2, is a critical issue for Palestinian residents, it supports a number of other institutions in the housing and infrastructure field. For example, the Municipal Development and Lending Fund, set up by the PNA, disbursed approximately $1.5 million in 2010–2011 on housing, road, and sanitation projects in the Palestinian Jerusalem governorate.[90] While these projects may not be directly inside the Jerusalem municipality, their impact is still felt in the municipal area as they help to relieve considerable pressures in these fields. Similarly, while the Palestine Housing Council is a nonprofit organization that operates at an arm's length from the PNA, it nevertheless informally coordinates its programs with the Palestinian ministries of housing and planning. Funded by the European Union, the Islamic Bank, Welfare Association, World Bank, USAID, and others, it has recently disbursed approximately $30 million on projects renovating historic residential properties in the Old City, constructed over thirty new apartments in the suburbs, and provided loans to over sixteen hundred individuals to construct houses.[91]

Despite the general oversight that the PNA may provide for these projects, most of the funds for them come from external sources. The revenue-raising capacity of the PNA may be improving, but it is still much too low for the kind of input required to either compete with Israeli investment or to meet the needs of the Palestinian residents in the city. At the same time, significant amounts of funds are channeled directly from these external sources into East Jerusalem in the form of various project grants. For example, one of the largest donors among Arab and Islamic bodies is the Al Quds Committee of the Organization of the Islamic Conferences. Between 2000 and 2010, it disbursed approximately $25 million on housing and renovation projects ($9.5 million), on education ($9.5 million), on health ($4 million), sport, and culture including Muslim-Christian associations ($600,000), and on general social welfare ($3 million).[92] As previously discussed, approximately another $25 million has been spent by the Welfare Association, the largest Palestinian NGO in the Middle East. The bulk of this has been invested in its Old City of Jerusalem Revitalisation Programme, which acts as a low-key but quasi-municipal body in the Palestinian areas of the Old City.[93] Approximately $12 million has been spent on renovation and cultural projects in the Old City, but other funds are spent on supporting civil society organizations, health and educational services, and youth employment projects.[94] Another large donor is the Islamic Development Bank, which has contributed in the past 5 years over $5 million toward health (Augusta Victoria Hospital) and educational facilities, including $3.1 million toward a new UNRWA school in Shu'afat refugee camp and $1.7 million for a vocational training center in Qalandia refugee camp.[95] Smaller donations and grants are channeled through philanthropic organizations such as the Faisal Husseini Foundation, which supports medical care in a range of Palestinian East Jerusalem hospitals including the Makassed Islamic Charitable Hospital (220 beds), the Augusta Victoria Hospital (100 beds), St. John's Ophthalmic Hospital (70 beds), St. Joseph Hospital (70 beds), the Palestine Red Cresent Maternity Hospital (30 beds), and the Princess Basma Center for Disabled Children (20 rehabilitation beds).[96] The foundation is also funding, to the tune of $70,000 to $80,000 a year, an ongoing program supporting libraries in East Jerusalem through a reading campaign called Let's Read.[97] Other organizations such as the Al-Quds Foundation for Medical Schools in Palestine and the Palestine Red Crescent Society have also channeled over $7 million into training, patient care, and hospital expansion since 2005.[98]

In addition to these forms of external support, we should not overlook the role of the Waqf Administration in this context. As we saw in chapter 3, the Waqf Administration in East Jerusalem is primarily a branch of the Jordanian Ministry of Waqfs and Religious Affairs. The details of the ebb and flow of pro-Jordanian and pro-Palestinian influences in the Waqf Administration need not concern us here, as the main point I wish to draw out is that in the heart of the city claimed by Israel as its capital we find a fully functioning Jordanian ministry funded by Jordanian and other Arab and Islamic sources, employing several hundred clerics, teachers, administrators, architects, archaeologists, builders, maintenance workers, guards and cleaners maintaining religious, historic, commercial, and residential properties in

East Jerusalem. We also saw in chapter 2 that the Waqf Administration was responsible for 38 schools employing approximately 850 staff and providing education to over 12,000 pupils.[99] At the same time, huge sums of money have been channeled into the restoration of the major monuments on the Haram al-Sharif, such as al-Aqsa Mosque and the Dome of the Rock.[100] The total sums of money covering all these activities by the Waqf Administration are difficult to compute, but it should be clear that its intervention as an externally funded body is significant.

From the evidence presented in this chapter, it seems clear that Jerusalem continues to hold an important position in the international relations of the world. Despite our Web site and Facebook survey revealing that it is no longer the center of the world, à la Mappae Mundi, there is no doubt it is still of prime concern to policy makers, activists, and worshippers across the globe. Through the involvement of the EU and the U.S. to the range of many other international actors, we see how the role of the Israeli state is affected and somewhat diminished and how the role of the Palestinians in East Jerusalem is, at the same time, buttressed. This external intervention provides Palestinians in East Jerusalem not only alternative sources of funding to the Israeli state but also competing if not parallel structures of organization to Israeli state agencies, which constrain the exercise of Israeli authority and jurisdiction over East Jerusalem. In this sense, the Israeli presence in Jerusalem is weakened and its power diluted. I should not overstate this phenomenon. The tentative and often erratic nature of external intervention is not sufficient to prise open the grip of the Israeli state over East Jerusalem. Nevertheless, it is sustained and pervasive enough to leave the question open of who does East Jerusalem belong to and thus open to negotiation. It is to this area that we turn in the following and last chapter.

5

JERUSALEM IN THE TWENTY-FIRST CENTURY

WHAT PROSPECT OF PEACE?

R UNNING AND DIVIDED cities are not an obvious mix. However, during the course of my research for the Conflict in Cities project, I have had the chance to run round and through the cities of Belfast, Brussels, Mostar, Nicosia, Beirut, and Jerusalem. I tend to run early in the morning, and it is remarkable what a different kind of city you see at that time from the one you encounter later in the day. In the first place, at that time of the day the city is a city of cleaners and garbage collectors, noisily loading trucks and dustbins sweeping piles of litter into even bigger mounds, focused on the job, and indifferent to a runner in shorts dodging between them. It is also a city of laborers and the working class. Professionals and schoolchildren both seem to rise later, and during that period just after dawn, but before the shops, offices, and schools open, you see the raw face of the city, the city of the informal economy. This is a side of the city that fades into the background later in the day amidst the hubbub of the city at full throttle with its busy private cars and taxis shooting past, stirring up dust, and confining pedestrians to the pavements. Before this, roughly clad men (it is mostly men) spill out of dirty battered buses; they move quietly across empty streets clutching their lunch in plastic bags; some group together in small clusters at street corners waiting for small vans and pickup trucks to come by, and tense negotiations over a day rate are conducted with the driver. Street vendors appear laden with small farm produce or secondhand clothing and goods and discretely pick a key spot beside a shady shop or road junction. You can often tell who is "up" and who is "down" in the city by the sellers of secondhand shoes. It is usually the new immigrants who are still struggling to get onto the first rung of regular employment and who have resorted to scavenging garbage cans ditto and rubbish tips to resell worn and discarded footwear—poor Russians in Jerusalem, North Africans in Greek Cypriot Nicosia, and Egyptians or Yemenis in Beirut.

So far these scenarios play out in most cities. What of occupied or divided cities? What similarities or differences have I noted on my early morning runs between occupied or divided cities and other cities? In the first place, while occupied or divided cities are generally much tenser, in the early morning, this is not always the case. In fact, like other cities, occupied or divided cities also have a different feel to them at that time than later; differences seem to emerge more later in the day. This is simply by virtue of the fact that in the early morning there are often fewer soldiers and border police in evidence or the ones who are in view are more relaxed and calmer. The reasons for this is partly something about the fact that fewer people and vehicles on the streets pose less of a security threat—there are so many less variables to deal with, so that the soldiers at checkpoints or in their stationary APCs can drink their coffee or smoke a cigarette contemplating the scene before them in a relaxed fashion, the safety catches on their weapons in the On position. It is also partly a tacit understanding between them and the laborers that, for all the political eruptions that take place for the rest of the day, for this initial period of the day and for this particular demographic the important business of getting to work or even getting work is paramount. Later on, with students, schoolchildren, white-collar workers and activists, and the unemployed all awake, the rules of the game change, the threat threshold is much lower. But, for the early-morning laborers and the early-morning checkpoint shift, both sides know that survival for them is too fragile for any other consideration apart from getting to work to be given much credence. The risk of a confrontation is, therefore, fairly remote. Later in the day, when the number of people on the streets increases and the number of the military and police also increases, the potential for confrontation and violence is heightened and the city get much more fraught.

Running in divided cities also presents you with other perspectives. Running one morning in Mostar, I found myself gravitating, surprisingly, upward, along roads that wound gradually round the back of the Croatian half of the city until I realized I was so high up I might as well continue up to a vantage point overlooking the city. There I found the huge thirty-to-forty-meter crucifix, painted white, that is visible from all parts of the city below. It declaims both a religious and political message to the non-Christian and non-Croatian residents of the city: this city belongs to "us"! The message has a vicious, nasty edge to it as well: it was from these heights that the Croatian army bombed the Bosniak Muslim and Serbian sections of the city, causing many deaths and extensive displacement. The bombardments also destroyed the Stari Most, the ancient bridge spanning the river that more or less separates the two sides of the city. As such, the cross acts as a constant symbolic reminder of the potential for genocidal violence that floats, as it were, in the sky above the daily lives of its inhabitants. Later on that day and on subsequent days in Mostar, I found that the cross subtly intruded into my consciousness so that I constantly felt as if I was in a sniper's crosshairs and, whenever I crossed the street or any open ground, I would automatically glance up at the cross on the hillside and register my exposure.

On another occasion, in Belfast, I ran across the city from where I was staying near Queen's University, over the River Langan into the predominantly Protestant part of East Belfast. Unlike my earlier run in Mostar, this time I had an agenda: I wanted to see both the birthplace of the greatest of all contemporary Irish singers, Van Morrison, and the inspiration of one of his most famous songs, "Cyprus Avenue." Stopping briefly outside his former home in Hyndford Street, a fairly nondescript terraced house with a motorbike in the small front yard, I made my way to the more middle-class area further up the hill. As I turned into Cyprus Avenue, which is a broad, shady boulevardlike street, with large houses set well back in mature gardens, I stopped to take in the scene, imagining the adolescent world of Van Morrison captured by his song and catching glimpses of the center of Belfast through the branches of the trees forming an arch over the road. I am sure Van Morrison would never have dreamed, thirty years later, after leaving Belfast, that another song of his, "Days Like This," would become the unofficial anthem of the Northern Irish peace movement and that he

FIGURE 5.1. Cross on top of hillside overlooking Mostar.

would be performing at a concert to celebrate the Anglo-Irish peace agreement in front of a mixed Protestant and Roman Catholic audience and the then president of the U.S., Bill Clinton.[1] The peace agreement that has put the deeply fragmented city of Belfast on the road to reintegration is fragile and beset with huge difficulties, not least the growing alienation of the working-class Protestant community from which Van Morrison came. But it is still holding, and the longer it holds, the greater are the chances that it will develop its own momentum. Standing at the top of the avenue, I could not help but contrast how much longer a road to peace Jerusalem has still to travel before there is anything like a celebratory concert or even a peace anthem. The abyss between the Israeli and Palestinian communities is still so wide.

The closest the two sides got to an agreement was in 2000 when the same Bill Clinton hosted a peace summit at the U.S. presidency's summer resort, Camp David. Much progress was made, but the unique multireligious nature of the city ultimately defeated the negotiators. As Ron Hassner puts it: "Negotiators reached some common ground on security issues, on Palestinian refugees, on Israeli withdrawal from Palestinian areas, even on dividing the modern city of Jerusalem, but reached an impasse on the issue of sovereignty over the sacred site at the heart of the old city."[2]

In this final chapter I shall explore why attempts to come to a peace agreement have failed. I shall offer in the first section a brief overview of the main stages of the peace negotiations to date. Then I shall examine two of the most salient proposals in more detail: the Geneva Initiative and the Jerusalem Old City Initiative. In the third section I shall examine what I perceive to be a more equitable proposal and evaluate its strengths and weaknesses, and, last, as a conclusion consider some of the longer-term issues that are both emerging and need to be resolved.

THE ROAD TO PEACE

Jerusalem has not been short of proposals to resolve the conflict. In 1995 a publication by Moshe Hirsch, Deborah Housen-Couriel, and Ruth Lapidoth cited 63 of the main ones, and since then there have been many more suggested.[3] I find it helpful to place the peace proposals on Jerusalem on a continuum between two poles. One pole of the continuum would be proposals that emphasize the unity and integrity of the city and toward the opposite pole are proposals that focus on structures that encompass the binary nature and diversity of the city.[4] For example, the UN General Assembly Resolution 181 and the Draft Statute for Jerusalem, also known as the *corpus separatum* or international zone, illustrates the unity and integrity end of the continuum. In this proposal the city would be internationalized and placed under a UN-appointed governor for a period of ten years, after which a referendum would be conducted to determine its final status. A legislative council with equal numbers from each religious community would be appointed and a judicial system be made responsible to the trusteeship council. Municipal functions would be delegated to autonomous units within the *corpus separatum*, but policing arrangements would be the prerogative of the governor.[5] At the opposite end of the continuum is a proposal contained in a letter by President Anwar Sadat of Egypt attached to the Camp David Agreement in 1978 between Israel and Egypt. Here the Egyptian president articulated the consensus Arab and PLO position of the time: West Jerusalem would remain Israeli and East Jerusalem would be under Arab (Palestinian) sovereignty and an integral part of the West Bank; all Israeli measures affecting East Jerusalem since 1967 would be rescinded. In recognition of the multifaith and multiethnic nature of the city, access to the religious sites and their internal administration would be respected. In addition, a joint municipal council would oversee the essential functions of the city, and, in this way, the city would remain politically separate at the national level, but there would be close cooperation at the municipal level.[6]

Within this overall continuum other proposals can be placed along the line between the two poles. For example, one of the most well-known proposals is that enunciated by Professor Walid Khalidi, a former adviser to the PLO chairman, Yasser Arafat, and other heads of state in the Middle East. He suggested a city of two capitals and two municipalities, but a "joint inter-state Great Municipal Council," which appears to lie at the midway point between the two poles of the continuum. His proposal also had a variant that included a degree of Third Party intervention: this is the "functional internationalisation" of the holy places.[7] Another example that would also sit on the midway point of the continuum is a joint proposal by the Palestinian academic and vice chancellor of al-Quds University, Professor Sari Nuseibeh, and the U.S. academic, Professor Mark Heller. They suggested devolving some functions and responsibilities to neighborhood councils, which they termed "scattered sovereignty," and other functions and responsibilities to a "metropolitan" government. This, they say, would "satisfy both the aspiration for distinctiveness/independence and the imperative of integration and unification."[8] Finally, the Israel Palestinian Center for Research and Information also suggested a similar form of political symmetry, but argued that the border of the joint municipal zone should be drawn in such a way as to ensure that there is parity between the Israeli and Palestinian populations of the city.[9] As a result, the area proposed is much larger than the existing borders to the extent it encompasses between 25–30 percent of the West Bank.

A subset of these proposals deals with the religious sites in the city. These can be placed along this continuum toward the unity and integrity end, but they are of a slightly different nature. Their focus is on the internationalization or the "extraterritorialization" of the holy places and to some degree all involve the intervention of a third party. The essence of these proposals is that religious sites are placed under a separate regime so that the international community can be assured that access to the holy sites and their protection is safeguarded. Until the Camp David summit of 2000, the Israeli position and most of its subsequent positions were derived from this starting point of focusing on international concerns over the holy sites while reserving Israeli political and military control over the rest of Jerusalem.[10]

A further variant of this approach, however, was put forward by the former Jordanian ambassador to the UN, Adnan Abu Odeh, who argued for the extraterritorialization of the whole of the Old City.[11] This received considerable media attention and was also discussed extensively in international policy circles. After some years in abeyance, this concept of a special regime for the Old City was developed with much more detail by a Canadian team based at the University of Windsor. Their proposal, the Jerusalem Old City Initiative, will be examined more thoroughly in the next section.[12]

After the signing of the Oslo Accords in 1993, we can see some variations that explore the notion of a dual capital in more detail. One of these is the "nonpaper" agreement between the former Israeli justice minister Yossi Beilin and the then-PLO general-secretary Mahmud Abbas (Abu Mazen), known as the Abu Mazen–Beilin Plan. The plan was never officially published, and it always remained a document for discussion. However, the detailed and wide-ranging nature of the plan and its status as the basis for Israeli and American proposals during the Camp David summit in July 2000 has made it a reference point for serious negotiations. The plan indicated a much greater flexibility on the Palestinian side than had been hitherto been the case. It proposed a joint higher municipal council and an Israeli and Palestinian submunicipality responsible for the concerns of their respective citizens and their property. The Old City would be under a "special regime," and the "preservation of the unique character of the Old City" was to be referred to a joint parity committee appointed by the two submunicipalities.[13] While Palestinians would have extraterritorial sovereignty over the Haram al-Sharif, it was significant and controversial that the submunicipal area designated as Palestinian did not come up to the 1967 borders, thus detaching the Old City and some of the Palestinian commercial and residential areas in East Jerusalem from the Palestinian submunicipality and capital. Nevertheless, despite these concessions, the Israeli government of the time was unable to swallow the prospect of a withdrawal from any part of East Jerusalem and the Plan remained a discussion paper.

In 2000, at the Camp David summit hosted by U.S. president Bill Clinton and attended by Israeli prime minister Ehud Barak and the president of the Palestinian National Authority, Yasser Arafat, we see the Israeli party offering less to the Palestinians than what was contained in the Abu Mazen–Beilin plan. The Israeli proposals comprised two main elements: first, that Israel would relinquish control over the northern Palestinian-dominated suburbs of the city to the Palestinian Authority and devolve administration in the central areas of East Jerusalem to Palestinian bodies. Second, Israel would retain overall sovereignty and security control over East Jerusalem, including the Old City and the Haram al-Sharif.

As these came nowhere close to Palestinian aspirations and did not take into account UNSC Resolution 242 in any meaningful way, they were rejected by Arafat. From a Palestinian perspective, the Israelis were not offering them much more than they already had in de facto terms. As we saw in chapter 2, a degree of Palestinian functional autonomy in parts of East Jerusalem was in already in place, and the Israeli concessions were seen as merely recognition of the situation at the time. Palestinian counterproposals were based upon Security Council Resolution 242, but also included a proposal for an "open city" with many shared municipal and security responsibilities, and were rejected out of hand by the Israelis as politically unfeasible.[14] Thus, despite the high hopes of the Americans, the Camp David summit ended in failure.

In the attempt to rescue the negotiations, President Clinton suggested some months later a framework known as the "Clinton Parameters," which would have led to the partition of the city, including the Old City, on demographic criteria. He further recommended Palestinian sovereignty over the Haram al-Sharif and Israeli sovereignty over the Western Wall and special arrangements for excavations underneath the Haram.[15] Neither side was happy with these ideas, but agreed to consider them further.

In a further attempt to consolidate what progress had been made at Camp David, negotiations were resumed at the Egyptian Red Sea resort at Taba in 2001. Building on the Clinton Parameters, there was further progress over the question of Jerusalem in the sense that both sides agreed that Jerusalem would be the capital of the two states. Furthermore, Palestinians were willing to discuss Israeli sovereignty over Israeli settlements in East Jerusalem and to accept Israeli sovereignty over parts of the Old City within the context of an "open city." In turn, Israel accepted Palestinian sovereignty over Palestinian suburbs up to the Green Line. In addition, an agreement to continue discussions on "special arrangements" regarding the Haram al-Sharif/Temple Mount and the concept of a Holy Basin to encompass religious sites in and outside the Old City was introduced.[16] From the Palestinian perspective, these discussions marked a significant shift from previously held Israeli positions and were important steps toward achieving the implementation of Resolution 242. Unfortunately, the Taba proposals were too little too late to both save the Barak administration, which fell in the subsequent elections, and/or to avoid the violence that was unleashed as the new Israeli administration of Prime Minister Ariel Sharon sought to pull back from these positions and weaken the Palestinian political leadership. As a result, there was an intensification of violent confrontation culminating in the Second Intifada, during which serious negotiations were suspended.

Indeed, since then we have witnessed the construction of the separation barrier and the continuation of the settlement policy in and around East Jerusalem which reveal an Israeli determination to revert to its maximalist positions. In fact, since Camp David in 2000, Israeli demands for sovereignty over the Haram al-Sharif have injected new obstacles into the possibilities for a negotiated agreement over Jerusalem. In 2006 the Israeli prime minister who succeeded Ariel Sharon, Ehud Olmert, declared that he "will never, never agree to a compromise on the complete control over the Temple Mount. And not only the Temple Mount but also the Old City, Mount of Olives and every place that is an inseparable part of Jewish history."[17]

Nevertheless, there is also clearly a shift from the previous Israeli position of no negotiations over the city. At the same press conference, Olmert went on to add, "We don't pray facing Bir Nabala or Issawiyya, or any of the other Palestinian neighbourhoods that have been added to Jerusalem by someone who drew a map one day." An illustration of this shift can be seen in the proposals by Knesset member Otniel Schneller, an adviser to Olmert, but also, and more significantly, a former leading figure in the Israeli settler movement. He suggested that while Israel would retain the Old City and immediate environs, it would not seek to hold onto some of the Palestinian suburbs.[18]

Two more recent rounds of negotiations have taken place following these indications of some flexibility—in Annapolis in 2007 and in Amman in 2011–2012. However, in neither of these rounds of talks has any significant progress been made. Reports on the Annapolis talks indicate that the discussion between the two sides made use of the Clinton Parameters as a basis for deciding on territorial division and land exchanges in the city.

In essence this meant that areas of predominantly Israeli Jewish residence, including settlements, would remain Israeli. At the same time, there was an Israeli acceptance of the Palestinian demand that Jerusalem be its capital. The difficult issue of the holy sites of the Old City would be dealt with by placing them under an international administration comprising Jordan, Saudi Arabia, Palestine, Israel, and the U.S. One version of this idea is that the area of international administration would extend beyond the Old City into an area that has already been referred to as the Holy Basin. In order to manage the changes such proposals would entail, a joint Palestinian-Israeli committee would administer East Jerusalem during a transitional period.[19]

One can see how, over time, both sides have shifted their positions. For Israel, it has moved from a position of no negotiations over Jerusalem to a consideration of land exchanges and the possibility of parts of East Jerusalem forming the capital of a Palestinian state. In this respect, since 1993, the return to the 1967 borders, as enunciated by UNSC Resolution 242, subject to some critical territorial exchanges, is not as distant a prospect as it had been a decade earlier. For its part, the Palestinian position has also evolved. From earlier demands of a complete withdrawal to the 1967 borders, it will now contemplate, provided that the recognition of East Jerusalem as the capital is forthcoming, land exchanges and some external involvement over the administration of religious sites. Both sides are willing to consider various coordinating bodies ranging from joint security coordination at a bare minimum to joint municipal committees to a supramunicipal council. The most important unresolved issues, however, remain exactly the same: the degree to which Israel will relinquish military control and security to either Palestinian bodies or third parties and the competing claims over control and management of the shared holy sites.

SHARING THE CITY

In this section I discuss two very different but partially overlapping proposals on Jerusalem that address these outstanding issues. The first, the Geneva Initiative (sometimes also known as the Geneva Accords) was launched with Swiss government support in December 2003.[20] It comprised two sets of negotiators, Israeli and Palestinian, and sought to flesh out in detail a possible agreement on the whole range of permanent status issues, from Jerusalem to refugees. Although having no official status, the negotiating teams comprised many of the leading figures in or advising the negotiating teams that had met in Camp David and Taba. As such it reflects some trends in thinking on both sides. Their work on Jerusalem encompasses the whole of the city of Jerusalem. The Jerusalem Old City Initiative was launched in 2004 by three former Canadian diplomats and supported by the Canadian Department of Foreign Affairs and International Trade.[21] In contrast to the work of the Geneva Initiative on Jerusalem, it focused specifically on exploring the ideas of Adnan Abu Odeh on a special regime for the Old City of Jerusalem and enlisted a wide range of experts and policy makers as contributors to its studies. As such, it is not a joint Israeli-Palestinian proposal, but a third-party intervention based on extensive consultations and dialogue with representatives of the two main sides. In terms of the continuum referred to earlier, the Geneva Initiative is closer to the binary pole and the Jerusalem Old City Initiative is a variant comprising an enclave that could be attached to either a binary or a unitary model.

Before looking at these two proposals in detail, we should recognize the lack of symmetry in the negotiations as a whole. In a nutshell, Israel is under much less pressure and has much less incentive to reach an agreement than the Palestinians. Israel has such a military, economic, and political dominance over the Palestinians that it does not need an agreement—certainly Israel does not need an agreement that relies on Palestinian security capabilities or one that would fracture its own national consensus and body politic, which would flow from making concessions either on settlements or on control over the Jewish holy sites. During the early 1990s and again in the early 2000s, the Palestinian uprising, the fear of eroding U.S. support, and the changing balance of power in the region all combined to provide a degree of motivation for the Israeli economic, political, and military elite to consider making limited concessions on territory in exchange for Palestinian cooperation on security and the management of resources and labor flows. Its approach then and now is, therefore, undergirded very much by a "take it or leave it" perspective. It can manage without an agreement. The political and economic costs of ongoing conflict, especially the low-level-intensity conflict that has existed since 1993, is much less than the costs of an agreement to Israel that would meet Palestinian aspirations. We should also recognize that even if Israel was so minded to make far-reaching concessions in the interests of a peace agreement, they have the major problem of entrusting elements of their security to an unreliable neighbor. Palestinian disunity and the influence of militant groups in Palestinian nationalism present Israeli decision makers with a dilemma. As they see it, they would be giving up land, resources, and control over a hostile people for a security cooperation—possibly illusory—and the Palestinian recognition of their right to be there. Both of which are easily withdrawn. In effect, they would be exchanging territory for a Palestinian promise of good behavior. The Israeli evaluation of the situation is that this is too high a risk to take.

For the Palestinians, an agreement is crucial for its national cohesion and state building project. They need the territory that Israel occupied in 1967 and the institutions and responsibilities Israel has controlled or restricted upon which a state of Palestine can be constructed. However, they are not prepared to pay any price for this, certainly not the price of accepting a bantustan masquerading as an independent state. To some extent, many Palestinians believe this is already occurring, that the PNA is a stooge of the Israeli government, that its leadership has been co-opted into a Zionist vision of the region, and that the Fatah movement is merely acting as the security enforcer for Israel. As a result, the Palestinian consensus has fractured during the course of the peace negotiations since 1993, with Hamas leading the powerful dissident movement. At the same time, while Fatah and its allies have shown a great deal of flexibility and pragmatism in the face of overwhelming Israeli odds, they too have their opportunities for leveraging concessions and also their red lines. For example, it is often overlooked how in the place of an air force, tanks, and extensive electronic and satellite surveillance, Palestinians have successfully enlisted the "soft power" of international law and international civil society. Despite some shortsighted departures from the corpus of UN resolutions which buttress the Palestinian position, on the whole, the main reason why the Palestinian nationalism has not faded away, like, for example, Armenian nationalism in Turkey, has been the mobilization of UN institutions and resolutions in its defense. However, the current PNA and PLO leadership has taken a huge gamble with its legitimacy and with the Palestinian national consensus in order to put in place a longer-term game plan of extracting an Israeli withdrawal from the territories it occupied in 1967 and a satisfactory resolution of the refugee issue. This game plan involves accepting Palestinians having a subordinate position with regard to Israel during a transitional period, on the condition that at the end of this period there will be a Palestinian state based upon UN resolutions. If this end goal is neither forthcoming nor looks like satisfying the aspirations of the Palestinians sufficiently, then cooperation during the transitional period is no longer tenable or desirable. In this case, no deal with the Israelis is preferable to a bad deal that would leave Palestinians divided and with a facade for a state. This is the gamble, and, if it fails, whether the current leadership survives will be an open question.

But what these considerations tell us is that, when it comes to the negotiation over Jerusalem, Israeli is unlikely to offer much more than fairly cosmetic change to its overall control of the city, both east and west. It has neither needed to in the past nor currently needs to do so. Its main drivers for some agreement with the Palestinians are twofold. First, the fear in Israel is that without an agreement it will end up incorporating too many Palestinians into the Israeli state, which will dilute the Jewish nature of the state. Second, that the ongoing occupation and conflict erodes its position as a liberal democracy in the international community. Nevertheless, these two considerations lose their force in the face of an increasingly volatile region and a disunited Palestinian leadership and minimum pressure from the U.S. and the rest of the international community. Whether the approach of minimum concessions is ultimately in the interests of the long-term future of Israel is debatable. In light of some emerging trends that will be discussed later, a peace agreement made from a position of strength may be a wiser option. However, during the period that the Geneva Initiative and the Jerusalem Old City Initiative were being worked out, the incentive for significant concessions was not immediately obvious, and this helps to frame our understanding of the nature of the two proposals.

THE GENEVA INITIATIVE

The Geneva Initiative was born out of the Taba negotiations in 2001. Rather than abandoning the progress that was made between Israeli and Palestinians negotiators there, key figures in those negotiations, such as the former Israeli minister of education, Yossi Beilin, and the Palestinian adviser to President Arafat, Yasser Abed Rabbo, were determined to continue on an unofficial nongovernmental basis. As such, the initiative was an attempt by Israeli and Palestinian former negotiators to ensure that the gains they had made could be consolidated and used to map out a possible trajectory for future official negotiations.

The Geneva Initiative proposed that Jerusalem be recognized as a city of two capitals for two states with two separate municipalities responsible for their respective areas.[22] To ensure that the two sides of the city worked in as much harmony as possible, a coordination committee would be appointed by the municipalities to oversee the economic development of the city as a whole. Within this overall framework, Israel would retain sovereignty over Israeli settlements in East Jerusalem, including Israeli "administration" of the Jewish cemetery on the Mount of Olives, with contiguity established through land corridors, bridges, and tunnels. Palestine would have sovereignty over the Haram al-Sharif (article 6.3). However, to tackle the issue of disputed holy and cultural sites, a special regime would be introduced for the Old City that would include Israeli sovereignty over the extended Jewish Quarter, the Western (Wailing) Wall, and the Western Wall tunnel.

A key instrument in the Geneva Initiative is third-party intervention and monitoring. This was intended to address, on the one hand, Israeli anxieties over the competence and capability of Palestinian security forces, and, on the other hand, Palestinian concerns over Israeli noncompliance. Thus the initiative proposes a number of channels for external intervention and involvement including an implementation and verification group and an interfaith council. Furthermore, UNESCO would be given a prominent role, with its protocols on conservation and heritage being established as benchmarks for cultural activities in the Old City. In addition, while Palestinian sovereignty over the Haram al-Sharif would be recognized by Israel, nevertheless, the compound would be subject to a multinational "presence" established to monitor security and conservation on the site (article 6.5(a)).

To some extent, the initiative has been an evolutionary process. Much of the detailed maps that were integral to a comprehensive agreement were not available at the time of the launch, as they were still being negotiated. It took a further six or seven years for them to appear. Nevertheless, the initiative marks an important progression. It indicates that a significant section of the political elite in Israel accept the possible role that the international community can play in monitoring and arbitrating complex issues such as access to religious sites and the conservation of heritage. Indeed, the establishment of an implementation and verification group offers a Palestinian state, which is likely to be much weaker than Israel, some support in confronting possible Israeli encroachments in the postagreement phases. In addition, in areas outside Jerusalem, the initiative recognizes many Palestinian demands including that of sovereignty over territory based on UNSCR 242 and provides for a corridor linking Gaza and the West Bank.

However, for the city of Jerusalem and its immediate hinterland, the initiative poses some major problems, not least that it falls dramatically short of Palestinian aspirations and is unlikely, therefore, to be accepted by the Palestinian political leadership. The shortcomings of the Initiative are not so obvious in the main text of the accord but can be clearly seen in the detailed "Annex 05, Jerusalem: Urban Challenges and Planning Proposals." This was developed later and also includes the essential maps which were absent in the outline agreement launched in 2003. For example, in Annex 05, the proposed Palestine-Israel state border is drawn around the Israeli settlements in the Jerusalem region in such a way as to link them to the main body of western half of the city (see map 5.1). The main text does not say specify this. Indeed, in contrast, it specifically refers to the general withdrawal of Israel from settlements (article 6.5). It is clear that, despite the main text of the initiative suggesting a withdrawal to the Green Line, in the Jerusalem region not a single settlement—from Pisgat Ze'ev to Gush Etzion, from Betar Illit to Maale Adumim—is evacuated or placed under Palestinian sovereignty. Rather than constructing a solution based on the principle in international law that no territory should be acquired through conquest or the use of force, the initiative is based upon recognizing the settlements as legitimate without requiring Israel to accept a range of other options such as partial evacuations, phased withdrawals, lease-back schemes, and administered enclaves under Palestinian sovereignty. Thus the divergence between what is in the main text and what is in Annex 05 dramatically shifts the balance of concessions made overall, so that serious and far-reaching concessions made by Palestinians in the main text, such as permitting a monitoring and inspection regime on the Haram al-Sharif itself, are compounded by the huge territorial concessions in Annex 05.

There are further shortcomings to the initiative. First, there is a great lack of clarity over definitions and terms. For example, it is not clear how the initiative defines a holy site. As we saw in chapter 3, estimates of the number of holy sites in Jerusalem range from thirty to over three hundred. In addition, there are clauses based upon "past practice" as a criterion for determining the type of visits that can be made on the Haram al-Sharif (article 6.5(b), no. iii). But this is a controversial issue, and it is not clear what past practice is being referred to—that which has been introduced by the Israelis since 1967 or previous Ottoman or British precedents? Another definition that demands clarity is the length of the Wailing Wall, since Israeli sovereignty is being conferred over it (article 6.6). Are the signatories referring to the 60 meters that have been exposed since 1967 or the full length of 147 meters? Similarly the text of the initiative deals only with the freedom of movement of people and not of goods in the Old City. Is this omission deliberate? If so, the implications for cross-city trade are enormous. These are all essential elements of a lasting and equitable agreement and need spelling out.

A second shortcoming is the how the border between the proposed Palestine state and Israel also fragments the city in ways that seriously compromise its integrity and its functioning as a single urban unit. The border will divide the city entirely along ethnic lines with Israeli and Palestinian residential, retail, and industrial areas kept completely separate. This is particularly incongruous and destructive in the Old City where the extended Jewish Quarter is separated out from the rest of the walled area. Despite claims in the main text that the city would remain a single planning and functional unit with strong coordination mechanisms, the border and separations proposed is unlikely to achieve such objectives. One should bear in mind that the separation barrier has already been place for nearly one decade, and, as we have already discussed earlier, its impact lies less in the physical presence of the structure itself but more in the way in which roads and patterns of lives have been directed away from the wall and away from previous connections with the other side of the wall to areas to the east, north, and south of the wall.[23] The Geneva Initiative border will only serve to reinforce this growing new orientation and the greater fragmentation of the city. The initiative attempts to ameliorate this fragmentation by providing a complex series of corridors, tunnels, and bridges so that Israeli areas are attached to other Israeli areas and Palestinian areas are similarly connected to each other. Annex 05 consists of several in-depth and quite imaginative studies on possible crossing points and connecting links. Yet they only serve to emphasize the disintegration of the city under these proposals.

A third shortcoming is the proposed border between the two sections of the city. The elongated and meanderings of the border proposed are a security expert's nightmare. Narrow necks or tongues of land, semi-enclaved clusters of houses, long tunnels with bends in them, and bridges over strategically important roads will require a huge investment in surveillance systems and security personnel on the ground.[24] It is not clear from either the text or Annex 05 whether all the borders will be impermeable, but, if so, the cost of maintenance and construction of barriers will be significant. The proposed international checkpoints will cause bottlenecks over the movement of tourists and may provide a disincentive to a vital part of the city's economy.

A final shortcoming concerns the Old City and its holy sites. The initiative proposes a wide range of restrictions upon Palestinian activity and sovereignty on the Haram al-Sharif, and it seems unlikely that these will meet the aspirations of religious-minded Palestinians. Indeed, the proposals also confer sovereignty of the Wailing Wall to Israel, but without similar constraints and oversights over its use and preservation. This appears unbalanced and provocative. More important, however, is the composition and role of the "Multinational Presence in al-Haram al-Sharif/Temple Mount Compound." Annex 04 of the Geneva Initiative offers a detailed breakdown

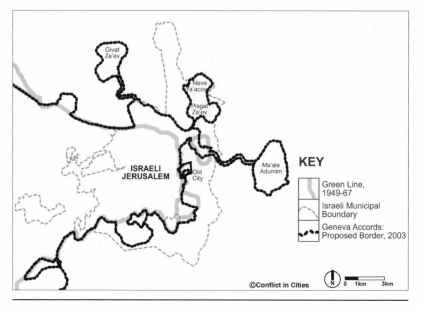

MAP 5.1. The Geneva Initiative: Proposed Israeli Jerusalem.

of its responsibilities and functions, which amount to a highly intrusive and domineering presence. In addition to 150 security personnel for the security and conservation unit, there will be 12 volunteers to the compound observation unit and ancillary administrative staff. On top of this, it is proposed that the presence itself be accountable to a number of other bodies including a donor's group. Ultimately the proposed multinational presence appears to be configured to operate in an atmosphere of little trust and the prospect of only minimal cooperation. It contains all the hallmarks of a peace-keeping operation based upon military coercion rather than a cooperative mechanism resulting from agreement between Israelis and Palestinians over the future of the Haram enclosure. In addition, despite the professed intention to preserve the freedom of movement of people in and into the Old City, some of the agreed provisions seem to make this difficult. For example, the allocation of gates of the Old City to either Israeli or Palestinian control and making nonresidents subject to security searches will cause complications in accessing different the Old City and deter nonresidents from entering it.[25] The end result may be to consign the Old City as a dead-end enclave and detach it from its urban hinterland. Further consideration of this point is made in the discussion on the Jerusalem Old City Initiative.

In essence, the Geneva Initiative has some imaginative approaches to the difficulties confronting an agreement based upon joint sovereignty and two municipal administrations. However, the emphasis is clearly on constructing an agreement based upon the changes introduced by Israeli policies over the past forty-five years, particularly with regard to the settlements both inside the city and in the hinterland. Little consideration is given to the possibility of either reversing them or extracting a greater parity in concessions. In this sense, the Geneva Initiative is focused on winning over Israeli public opinion by not touching the sacred cows of settlement and Israeli sovereignty over the Jewish holy places. What is quite remarkable is the credence that the initiative has obtained in many Palestinian circles. One might dismiss this engagement as a reflection of the limited views of a Ramallah elite who have been seduced by the siren call of meetings and workshops in five-star hotels, of international travel, and the media spotlight. Others have suggested that, for the Palestinians, the initiative is part of a slow process of dialogue and engagement with Israelis that will eventually inform them of the Palestinian perspective. Some years ago a senior Fatah member and former PNA cabinet minister consulted me on whether he should declare his support for the initiative as he was being put under pressure to do so by its Palestinian supporters. We went through all the pros and cons, and after several meetings he eventually decided against, preferring in the end to keep his powder dry so that he could throw his political weight behind something he thought had a better prospect of providing a breakthrough. The Geneva Initiative was not it.

THE JERUSALEM OLD CITY INITIATIVE

The Jerusalem Old City Initiative (JOCI) is based on the view that a negotiated agreement between the governments of Palestine and Israel on Jerusalem is not possible unless there is a resolution over the disputes over access, management, and use of the holy sites in the city. The best way forward in breaking the impasse over these sites is to have a separate agreement or a special administrative regime for them. As the overwhelming majority of religious sites are located in the Old City and as the Old City is also the location of the two main sites under dispute—the Haram al-Sharif/Temple Mount and the al-Buraq/Wailing Wall, the separate agreement or special regime should focus on the Old City. In this way, progress in the negotiations over other parts of the city will not be impeded.[26]

In advancing this view, a team of former Canadian diplomats based at Windsor University, Canada, explored the idea of a special regime for the Old City in considerable detail. We should note that the JOCI proposals differ from the Geneva Initiative in a number of ways: First, the focus is on the Old City only, although the team does raise the possibility that, as a template, it could be extended to other areas such as the Holy Basin. Second, the integrity of the Old City is preserved with no physical division between the quarters. The proposed borders between the states of Palestine and Israel will be limited to "within and including the walls" of the Old City.[27] Third, JOCI gives a much stronger role to third parties whose mandate will be supported by the Security Council. In the Geneva Initiative, most of the roles conferred on third parties are those of monitoring and dispute management, while in JOCI the third party is given a direct role in administration and security.

In separating out the Old City in this way, the JOCI proposal recognizes that a body, known as the Old City Administration, should be given overall responsibility for a range of quasi-state and quasi-municipal responsibilities. These would include security and policing, access to and from the Old City, oversight over heritage and archaeological activities, planning and zoning within the walls, property registration and transfer, and ensuring that residents and visitors are treated with equality and respect. In order to manage these responsibilities, the special regime for the Old City will establish a chief administrator appointed by the governments of Palestine and Israel for a fixed but renewable term. The chief administrator will have extensive proconsular powers and receive sufficient funds to run a small bureaucracy. In addition, he or she will appoint a chief of police that will be accountable to the chief administrator. As much of the property and key buildings in the Old City are owned by religious communities, and much of the life of the Old City is geared to supporting the many religious activities that take place there, the chief administrator will also consult with a religious council that will be independent of the OCA. All responsibilities not taken up by the Old City Administration will be the responsibility of the governments of Israel and Palestine. In this way it is thought that the special regime for the Old City will retain its quotidiennial connections to the city outside the walls.

The JOCI team regarded the creation of an effective and convincing security framework as critical, particularly in ensuring Israeli participation in the regime. It was therefore made the subject of a separate study by authoritative international experts including two who had worked on the peace agreement for Northern Ireland.[28] Their study emphasized the importance of strong liaison mechanisms between the Old City chief of police and Palestinian and Israeli security agencies and the need to have an arrangement where there was backup from Palestinian and Israeli police services. At the same time, they argued that the chief administrator and chief of police should have complete operational autonomy. The success of a security regime in the Old City would depend on the residents perceiving the police as a service rather than as a force imposed upon them and thus the need to follow a community policing approach. In this regard, what would be called the Old City police service would have separate but ethnically mixed police units for the religious sites and stress the importance of training in human rights norms and cultural awareness.[29]

In a marked fashion, the JOCI proposal broke new ground and contained many elements that can be used in a broader and more comprehensive agreement for the city. What was remarkable was the team's methodology and program of activities. Not only did it commission original research on legal, economic, and social conditions in the Old City, it also carried out an extended and intensive program of consultations with a wide range of people reaching up to the highest levels in Palestinian and Israeli political and security circles. This painstaking yet inclusive approach provided opportunities to carefully consider the advantages and disadvantages of the special regime formula, and the drafts went through numerous formulations as new ideas or concerns were expressed. I was an active member of the Governance Working Group of the JOCI team for part of its existence and was struck by the conscientiousness with which the team members sought to draw out the objections to their vision and try to address them openly. Even if ultimately I, like many others, was not happy with the final report and set of proposals, nevertheless, the concepts and terminologies developed by the JOCI team have clarified the debate over a special regime for the Old City. In addition, the discussion processes and networks that evolved in Israel and the occupied Palestinian territories, as well as the advocacy work undertaken by the JOCI team in the North American and European policy community during the period of its existence, kept the possibility of a negotiated solution to Jerusalem alive during the period of profound skepticism of both the negotiations and the two-state solution.

The weaknesses of the JOCI proposal are nonetheless profound and highlight the difficulties of arriving at a negotiated solution. They can be grouped around three main issues: sovereignty, administration, and duration. On the sovereignty issue, it is significant that the final JOCI text makes no reference either to UN Security Council Resolution 242 or to Palestinian sovereignty over East Jerusalem as the basis of an agreement. The proposal is presented as an interim measure specifically for a regime for the Old City pending a final agreed solution on the whole city, so its authors can argue that no sovereignty issues have been prejudged. But the absence of this recognition of Palestinian sovereignty over the Old City implicitly incorporates a Palestinian concession. By agreeing to a suspension of the sovereignty issue and the creation of a special legal status for the Old City, mandated by the UN Security Council, Palestinians will be accepting that it is different from other parts of East Jerusalem. While there is no territorial gain for Israel, there is a loss for the Palestinians, and it is a loss on the most valuable and important part of the city. I would argue that it is fundamental for a successful negotiation process on Jerusalem that Palestinian sovereignty should be recognized in all of East Jerusalem and that a special regime in the Old City, while taking into account Israeli security concerns, can contribute to this. But such a regime for the Old City would be a special regime only in the sense of providing "special arrangements" for access to the holy sites, and, importantly, in the overall context of Palestinian sovereignty. In the early stages of discussion on the special regime, the JOCI papers included references to UN resolutions, but these were dropped as the rolling draft rolled forward. The reason for this change in tack is that the core team felt it was a prerequisite for progress in their discussions if the sovereignty issue were not predetermined. The importance of this became clearer later: as the report came to its final version, more power and authority was being conferred onto the special regime administration than I and others had originally envisaged the core team would recommend. It thus became clear that in a scenario in which a strong semiautonomous special regime administration was being created, as the JOCI proposed, the principle of Palestinian sovereignty over the Old City would be even more important to adhere to. Without it, the Old City special regime would become a Trojan horse for the ceding of Palestinian sovereignty.

On the second issue of the administrative structures for the Old City special regime, the JOCI team was concerned about the dangers inherent in third-party interventions: the question of legitimacy. It concluded that, unless the special regime had strong and extensive administrative powers, its main function, which is to ensure the security of the religious sites there, would not receive the essential support of the residents. The proposal therefore extends the role of the Old City special regime to areas that are normally regarded as a function or responsibility of a municipality. In addition to policing roles already mentioned, there would be a legal system and court system, a planning and zoning department, a land registry committee, a heritage and archaeology department, and various advisory and representative councils. I characterized this structure as the "mini-municipality" model in which the special regime constitutes a separate and well-developed administrative framework in its own right. The result would be to create a distinct administrative and political entity that can be clearly seen as separate from the rest of East Jerusalem.

This, I argued, would compound the balance in concessions being asked of the different parties. Not only would there be a loss of sovereignty but there would also be a significant loss of governance. An alternative model, which I termed the "light touch" model, was not explored sufficiently in the JOCI debates and its final proposals. In the light touch model, the differences in jurisdiction between the life inside and outside the wall would be kept to a minimum. Palestinian sovereignty and municipal administration and services would extend to all parts of the Old City, with the special regime element comprising third party involvement being focused solely on the access to and management and use of religious sites. It would be important to recognize that under this light touch model the Jewish Quarter presents a formidable challenge. But, as the Geneva Initiative has shown, variations are possible, and the JOCI proposals could be amended to show how the Jewish Quarter would similarly enjoy many aspects of this light-touch special regime, but could also have a separate status by virtue of its likely incorporation into the Israeli state through territorial exchanges.[30]

The final difficulty in the JOCI proposal is the question of the duration of the special regime. The JOCI proposal recommends that the duration of the special regime would be for a "generation"—to allow time for the peace to be consolidated.[31] It could end sooner or be extended, depending upon the wishes of the party. I do not think this vagueness is constructive. The lack of clarity over the termination of the special regime introduces an unnecessary and damaging operational weakness. Administrators need to know how long they have in order to implement projects or address problems or manage a budget. The duration of a project affects the structures that are created and the funding that is required. The absence of a termination date is also a recipe for disputes between the parties, and, as a result, the international community, as guarantor of the agreement, will be drawn into the minutiae of the administration. Nothing is more certain to draw in the great powers on the Security Council than ambivalence over the duration of the special regime. The success of the Old City special regime will become contingent on the ebb and flow of high politics which may have nothing to do with the dramas taking place in the narrow street of the Old City. Furthermore, any special regime that lasts longer than ten years gives a sense of permanence and establishes a *new* status quo for the Old City. The effect of the JOCI proposal is that the current international position, which demands that Israel should withdraw from territory acquired in 1967, will be supplemented, if not replaced, by a Security Council mandate for a special regime whose termination is in effect indefinite. Any new negotiations will be based upon this situation as a starting point.

There are two other aspects of the JOCI proposal which demand further consideration: The first consideration regards planning and development in the Old City. The focus in the JOCI proposal on the Old City and the area within the walls reinforces a conception of the Old City as a separate and distinct physical entity. Historically, as we have seen in previous chapters, the Old City has been the center of the city of Jerusalem, and the links and connections between life within and without the walls have been seamless and organically evolving. The proposal contains strong tendencies, through its "mini-municipality" approach and planning powers conferred on the Old City Administration, to cut that link and set it adrift from the city. This would add to the already fragmented nature of the city as a result of its division in 1949 and the introduction of Israeli enclaves after 1967. Thus, in attempting to address a political problem of governance and a security problem of ensuring access to holy sites, the JOCI proposal is likely to accentuate the current fragmentation of the city into enclaves and segregated areas. I know this was not the intention of the JOCI team, but it is one of the probable unintended consequences.

The second consideration is the need for an overall negotiation framework to contextualize the JOCI proposal. By definition, the JOCI proposal is focused on the Old City, but it cannot be fully evaluated without taking into account the nature of an agreement in other areas outside the Old City or, similarly, the impact of a special regime in the Old City on arrangements for the rest of Jerusalem. For example, how would the security cooperation between the OCA and the Israeli and Palestinian security service, which is envisaged in JOCI, have an impact or differ from security cooperation between Israel and Palestine in the rest of the city and, indeed, relate to any third party role that is introduced in monitoring the borders of the city? Or, how would joint Israel and Palestine municipal coordination in other parts of the city impinge on the services provided by the proposed OCA? Would the city emerge in a postconflict period with a set of Israeli services, Palestinian services, some joint services, and a set of Old City services? These are not insurmountable challenges, but, in this way, JOCI offers ideas for a partial vision of the city that need to be developed further to take in broader citywide issues.

Finally, perhaps the overall conclusion one can come to on the JOCI proposal is that it constructs a framework with many useful ideas, but one that does not challenge the balance of power which at present favors the Israeli side. It seems to me that, in introducing an intrusive external intervention that may last up to twenty-five years or more, the JOCI proposals will detach the Old City from the Palestinian East Jerusalem hinterland, and, given the dominance of Israel in the city, this will pave the way for a semi-Israelized enclave. This may account for the reason why Israeli reactions to the JOCI proposal are much more favorable than those of the Palestinians. It may also account for the fact that, while they are willing to discuss a special regime for the Old City, Palestinians will do so only in the context of recognition of Palestinian sovereignty over the Old City. They neither trust the Israelis nor any third parties nor their own capabilities to ensure that the Old City remains within the Palestinian Arab orbit. My own view is that the JOCI proposal should instead have focused on delineating a limited role for third parties which was directed toward the protection of and safeguarding access to the holy sites of the city. Others responsibilities and functions of the third party would be extended only insofar as they were necessary to meet that limited goal.

PROSPECTS FOR PEACE IN JERUSALEM

In view of the limitations of both the proposals presented in the previous section, we should turn to a discussion of the likelihood of a possible peace agreement for Jerusalem and the obstacles that line the route. A realistic assessment of the current situation, that is, during 2012–13, surely must conclude that an agreement over the city in the near future is highly unlikely. Despite occasional outbreaks of violence and disorder, and despite the continued local, national, and international opposition to unilateral Israeli measures in East Jerusalem, there is, as we discussed earlier in this chapter, no urgent reason for Israel to make concessions sufficiently far-reaching to meet Palestinian aspirations. The main priority of successive Israeli governments in this situation seems to be to breathe enough life into the process of dialogue and engagement with the Palestinians to encourage their continued cooperation over security and their avoidance of violent resistance to further Israeli encroachments on land and other resources. In effect, Israel wishes to and is able to signal the possibility of an agreement without being obliged to deliver one. For their part, the Palestinians have reached a crossroads. The gamble taken by the Fatah leadership mentioned earlier does not look like it is paying off. The fruits of the peace process have been so insubstantial, with the prospect of a possible agreement constantly receding, that the overall result is a profoundly negative one for them. Disagreements over strategy and tactics in the national movement have become major and possibly irreversible divisions. In addition, the credibility of the Fatah leadership is so undermined that their ability to deliver an agreement, if ever one took place, is questionable. A growing number of senior decision makers are no longer bluffing when they say that the two-state solution, the foundation of the peace process, is no longer viable and that the only alternative left to them is to seek greater rights within an Israeli state.[32] It is quite likely, therefore, that there may even be a further split in the Fatah ranks, as those disillusioned with the peace negotiations try to reestablish cooperation with Hamas and its allies in order to reverse Israeli gains of the post-Oslo period. Others who see no future in resistance or militancy will continue to be gradually co-opted by the Israeli state.

In this scenario, it does seem that without any major changes in the current balance of power the prospect of a peace agreement on Jerusalem is a distant possibility. Unless there is a dramatic reversal in the balance of power away from Israel that would oblige it to quickly settle with the Palestinians in order to forge new regional alliances, or unless there is a shift in perceptions of tectonic proportions by the Israeli public of Palestinian rights, the only prospect on offer for Jerusalem in the near to medium future is an archipelago of Palestinian enclaves in and around Jerusalem with cultural autonomy and responsibility for most municipal services. Security, planning, zoning, and labor and population flows would all remain under Israeli control.

Having laid out this bleak prognosis of the current situation, we should nevertheless recognize both some long-term emerging trends and the possibility of some dramatic event thatwill present unexpected twists in the current trajectory. After all, as I observed in the introduction, few political scientists predicted the tearing down of the Berlin Wall in 1989 and the rapidity of the dismemberment of the Soviet Union and the Soviet bloc; even fewer predicted that Nelson Mandela would become the president of the state that had imprisoned him for twenty-six years, and very few predicted the near collapse of the world economy in 2008. The reordering of the Middle East after the Arab Spring is quite likely to throw up some unexpected new developments that will precipitate a major realignment of forces in the Arab-Israeli conflict and thus impinge on the unfolding of arrangements for Jerusalem. In light of this we should turn to a number of long-term issues that should be taken into consideration in assessing the prospects for a peace agreement over Jerusalem. This is particularly the case in view of the growing acceptance that the two-state solution may no longer be a feasible goal and that alternatives should be considered.

JERUSALEM AND THE BINATIONAL MODEL

In recent years, discussion on the binational option as a solution to the Palestinian-Israeli conflict has become much more prolific. In addition to numerous newspaper articles, there are now a number of academic journal articles, monographs, and edited volumes available.[33] The main reason for this proliferation has been, as we discussed earlier, the growing view that the two-statesolution, as envisaged in the Oslo Accords and the road map promoted by the Quartet (U.S., Russia, UN, and EU), has failed. Academics, activists, and policy makers have agreed that there is an urgent need to explore other models in order to offer alternatives to the maximalist positions outlined either by the Israeli right or the Palestinian Islamic movement.[34]

What is significant about this debate is that, while it still remains a minority position, it is no longer confined solely to the margins of debate and dismissed as the fantasy of naive utopians. It is still true that most Israelis and Zionists characterize binationalism as a code for the extinction of Israel and accuse its supporters of anti-Semitism. Similarly, some Palestinian nationalists have seen it as either an accommodation to the defeat and dispossession of the Palestinians that occurred in 1948 or presaging an unwelcome dilution of Arab identity in the new state of Palestine, having repercussions for Palestinian relations with the surrounding Arab states.[35] Policy makers and diplomats regard discussion of it as unrealistic and fruitless in the face of overwhelming Israeli military superiority.

Indeed, while its rejection by the Zionist and Israeli establishment is equally vehement as when the idea was first mooted during the mandate period, there is a difference in the current tenor of the debate. The realization that Israeli actions themselves are undermining the two-state model and leaving Palestinians with little choice but to embrace the idea of binationalism has brought the discussion over binationalism more into the mainstream. For example, at an Israeli postmortem on the Camp David summit of 2000, this was one of the main observations that emerged. The conference, attended by the former Israeli prime minister, Ehud Barak, his chief negotiators, among them Gilead Sher, Itamar Rabinovich, and former Israeli intelligence officials, as well as senior U.S. participants in the negotiations such as Aaron Miller, Martin Indyk, and Robert Malley, was presented with several analyses that emphasized that, if the two-state solution were not regarded as a feasible and desirable goal for the Palestinians, by default they would be driven to the alternative option. If Palestinians drew the conclusion from Israeli negotiation tactics and strategies that a Palestinian state in the occupied Palestinian territories was not viable, and did not meet the minimum benchmarks of sovereignty, then they would have little choice to either defer an agreement or work toward a one-state solution.[36]

Before proceeding further, we should be clearer about the use of some of the terms in the binationalism debate; the terms *bi-nationalism* and the *one-state* model have been used loosely and often interchangeably. In this discussion I will confine myself to the term *binationalism* as I feel the term *one state* does not allow for enough differentiation. As we will see, there are different ways in which a state comprising two ethnopolitical groups can govern itself, and the term *binationalism* offers more a sense of possible variety than the term *one state*. In essence, the term *binationalism* is used to describe a political system comprising two national groups sharing the same territory and borders. At the same time, however, it includes a number of possible models such as confederalism, federalism, and consociationalism. Examples of these can be found in Switzerland, Belgium, Lebanon, Malaysia, and Germany. In this sense binationalism does not necessarily mean the elision or submergence of separate national identities or of communally based decision making. At a minimum, it is an attempt to provide institutional mechanisms to reconcile competing ethnonational identities within a unitary political system. These coordinating mechanisms can and often do have a territorial basis to them which allows national identities to be associated with certain geographical areas, as in the Swiss, Belgian, and Lebanese examples.[37] In Switzerland, for example, you have German- or French-speaking cantons, territorially separate but working through confederal structures over a range of national issues.

One leading proponent of the binational model is a Palestinian with Israeli citizenship, Dr. As'ad Ghanem. He has sought to delineate the elements that make up variants of the binational model. Recognizing the fundamental changes in the balance of power and mindsets required before such a model would be acceptable not only to Israelis but also to Palestinians, he has tried, nevertheless, to peer into the future and construct a vision of Israelis and Palestinians that combines both confederal and consociational structures. These structures include a broad coalition drawn from Israeli and Palestinian political elites, a right of veto in certain areas, fair representation in whatever legislative assembly is agreed upon, which would be balanced by a quota of offices in state agencies and, importantly, a degree of internal autonomy.[38] From this angle, one can see that there is a continuum of options in the binationalism vision that range from equal citizenship within a single centralized state through to a "binational framework" comprising two territorially separate ethnonational entities with some degree of cooperation and functional interconnectedness.[39] This kind of disaggregation of the binational idea offers possibilities for the kinds of unitary structures that would be appropriate for an entity comprising different ethnicities, cultural backgrounds, and historical narratives. A binational Palestine and Israel would not necessarily be conflated within a single state with a single legislative council, presidency, judiciary, etc., but would retain sufficient differentiation to satisfy the national, cultural, and religious aspirations of their citizens within strong coordinating structures and a supranational level. In essence, there would be a predominantly Palestinian territory and a predominantly Israeli territory bound together with strong coordinating mechanisms in governance, administration, and the economy.

The long, etiolated process of negotiations between Israelis and Palestinians since 1993 has also played, perhaps inadvertently, an important part in giving ballast to the binationalism debate. In discussing the fine print of a possible agreement, analysts, policy makers, and academics in the different behind-the-scenes (or Track 2) negotiations have come to the realization that an extraordinarily high degree of cooperation will be required between the two parties and the two states. There is a growing understanding that if a peace agreement is to avoid the total separation suggested by the separation barrier running through the West Bank and the fences surrounding Gaza, and if it is to avoid the alienation of the vast majority of Palestinian refugees, it will be essential to have state-to-state coordination across a wide range of responsibilities.[40]

Cooperation on such a comprehensive scale points to coordinating arrangements that are much more than a standard bilateral treaty between two states and much closer to an EU model of partial integration. It has already been accepted in the various meeting at Camp David and Taba that the two-state model in the Palestinian-Israeli conflict will consist of a range of agreements that will extend beyond intelligence and security cooperation, also encompassing the economy and trade, the environment, including the extraction of water, regional urban planning, tourism, immigration, etc. There are agreements also in place for a single economic zone for Israel and Palestine, for a customs union, for the sharing of water, which point to a merging of the two states at some fundamental levels. In this sense the binationalism debate poses a false dichotomy because the one-state model with its institutional cooperative structures and functional interconnectedness is not so distant from the more idealized vision of the two-state model with its proposals for open borders, economic unions, and security cooperation. Both require a degree of coordination leading to a dilution or a sharing of sovereignty. It is this degree of inter-state penetration which suggests that in essence what is being discussed as a two-state model is in fact a sort of "two-state-plus" model, which, on further analysis, looks remarkably close to some variants of the binational model.

I would also like to put this binationalism debate into a longer historical perspective, as I think it reveals some underlying trends that are not immediate apparently when one is immersed in current affairs. From a longer perspective on the Arab-Israeli conflict, one can conclude two things: first, there are strong indications that political Zionism, as a project promoting religious and ethnic dominance over the land of former Palestine, is a project in retreat. Second, the most likely guarantor of continued Jewish presence in its biblical homeland is an accommodation with the indigenous Palestinian population. Taking the contention of Israeli retreat, few would want to dispute the facts of physical and geographical withdrawal from territory. The peak of Israel's expansion was in 1967 with its conquest of the Golan Heights, West Bank, Gaza Strip, and Sinai Peninsula. Recall that, having withdrawn from the Sinai Peninsula in 1977, in 1982 Israel controlled all the land from the Egyptian border up to and including Beirut. Since then it has withdrawn incrementally from south Lebanon, all of the Gaza Strip, parts of the West Bank, and is contemplating further withdrawals from the West Bank. More important, it has made these later withdrawals without coming to a final agreement with the Palestinians and without agreement with most of the Arab world, also refusing until quite recently to recognize Palestinian rights to an independent Palestinian state. The withdrawals may have been presented as an exhibition of strength, and Israeli politicians have conferred upon them a grand term—*unilateralism*—but this cannot mask the strategic retrenchment at their core. The observation and contention that Zionism is a project in retreat does not ignore the fact that there are other forms of domination possible and that a territorial retreat does not mean that Israel is no longer the military supremo or economic powerhouse of the region. For example, while it has withdrawn its troops from the Gaza Strip and evacuated its colonies there, it still controls access to the strip and the airspace above it and the waters around it. It is still able to project force remotely and effectively. Nevertheless, one cannot escape the fact that an overall territorial retreat has taken place and, more important, that any further agreement with the Palestinians, however limited, will lead to further withdrawals.

These unilateral withdrawals suggest both a strategic and an intellectual confusion in the political establishment of Israel over the future of both Zionism and of the direction of the state. An example of this strategic confusion is the separation barrier constructed around the West Bank. As we saw in chapter 1, over one-third of the wall is not congruent with the Armistice Lines of 1949. Indeed, some sections cut deep into the West Bank and encircle large parts of East Jerusalem.[41] This departure from the Armistice Lines of 1949 opens up a Pandora's box: by abandoning the internationally recognized borders through the construction of the separation barrier, Israeli has opened up the question of the sanctity of these lines. By unraveling the consensus on the 1967 borders, the Israeli political elite has inadvertently raised the question of the future of Galilee and the Triangle. These are both predominantly Palestinian areas inside Israel and close to the West Bank and were both designated part of the Palestinian Arab state in the UN partition plan of 1947. In this way one can see that once one departs from the Armistice Lines of 1949 as the agreed border, the Israeli argument for a border further east based on demography, that is, along the Jordan River, can be matched by a Palestinian argument for a border further west based on demography incorporating the Triangle and the Galilee.

A similar strategic confusion is also apparent over Israeli positions on Jerusalem. In the broader negotiations, Israel opposes the return of significant numbers of Palestinian refugees to their ancestral homes in what is now Israel on demographic grounds. A large influx of Palestinian refugees would swamp the Jewish population and render them a minority in their own country. At the same time, it insists on controlling over two hundred thousand Palestinians in East Jerusalem and the surrounding suburbs on the grounds that they are residing in the "eternal" capital of Israel, although these numbers of Palestinians impact upon its efforts to maintain a Jewish majority in the city. These contradictory responses to Palestinian presence in the state reflect a lack of clarity as to its long-term relationship with them. This confusion points to the long-term Zionist dilemma concerning Israeli identity and the fate of the people it replaced: who are, ultimately, the inhabitants of this land and the citizens of the new state? Who should be kept in and who should be locked out? In this "long view" of the Zionist trajectory in Palestine, the Palestinians have demonstrated that they cannot be compared to the Native American Indians who were defeated militarily and finally contained by European settlers to the U.S. in reservations. Instead, the Palestinians have established themselves as a political force and are demanding the same rights to a state as the Zionist settlers did.

Addressing this dilemma is closely connected to the debate on binationalism. A useful way of understanding how the current impasse in the negotiations is related to the longer trends and broader issues is to turn to the literature on democratization in political science.[42] A leading theorist of this school, Dankwort Rustow (1970), identified four phases in which a divided society has to pass before democracy is established.[43] The first phase is that of defining what is the nation. During this phase groups compete with each other to have their identity and rights recognized in the political arrangements of the new state. In addition, there is debate and conflict over the borders of the new state, with some areas included and others excluded. The second phase is known as the historic compromise phase. Here, after a long struggle, the political elites of the competing groups recognize that neither side can achieve supremacy over the others, and they finally agree to negotiate a grand bargain specifying their roles and rights. This bargain forms the basis of the new political system. The third phase is called the habituation phase. In this phase the political elites begin to work out how the new system can be used to their advantage without jeopardizing the overall bargain. The final phase, the consolidation phase, is where these systems are embedded and group competition is mediated through normal democratic political processes.[44]

In the context of the binational model and the retreat of Zionism I have outlined, I would argue that the Palestinian-Israeli conflict is going through the first phase of Rustow's model. The conflict is ultimately about defining who comprises the emerging nation based on the land of former mandatory Palestine and what its borders are. But it is also moving gradually into the second phase of historic compromise whereby the competing groups recognize that the other side cannot be eliminated or neutralized. The Oslo Accord marked the end of the first phase and the beginning of the second phase, but its impending failure show that the accords did not sufficiently encompass the concerns of all those involved, and since 2000 we are seeing a return to the first phase. The Oslo Accord implied the establishment of a Palestinian state, but it was not sufficiently credible enough to Palestinians to constitute the "historic compromise" that would allow a new composite state. In Rustow's scheme there will not be movement toward the second phase without an agreement between the two groups that incorporates the following compromises: First, Palestinians of all political groupings will need to agree to share the land of Palestine and recognize the permanent presence of Israeli Jewish migration. For their part, the Israeli political groups need to recognize Palestinian rights to the land of historic Palestine and reconcile themselves to a more inclusive vision of a Jewish national home and of Zionism in which the state is not defined by its Jewishness although Judaism will still play an important role. Without these two fundamental prerequisites, it is unlikely that the Palestinian-Israeli case can move from phase one to phase two. As the debate on binationalism reflects the ebb and flow of the negotiations between the two sides, the potential role played by Jerusalem as both major city and capital of both states will continue to be crucial.

The role of Jerusalem in this debate is central.[45] If Jerusalem is to become a functioning city and the capital of both the Israeli and the Palestinian state, it will require a sophisticated degree of coordinating structures between the two sides of the city that will, in turn, have a significant impact on interstate relations between Israel and Palestine. My argument is that this would be the case in either of the two models—binational or two state—under discussion and for Jerusalem is thus a false dichotomy. If there is a complete separation between the two states which will be divided by a "hard" border and a "cold" peace, then these coordinating arrangements are less likely to occur. Indeed, my argument goes further in that the creation of coordinating structures will transform the two-state model into what I have termed the "two-state plus model."

TOWARD AN AGREEMENT

In my previous books on Jerusalem I have avoided presenting a plan for the resolution of the Jerusalem issue. There were two reasons for this. First I was aware of the large number of plans already in circulation, many of them containing useful and important possibilities, and I did not wish to clutter up the discussion with yet another variant. Rather, I felt that my contribution could be to draw out some of the underlying issues that needed addressing and some of the overarching principles that would frame a viable agreement. The second reason is the awareness from my research and discussions with people involved in the negotiations over Jerusalem across many years that I never quite had the complete picture, that there were always variables I did not know about and pressures and trends emerging that I had not considered. My view always seemed to be obscured and veiled, and it was pointless, therefore, to present a plan based on a partial knowledge of the overall situation. I realize, now, that this sense of "more to find out" goes with the territory. Neither an academic, however much she or he is engaged with policy makers, nor even policy makers at the heart of the negotiation process themselves will have the complete picture, and ultimately all they can only offer is their best shot. Indeed, it may be the case that an academic, slightly detached by vocation, by geographical and political distance, should be able to offer insights and ideas that would not be obvious to someone who has to roll her sleeves up on a daily basis to address and confront demands and claims from the other side. So in this last section I take the plunge and suggest a possible way of dealing with two of the most contentious issues confronting negotiators on Jerusalem: the security concerns of Israel and the question of the holy sites in the Old City.

Before entering into any details, we have to be clear from the outset that any agreement would be based upon the assumption that Palestinian sovereignty will be recognized in all areas east of the 1949 Armistice Lines and the de facto borders that existed in 1967 and that Israeli sovereignty will be recognized on the western side of these lines, subject to mutual territorial exchanges equal in size and value. While there is a great likelihood that there may be arrangements imposed upon Palestinians or a series of transitional or interim agreements, I do not foresee there being any prospect of a lasting or comprehensive agreement between the two parties without this recognition as a prerequisite. Following on from this, we can also assume that the governance of Jerusalem will comprise two municipalities: a Palestinian East Jerusalem municipality and an Israeli West Jerusalem municipality, and there will be a supramanagement body to coordinate the activities of these municipalities. This basic framework has emerged as the only workable one in nearly all the discussions and proposals presented hitherto.

In addressing the security concerns of the Israelis without compromising Palestinian sovereignty, I believe that it is possible to reconsider the vision of an "open city" that was proposed in the mid-1990s, making use of much of the valuable work carried out by the various Track 2 activities such as the Geneva Initiative and the Jerusalem Old City Initiative and learning from international precedents including the EU Schengen Agreement. The open city concept for Jerusalem was a response to Israeli fears that Palestinian sovereignty over East Jerusalem would lead to its division and consequently the lack of access to Jewish holy sites and property there.[46] The open city concept also promoted the vision of an inclusive city incorporating different nationalities and religions. The basic operational element is that an open city will permit the free movement of persons and goods within a zone through which the national border between Israel and Palestine also runs, and this zone will be, to all intents and purposes, invisible. All controls appropriate to national borders will be exercised at the exits of the open city zone.[47] Despite this, there would be an internal border running through the open city zone, and full sovereignty will be exercised by Palestine and Israel in those sections of the open city zone on their sides of that internal border. In order to oversee this zone, a set of institutions and agencies would be developed to coordinate functions and activities on the two sides the open city zone. In this way, the Jerusalem open city zone should permit free movement of persons and goods throughout the city of Jerusalem, without putting in question the sovereignty of Palestine and Israel over those portions of Jerusalem within their national boundaries. Following the wave of attacks on Israeli targets by Palestinian militants and the construction of the separation barrier, Israeli interest in the open city concept waned dramatically. Nevertheless, the concept continues to hold sway in some circles as the only means by which the city can remain viable as an urban unit, and it continues to be the preferred option of the current PLO leadership.[48]

What is required in a reconsideration of this idea is a greater emphasis on the security aspects of the open city and the mechanics of how the zone will work. An open city zone will involve cross-border cooperation in many areas—ranging from the provision of services to planning and zoning of construction to measures to stimulate economic development—but the focus of this section will be on what is surely the prerequisite for any of these activities to take place, that is, the provision of security and the establishment of an effective policing system. At the same time, such provision needs to take place within a political framework that meets the aspirations of both the Israelis and the Palestinians.

In this context, then, I want to explore the idea of delineating an open city "security zone" for security purposes within which movement across the city for people, goods, and vehicles will be unimpeded. In the first place, we should recognize that the open city security zone will not necessarily be identical with the borders of the two municipalities or of any interstate coordinated regional planning zones. As we saw in previous chapters and in the experience of other divided cities, borders with different functions are not always congruent with each other. In this scenario Jerusalem would have a security cordon running round the city irrespective of the location of the political borders. In addition, the governments of Palestine and Israel would draw up two conventions, a legal convention and a policing convention, that would apply to this zone and comprise a strong cooperative framework between the two states. A final feature of the zone would be that the governments of Palestine and Israel would agree on a mandate for third party assistance in liaison, coordination, and oversight activities.

In order to understand how this zone would work in practice, I spell out some details of the essential elements. These are drawn from discussion with members of the security services and police forces, from papers submitted to various Track 2 workshops, and from the security report of the JOCI proposal. The first detail to consider is the route of the security cordon itself. This would make use of suitable urban and topographical features such as road systems, junctions, barriers, and perimeters of the residential areas and valleys. In deciding on the size of the open city zone and the location of the perimeter of the cordon, there is a balance that needs to be struck between urban planning issues, such as the location of roads, junctions, and major traffic flows, and political and security issues. The optimum conditions for such a zone would be if there was a "warm" peace between the two states where there is a "soft" permeable border between Palestine and Israel. In this situation there would be easy passage between the two states, and it would be more beneficial to have a smaller open city security zone. Since, in this scenario, the free flow of traffic between Palestine and Israel would not have many obstacles, the zone need not, therefore, be so extensive.

If there is a "hard" border between the two countries, then the open city security zone would need to be larger in order to maximize the urban space in Jerusalem which is unimpeded by controls. However, a hard border is the most likely result of a "cold" peace between the two parties, and a cold peace will make the security coordination between the two parties more difficult. In addition, a larger open city security zone would require more security coordination over a greater area and over a greater number of people. Thus there would be greater potential for disagreements and problems. For these reasons I do not imagine that an open city would be feasible in any conditions other than a warm peace and a "soft" border between the two states. However, it is likely that in any agreement there will be a transitional phase that will involve some elements of a cold peace and a hard border for a limited period of time.

Planners and security experts recommend that any security cordon should be as close to the shape of a circle as possible in order to keep it compact and minimize difficult areas for surveillance, and this consideration should be taken seriously. In particular, the Jerusalem open city security zone should avoid, as we saw in the Geneva Initiative, extended "tongues" of land that are difficult to patrol and monitor. Most important, the security cordon should be aligned along existing features such as major roads with few junctions. Similarly, in order to minimize resentment by local residents, the cordon should avoid going through areas of visual and environmental importance. The route should also avoid dividing residential areas from local commercial centers, as this would have the beneficial impact of reducing the volume of traffic between points inside and outside the security cordon A further consideration is that territorial exchanges in the agreement between Palestine and Israel may result in the creation of Israeli enclaves (former settlements) inside the East Jerusalem municipality. These areas would remain under Israeli legal jurisdiction and receive services from the Israeli West Jerusalem municipality and will be surrounded by an internal border identical to that separating East and West Jerusalem. Where these Israeli enclaves are contiguous with the Israeli West Jerusalem, consideration should be given for these to be ceded to Israel in exchange for comparable territory for the state of Palestine. The connecting transportation routes between the Israeli enclaves and the Israeli West Jerusalem municipal area will remain the sovereignty of Palestine, although mechanisms for joint patrols should be in place to respond to times of high tension. A final consideration regarding the route of the cordon would be that the existing ring-road system may require alteration to avoid north-south traffic entering the open city zone unnecessarily. Some access roads may have to be closed in order to ensure traffic and people enter and exit only through the control points.

The smooth running of well-placed control points for entry and exit to the open city security zone of Jerusalem are a critical part of its feasibility. In this scheme they will function in the same way as national entry and exit on the international borders. In terms of exiting the Jerusalem security zone into Israel or Palestine, the operation of the exit control points will be the responsibility of either the Israeli or Palestinian governments and need not be identical. It is their responsibility how they wish to monitor those leaving Jerusalem and entering their territory. The entry into the open city security zone will be a different matter. This will be a coordinated activity between Israel and Palestine police and security services. A border entry coordination body will be established, with the option of international third party oversight, to ensure that the communication of risks and threats are direct and responded to in an agreed manner.

While the operational details of these control points are beyond the scope of this chapter, some examples can be given to indicate the nature of the coordination required. For example, it is clear that only persons and vehicles with valid authorization will be permitted to enter or exit the zone. A study for the PLO's Negotiations Support Unit in 2001 by an urban planner, Professor Antony Coon, estimated that ninety thousand people would be crossing into a Jerusalem open city zone based upon the inner ring-roads of the city. Nine thousand an hour will cross at peak periods in the morning and early evening.[49] These figures will need to be updated, but they give an idea of the scale of the challenge. Coon estimated that, with twenty control points (four on the Israeli side and sixteen on the Palestinian—the difference is due to the road systems), they would need to process fifteen persons every minute at peak times. One way to speed up the flow of persons and traffic would be to make available separate entry and exit points to permanent residents of the open city zone and also to allow people without bags to enter through an "express" line. Another way would be to construct good public transportation between control points and the city center, with park and ride facilities on the outside. For vehicles passing through the control points, automatic number plate reading systems (ANPRS) would be connected to national police databases to speed up identification. A joint Palestinian-Israeli "hot list" should be established to remove any potential disagreements over a range of individuals.

The EU Schengen model has set useful precedents which could be emulated in these areas, and a brief discussion of its achievements is worth including here. In May 1999, at the Treaty of Amsterdam, the Schengen Agreement was incorporated into the first pillar of the EU and expressed the aim to establish in the EU a borderless "area of freedom, security and justice."[50] In essence, the agreement, which includes all members of the EU (except the UK), provides for closer cooperation between member states in the police, customs, and the judiciary. Part of this cooperation was the establishment of the Schengen Information System (SIS) and other institutions and mechanisms for shared intelligence and border controls. These institutions and mechanisms include the designation of a "central authority" as a single point of contact responsible for all international police cooperation. The central authority, it was agreed, should be reachable by all national police and border services on a twenty-four hour basis; it should provide for the location of all liaison officers on a single site; it should have all relevant information on cooperation including a centralized list of requests for assistance, and, finally, it should have analytical capacity on criminal intelligence data. Not all aspects of the Schengen Agreement are applicable to the running of a security zone in Jerusalem, but of the features most relevant are those which include the establishment of joint police stations to which are devolved policing responsibilities. In the same way, the Schengen Agreement established police and customs cooperation centers, which have no operational jurisdiction but provide assistance and advice to units responsible for police, border, and customs tasks in cross-border relations. The agreement also lays down operational guidelines in which joint teams and patrols guarantee the protection of the officers of the adjoining state as if they were of their own. Finally, an essential component of these administrative and legal coordinating frameworks in the Schengen Agreement provides for the compatibility of communication equipment and information technology systems.[51]

The Schengen Agreement has evolved, and emphasis is placed on evaluative studies, on extensive liaison and better communication, and on a high level of training. Recent recommendations, for example, suggest that police, custom, and border authorities of the participant states should work "towards a common strategy for training in Schengen matters."[52] At first sight the Schengen Agreement seems a highly improbable precedent. It is a highly complex and evolving agreement that encompasses a wide range of policing responsibilities involving many countries.[53] The likelihood of it being effective appears remote. Nevertheless, the strong interests of the parties involved have made it succeed. What is remarkable and significant for the Jerusalem case is the willingness of the policing and technocratic professionals in over twenty states to create workable operational coordinating systems. A security coordination agreement for Jerusalem would only involve two parties and a much smaller population and geographic spread. There are, of course, special issues to take into account in Jerusalem, such as the sensitivity of the holy sites in the city and the high number of tourists on which intelligence data is limited, but these are no more complex than those and other issues being dealt with in the Schengen zone. In a culture of political agreement, this kind of cross-border cooperation in policing, security, and customs in Jerusalem is not unattainable.

Within the zone itself, security will be enforced through a combination of joint and coordinated Israeli-Palestinian policing, agreed parameters where Israeli and Palestinian police have sole responsibility, and some areas where there would be third party participation. Palestinian and Israeli courts would be responsible for personal jurisdiction, that is, Palestinian law would apply to Palestinian nationals and Israeli law to Israeli nationals, but subject to the legal and policing conventions applying to the zone. This would reassure those most politically opposed to such a zone that their nationals will be fairly treated within the overall agreement that encompasses the conventions. Crimes committed by third party nationals would be the jurisdiction of the law of the country through which they entered into Jerusalem. While there may be some evidential problems associated with this, such as Israeli courts relying on evidence from Palestinian police and vice versa, the shortcomings of this approach are generally outweighed by the advantages of such a system ensuring that Israel and Palestine border controls are responsible for whom they allow into the security zone. Commercial crimes committed on the other side of the internal border and crimes against property belonging to persons of the nationality on the other side will be placed under the jurisdiction of special joint criminal courts. Clearly these guidelines cannot encompass all eventualities, so, for matters where there is a dispute between the two parties over whose competence should take priority, a tribunal will be established whose chair will be an international judge.

The success of the zone will depend greatly on coordination between Israel and Palestine on all levels—municipal services, planning, economic development—but security coordination will be paramount and a prerequisite. In order to clarify this, there should be a Palestinian-Israeli convention on legal and policing cooperation and assistance covering, for example, routine extradition, rights of hot pursuit, definitions of criminal activity, convergence on status of evidence, and investigative procedures. There should also be a joint Palestinian and Israeli liaison unit based in a central location of the city with some joint units established for serious crimes such as smuggling, organized crime, narcotics, murder, and kidnapping. As is usual in such postconflict policing coordination, there would be daily risk assessment meetings between Israeli and Palestinian counterparts so that threat levels are communicated regularly to the border control points. Additional specialized joint Palestinian-Israeli joint units for surveillance and counterterrorism would have third party oversight and monitoring and develop close connections with both national agencies and with Interpol.

In general, policing in the city will be what is termed "intelligence led" with emphasis placed on establishing good relations with the different communities of the city. Overtly armed police would be kept to a minimum, but, in the event of extreme events or public disorder, both parties should have recourse to backup forces. Their deployment will be according to criteria established by the conventions already mentioned. The area within the security cordon would be a weapons-free area in which only authorized police, security and army personnel will be permitted to bear arms, and no civilians would be allowed to carry weapons. Israeli enclaves in East Jerusalem that in this scenario have been either ceded to Israel or leased for an extended period will be subjected to Israeli law and criminal code, but all other Israeli residence or land use shall be subject to the Palestinian criminal code in the framework of the conventions agreed with Israel. In areas of potentially high friction, such as adjacent Palestinian and Israeli areas and on the perimeter of Israeli enclaves, community policing approaches should be introduced in order to prioritize the concerns of residents. One way to achieve this could be the creation of neighborhood police councils and an online complaints procedure, monitored by third party officials, made available for all residents and visitors to the open city zone.[54]

Finally, police officers from both states working in the security zone would be members of the Jerusalem police service and would be given a distinct uniform to indicate the additional and separate responsibilities its officers carry out. The logo or crest or other distinguishing features could be devised so that a joint symbol is attached to the uniforms of both police services. Recruits to the Jerusalem police service would undergo additional training for their special responsibilities in Jerusalem. This will include training with their Israeli and Palestinian counterparts in specific area such as investigative procedures, definitions of crime, judicial systems, as well as in language, social customs, and public expectations of policing.

A particular issue is, of course, the policing of the holy sites of the city. During Ramadan, the Friday prayers in the Haram al-Sharif can attract up to 250,000 worshippers crowded into a very small space and with difficult points of entry and exit. During the Jewish High Holy Days, crowds of some 30,000 Jews can file through the Old City toward the Wailing Wall. Similarly, on Easter Saturday some 50 to 60,000 Christian worshippers will flock to the courtyard in front of the Church of the Holy Sepulchre. All these festivities and observances put enormous strains upon security and police services and require close coordination and planning with the heads of the different communities. When there is a breakdown in coordination and public trust, then incidents and confrontations occur. In chapter 4, in discussing the role of UNESCO in the city, we referred to controversy provoked by the Mughrabi ascent incident in 2007. In this incident over three thousand Israeli policemen and women were required to deal with the threat to public order it caused. This was estimated to be between 100–150 percent larger than routine Israeli security forces. One particular trigger point can be the clash of dates, as some holidays are fixed by the solar calendar, while others by the lunar one.

Under this open city security zone, a special unit, possibly called the Holy Sites Police Unit (HSPU), will be created for the policing of the holy sites. The role of the HSPU would be to ensure respect for the sanctity of the holy sites, to ensure unimpeded access by residents, pilgrims, and tourists to the chief holy sites in the city, and to prevent any damage to them or any incidents that may disturb their operations. An initial task would be the compiling of a list of key sites and the procedures for responding to security threats. What would be essential and declared at the outset is that the HSPU would preserve the "status quo" arrangements established by the Ottoman authorities and those supplementary arrangements that have been in operation following the British mandate period. Any changes or revisions will be based upon agreements between the governments of Palestine and Israel and other international bodies or submitted to a special arbitration tribunal. The HSPU will be led by international third party police officers. For policing matters related to sites of a particular religious community, the unit involved should include personnel from the relevant police service. For example, anything to do with the Wailing Wall should involve Israeli members of the Jerusalem police service. To reassure the custodians of the holy places and to obtain the support of the religious hierarchies and lay members of the different communities, there should be a clear prohibition of the entry of armed units into the holy sites with the exception of extreme circumstances such as the threat to fabric of the buildings or the lives of those within it. In liaison with the religious authorities in the city, members of this unit would have additional training in religious and cultural issues involved in the protection of these sites. In general, the HSPU would maintain good relations with the relevant religious authorities and draw up plans for the protection of holy sites that involve them where it would be appropriate.

The conditions for negotiating an open city security zone as I have described are currently lacking. As I discussed earlier, the incentive for Israel to make the kinds of concessions that would come close to Palestinian "red lines" and aspirations is just not there. However, the main thrust of my argument in this book is that, since it is clear that the borders of the city are not sacrosanct and immutable, all is not lost in the search for a negotiated agreement. Indeed, the span of history under review has shown how very movable the borders of the city have been. And this fluidity over time holds out prospects that areas which were once seen to be irreversibly on one side or the other are, in reality, open to compromise and negotiation. But, more significantly, this book has highlighted the fluidity of the city's borders both within and throughout the city. Much of the argument around this point has been based upon empirical evidence and analysis that the city is criss-crossed with a variety of hard, soft, permeable, and impermeable borders whose relevance and resonance come to the fore or recede depending upon the political circumstances. In times of violence between the two communities, the lines that demarcate the residential segregation of Israelis and Palestinians take on a defensive protective role and may emerge as the future lines dividing the city. During the more recent phase of Palestinian state building in the West Bank and Gaza Strip, the borders of the Palestinian electoral district running through East Jerusalem and the educational curricula taught in Palestinian schools—both virtual borders—take on much greater meaning in terms of identity construction and culture than, for example, those of the Israeli municipal border which has become increasingly defunct in the eastern part of the city.

This fluidity has been engendered partly by the graduated and selective way in which the Israeli state has inserted itself into East Jerusalem. Primarily concerned with establishing military control and the utilization of land, other state and municipal functions were neglected. A key element in this differentiated approach to state and municipal provision on the part of Israel has been ideological. The militant form of Zionism that has come to dominate Israeli politics in and concerning the city has excluded Palestinians from a national Israeli vision and led Palestinians to rely not upon the Israeli state but rather alternative sources for political representation, for funding, and for parallel, if not competing, forms of organizational structure.

An important addition to this dynamic of fluid borders is the presence of the holy sites. The physical area they encompass, the relatively independent clerical superstructure that acts as their guardian, the regional and international networks of social and political relationships created as a result of their centrality in three of the world's religions have an impact on

Israel's role in the city. They all combine to dilute the power of the Israeli state and to allow an archipelago of institutions across the city to operate quasi-autonomously and below the radar. Supporting these institutions and the Palestinian presence in the city are a wide range of international actors from the UN and its daughter agencies to the EU, the U.S. (more half-heartedly), and states and foundations in the Arab and Islamic world. By affirming international law and international benchmarks in the modes of operation, these actors also add to the constraints on the Israeli exercise of its sovereignty.

The argument has also drawn some of its strength from the recognition that these are attributes and processes that Jerusalem holds in common with a number of other divided and occupied cities. Divided cities such as Belfast, Beirut, Mostar, and Nicosia are overshadowed by the same ethnonational rivalries that attract chauvinistic politicians and ideologues who seek to contain and control subordinate groups within their cities, often by denying them a role or constraining their activities. Looking for external support, these subordinate groups draw in the international community and regional actors, who all contribute to the emergence of the many-borders syndrome seen in Jerusalem with a range of functions on different levels. In this area Jerusalem may have a longer sustained institutional presence of the UN and other international bodies than any of the other cities studied in the Conflict and Cities project, but it is not unique. The UN presence in Nicosia is essential and far-reaching; the role of international agencies and the EU in Mostar has been profound. The one area in which Jerusalem can claim unquestionable uniqueness is, of course, the impact of religion and the presence of the holy sites. By virtue of increasing the number of significant actors, the presence of religion has introduced a far more complex dynamic between the Israeli and Palestinian protagonists. Nevertheless, the examination of the city of Jerusalem in light of not only its differences but also its similarities with other cities that are divided or occupied has thrown into sharp relief the pattern of external involvement and constraints of state power that all of them experience in different ways.

The overall argument of this book has been that the borders we have highlighted, which exist and function in different ways and on different levels, and the constraints on Israeli power in the city all combine to explain the resilience of the Palestinian enclaves in Jerusalem after forty-five years of Israeli occupation. They also, cumulatively, point to an argument that the presence of the enclaves will be enduring, dynamic, and, in some aspects, possibly threatening to Israeli control over the city. Short of a spate of cataclysmic ethnic cleansing of Palestinians, a wholly Jewish Jerusalem is, consequently, an unrealistic fantasy. A quiescent and docile Palestinian population for all time is only a slightly less fantastical option. The Palestinian challenge to Israeli dominance in Jerusalem, therefore, will have to be confronted. The roots of the Palestinian community in the city are too deep and its support too widespread and pervasive to be dealt with effectively by zoning, by imposing changes in residency status, by sequestering property, by the neglect of services, and by brute intimidation. The city will ultimately have to be shared. Currently the political elites on both sides are tempted by the possibility of some *deus ex machina* intervention that will provide the decisive blow which either recognizes the new Israeli presence in the city or returns the Palestinians to their previous state of preeminence, at least in the central area of the city. Nevertheless, there is enough evidence ranging from participants in various Track 2 negotiations over the city to suggest that some sections of both those elites understand that Jerusalem is an ethnically and religiously mixed city. By its very nature, the future stability and prosperity of the city is dependent on the capacity of Israelis and Palestinians to accommodate each other in the same city.

In closing, we return to our observer, possibly even a morning runner, standing on the brow of the Mount of Olives. Having read this book, what should she or he now see? My hope is that the observer can now see how the city is one of many fragments and more than just of two parts; how visible and invisible lines crisscross its face creating myriad different social, economic, and political groupings; how its streets change from Friday to Saturday to Sunday, from Christmas to Pesach to 'Eid al Adha. I also hope the observer would realize that these fragments and changing facades cumulatively reveal a complex political dynamic concerning the future of the city. While the city is being fought over by two ethnonational camps, a simple territorial partition will be damaging for the city as a whole and also for the two parts that would result. A negotiated agreement will need to reflect its heterogeneous makeup and overlapping histories. I also would imagine the observer would see, over the past forty-six years since the Israeli occupation of the city, how the gold of the Dome of the Rock remains the iconic monument of the city, and there is, as yet, no other monument or park or institution that has replaced it. But our observer would also be aware that the dark brooding presence of the separation barrier is lining itself up to do so.

APPENDIX: WEB SITE AND FACEBOOK SURVEYS

TABLE AP1.1

JERUSALEM: WEB SEARCH RESULTS (MAY 18–23, 2012)

JERUSALEM

SEARCH ENGINE	ANY	ENGLISH	FRENCH	ARABIC	FARSI	RUSSIAN	CHINESE
Google	137,000,000	219,000,000	11,200,000	1,360,000	273,000	2,370,000	1,010,000
Bing	167,000,000	100,000,000	13,000,000	901,000	44,100	429,000	96,300
Yahoo	182,000,000	127,000,000	914,000	924,000	0	553	91,400
AOL,	137,000,000	258,000,000	17,800,000	1,950,000	277,000	3,270,000	1,010,000
Youtube	119,000						

TABLE AP1.2

MAJOR CITIES OF THE WORLD: WEB SEARCH RESULTS (MAY 18–23, 2012)

1. NEW YORK

SEARCH ENGINE	ANY	ENGLISH	FRENCH	ARABIC	FARSI	RUSSIAN	CHINESE
Google	3,000,000,000	8,200,000,000	455,000,000	8,660,000	2,710,000	26,000,000	19,500,000
Bing	44,700,000	1,610,000,000	40,400,000	1,020,000	383,000	3,670,000	1,760,000

	ANY	ENGLISH	FRENCH	ARABIC	FARSI	RUSSIAN	CHINESE
Yahoo	41,500,000	1,920,000,000	77,100,000	3,430,000	-	6,060,000	17,300,000
AOL	3,000,000,000	6,980,000,000	487,000,000	105,000,000	3,660,000	87,900,000	63,900,000
Youtube	1,780,000						

2. LONDON

SEARCH ENGINE	ANY	ENGLISH	FRENCH	ARABIC	FARSI	RUSSIAN	CHINESE
Google	2,150,000,000	5,450,000,000	170,000,000	15,200,000	3,590,000	35,000,000	22,300,000
Bing	1,130,000,000	1,430,000,000	21,300,000	4,440,000	1,030,000	5,940,000	1,970,000
Yahoo	1,300,000,000	1,260,000,000	23,200,000	4,110,000	-	5,840,000	1,810,000
AOL	2,170,000,000	4,530,000,000	219,000,000	27,000,000	21,000,000	62,900,000	44,800,000
Youtube	1,350,000						

3. TOKYO

SEARCH ENGINE	ANY	ENGLISH	FRENCH	ARABIC	FARSI	RUSSIAN	CHINESE
Google	606,000,000	904,000,000	52,400,000	1,210,000	349,000	26,000,000	14,500,000
Bing	341,000,000	196,000,000	11,400,000	492,000	129,000	956,000	1,590,000

	ANY	ENGLISH	FRENCH	ARABIC	FARSI	RUSSIAN	CHINESE
Yahoo	366,000,000	221,000,000	13,300,000	485,000	-	1,170,000	1,860,000
AOL	606,000,000	1,070,000,000	121,000,000	1,700,000	357,000	29,700,000	14,500,000
Youtube	454,000						

4. PARIS

SEARCH ENGINE	ANY	ENGLISH	FRENCH	ARABIC	FARSI	RUSSIAN	CHINESE
Google	1,960,000,000	2,200,000,000	873,000,000	20,000,000	2,390,000	24,800,000	28,200,000
Bing	1,010,000,000	596,000,000	225,000,000	2,340,000	675,000	3,380,000	1,750,000
Yahoo							
AOL							
Youtube	1,290,000						

5. HONG KONG

SEARCH ENGINE	ANY	ENGLISH	FRENCH	ARABIC	FARSI	RUSSIAN	CHINESE
Google	1,040,000,000	1,340,000,000	117,000,000	7,180,000	702,000	90,900,000	26,400,000
Bing	368,000,000	262,000,000	8,980,000	1,540,000	63,400	701,000	2,380,000

	ANY
Yahoo	
AOL	
Youtube	228,000

6. CHICAGO

SEARCH ENGINE	ANY	ENGLISH	FRENCH	ARABIC	FARSI	RUSSIAN	CHINESE
Google	1,210,000,000	3,900,000,000	56,400,000	5,220,000	987,000	8,640,000	17,100,000
Bing	646,000,000	802,000,000	13,600,000	216,000	192,000	1,790,000	572,000
Yahoo							
AOL							
Youtube	632,000						

7. LOS ANGELES

SEARCH ENGINE	ANY	ENGLISH	FRENCH	ARABIC	FARSI	RUSSIAN	CHINESE
Google	1,250,000,000	3,170,000,000	172,000,000	2,030,000	935,000	12,100,000	20,000,000
Bing	787,000,000	602,000,000	13,800,000	198,000	143,000	597,000	524,000
Yahoo							

SEARCH ENGINE							
AOL							
Youtube	1,980,000						

8. SINGAPORE

SEARCH ENGINE	ANY	ENGLISH	FRENCH	ARABIC	FARSI	RUSSIAN	CHINESE
Google	1,120,000,000	1,100,000,000	19,600,000	4,520,000	573,000	11,100,000	20,100,000
Bing	260,000,000	363,000,000	3,810,000	1,680,000	127,000	792,000	2,000,000
Yahoo							
AOL							
Youtube	650,000						

9. SYDNEY

SEARCH ENGINE	ANY	ENGLISH	FRENCH	ARABIC	FARSI	RUSSIAN	CHINESE
Google	2,450,000,000	1,210,000,000	17,300,000	1,010,000	319,000	4,470,000	4,780,000
Bing	343,000,000	330,000,000	8,690,000	146,000	78,500	522,000	638,000
Yahoo							
AOL							
Youtube	382,000						

10. SEOUL

SEARCH ENGINE	ANY	ENGLISH	FRENCH	ARABIC	FARSI	RUSSIAN	CHINESE
Google	171,000,000	196,000,000	4,060,000	544,000	2,580,000	1,370,000	4,110,000
Bing	71,500,000	50,800,000	2,860,000	96,900	44,800	142,000	463,000
Yahoo							
AOL							
Youtube	122,000						

TABLE AP1.3

DIVIDED CITIES (CONFLICT IN CITIES AND THE CONTESTED STATE PROJECT) WEB SEARCH RESULTS (MAY 18–23, 2012)

1. BEIRUT

SEARCH ENGINE	ANY	ENGLISH	FRENCH	ARABIC	FARSI	RUSSIAN	CHINESE
Google	63,300,000	122,000,000	2,810,000	25,700,000	83,400	814,000	364,000
Bing	46,300,000	39,700,000	739,000	1,440,000	16,300	74,000	40,000
Yahoo							
AOL							
Youtube	56,800						

2. KIRKUK

SEARCH ENGINE	ANY	ENGLISH	FRENCH	ARABIC	FARSI	RUSSIAN	CHINESE
Google	5,170,000	4,920,000	65,500	443,000	17,200	39,900	206,000
Bing	3,750,000	2,620,000	11,400	57,200	526	26,500	17,000
Yahoo							
AOL							
Youtube	9,550						

3. NICOSIA

SEARCH ENGINE	ANY	ENGLISH	FRENCH	ARABIC	FARSI	RUSSIAN	CHINESE
Google	29,900,000	40,600,000	542,000	178,000	32,200	539,000	124,000
Bing	22,100,000	14,000,000	144,000	16,500	8,710	33,500	23,200
Yahoo							
AOL							
Youtube	17,200						

4. BERLIN

SEARCH ENGINE	ANY	ENGLISH	FRENCH	ARABIC	FARSI	RUSSIAN	CHINESE
Google	1,050,000,000	1,450,000,000	74,900,000	2,460,000	635,000	24,700,000	8,000,000
Bing	447,000,000	242,000,000	22,100,000	525,000	125,000	2,080,000	710,000
Yahoo							
Youtube	547,000						

5. BRUSSELS

SEARCH ENGINE	ANY	ENGLISH	FRENCH	ARABIC	FARSI	RUSSIAN	CHINESE
Google	146,000,000	252,000,000	11,100,000	377,000	109,000	1,730,000	910,000
Bing	101,000,000	98,500,000	3,930,000	62,200	24,500	164,000	94,800
Yahoo							
AOL							
Youtube	139,000						

6. BELFAST

SEARCH ENGINE	ANY	ENGLISH	FRENCH	ARABIC	FARSI	RUSSIAN	CHINESE
Google	136,000,000	237,000,000	4,930,000	297,000	51,400	1,690,000	615,000
Bing	130,000,000	157,000,000	1,380,000	12,900	16,600	74,400	77,200
Yahoo							
AOL							
Youtube	131,000						

7. TRIPOLI (LEBANON)

SEARCH ENGINE	ANY	ENGLISH	FRENCH	ARABIC	FARSI	RUSSIAN	CHINESE
Google	1,780,000	11,300,000	35,200	166,000	7,740	6,860	18,400
Bing	10,300,000	7,000,000	31,700	57,600	357	17,000	11,100
Yahoo							
AOL							
Youtube	4,460						

8. MOSTAR

SEARCH ENGINE	ANY	ENGLISH	FRENCH	ARABIC	FARSI	RUSSIAN	CHINESE
Google	23,600,000	11,400,000	505,000	28,600	8,150	250,000	43,200
Bing	9,100,000	4,010,000	89,600	11,100	414	12,800	15,400
Yahoo							
Youtube	21,600						

TABLE AP1.4
OTHER HOLY CITIES WEB SEARCH RESULTS (MAY 18–23, 2012)

1. MECCA

SEARCH ENGINE	ANY	ENGLISH	FRENCH	ARABIC	FARSI	RUSSIAN	CHINESE
Google	49,800,000	72,500,000	705,000	813,000	138,000	299,000	257,000
Bing	59,000,000	52,500,000	581,000	542,000	26,400	34,900	77,300
Yahoo	64,900,000	58,300,000	651,000	531,000	–	38,400	43,800
AOL	49,800,000	90,600,000	921,000	1,020,000	142,000	619,000	312,000
Youtube	90,300						

2. ROME

SEARCH ENGINE	ANY	ENGLISH	FRENCH	ARABIC	FARSI	RUSSIAN	CHINESE
Google	69,200,000	782,000,000	50,800,000	1,770,000	752,000	5,250,000	4,920,000
Bing	343,000,000	333,000,000	41,000,000	341,000	366,000	933,000	1,610,000
Yahoo	492,000,000	412,000,000	43,600,000	466,000	-	1,130,000	758,000
AOL	393,000,000	783,000,000	50,800,000	1,780,000	753,000	36,900,000	4,900,000
Youtube	250,000						

3. LOURDES

SEARCH ENGINE	ANY	ENGLISH	FRENCH	ARABIC	FARSI	RUSSIAN	CHINESE
Google	103,000,000	72,900,000	32,600,000	160,000	13,000	477,000	266,000
Bing	410,000,000	342,000,000	42,000,000	341,000	366,000	933,000	705,000
Yahoo	486,000,000	424,000,000	41,500,000	489,000	-	1,100,000	738,000
AOL	19,600,000	72,900,000	31,700,000	160,000	12,700	794,000	265,000
Youtube	48,500						

4. KYOTO

SEARCH ENGINE	ANY	ENGLISH	FRENCH	ARABIC	FARSI	RUSSIAN	CHINESE
Google	104,000,000	120,000,000	6,830,000	183,000	58,300	1,210,000	1,630,000
Bing	65,400,000	35,900,000	2,420,000	28,600	8,500	144,000	329,000
Yahoo	70,100,000	38,800,000	2,600,000	27,100	-	147,000	334,000
AOL	104,000,000	120,000,000	15,500,000	237,000	58,300	4,410,000	1,630,000
Youtube	92,000						

5. VARANASI

SEARCH ENGINE	ANY	ENGLISH	FRENCH	ARABIC	FARSI	RUSSIAN	CHINESE
Google	34,400,000	51,100,000	470,000	38,200	5,130	125,000	101,000
Bing	13,800,000	10,800,000	158,000	37,400	493	13,900	12,300
Yahoo	14,500,000	11,200,000	161,000	36,700	-	19,000	11,000
AOL	34,500,000	51,100,000	930,000	38,500	4,970	125,000	99,900
Youtube	20,800						

6. QOM

SEARCH ENGINE	ANY	ENGLISH	FRENCH	ARABIC	FARSI	RUSSIAN	CHINESE
Google	1,150,000	9,740,000	244,000	112,000	788,000	101,000	1,120,000
Bing	13,500,000	13,500,000	83,900	42,300	276,000	24,200	22,300
Yahoo	17,100,000	12,100,000	72,700	29,000	-	39,400	24,800
AOL	9,080,000	9,760,000	244,000	112,000	788,000	102,000	134,000
Youtube	12,500						

7. NAJAF

SEARCH ENGINE	ANY	ENGLISH	FRENCH	ARABIC	FARSI	RUSSIAN	CHINESE
Google	5,030,000	6,980,000	125,000	448,000	141,000	63,900	210,000
Bing	4,130,000	2,950,000	24,300	140,000	24,200	23,400	25,700
Yahoo	4,080,000	3,030,000	24,900	165,000	-	13,200	12,200
AOL	5,030,000	6,990,000	135,000	443,000	141,000	63,900	209,000
Youtube	18,200						

TABLE AP1.5
JERUSALEM WEB SEARCH RESULTS PER CAPITA (MAY 18–23, 2012)

JERUSALEM

SEARCH ENGINE	ANY	ENGLISH	FRENCH	ARABIC	FARSI	RUSSIAN	CHINESE
Google	171.0362047	273.4082397	13.9825218	1.6978776	0.340823	2.95880149	1.26092384
Bing	208.4893883	124.8439451	16.2297128	1.1248439	0.055056	0.53558052	0.12022471
Yahoo	227.2159800	158.5518102	1.14107365	1.1535580	0	0.00069038	0.11410736
AOL	171.0362047	322.0973783	22.2222222	2.4344569	0.345817	4.08239700	1.26092384
Youtube	0.148564295						

TABLE AP1.6
MAJOR CITIES OF THE WORLD WEB SEARCH RESULTS PER CAPITA ((MAY 18–23, 2012)

NEW YORK

SEARCH ENGINE	ANY	ENGLISH	FRENCH	ARABIC	FARSI	RUSSIAN	CHINESE
Google	154.121225	421.264681	23.375052	0.444897	0.139223	1.335717	1.001788
Bing	2.296406	82.711724	2.075499	0.052401	0.019676	0.188542	0.090418
Yahoo	2.132010	98.637584	3.960915	0.176212	0.000000	0.311325	0.888766

	ANY	ENGLISH	FRENCH	ARABIC	FARSI	RUSSIAN	CHINESE
AOL	154.121225	358.58716	25.019012	5.394243	0.188028	4.515752	3.282782
Youtube	0.091445						

LONDON

SEARCH ENGINE	ANY	ENGLISH	FRENCH	ARABIC	FARSI	RUSSIAN	CHINESE
Google	263.025899	666.740069	20.797397	1.859532	0.439192	4.281817	2.728129
Bing	138.241519	174.942807	2.605791	0.543179	0.126008	0.726686	0.241005
Yahoo	159.038916	154.145411	2.838233	0.502808	0.000000	0.714452	0.221431
AOL	265.472651	554.189452	26.791940	3.303116	2.569090	7.695037	5.480726
Youtube	0.165156						

TOKYO

SEARCH ENGINE	ANY	ENGLISH	FRENCH	ARABIC	FARSI	RUSSIAN	CHINESE
Google	45.959570	68.560150	3.974062	0.091767	0.026468	1.971863	1.099693
Bing	25.861738	14.864811	0.864586	0.037314	0.009783	0.072504	0.120587
Yahoo	27.757760	16.760833	1.008684	0.036783	0.000000	0.088734	0.141064
AOL	45.959570	81.149736	9.176746	0.128929	0.027075	2.252474	1.099693
Youtube	0.034432						

PARIS

SEARCH ENGINE	ANY	ENGLISH	FRENCH	ARABIC	FARSI	RUSSIAN	CHINESE
Google	188.219279	211.266537	83.834403	1.920605	0.229512	2.381550	2.708053
Bing	96.990547	57.234026	21.606805	0.224711	0.064820	0.324582	0.168053
Yahoo	0.000000	0.000000	0.000000	0.000000	0.000000	0.000000	0.000000
AOL	0.000000	0.000000	0.000000	0.000000	0.000000	0.000000	0.000000
Youtube	0.123879						

HONG KONG

SEARCH ENGINE	ANY	ENGLISH	FRENCH	ARABIC	FARSI	RUSSIAN	CHINESE
Google	147.283748	189.769444	16.569422	1.016824	0.099417	12.873166	3.738741
Bing	52.115788	37.104175	1.271739	0.000000	0.008979	0.099275	0.337053
Yahoo	0.000000	0.000000	0.000000	0.000000	0.000000	0.000000	0.000000
AOL	0.000000	0.000000	0.000000	0.000000	0.000000	0.000000	0.000000
Youtube	0.032289						

CHICAGO

SEARCH ENGINE	ANY	ENGLISH	FRENCH	ARABIC	FARSI	RUSSIAN	CHINESE
Google	448.8799888	1446.80	20.92300	1.93649053	0.36615252	3.205225	6.34367587
Bing	239.6499775	297.5221	5.045262	0.080130643	0.071227238	0.664045	0.21219781
Yahoo	0.000000	0.000000	0.000000	0.000000	0.000000	0.000000	0.000000
AOL	0.000000	0.000000	0.000000	0.000000	0.000000	0.000000	0.000000
Youtube	0.234456325						

LOS ANGELES

SEARCH ENGINE	ANY	ENGLISH	FRENCH	ARABIC	FARSI	RUSSIAN	CHINESE
Google	329.5873751	835.83358	45.351222	0.5352498	0.2465313	3.1904057	5.273398001
Bing	207.5082113	158.72927	3.6386446	0.052206	0.0377047	0.157410	0.13816302
Yahoo	0	0	0	0	0	0	0
AOL	0	0	0	0	0	0	0
Youtube	0.522066402						

SINGAPORE

SEARCH ENGINE	ANY	ENGLISH	FRENCH	ARABIC	FARSI	RUSSIAN	CHINESE
Google	216.0618863	212.20363	3.781083	0.8719640	0.1105388	2.1413276	3.877539209
Bing	50.1572236	70.027200	0.7349962	0.3240928	0.0244998	0.152786	0.385824797
Yahoo	0	0	0	0	0	0	0
AOL	0	0	0	0	0	0	0
Youtube	0.12539305						

SYDNEY

SEARCH ENGINE	ANY	ENGLISH	FRENCH	ARABIC	FARSI	RUSSIAN	CHINESE
Google	529.4612786	261.48903	3.7386449	0.2182677	0.068938	0.965996	1.03298976
Bing	74.12457	71.315192	1.8779667	0.031551	0.0169643	0.1128076	0.137876039
Yahoo	0	0	0	0	0	0	0
AOL	0	0	0	0	0	0	0
Youtube	0.0825527						

SEOUL

SEARCH ENGINE	ANY	ENGLISH	FRENCH	ARABIC	FARSI	RUSSIAN	CHINESE
Google	17.45912726	20.011631	0.4145266	0.0555424	0.2634184	0.1398772	0.41963165
Bing	7.3001614	5.1866881	0.2920064	0.0098935	0.0045740	0.0144982	0.047372374
Yahoo	0	0	0	0	0	0	0
AOL	0	0	0	0	0	0	0
Youtube	0.01245621						

TABLE AP1.7

DIVIDED CITIES (CONFLICT IN CITIES AND THE CONTESTED STATES PROJECT)
WEB SEARCH RESULTS PER CAPITA (MAY 18–23, 2012)

BEIRUT

SEARCH ENGINE	ANY	ENGLISH	FRENCH	ARABIC	FARSI	RUSSIAN	CHINESE
Google	175.1688656	337.60785	7.7760497	71.119031	0.2307909	2.2525638	1.007289009
Bing	128.12494	109.86091	2.045018	3.9848795	0.0451066	0.2047785	0.1106911
Yahoo	0	0	0	0	0	0	0
AOL	0	0	0	0	0	0	0
Youtube	0.1571813						

KIRKUK

SEARCH ENGINE	ANY	ENGLISH	FRENCH	ARABIC	FARSI	RUSSIAN	CHINESE
Google	6.0767266	5.7828810	0.0769875	0.5206943	0.0202165	0.0468977	0.2421287
Bing	4.4076837	3.0795016	0.0133993	0.0672318	0.0006182	0.0311476	0.0199814
Yahoo	0	0	0	0	0	0	0
AOL	0	0	0	0	0	0	0
Youtube	0.0112249						

NICOSIA

SEARCH ENGINE	ANY	ENGLISH	FRENCH	ARABIC	FARSI	RUSSIAN	CHINESE
Google	96.341286	130.81793	1.7463872	0.5735367	0.1037521	1.7367208	0.399542459
Bing	71.208777	45.109632	0.4639847	0.0531649	0.0280646	0.1079409	0.074753105
Yahoo	0	0	0	0	0	0	0
AOL	0	0	0	0	0	0	0
Youtube	0.0554204						

BERLIN

SEARCH ENGINE	ANY	ENGLISH	FRENCH	ARABIC	FARSI	RUSSIAN	CHINESE
Google	299.83962	414.06424	21.388560	0.7024814	0.1813315	7.0533703	2.2844924
Bing	127.64601	69.105895	6.3109102	0.1499198	0.0356951	0.5939680	0.2027487
Yahoo	0	0	0	0	0	0	
Youtube	0.1562021						

BRUSSELS

SEARCH ENGINE	ANY	ENGLISH	FRENCH	ARABIC	FARSI	RUSSIAN	CHINESE
Google	130.4633773	225.18336	9.9187910	0.3368814	0.0974007	1.5459016	0.813162146
Bing	90.252062	88.018100	3.511788	0.0555809	0.0218928	0.1465479	0.084711837
Yahoo	0	0	0	0	0	0	0
AOL	0	0	0	0	0	0	0
Youtube	0.1242082						

BELFAST

SEARCH ENGINE	ANY	ENGLISH	FRENCH	ARABIC	FARSI	RUSSIAN	CHINESE
Google	508.411215	885.98130	18.429906	1.1102803	0.1921495	6.3177570	2.2990654
Bing	485.98130	586.91588	5.1588785	0.0482242	0.0620560	0.2781308	0.2885981
Yahoo	0	0	0	0	0	0	0
AOL	0	0	0	0	0	0	0
Youtube	0.4897196						

TRIPOLI (LEBANON)

SEARCH ENGINE	ANY	ENGLISH	FRENCH	ARABIC	FARSI	RUSSIAN	CHINESE
Google	3.3584905	21.320754	0.0664150	0.3132075	0.0146037	0.0129433	0.0347169
Bing	19.433962	13.207547	0.0598113	0.1086792	0.0006735	0.0320754	0.0209433
Yahoo	0	0	0	0	0	0	0
AOL	0	0	0	0	0	0	0
Youtube	0.0084150						

MOSTAR

SEARCH ENGINE	ANY	ENGLISH	FRENCH	ARABIC	FARSI	RUSSIAN	CHINESE
Google	183.73909	88.755323	3.9317051	0.2226668	0.0634522	1.946388	0.3363359
Bing	70.84854	31.220074	0.6975856	0.0864196	0.003223	0.09965	0.1198975
Yahoo	0	0	0	0	0	0	
Youtube	0.1681679						

TABLE AP1.8

OTHER HOLY CITIES WEB SEARCH RESULTS PER CAPITA (MAY 18–23, 2012)

MECCA

SEARCH ENGINE	ANY	ENGLISH	FRENCH	ARABIC	FARSI	RUSSIAN	CHINESE
Google	24.900000	36.2500000	0.3525000	0.4065000	0.06900	0.1495000	0.128500
Bing	29.500000	26.2500000	0.2905000	0.271000	0.0132	0.0174500	0.0386500
Yahoo	32.450000	29.1500000	0.3255000	0.2655000	0.00000	0.0192000	0.021900
AOL	24.900000	45.300000	0.46005000	0.51000	0.071000	0.309500	0.15600
Youtube	0.045150						

ROME

SEARCH ENGINE	ANY	ENGLISH	FRENCH	ARABIC	FARSI	RUSSIAN	CHINESE
Google	24.910195	281.49960	18.28667	0.63715	0.2707	1.8898630	1.771071
Bing	123.47105	119.87131	14.75893	0.12275	0.1317	0.335856	0.579558
Yahoo	177.10717	148.30925	15.69486	0.16774	0.0000	0.406705	0.272860
AOL	141.46597	281.85988	18.28667	0.64075	0.2710	13.283037	1.763872
Youtube	0.0899934						

KYOTO

SEARCH ENGINE	ANY	ENGLISH	FRENCH	ARABIC	FARSI	RUSSIAN	CHINESE
Google	59.641714	68.817362	3.916855	0.104946	0.033434	0.693908	0.934769
Bing	37.505462	20.587861	1.387817	0.016401	0.004875	0.082581	0.188674
Yahoo	40.200809	22.250947	1.491043	0.015541	0.000000	0.084301	0.191542
AOL	59.641714	68.817362	8.888909	0.135914	0.033434	2.529038	0.934769
Youtube	0.052760						

VARANASI

SEARCH ENGINE	ANY	ENGLISH	FRENCH	ARABIC	FARSI	RUSSIAN	CHINESE
Google	9.342256	13.877596	0.127641	0.010374	0.001393	0.033947	0.027429
Bing	3.747766	2.933034	0.042909	0.010157	0.000134	0.003775	0.003340
Yahoo	3.937870	3.041665	0.043724	0.009967	0.000000	0.005160	0.002987
AOL	9.369414	13.877596	0.252567	0.010456	0.001350	0.033947	0.027131
Youtube	0.005649						

QOM

SEARCH ENGINE	ANY	ENGLISH	FRENCH	ARABIC	FARSI	RUSSIAN	CHINESE
Google	0.932685	7.899432	0.197891	0.090835	0.639092	0.081914	0.908354
Bing	10.948905	10.948905	0.068045	0.034307	0.223844	0.019627	0.0180886
Yahoo	13.868613	9.813463	0.058962	0.023520	0.000000	0.031955	0.020114
AOL	7.364152	7.915653	0.197891	0.090835	0.639092	0.082725	0.108678
Youtube	0.010138						

NAJAF

SEARCH ENGINE	ANY	ENGLISH	FRENCH	ARABIC	FARSI	RUSSIAN	CHINESE
Google	8.982143	12.464286	0.223214	0.800000	0.251786	0.114107	0.375000
Bing	7.375000	5.267857	0.043393	0.250000	0.043214	0.041786	0.045893
Yahoo	7.285714	5.410714	0.044464	0.294643	0.000000	0.023571	0.021786
AOL	8.982143	12.482143	0.241071	0.791071	0.251786	0.114107	0.373214
Youtube	0.032500						

TABLE AP1.9
POPULATION TOTALS UTILIZED IN CALCULATING TABLE FIGURES

HOLY CITY	POPULATION
Mecca	2,000,000
Rome	2,777,979
Kyoto	1,473,746
Varanasi	3,682,194
Qom	1,233,000
Najaf	560,000

MAJOR CITY	POPULATION
Jerusalem	81,100
New York	19,465,197
London	8,174,100
Tokyo	13,185,502
Paris	10,413,386
Seoul	9,794,304,
Hong Kong	7,061,200
Chicago	2,695,598
Los Angeles	3,792,621
Singapore	5,183,700
Sidney	4,627,345

DIVIDED CITY	POPULATION
Beirut	361,366
Kirkuk	850,787
Nicosia	310,355
Berlin	3,501,872
Brussels	1,119,088
Belfast	267,500
Tripoli	530,000
Mostar	128,443

NOTES

ACKNOWLEDGMENTS

1. See maps on Jerusalem produced by the Jerusalem Institute of Israel Studies, http://jiis.org.

INTRODUCTION

1. For approximate comparative purposes we can note that in 2000 Cairo had over 10.7 million inhabitants, Istanbul 9.5 million, Tehran 7.4 million, Damascus 2.3 million, Tel Aviv 2.1 million, and Aleppo 2.1 million. See *The Times Concise Atlas of the World* (New York: Times, 2000), p. 35. Despite being center stage for so much of the time, Jerusalem is still a very small city.
2. Michael Dumper, *The Politics of Jerusalem Since 1967* (New York: Columbia University Press, 1997) and *The Politics of Sacred Space: The Old City of Jerusalem in the Middle East Conflict* (Boulder: Lynne Rienner, 2002).
3. Meron Benvenisti, *Jerusalem: The Torn City* (Minneapolis: Israel Typeset and the University of Minneapolis, 1976).
4. Israel Kimhi, *A Socio-Economic Survey of Jerusalem, 1967–1975* (Jerusalem: Jerusalem Committee, 1978); Michael Romann and Alex Weingrod, *Living Together Separately* (Princeton: Princeton University Press, 1991).
5. The list of books on Jerusalem is now quite extensive. Here are just a few of the more well known: Karen Armstrong, *Jerusalem: One City, Three Faiths* (London: Harper Collins, 1996); Kamil Jamil Asali, *Jerusalem in History: 3000 BC to Present* (London: Routledge and Kegan Paul, 2002); Meron Benvenisti, *City of Stone: The Hidden History of Jerusalem* (Berkeley, University of California Press, 1996); Roger Friedland and Roger D. Hecht, *To Rule*

Jerusalem (Berkeley: University of California Press, 2000); Ruth Kark, *Jerusalem and Its Environs: Quarters, Neighbourhoods, Villages, 1800–1948* (Detroit: Wayne State University Press, 2001).

6. Menachem Klein, *Jerusalem the Contested City* (London: Hurst, 2001).

7. Marshall J. Breger and Ora Ahimer, *Jerusalem: A City and Its Future* (Syracuse, NY: Syracuse University Press, 2002); Phillip Misselwitz and Tim Rieniets, *City of Collision: Jerusalem and the Principles of Conflict Urbanism* (Basel: Birkhäuser, 2006).

8. Yitzhak Reiter, *Jerusalem and Its Role in Islamic Solidarity* (New York: Palgrave Macmillan, 2008); Sami Musallem, *The Struggle for Jerusalem* (Jerusalem: PASSIA, 1996); Simone Ricca, *Reinventing Jerusalem: Israel's Reconstruction of the Jewish Quarter After 1967* (London: I. B. Tauris, 2007).

9. See, for example, Yehezkel Lein and Alon Cohen-Lifshitz, *Under the Guise of Security* (Jerusalem: Bimkom and B'Tselem, 2005); Ibrahim Habib, *A Wall in Its Midst: The Separation Barrier and Its Impact on the Right to Health and on Palestinian Hospitals in East Jerusalem* (Tel Aviv: Physicians for Human Rights, 2005); Mustafa Al-Barghuti, *Health and Segregation: The Impact of the Israeli Separation Wall on Access to Health Care Services* (Ramallah: Health Development, Information and Policy Institute, 2004); UN-OCHA , *East Jerusalem: Key Humanitarian Concerns* (March 2011), p. 76, available online at www.ochaopt. org/documents/ocha_opt_Jerusalem_FactSheet_December_2011_english.pdf; Al-Haq, *Redrawing Occupied East Jerusalem* (Ramallah: al-Haq, n.d.), p. 11. Michael Dumper and Wendy Pullan, "Jerusalem: The Cost of Failure" (London: Chatham House, Royal Institute of International Affairs, February 2010), available online at www.chathamhouse. org.uk/publications/papers/view/-/id/835/; Jerusalem Institute for Israel Studies, *2011 Jerusalem Statistical Yearbook*. Further details are available online at http://jiis.org/.upload/ yearbook/10_11/C/shnaton%20C0111.pdf: International Peace and Cooperation Center, *Jerusalem on the Map III* (Jerusalem: International Peace and Cooperation Center, 2007); Masry-Herzalla Asmahan, Razin Eran, and Choshen Maya, "Jerusalem as an Internal Migration Destination for Israeli-Palestinian Families," (Jerusalem: Floersheimer Institute for Policy Studies, 2011); Nadav Shragai, *Jerusalem, the Dangers of Division: An Alternative to Separation from the Arab Neighbourhoods* (Jerusalem Center for Public Affairs), p. 9, available online at http://www.jcpa.org/text/shragai_last2.pdf.

10. Ian Lustick, "Has Israel Annexed Jerusalem?" *Middle East Policy* 5, no. 1 (1997): 34–45; and "Reinventing Jerusalem," *Foreign Policy*, no. 93 (1993–94): 41–59.

11. For project details see: www.conflictincities.org.

12. Wendy Pullan, P. Misselwitz, R. Nasrallah, H. Yacobi, "Jerusalem's Road 1," *City* 11 (2007): 187–88.

13. Almost 80 percent of Israeli settlers on the West Bank live in this Greater Jerusalem area.

14. Ron E. Hassner, "'To Halve and to Hold': Conflicts Over Sacred Space and the Problem of Indivisibility," *Security Studies* 12, no. 4 (Summer 2003): 1–33; Isak Svensson, "Fighting with Faith: Religion and Conflict Resolution in Civil Wars," *Journal of Conflict Resolution* 51, no. 6 (2007): 930–49.

15. See examples in Scott Bollens, *Cities, Nationalism, and Democratization* (New York: Routledge, 2007); and Anthony Hepburn, *Contested Cities in the Modern West* (Basingstoke: Palgrave Macmillan 2004).

16. The designation of the separation barrier is controversial. It has been given several different names, usually reflecting a political perspective: security fence, the Wall, the Apartheid Wall, etc. I have adopted the term *separation barrier* as it is less emotive and also encompasses the fact that in some places the barrier is a fence and in other places it is a wall. This does not minimize its destructive impact on the communities affected by it or on the environment.

17. I explore this aspect of my many-bordered thesis more fully in Michael Dumper, "A False Dichotomy? The Binationalism Debate and the Future of Divided Jerusalem," *International Affairs* 87, no. 3 (May 2011): 671–86.

18. For further details on this topic, see Ann Lesch and Ian Lustick, *Exile and Return: Predicaments of Palestinians and Jews* (Philadelphia : University of Pennsylvania Press, 2005); Michael Fischbach, *The Peace Process and the Palestinian Refugee Claims* (Washington, DC: United States Institute for Peace, 2006); Donna Arzt, *Refugees into Citizens: Palestinians and the End of the Arab-Israeli Conflict* (New York: Council on Foreign Relations, 1997); Rex Brynen and Roula El Rifai, *Palestinian Refugees: Challenges of Repatriation and Development* (London: I. B. Tours, 2007); Michael Dumper, *The Future of Palestinian Refugees* (Boulder: Lynne Reinner, 2007) and *Palestinian Refugee Repatriation: Global Perspectives* (London: Routledge, 2006); Joseph Ginat and Edward Perkins, *The Palestinian Refugees: Old Problems, New Solutions* (Brighton: Sussex Academy, 2001); Lex Takkenberg, *The Status of Palestinian Refugees in International Law* (Oxford: Clarendon, 1998); Ghada Talhami, *Palestinian Refugees Pawns to Political Actors* (New York: Nova Science, 2001).

19. Even the great guru of urban studies, Lucien Febvre, ascribes to this view. See Lucien Febvre, "Frontière: The Word and the Concept," in *A New Kind of History: From the Writings of Febvre,* ed. Peter Burke (London: Routledge and Kegan Paul, 1973).

20. Paul Hirst, *Space and Power: Politics, War and Architecture* (Cambridge: Polity, 2005).

21. Annsi Paasi, "Boundaries as Social Processes: Territoriality in the World of Flows," *Geopolitics* 3, no. 1 (1998): 69–88, special issue: "Boundaries Territory and Postmodernity."

22. Scott A. Bollens, *Cities, Nationalism, and Democratization* (New York: Routledge, 2007), p. 249.

23. Peter Marcuse, "Not Chaos But Walls: Postmodernism and the Partitioned City," in *Post-Modern Cities and Spaces,* ed. Sophie Watson and Katherine Gibson (Oxford: Blackwell, 1995), pp. 243–53, cited in Menachem Klein, "Old and New Walls in Jerusalem," *Political Geography* 24 (2005): 58.

24. See, for example, the research on how acts of "grotesque" violence can act as area demarcations in T. Wilson, *Frontiers of Violence: Conflict and Identity in Ulster and Upper Silesia, 1918–1922* (Oxford: Oxford University Press, 2010).

25. See chapter 5 for a fuller explanation of the Schengen Agreement.

26. Dumper, *The Politics of Jerusalem Since 1967,* p. 261ff.
27. Klein, "Old and New Walls in Jerusalem," pp. 53–76.

1. THE HARD BORDERS OF THE CITY

1. Suzanne Goldenberg, "The Street Was Covered with Blood and Bodies: The Dead and the Dying," *Guardian,* August 10, 2001.
2. The Palestinian National Authority is the administrative arm of the Palestinian Liberation Organization (PLO), which was set up in the West Bank and Gaza Strip (also known as the occupied Palestinian territories or OPTs) after the Oslo Accord in 1993. Palestinians were anxious to vest in this body quasi-state responsibilities and recognition by calling it the Palestinian National Authority. Its official documentation included a crest with this nomenclature.
3. The first uprising, the Intifada, was between 1987 and 1993.
4. Nadav Shragai, *Jerusalem: The Dangers of Division: An Alternative to Separation from the Arab Neighbourhoods* (Jerusalem: Jerusalem Centre for Public Affairs, 2008), p. 10, available online at www.jcpa.org/text/shragai_last2.pdf. Of the 173 different bombing incidents, as opposed to other forms of violent attack, 11 of them were car bombs, 32 were petrol bombs, ten grenade attacks, and 12 incidents of mortar shelling.
5. Hank Savitch, "Anatomy of Urban Terror: Lessons from Jerusalem and Elsewhere," *Urban Studies* 42, no. 3 (2005): 371.
6. This phrase is taken from the evocative title of Yiannis Papadakis's book *Echoes from the Dead Zone: Across the Cyprus Divide* (London: I. B. Tauris, 2005).
7. Hank Savitch and Yaakov Garb, "Terror, Barriers, and the Changing Topography of Jerusalem," *Journal of Planning Education and Research* 26, no. 2 (2006): 161. See also Savitch, "Anatomy of Urban Terror," p. 386.
8. An armistice agreement was signed between Israel and Jordan on April 3, 1949, ending hostilities between the two countries. Jordan retained control over the West Bank and later annexed it by "invitation" in 1950. The Armistice Lines also became known as the "Green Line," and, after the Israeli occupation of the West Bank in 1967, they became known as the 1967 borders. They are all the same line.
9. Writings critical of the Oslo Accords abound. The list below is a small selection: Edwin G. Corr, Joseph Ginat, Shaul Gabbay, *The Search for Israeli-Arab Peace: Learning from the Past and Building Trust* (Brighton: Sussex Academic, 2007); Edward Said, *The End of Peace Process: Oslo and After* (New York: Pantheon, 2000); Jamil Hilal, *Where Now for Palestine? The Demise of the Two-State Solution* (New York: Zed, 2007); George Giacaman and Dag Jorund Lønning, *After Oslo: New Realities, Old Problems* (London: Pluto, 1998); Clayton E. Swisher, *The Truth About Camp David: The Untold Story About the Collapse of the Middle East Peace Process* (New York: Nation, 2004).
10. "Israeli Settlements in the Occupied Territories: A Guide," *Foundation for Middle East Peace,* Settlement Report 12, no. 7 (2002), available online at www.fmep.org/reports/special-reports/a-guide-to-israeli-settlements-in-the-occupied-territories/israeli-settlements-in-the-occupied-territories-a-guide.

11. Further details can be found in Geoffrey Watson, *The Oslo Accords, International Law, and the Israeli-Palestinian Peace Agreement* (Oxford: Oxford University Press, 2000). See also George Giacaman and Dag Lønning, *After Oslo*; David Makovsky, *Making Peace with PLO: The Rabin Government's Road to the Oslo Accord* (Boulder: Westview, 1995); Yossi Beilin, *Touching Peace: From the Oslo Accord to a Final Agreement* (London: Weidenfeld and Nicolson, 1999).

12. UNOCHA, "Special Focus: Barrier Update" (July 2011), p. 3, available online at www.ochaopt.org/documents/ocha_opt_barrier_update_july_2011_english.pdf. Requisitions are by military order, valid for three years and renewable. See also UNOCHA , "East Jerusalem: Key Humanitarian Concerns," special focus (March 2011), available online at http://unispal.un.org/pdfs/OCHASpFocus_230311.pdf.

13. Savitch and Garb, "Terror, Barriers, and the Changing Topography of Jerusalem," p. 156.

14. Regarding the Armistice Lines, see note 8, this chapter.

15. UNOCHA, "Special Focus: Barrier Update," p. 3. The reasons for the delay are partly due to legal challenges over the route, political considerations regarding stretches of the Jerusalem section and budgetary constraints. As of July 2011, 61.8 percent of the barrier is complete and a further 8.2 percent under construction. The other 30 percent is planned but not constructed.

16. UNOCHA, "Special Focus: Barrier Update." See note 12, this chapter.

17. UNOCHA, "East Jerusalem: Key Humanitarian Concerns," p. 68.

18. See, for example, Yehezkel Lein and Alon Cohen-Lifshitz, *Under the Guise of Security: Routing the Separation Barrier to Enable the Expansion of Israeli Settlements in the West Bank* (Jerusalem: Bimkom and B'Tselem, 2005), available online at www.btselem.org/download/200512_under_the_guise_of_security_eng.pdf; Ibrahim Habib, *A Wall in Its Midst: The Separation Barrier and Its Impact on the Right to Health and on Palestinian Hospitals in East Jerusalem* (Tel Aviv: Physicians for Human Rights, 2005); Mustafa Al-Barghuti, *Health and Segregation: The Impact of the Israeli Separation Wall on Access to Health Care Services* (Ramallah: Health Development, Information and Policy Institute, 2004). See also Negotiations Affairs Department (PLO), *Israel's Wall* (Ramallah: Palestinian Liberation Organization, 2004). For the position of the international community, see International Court of Justice, "Legal Consequences of the Construction of a Wall in the Occupied Palestinian Territory," advisory opinion (2004), p. 136, available online at www.icj-cij.org; UNOCHA, "East Jerusalem: Key Humanitarian Concerns," pp. 9, 66–82.

19. UNOCHA, "East Jerusalem: Key Humanitarian Concerns," p. 13.

20. Ibid., p. 16.

21. UNGAOR, *Report of the Special Committee to Investigate Israeli Practices Affecting the Human Rights of the Palestinian People and Other Arabs of the Occupied Territories: Note By the Secretary-General*, 61st session, UN Doc. A/61/500 (2006).

22. UNOCHA, "East Jerusalem: Key Humanitarian Concerns," p. 76.

23. Savitch and Garb, "Terror, Barriers, and the Changing Topography of Jerusalem," p. 166. See also UNOCHA, "East Jerusalem: Key Humanitarian Concerns," p. 76.

24. Ibid., p. 167.

25. UNOCHA, "East Jerusalem: Key Humanitarian Concerns," p. 76.

26. UNOCHA, *Special Focus: Barrier Update* (July 2011): pp. 3–4 and pp. 21–22.

27. Ibid., p. 15; cf. UNOCHA, "East Jerusalem: Key Humanitarian Concerns," p. 75. See also Nir Hasson, "Israel Sanctions East Jerusalem Family for Straddling Palestinian Border," *Haaretz*, September 27, 2011, available online at www.haaretz.com/print-edition/news/israel-sanctions-east-jerusalem-family-forstraddling-palestinian-border-1.386897.

28. UNOCHA, "East Jerusalem: Key Humanitarian Concerns," pp. 69–70. Qalandiya checkpoint, for example, has offices of the National Insurance, Ministry of Interior, Ministry of Labor, and the postal service. See also Al-Haq, *Redrawing Occupied East Jerusalem* (Ramallah: Al-Haq, n.d.), p. 11.

29. See statement by Yakir Segev, holder of the East Jerusalem portfolio in the Israeli Jerusalem Municipality, in which he declared that "the Jerusalem municipality has no hand in managing these neighbourhoods. . . . The State of Israel has given up, [the neighbourhoods] are outside the jurisdiction of the state, and certainly the municipality. For all practical purposes, they are Ramallah." Quoted by Nir Hasson, "Jerusalem Official: Areas East of the Fence Not Part of the City," *Haaretz*, January 8, 2010, available online at www.haaretz.com/hasen/spages/1141313.html.

30. Personal e-mail communications with resident of Kufr Aqab, May 2012.

31. The Palestinian police service has set up a specific district called the Jerusalem Periphery District which reports to the chief of police directly. While abiding by Israeli restrictions on their operations in Israeli municipal areas such as Kufr Aqab and Semiramis, they are able to assist "remotely." Interview with Major-General Hazem Attallah, chief of Palestinian Police Service, March 13, 2012. For more information on the Palestine Police Service, see Yezid Sayigh, "Policing the People, Building the State: Authoritarian Transformation in the West Bank and Gaza," *Carnegie Middle East Center*, Carnegie Papers (February 2011), and "'We Serve the People': Hamas Policing in Gaza," *Crown Center for Middle East Studies*, Crown Paper 5 (Brandeis University, April 2011); International Crisis Group, "Squaring the Circle: Palestinian Security Reform Under Occupation," *Middle East Report*, no. 98 (September 7, 2010): 12.

32. Michael Dumper and Wendy Pullan, "Jerusalem: The Cost of Failure," Chatham House Briefing Paper, Chatham House: The Royal Institute of International Affairs (February 2010), available online at www.chathamhouse.org.uk/publications/papers/view/-/id/835/. Cf. UNOCHA, "East Jerusalem: Key Humanitarian Concerns," p. 71. See also Lorenzo Kamel, interview with Dr Salim Anati of Shu'afat camp: "Interview: A Day in the Life of a Jerusalem Refugee Camp Doctor," *+972Magazine*, December 28, 2011, available online at http://972mag.com/interview-a-day-in-the-life-of-a-jerusalem-refugee-camp-doctor/31427/.

33. Al-Haq, *Redrawing Occupied East Jerusalem*, p. 11. See also the municipality statement of December 23, 2011, reported in Xinhua News agency, that the Israeli mayor, Nir Barakat, was contemplating reducing municipal services to the east of the barrier, leaving them to be dealt with by the Israeli Ministry of Defense's Civil Administration for the West Bank, available online at http://news.xinhuanet.com/english/world/2011–12/23/c_131323390.htm.

34. UNOCHA, *Special Focus: Barrier Update*, pp. 17–18.

35. Ibid., pp. 19–20.

36. Savitch and Garb, "Terror, Barriers, and the Changing Topography of Jerusalem," p. 166.

37. In 2003 the Palestinian population was 228,700. By 2009 it was estimated to be 275,900. See Jerusalem Institute for Israel Studies, *Jerusalem Statistical Yearbook (2011)*; further details are available online at http://jiis.org/.upload/yearbook/10_11/C/shnaton%20C0111. pdf. Note that these figures refer to the municipal borders established in 1967 and not only those areas inside the Separation Wall.

38. International Peace and Cooperation Centre, *Jerusalem on the Map III* (Jerusalem: International Peace and Cooperation Centre, 2007), p. 19.

39. Savitch and Garb, "Terror, Barriers, and the Changing Topography of Jerusalem," p. 164. The authors also write about some young Palestinians, mostly men, moving to the Tel Aviv region and to Palestinian areas inside Israel such as "the triangle." (The Triangle, *al-muthallath* in Arabic, is an strip of land in Israel abutting the northwestern border of the West Bank and comprising the large Palestinian town Umm al-Fahm and others such as Tira and Taibe. It is a territory that was ceded to Israel by King Abdullah of Jordan in the 1949 Armistice Agreements in exchange for land held by Israel in the Hebron district.

40. Savitch and Garb, "Terror, Barriers, and the Changing Topography of Jerusalem," p. 167.

41. Conflict in Cities, fieldwork site observations, 2006.

42. Masry-Herzalla Asmahan, Razin Eran, and Choshen Maya, "Jerusalem as an Internal Migration Destination for Israeli-Palestinian Families," *Floersheimer Institute for Policy Studies* (2011), abstract available at www.fips.org.il/site/p_publications/item_en.asp?doc=&iss=&iid=852. See also Nadav Shragai, "Jerusalem: The Dangers of Division, an Alternative to Separation from the Arab Neighbourhoods," *Jerusalem Centre for Public Affairs*, p. 9, available online at www.jcpa.org/text/shragai_last2.pdf.

43. Choshen Maya and Israel Kimhi, "Migration to and from Jerusalem," *Jerusalem Institute for Israel Studies* (1991): 8.

44. Shragai, "Jerusalem," p. 7.

45. Bill Hutman, "Jerusalem Losing Best of Its Young People," *Jerusalem Post*, May 25, 1992.

46. Jerusalem Institute for Israel Studies, "Sources of Population Growth in Jerusalem by Population Groups and Sub-Quarters," table III//8, *Jerusalem Statistical Yearbook (2009)*; further details are available online at http://jiis.org/.upload/yearbook/10_11/C/shnaton%20 C0111.pdf. Note that these figures refer to the municipal borders established in 1967 and not only those areas inside the barrier.

47. The removal of sections of the barrier near the Israeli settlement of Gilo attests to this. Conflict in Cities, fieldwork observations in 2012.

48. Wendy Pullan, P. Misselwitz, R. Nasrallah, H. Yacobi, "Jerusalem's Road 1," *City* 11, no. 2 (July 2007): 188.

49. See Virginia Tilley, *Beyond Occupation: Apartheid, Colonialism, and International Law in the Occupied Palestinian Territories* (London: Pluto, 2012): p. 181ff; "Schools in Jerusalem," *Tanmiya* 73 (2006): 5 (quarterly newsletter of the Welfare Association).

50. The Association for Civil Rights in Israel, "The State of Human Rights in East Jerusalem 2009: Facts and Figures" (May 2009), available online at www.acri.org.il/en/2010/10/27/publications/.

51. Ray Dolphin, *The West Bank Wall: Unmaking Palestine* (London: Pluto, 2006), pp. 129–130.

52. Ibid., pp. 126–27.

53. See www.banksy.co.uk/outdoors/index.html. For a fascinating study of the way in which the concrete sections of the barrier are utilized for mobilization, propaganda, territory marking, and retail purposes, see Craig Larkin, "Resisting the Separation Barrier—Graffiti, Protest Art, and Conflict Tourism," British Society for Middle East Research (BRISMES) and European Association for Middle Eastern Studies (EURAMES) Annual Conference, University of Exeter, June 27–29, 2011. See also Mark Thomas, *Extreme Rambling: Walking Israel's Separation Barrier. For Fun.* (London: Ebury, 2011). See also the short film produced by UNOCHA entitled *Walled Horizons*, narrated by Roger Waters (founding member of the UK rock group Pink Floyd), available online at www.ochaopt.org/videos .aspx#.

54. UNGAOR, "Illegal Israeli Actions in Occupied East Jerusalem and the Rest of the Occupied Palestinian Territory," *General Assembly Resolution ES-10/13*, 10th emergency session, UN Doc. A/RES/ES/10–13 (2003).

55. International Court of Justice, "Legal Consequences of the Construction of a Wall in the Occupied Palestinian Territory, Advisory Opinion of 9 July 2004," para. 141. The full text of the ICJ opinion is available online at www.icjcij.org/docket/index.php?p1=3&p2=4&k=5a &case=131&code=mwp&p3=4.

56. Stephanie Koury, "Legal Strategies at the United Nations: A Comparative Look at Namibia, Western Sahara, and Palestine," in *International Law and the Israeli-Palestinian Conflict: A Rights-Based Approach to Middle East Peace*, ed. Susan Akram, Michael Dumper, Michael Lynk, and Iain Scobbie (Abingdon: Routledge. 2011), p. 161.

57. Danny Seidemann, "The Separation Barrier and the Abuse of Security," *Foundation for Middle East Peace*, cited in Dolphin, *The West Bank Wall: Unmaking Palestine*, pp. 132–33.

58. Ibid. See also Ir Amim, "State of Affairs—Jerusalem 2008: Political Developments and Changes on the Ground" (December 2008), p. 34, available online at http://eng.ir-amim .org.il/_Uploads/dbsAttachedFiles/AnnualReport2008Eng(1).pdf.

59. This period is well covered by Kamal al-'Asali, *Jerusalem in History* (London: Scorpion, 1989); and two books by Yehoshua Ben Arieh, *Jerusalem in the Nineteenth Century: Emergence of the New City* (New York: St. Martins, 1989); and Yehoshua Ben Arieh, *Jerusalem in the Nineteenth Century: The Old City* (New York: St. Martins, 1984).

60. Rami Nasrallah, "Transformations in Jerusalem: Where Are We Heading?" in *Divided Cities in Transition: Challenges Facing Jerusalem and Berlin*, ed. Michele Auga, S. Hasson, R. Nasrallah, and S. Stetter (Jerusalem, 2005), pp. 206–7.

61. Ruth Kark, *Jerusalem Neighbourhoods: Planning and By-Laws (1855–1930)* (Jerusalem: Magnes, 1991), and *Christians in the Holy Land,* ed. Michael Prior and William Taylor (London: World of Islam Festival Trust, 1994).

62. Alexander Scholch, "Jerusalem in the Nineteenth Century, 1831–1917," in al-'Asali, *Jerusalem in History.*

63. Uriel O. Schmelz, *Modern Jerusalem's Demographic Evolution* (Jerusalem: Hebrew University of Jerusalem, 1987), p. 28.

64. Michael Dumper, *The Politics of Jerusalem Since 1967* (New York: Columbia University Press, 1996), pp. 61–64.

65. Ibid., p. 65.

66. Hadawi estimated that 31 percent of the area that became West Jerusalem after 1949 was Jewish owned. Given that Jewish residential areas in the eastern part of the city was confined to the small Jewish Quarter in the Old City and to scattered residences in Silwan and Shaykh Jarrah, it is reasonable to estimate that taken in total this would not exceed 35 percent. See discussion in Dumper, *The Politics of Jerusalem Since 1967*, pp. 36–37.

67. Ad Hoc Committee on Palestinian Question, "Future Government of Palestine," General Assembly Resolution A/RES/181(II), 2d session (1947), available online at www.un.org/depts/dhl/resguide/r2.htm. This has been recently recalled in UNGAOR, Jerusalem, General Assembly Res. 60/41, 60th session, UN Doc. A/RES/60/41 (2005).

68. Walid Khalidi, *All That Remains: The Palestinian Villages Occupied and Depopulated by Israel in 1948* (Washington DC: Institute for Palestine Studies, 1992), p. 583; see also Janet L. Abu-Lughod, "The Demographic Transformation of Palestine," in *The Transformation of Palestine by Ibrahim Abu-Lughod* (Evanston: Northwestern University Press, 1971), p. 159. Janet Abu-Lughod puts the figure at about eighty thousand.

69. See details in Israeli Raphael, *Jerusalem Divided: The Armistice Regime, 1947–1967* (London: Frank Cass, 2002).

70. Dumper, *The Politics of Jerusalem Since 1967*, p. 31. See also other calculations which show 80.5 percent. International Peace and Cooperation Centre, *Jerusalem on the Map III* (Jerusalem: International Peace and Cooperation Centre, 2007), p. 12. I imagine the discrepancy stems from whether the UN enclaves are included in the calculations or not.

71. In November 1948 the population was approximately 58, 600 Jews, a drop of over 40,000 from official estimates of 99,300 in 1946. See Schmelz, *Modern Jerusalem's Demographic Evolution*, p. 43.

72. Meron Benvenisti, *Jerusalem: The Torn City* (Minneapolis: Israel Typeset and the University of Minneapolis, 1976), p. 43.

73. Schmelz, *Modern Jerusalem's Demographic Evolution*, p. 44.

74. Details of how the Armistice Agreements worked and the operations of the Mixed Armistice Commission can be found in Raphael, *Jerusalem Divided*. Chapter 8 provides a colorful description of life alongside the dividing line.

75. Law and Administration Ordinance (Amendment No. 11), Law 5727/1967, *Laws of the State of Israel* 21 (1966/67): 75.

76. Municipalities Ordinance (Amendment No. 6) Law, 5727/1967, ibid., pp. 75–76.

77. Benvenisti, *Jerusalem*, p. 112. See also Ian Lustick, "The Fetish of Jerusalem: A Hegemonic Analysis," in *Israel in Comparative Perspective*, ed. Michael N. Barnett (Albany: State University of New York Press, 1996), pp. 143–72. Some Israeli planners argue that the security aspect is overstated. See Michael Dumper, *The Politics of Jerusalem Since 1967* (New York: Columbia University Press, 1997), p. 42n58.

78. Letter of Israel's foreign minister, Abba Eban, to the UN secretary-general concerning General Assembly Resolution 2253 (ES-V), July 10, 1967, cited in Ruth Lapidoth and

Moshe Hirsch, *The Jerusalem Question and Its Resolution: Selected Documents* (Dordrecht: Kluwer Academic, 1994), p. 172.

79. Ian Lustick, "Has Israel Annexed Jerusalem?" *Middle East Policy* 5, no. 1 (1997): 34–45.

80. A selection of relevant publications include Rodman Bundy, "Legal Approaches to the Question of Jerusalem" in *Jerusalem Today: What Future for the Peace Process?* ed. Ghada Karmi (Reading: Ithaca, 1996): p. 46; Henry Cattan, *Jerusalem* (London: Croom Helm, 1981); John Quiqley, "Jerusalem in International Law," in Karmi, *Jerusalem Today*, p. 25; Lapidoth and Hirsch, *The Jerusalem Question and Its Resolution*; Yehuda Zvi Blum, *The Juridical Status of Jerusalem* (Jerusalem: Hebrew University, 1974); Elena Molaroni, Report of the Third Committee, "Right of Peoples to Self-Determination: Draft Resolution III," The Right of the Palestinian People to Self-Determination in UNGAOR 61st session, UN Doc. A/61/442 (2006), pp. 12–13. Antonio Cassese, "Legal Considerations on the International Status of Jerusalem," in *The Legal Aspects of the Palestine Problem with Special Regard to the Question of Jerusalem*, ed. Hans Koechler (Vienna: International Progress Organization, 1981), pp. 149–51; Elihu Lauterpacht, *Jerusalem and the Holy Places* (London: Anglo-Israel Association, 1968); Julius Stone, *Israel and Palestine: Assault on the Law of Nations* (Baltimore: Johns Hopkins University Press, 1981). Yehuda Zvi Blum, "The Missing Revisioner: Reflections on the Status of Judea and Samaria," *Israel Law Review* 3 (1968): 279; Meir Shamgar, "The Observance of International Law in the Administered Territories," *Israel Yearbook on Human Rights* 1 (1971): 262. Watson, *The Oslo Accords*, p. 268*n*12. Dumper, *The Politics of Jerusalem Since 1967*, pp. 231–49. See also Shlomo Slonim, "The United States and the Status of Jerusalem, 1947–1984," *Israel Law Review* 19 (1984): 179; William T. Mallison and Sally V. Mallison, *An International Law Analysis of the Major United Nations Resolutions Concerning the Palestine Question: Study Prepared and Published at the Request of the Committee on the Exercise of the Inalienable Rights of the Palestinian People* (New York: United Nations, 1979).

81. In a collection of UN documents from between 1947 and 1997, there are no less than 66 Security Council, General Assembly Council, and UNESCO resolutions on Jerusalem. See Palestinian Academic Society for the Study of International Affairs, *Documents on Jerusalem* (Jerusalem: PASSIA, 1996), pp. 225–291.

82. The United Kingdom and Pakistan were the only two countries in the UN to recognize the Jordanian annexation of the West Bank including East Jerusalem. Lapidoth and Hirsch, *The Jerusalem Question and Its Resolution*, p. 23.

83. Palestinians have succeeded in thwarting Israeli attempts to avoid parity in territorial exchanges. Initial proposals at Camp David, where the proportion proposed by Israeli negotiators was approximately 9:1, have been whittled down to 1:1, that is, for every square kilometer of the OPTs that Israel acquires, Palestinians should receive a square kilometer of land located in Israel of equal quality and value. This is now accepted by all the major sponsors of the negotiations, such as the Quartet.

84. International Court of Justice, "Legal Consequences of the Construction of a Wall in the Occupied Palestinian Territory," advisory opinion, para. 141, July 9, 2004. The full text of the ICJ opinion is available online at www.icj-cij.org/docket/index.php?p1=3&p2=4&k=5a

&case=131&code=mwp&p3=4. A similar view is also adopted by Professor Robbie Sabel, former adviser to the Israeli Ministry of Foreign Affairs. See his "The International Court of Justice Decision on the Separation Barrier and the Green Line," *Israel Law Review* 38 (2005): 316.

85. UNOCHA, Special Focus: Barrier Update, p. 23.

2. THE "SOFTER" BORDERS OF THE CITY

1. Tovi Fenster, *The Global City and the Holy City: Narratives on Knowledge, Planning and Diversity* (Essex: Pearson Education, 2004), p. 126ff. Fenster, an Israeli academic, describes similar shifts in "comfort" from an anthropological and planning perspective.

2. Violence is also a manifestation and consolidator of identities and can act as a demarcation symbol between communities. See T. Wilson, *Frontiers of Violence: Conflict and Identity in Ulster and Upper Silesia, 1918–1922* (Oxford: Oxford University Press, 2010).

3. The literature on the conflict in Belfast is extensive. A selection of useful publications is Frederick Boal and Stephen Royle, *Enduring City: Belfast in the Twentieth Century*, (Belfast: Blackstaff, 2007); Emrys Jones, *A Social Geography of Belfast* (London: Oxford University Press, 1960); Anthony C. Hepburn, "The Failure of Chronic Violence: Belfast," in Anthony C. Hepburn, *Contested Cities in the Modern West* (Basingstoke: Palgrave Macmillan, 2004), pp. 158–88; Peter Shirlow and Brendan Murtagh, *Belfast: Segregation, Violence and the City* (London: Pluto, 2006), chapter 3. The last is very instructive on the enduring impact of enclaving.

4. John Yarwood, *Rebuilding Mostar: Urban Reconstruction in a War Zone* (Liverpool: Liverpool University Press, 1999).

5. Scott Bollens, *City and Soul in Divided Societies* (Routledge: London, 2012); see chapters 12 and 13.

6. The term *reunification* is a controversial term and tends to be used by Israeli officials to describe the incorporation of East Jerusalem into the Israeli state and thus, it is argued, glossing over the conquest and implying a return to a more normal situation. For Palestinians, East Jerusalem was not reunited but occupied, and they perceive its integration into West Jerusalem as a national loss and a landgrab by Israel. I use the term here in a technical sense.

7. In a policy decision of monumental folly and strategic myopia by Israeli planners, the Green Line was partially reinstated in the mid-1990s by the construction of an eight-lane expressway, Road No. 1, along much of the former Green Line. See the critique of this expressway in Wendy Pullan, P. Misselwitz, R. Nasrallah, H. Yacobi, "Jerusalem's Road 1," *City* 11, no. 2 (2007): 176–98.

8. One of the anonymous reviewers of this volume has pointed out that the standard legal view is that occupation is neither legal nor illegal, but simply a question of fact which calls for regulation (that is "occupation is a factual situation which gives rise to normative consequences but is itself not normatively qualified"). In this way acts undertaken in the conduct of an occupation may be unlawful, such as racial discrimination or other human

rights violations, but the conventional view, the reviewer argues, is that this does not, in itself, make the occupation unlawful. This is a nuanced legal distinction I and others sometimes fail to make clear, not because it is not accurate, but because the effect of committing acts that are illegal and the act of occupation are politically indistinguishable. In this respect, references in this book to the "illegality of the Israeli occupation" are utilized as a short form that would be acceptable to most political scientists, but not, I now understand, to legal scholars.

9. See chapter 1n54.

10. An example can be seen in the 2009 EU Heads of Mission Report on East Jerusalem in which EU states were recommended to emphasize the illegality of the Israeli occupation through by not accepting Israeli protocols for visiting politicians and coordinating such visits with the PNA in Ramallah. This is available online at www.scribd.com/doc/23721677/ EU-heads-of-missionreports-on-East-Jerusalem-Jerusalem-and-the-Middle-East -peace-process.

11. See also note 7, this chapter.

12. Jeremy Waldron, professor of law at New York University, has wrestled with this issue of what rights accrue to settlers over time. See his articles: Jeremy Waldron, "Superseding Historical Injustice," *Ethics* 103, no. 1 (October 1992): 4–28, and "Settlement, Return, and the Supersession Thesis," *Theoretical Inquiries in Law* 5, no. 2 (July 2004): 237–59. I shall return to his arguments in my final chapter.

13. See my contribution to this debate in Michael Dumper, "Constructive Ambiguities? Jerusalem, International Law and the Peace Process" in Susan Akram, Michael Dumper, Michael Lynk, and Iain Scobbie, *International Law and the Israeli-Palestinian Conflict: A Rights-Based Approach to Middle East Peace* (Abingdon: Routledge. 2011).

14. There are a very large number of publications on the situation of Palestinian citizens of Israel. See for example: Ian Lustick, *Arabs in the Jewish State: Israel's Control of a National Minority* (Austin: University of Texas Press, 1980); Sabri Jiryis, *The Arabs in Israel* (London: Monthly Review, 1976); Nadim Rouhana, *Palestinian Citizens in an Ethnic Jewish State: Conflict in Identities* (New Haven: Yale University Press, 1997); see also Ephraim Nimni, *The Challenges of Post-Zionism: Alternatives to Fundamentalist Politics in Israel* (London: Zed, 2003); Adam Garfinkle, *Politics and Society in Modern Israel: Myths and Realities*, 2d ed. (New York: Sharp, 2000); Ehud Sprinzak and Larry Diamond, *Israeli Democracy Under Stress* (Boulder: Lynne Rienner, 1993); Michael Dumper, "Israel: Constraints on Consolidation" in David Potter, David Goldblatt, Margaret Kiloh, and Paul Lewis, eds., *Democratization* (London: Polity, 1997); Calvin Goldscheider, *Israel's Changing Society Population, Ethnicity, and Development*, 2d ed. (Colorado: Westview, 2002); Emma C. Murphy and Clive Jones, *Israel: Challenges to Identity, Democracy and the State* (London: Routledge, 2002); Peter Medding, *The Founding of Israeli Democracy, 1948–67* (Oxford: Oxford University Press, 1990); Keith Kyle and Joel Peters, *Whither Israel: The Domestic Challenges* (London: Royal Institute for International Affairs, 1993).

15. Thirty-five percent of Palestinian land in East Jerusalem has been confiscated by the Israeli state. Another 30 percent has been designated green areas and cannot be developed

by Palestinians. Akiva Eldar, "Discrimination Is Flourishing in East Jerusalem," *Ha'aretz,* May 3, 2010, available online at www.haaretz.com/print-edition/opinion/disrimination-is -fluorishing-in-east-jerusalem-1.287733. Further details of these policies will be examined later on in this chapter. The impact Israeli exclusivism can be found in Moshe Amirav, *Jerusalem Syndrome: The Palestinian-Israeli Battle for the Holy City* (Eastbourne: Sussex Academic, 2009); Amir Cheshin, Bill Hutman, and Avi Melamed, *Separate and Unequal: The Inside Story of Israeli Rule in East Jerusalem* (Cambridge: Harvard University Press, 1999).

16. Michael Dumper and Wendy Pullan, "Jerusalem: The Cost of Failure," Chatham House Briefing Paper, Chatham House: The Royal Institute of International Affairs (February 2010), p. 11, available online at www.chathamhouse.org.uk/publications/papers/view/-/ id/835/.

17. Ian Lustick, "Reinventing Jerusalem," *Foreign Policy* 93 (Winter 1993): 41–59; and "Has Israel Annexed Jerusalem?" *Middle East Policy* 5, no. 1 (1997): 34–45.

18. In a later personal communication to me, Lustick answered this rhetorical question in more detail: the strategy was to create the "hegemony of annexation" without the formal deed that would expose the hegemonic project to fatal attack. East Jerusalem could be then ruled by Israel as if it had been annexed without having to pay the political costs of formally annexing it. E-mails October 3 and 9, 2012.

19. See chapter 1*n*77.

20. A leading Palestinian scholar of 1970s, the late Sabri Jiryis, referred to this raft of Israeli legislation as "the laws of absorption" to indicate the objective of making Israeli sovereignty more palatable to East Jerusalemite Palestinians. See Sabri Jiryis, "Israeli Laws as Regards Jerusalem," in *The Legal Aspects of the Palestine Problem with Special Regard to the Question of Jerusalem,* ed. Hans Kochler (Vienna: Wilhelm Braumuller, 1981), p. 187.

21. Dumper, *The Politics of Jerusalem Since 1967,* pp. 43–46*n*29; Terry Rempel, "The Significance of Israel's Partial Annexation of East Jerusalem," *Middle East Journal* 51, no. 4 (1997). The anonymous reviewer informs me that it is now the case that money changers are allowed to operate in Israel. See"Travelers Balk at New Money-changing Rates at Israel's Airport," *Ha'aretz,* April 6, 2012, available at www.haaretz.com/weekend/anglo-file/ travelers-balk-at-new-money-changing-rates-at-israel-s-airport-1.422937.

22. Article 4, Legal and Administrative Matters (Regulation) Law (Consolidated Version), 5730–1970, *Laws of the State of Israel* 24 (1968/70): 144–283.

23. See Jiryis, "Israeli Laws as Regards Jerusalem," pp. 181–91; cf. Yehuda Bar-Sela, "Law Enforcement in the Eastern Sector of Jerusalem" in *Jerusalem—Aspects of Law,* ed. Ora Ahimeir (Jerusalem: Jerusalem Institute for Israel Studies, 1983), p. xx; see also Michael Dumper, *Islam and Israel: Muslim Religious Endowments and the Jewish State* (Washington, DC: Institute for Palestine Studies, 1994), p. 109. The same law also prevented Palestinian residents of East Jerusalem from claiming their property in West Jerusalem.

24. There is also a weak cultural life for the Palestinian intelligentsia in East Jerusalem provided by the al-Hakawati Theatre, the Educational Bookshop, with its frequent public meetings and "meet the author" sessions, and the various fora of the Palestinian Academic Society for the Study of International Affairs.

25. Amirav, *Jerusalem Syndrome*, p. 113.

26. Hillel Cohen, *The Rise and Fall of Arab Jerusalem: Palestinian Politics and the City Since 1967* (New York: Routledge, 2011), p. 17.

27. Amirav, *Jerusalem Syndrome*, p. 114; and Cohen, *The Rise and Fall of Arab Jerusalem*, p. 95.

28. See the report on the 1998 elections: Badil Resource Centre for Refugees and Residency Rights, "Palestinians Boycott Israeli Municipal Elections in Jerusalem" (1998), available online at www.badil.org/fr/ressources-en-francais/51-press-releases-1998/87-press32–98.

29. See the argument over the futility of such expectations in Menachaem Klein, "The Good and Bad News About Israel's 'Peace Index,'" *Ha'aretz*, May 23, 2012.

30. Majid Al-Haj and Henry Rosenfeld, *Arab Local Government in Israel* (Boulder: Westview, 1990); Ian Lustick, *Arabs in the Jewish State* (1980); Oren Yiftachel, "State Policies, Land Control, and an Ethnic Minority: The Arabs in the Galilee Region, Israel," *Society and Space* 9 (1991): 329–62.

31. There is, in addition, the argument that an anti-Zionist alliance comprising ultra-Orthodox Jewish and Palestinian groups could dominate the Municipal Council. However, a leading Israeli scholar on the ultra-Orthodox community in Jerusalem, Menachem Friedman, is dismissive of this potential. See Menachem Friedman, "Haredim and Palestinians in Jerusalem," in *Jerusalem: A City and Its Future*, ed. Marshall J. Breger and Ora Ahimeir (Syracuse: Syracuse University Press, 2002). See also Amirav, *Jerusalem Syndrome*, pp. 99–100.

32. Declaration 1993, Annex 1, para.1.

33. Ruth Lapidoth, "Jerusalem: Some Legal Aspects," in Breger and Ahimeir, *Jerusalem*, p. 80.

34. See Central Elections Commission for Palestine, "Voting Procedures for Jerusalem Residents PLC Elections 2006," available online at www.elections.ps:90/template.aspx?id=266.

35. An in-depth description of the tortuous negotiations over how the Israeli post offices would function during election day can be found in Menachem Klein, *Jerusalem: The Contested City* (London: Hurst, 2001), pp. 230–31.

36. Israeli-Palestinian Interim Agreement on the West Bank and the Gaza Strip (Oslo II), Annex 2, Article 6, no.1, September 28 (1995), available online at www.cfr.org/israel/oslo-ii-accords-interim-agreement-west-bank-gaza-strip/p9676.

37. Cohen, *The Rise and Fall of Arab Jerusalem*, p. 33. See also Klein, *Jerusalem*, pp. 235–36.

38. Klein, *Jerusalem*, p. 234.

39. Cohen makes the point that the youth of Palestinian population of East Jerusalem have grown up with no experience of PNA, unlike their compatriots in Hebron, Ramallah, and Nablus. See Cohen, *The Rise and Fall of Arab*, p. 36.

40. *System* may be too strong a word as the provision of education in East Jerusalem is, as we shall see, a hodgepodge of providers both inside and outside of Israeli and Palestinian state control.

41. See, for example, Kenneth D. Bush and Diana Saltarelli, *The Two Faces of Education in Ethnic Conflict* (Florence: United Nations Children's Fund, Innocenti Research Centre, 2000); Sobhi Tawil and Alexandra Harley, "Education and Identity-based Conflict: Assessing Curriculum Policy for Social and Civic Reconstruction," in *Education, Conflict and Social Cohesion*, ed. UNESCO International Bureau of Education 9, no. 39 (April 27, 2004).

42. The education of Palestinians inside Israel is a subject of great controversy and of Palestinian efforts to improve both their representation in the curriculum and to provide a deeper understanding of the Palestinian, Arab, Muslim, and Christian heritage of the country. See Nadim Rouhana, *Palestinian Citizens in an Ethnic Jewish State: Conflict in Identities* (New Haven: Yale University Press, 1997), p. 86. A fuller discussion of this issue can be found in Sami Mar'i, *Arab Education in Israel* (Syracuse: Syracuse University Press, 1978); Majid al-Haj, *Education, Empowerment and Control: The Case of the Arabs in Israel* (Albany: State University of New York Press, 1995).

43. Klein, *Jerusalem*, p. 68.

44. Cohen, *The Rise and Fall of Arab Jerusalem*, p. 86.

45. Amirav, *Jerusalem Syndrome*, p. 113.

46. Cohen, *The Rise and Fall of Arab Jerusalem*, pp. 86–87.

47. Klein, *Jerusalem*, p. 70.

48. Ibid., p. 71.

49. UNOCHA, East Jerusalem: Key Humanitarian Concerns, Special Focus (March 2011), p. 86, available online at www.ochaopt.org/documents/ocha_opt_Jerusalem_FactSheet_December_2011_english.pdf.

50. Association for Civil Rights in Israel and Ir Amim, The East Jerusalem School System—Annual Status Report (September 2011), available online at www.ir-amim.org.il/Eng/?CategoryID=254.

51. See Jalal Abu Khater, Israel Censors Palestinian Textbooks in East Jerusalem, Electronic Intifada, http://electronicintifada.net/blog/jalal-abukhater/israel-censors-palestinian-text books-east-jerusalem; The Civic Coalition for Defending the Palestinians' Rights in Jerusalem: The Municipality of Jerusalem Seeks Controlling the Palestinian Education System in the City, press release, available at www.badil.org/phocadownload/Press_Releases/2010–2015/THe%20Civic%20Coalition%20for%20Defending%20the%20Pal estinians%27%20Rights%20in%20Jerusalem_The%20Municipality%20of%20Jerusalem% 20seeks%20controlling%20the%20Palestinian%20Education%20System%20in%20 the%20City.pdf; www.facebook.com/note.php?note_id=10150313962466017.

52. Interview with Meir Margalit, Meretz muncipal councillor, March 17, 2012. One explanation for the reversal of the proposals to amend the curriculum in Palestinian schools in East Jerusalem was electoral. It has been estimated that the incumbent Israeli mayor of the city, Nir Barakat, is short of ten thousand votes to be reelected. The previous election was boycotted by the ultra-Orthodox, which allowed Barakat to defeat his main rival. However, the indications are that the ultra-Orthodox will field their own candidate at the next election thus eroding Barakat's support. The curriculum issue is one that will deter any wavering Palestinian voters, and he does not wish to antagonize them.

53. Association for Civil Rights in Israel, The East Jerusalem School System.

54. According to their report in 2011, there were twenty-one times more educational advisers in West Jerusalem than in the Palestinian sector in East Jerusalem. Association for Civil Rights in Israel, The East Jerusalem School System.

55. Compulsory Education Law, 1949, Laws of the State of Israel, 3:125. Cited in UNOCHA, East Jerusalem: Key Humanitarian Concerns, p. 85.

56. Ibid.

57. Ibid., p. 91.

58. Many graduates from al-Quds University, particularly in the medical field, are not able to find employment in Jerusalem medical institutions as their certificates are not recognized by the Israeli authorities. See ibid., p. 95. See also Joel Greenberg, "Premier Palestinian Medical School Graduates Struggle to Work in Jerusalem," *Washington Post,* July 16, 2012, available online at www.washingtonpost.com/world/middle_east/premier-palestinian-medical -school-graduates-struggle-to-work-in-jerusalem/2012/07/15/gJQAlzpDoW_story.html.

59. Cohen, *The Rise and Fall of Arab Jerusalem,* p. 104.

60. See discussion in chapter 1nn64–65. See also discussion in Michael Dumper, *The Politics of Jerusalem Since 1967* (New York: Columbia University Press, 1996), pp. 36–37.

61. For further details, see, for example, Foundation for Middle East Peace, "Israeli Settlements in the Occupied Territories: A Guide," *Settlement Report* 12, no. 7 (March 2002), available online at www.fmep.org/reports/special-reports/a-guide-to-israeli-settlements-in-the-occupied-territories/israeli-settlements-in-the-occupied-territories-a-guide; UNOCHA, East Jerusalem: Key Humanitarian Concerns, pp. 50–65; International Peace and Cooperation Centre, *Jerusalem on the Map III* (Jerusalem: International Peace and Cooperation Centre, 2007).

62. Meir Margalit, *Seizing Control of Space in East Jerusalem* (Tel Aviv: Sifrei Aliat Gag, 2010); Dumper and Pullan, "Jerusalem: The Cost of Failure," p. 7; UNOCHA, East Jerusalem: Key Humanitarian Concerns, pp. 53–58.

63. UNOCHA , East Jerusalem: Key Humanitarian Concerns, p. 29.

64. Eyal Weizman, *Hollow Land: Israel's Architecture of Occupation* (London: Verso, 2007). Rafi Segal, Eyal Weizman, and David Tartakover, eds., *A Civilian Occupation: The Politics of Israeli Architecture* (London: Verso, 2003).

65. See the map in Philip Misselwitz and Tim Rieniets, *City of Collision: Jerusalem and the Principles of Conflict Urbanism* (Basel: Birkhäuser, 2006), pp. 206–7.

66. UNOCHA , East Jerusalem: Key Humanitarian Concerns, pp. 26–39.

67. Yael Stein, "The Quiet Deportation: Revocation of Residency of East Jerusalem Palestinians," joint report by HaMoked and B'Tselem (April 1997), p. 4, available at www.hamoked .org/items/10200_eng.pdf, cited in UNOCHA, East Jerusalem: Key Humanitarian Concerns, p. 13.

68. Charles B. Keely, "The International Refugee Regime(s): The End of the Cold War Matters," *International Migration Review* 35, no. 1 (2001): 303–14. Arthur Helton, *The Price of Indifference: Refugees and Humanitarian Action in the New Century* (Oxford: Oxford University Press 2002).

69. Hilal Khasan, "Palestinian Resettlement in Lebanon: Behind the Debate," Palestinian Refugee ReseachNET (April 1994), available online at www.arts.mcgill.ca/mepp/new _prrn/research/papers/khashan_9404.htm.

70. Danielle Jefferis, "Institutionalising Statelessness: The Revocation of Residency Rights of Palestinian in East Jerusalem," *International Journal of Refugee Law* 24, no. 2 (May 2012): 202–30.

71. See chapter 5 of Dumper, *The Politics of Jerusalem Since 1967,* especially pp. 128–59.

72. For further details of the restrictions on health provision in the Palestinian enclaves in East Jerusalem see UNOCHA, East Jerusalem: Key Humanitarian Concerns, pp. 100–11.

73. Exceptions: Uzi Benziman and Meron Benevisti, *Jerusalem: The Torn City* (Minneapolis: Israel Typeset and the University of Minneapolis, 1976); Meron Benvenisti, *City of Stone: The Hidden History of Jerusalem* (Berkeley: University of California Press, 1996).

74. Amir Cheshin, Bill Hutman, and Avi Melamed, *Separate and Unequal: The Inside Story of Israeli Rule in East Jerusalem* (Cambridge: Harvard University Press, 1999). Amirav, *Jerusalem Syndrome.*

75. The most well known of these are Bimkom, HaMoked, B'Tselem, the Association of Civil Rights in Israel (ACRI), and the International Campaign Against Housing Demolitions (ICAHD).

76. Meir Margalit, *Discrimination in the Heart of the Holy City* (Jerusalem: International Peace and Cooperation Centre, 2006).

77. An EU Heads of Mission report in December 2008 suggested that as little as 5–10 percent of the Jerusalem municipal budget is spent in Palestinian East Jerusalem. See Rory Mc-Carthy, "Israel Is Annexing East Jerusalem Says EU," *Guardian,* March 7, 2009, available online at www.guardian.co.uk/world/2009/mar/07/israelpalestine-eu-report-jerusalem.

78. Bill Hutman and Amir Cheshin, "Living Together and Apart in Jerusalem," in *Jerusalem: A City and Its Future,* ed. Marshall J. Breger and Ahimeir Ora (Syracuse: Syracuse University Press, 2002), pp. 410–11.

79. *Maariv,* October 10, 1990, cited in Amirav, *Jerusalem Syndrome,* p. 115.

80. Ibid., p. 116.

81. Jerusalem Municipality, Report on Comparisons of Services and Infrastructure Between East and West of the City (Jerusalem: Office of the Director-General of the Municipality, 2000), cited in Amirav, *Jerusalem Syndrome,* p. 117.

82. Ibid.

3. THE SCATTERED BORDERS OF HOLINESS

1. Yitzhak Reiter, Marlen Eordegian, and Marwan Abu Khallaf, "Between Divine and Human: The Complexity of Holy Places in Jerusalem," in *Jerusalem: Points of Friction—and Beyond,* ed. Moshe Maoz and Sami Nusseibeh (Boston: Kluwer Law International, 2000), pp. 95–153. David E. Guinn, *Protecting Jerusalem's Holy Sites: A Strategy for Negotiating a Sacred Peace* (Cambridge: Cambridge University Press, 2006).

2. Gavin Young, *Iraq Land of Two Rivers* (London: Collins St. James Place, 1980); Meir Litvak, *Shi'i Scholars of Nineteenth-century Iraq: The 'Ulama' of Najaf and Karbala',* (Cambridge: Cambridge University Press, 1998); Yitzhak Nakash, *The Shi'is of Iraq* (Princeton: Princeton University Press, 1994).

3. Julia Clancy-Smith, *Rebel and Saint: Muslim Notables, Populist Protest, Colonial Encounters (Algeria and Tunisia, 1800–1904)* (Berkeley: University of California Press, 1997); Juan Cole, *Sacred Space and the Holy War: The Politics, Culture and History of Shi'ite Islam* (London:

I. B.Tauris, 2002); Roger Owen, *State, Power and Politics in the Making of the Modern Middle East* (London: I. B.Tauris, 2000).

4. Dale Eickelman, "Is There an Islamic City? The Making of a Quarter in a Moroccan Town," *International Journal of Middle East Studies* 5 (1974): 274–94.

5. Masashi Haneda and Toru Miura, *Islamic Urban Studies: Historical Review and Perspectives* (London: Kegan Paul International, 1994). See also Kenneth Brown, *People of Sale: Tradition and Change in a Moroccan City, 1830–1930* (Manchester: Manchester University Press, 1976).

6. She argues, "How is it that we have a large body of literature about an intellectual construction of reality called the 'Islamic city' while we have few or no articles, books and conferences about the Christian city, the Buddhist City, the Hindu City, or the Pagan City?" Cited by Masatoshi Kisaichi, "Maghrib," in *Islamic Urban Studies: Historical Review and Perspectives*, ed. Masashi Haneda and Toru Miura (London: Kegan Paul International, 1994), p. 41. See also Janet Abu-Lughod, "Islamic City: Historical Myth, Islamic Essence, and Contemporary Relevance," *International Journal of Middle East Studies* 19 (1987): 155–76, "What Is Islamic About a City? Some Comparative Reflections," in Yukawa Takeshi, ed., *Urbanism in Islam: The Proceedings of the International Conference on Urbanism in Islam* 1 (Tokyo: Research Project Urbanism in Islam, 1989), pp. 193–217, and "Urbanisation in the Arab World and the International System," in *The Urban Transformation of the Developing World*, ed. Josef Gugler (Oxford: Oxford University Press, 1996), p. 193.

7. Francis E. Peters, *Jerusalem and Mecca: The Typology of the Holy City in the Near East* (New York: New York University Press, 1986).

8. See the Web site of the Council of Religious Institutions of the Holy Land: www.crihl.org. Some detailed discussions have taken place on how to extend the responsibilities of this council. See Michael Dumper, *An Inter-religious Council for Jerusalem* (Madrid: Toledo International Centre for Peace, 2011), available online at www.toledopax.org/uploads/Religious%20Council%20of%20Jerusalem.pdf.

9. Council of Religious Institutions of the Holy Land, "Statement Condemning Desecration of St Francis Convent," October 3, 2012, available online at www.crihl.org/view/updates.

10. Joel P. Brereton, "Sacred Space" in *The Encyclopaedia of Religion*, ed. Mircea Eliade (New York: Macmillan, 1987).

11. A depressing yet excellent example of this is the imposed partition of the al-Ibrahimi Mosque in Hebron, which I will discuss in more detail at the end of this chapter.

12. There is an exception to this rule with nomadic societies. The Hebrew Ark of the Covenant and the Holy of Holies was initially a movable sacred space which only became associated with the Temple Mount/Haram al-Sharif when the Hebrew tribes settled in Canaan. The Mongol adoration of Genghis Khan was for centuries based upon artifacts associated with him placed in tents, or *gers*, which could be and were moved in times of danger. See John Man, *Genghis Khan: Life, Death and Resurrection* (London, Transworld, 2005).

13. Ron E. Hassner, "'To Halve and to Hold': Conflicts over Sacred Space and the Problem of Indivisibility," *Security Studies* 12, no.4 (Summer 2003): 1–33.

14. Isak Svensson, "Fighting with Faith: Religion and Conflict Resolution in Civil Wars," *Journal of Conflict Resolution* 51, no. 6 (2007): 930–49.

15. See, for example, Article 77 of the United Nations Convention on the Law of the Sea, December 10, 1982, available online at www.un.org/Depts/los/convention_agreements/convention_overview_convention.htm. For further discussion on this topic see also Ruth Lapidoth, "Jerusalem: Some Legal Aspects," in *Jerusalem: A City and Its Future*, ed. Marshall J. Breger and Ora Ahimeir (Syracuse: Syracuse University Press, 2002), pp. 85–87.

16. Eyal Weizman, "The Subversion of Jerusalem's Sacred Vernaculars: Four New Planning Tools for a Holy Environment," in *The Next Jerusalem: Sharing the Divided City*, ed. Michael Sorkin (New York: Monacelli, 2002). Sophie Calle, *L'erouv de Jerusalem* (Arles Cedex: Actes Sud, 1996).

17. Eruvs are not particular to Israel. They also exist in other cities such as London, New York, St. Louis, and many other cities across the USA. See Sophie Watson, "Symbolic Spaces of Difference: Contesting the Eruv in Barnet, London and Tenafly, New Jersey," *Environment and Planning D: Society and Space* 23 (2005): 597–643; Barbara Mann, *Space and Place in Jewish Studies* (New Jersey: Rutgers University Press, 2012); Yosef Gavriel Bechhofer, *The Contemporary Eruv: Eruvin In Modern Metropolitan Areas* (Jerusalem: BookSurge, 2006). An extension to the Manhattan Island, New York, eruv was recently approved by the New York City authorities. This is available online at http://sites.google.com/site/manhattaneruv/extension. In order to prevent repeated storm damage to eruvs, which can cause great stress to Jewish communities over whether they are breaking religious law, one observant Jew has introduced the idea of a laser eruv. See http://dziga.com/laser/.

18. Michael Dumper, *The Politics of Jerusalem Since 1967* (New York: Columbia University Press), p. 204.

19. Tzvi Ben Gedalyahu, "Jerusalem Arabs View 'Eruv' as New Political Border," *Arutz Sheva*, October 8, 2010, available online at www.israelnationalnews.com/News/News.aspx/139040.

20. Studies on this relationship include Shlomo Hasson, *The Cultural Struggle Over Jerusalem* (Jerusalem: Floersheimer Institute for Policy Studies, 1996); Menachem Friedman, *The Haredi (Ultra-Othodox) Society: Sources, Trends and Processes* (Jerusalem: Jerusalem Institute for Israeli Studies, 1991). The British Mandate period is well covered in Jeff Halper, "Jewish Ethnicity in Jerusalem," in *Jerusalem: City of the Ages*, ed. Alice Eckhardt (New York: University Press of America, 1987).

21. These terms have been used in different ways over the past decades by the Israeli Central Bureau of Statistics in its annual Social Survey, which is available online at www1.cbs.gov.il/reader/?MIval=cw_usr_view_SHTML&ID=576.

22. Uziel O. Schmelz, *Modern Jerusalem's Demographic Evolution* (Jerusalem: Jerusalem Institute for Israel Studies, 1987), pp. 110–11; Benjamin Hyman, Israel Kimhi, and Joseph Savitzky, *Jerusalem in Transition: Urban Growth and Change, 1970's and 1980's* (Jerusalem: Jerusalem Institute for Israel Studies, 1985), p. 20.

23. "Table III/17—Jewish Population in Jerusalem, Aged 20 and Over, by Level of Religious Observance, 2003–2005—2007–2009," in Jerusalem Institute for Israel Studies, *Statistical*

Yearbook 2011 (Jerusalem: Jerusalem Institute for Israel Studies, 2012), available online at http://jiis.org/.upload/yearbook/10_11/C/shnaton%20C1711.pdf.

24. According to a report released by the Jerusalem Institute for Israel Studies, 59,900 pupils are enrolled in the state-run secular and religious school systems (40 percent), while 90,200 are enrolled in haredi-religious schools (60 percent). The same report reveals that, over a five-year period between 2003 and 2008, the number of students enrolled in the state-run religious and secular school system has decreased by 6 percent and the number of students enrolled in haredi-religious schools has increased by 11 percent. See "Most Jerusalemites Attend Haredi-Religious Schools," *Arutz Sheva*, May 25, 2009, available online at www.israelnationalnews.com/News/Flash.aspx/165421#.T5VdWNkrLEE. One should note that these figures only apply to Jewish Jerusalemites.

25. Nir Hasson, "J'lem Police 'Waging War' on Secular Protests, Activists Say," *Haaretz*, February 23, 2010, available online at www.haaretz.com/hasen/spages/1151398.html.

26. Joseph Glass and Rassem Khamaisi, "Report on the Socio-Economic Conditions in the Old City of Jerusalem," unpublished MS (Jereslem Project, Munk Centre for International Studies, University of Toronto, 2005), p. 24, available online at www.uwindsor.ca/joci/system/files/section1.pdf. A full copy is in my possession.

27. Dumper, *The Politics of Jerusalem Since 1967*, p. 204.

28. Figures for the Christian population are difficult to collate. Israeli figures differentiate between "Arab" and "non-Arab" Christians while other sources lump them together. The figures cited in this chapter have been taken from several sources: Daphne Tsimhoni, *Christian Communities in Jerusalem and the West Bank Since 1948: An Historical, Social and Political Study* (Westport, CT: Praeger, 1993), p. 26; Bernard Sabella, "Palestinian Christians: Realities and Hopes," unpublished MS (1998); Amnon Ramon, *Christians and Christianity in Jerusalem* (Jerusalem: Jerusalem Institute for Israel Studies, 2011), unpublished MS, available online at http://jiis.org/?cmd=newse.444&act=read&id=780.

29. Ramon, *Christians and Christianity*.

30. These figures do not refer to Jews from the former Soviet Union who immigrated to Israel in the late 1990s. It is estimated that one-third of these largely Russian immigrants are actually Christian, but met the criteria for immigration as they were able to identify one grandmother as Jewish. Most of these have settled in the coastal areas of Israel, but a few score are living in Jerusalem, leading to a revival of the Russian Orthodox Church there. There is a similar unrecorded presence of Eritrean Christians, usually practicing Ethiopian Orthodox, who have immigrated to Israel, an unknown number of whom are residing in Jerusalem. Conflict in Cities interview with Amnon Ramon, researcher at the Jerusalem Institute for Israel Studies, February 4, 2011.

31. The literature on the challenges facing Christians and Christian Palestinians in Jerusalem is extensive. The following are amongst the most informative: Karen Armstrong, *Jerusalem: One City, Three Faiths* (London: HarperCollins, 1996); Naim Ateek, Cedar Duaybis, and Maurine Tobin, *The Forgotten Faithful: A Window Into the Life and Witness of Christians in the Holy Land* (Jerusalem: Sabeel Ecumenical Liberation Theology Center, 2007); Raymond Cohen, *Saving the Holy Sepulchre: How Rival Christians Came Together to Rescue Their*

Holiest Shrine (New York: Oxford University Press, 2008); Saul P. Colbi, "The Christian Establishment in Jerusalem." in *Jerusalem: Problems and Prospects*, ed. Joel L. Kraemer (New York: Praeger, 1980); Michael Dumper, *The Politics of Sacred Space: The Old City of Jerusalem in the Middle East Conflict* (Boulder: Lynne Rienner, 2002). Kevork Hintlian, *History of the Armenians in the Holy Land.* (Jerusalem: Armenian Patriarchate, 1989); G. Linden, *Church Leadership in a Political Crisis: Joint Statements from the Jerusalem Heads of Churches, 1988–1992* (Uppsala: Swedish Institute for Missionary Research, 1994); Anthony O'Mahoney, Goran Gunner, and Kevork Hintlian, *The Christian Heritage in the Holy Land* (London: Scorpion Cavendish, 1995); Michael Prior and William Taylor, *Christians in the Holy Land* (London: World of Islam Festival Trust, 1994); Alisa Peled, "The Chrystallization of an Israeli Policy Towards Muslim and Christian Holy Places, 1948–1955," *Muslim World* 84, nos. 1–2 (January-April 1994); Amnon Ramon, "The Christian Element and the Jerusalem Question." *Background Papers for Policy Papers*, no. 4, unofficially translated by the Society of St. Ives (Jerusalem: Jerusalem Institute for Israel Affairs, 1996); Albert Rock, *The Status Quo in the Holy Places* (Jerusalem: Franciscan, 1989); Tsimhoni, *Christian Communities in Jerusalem and the West Bank Since 1948*; Walter Zander, *Israel and the Holy Places of Christendom* (London: Weidenfield and Nicolson, 1971).

32. Lionel G. A. Cust, *The Status Quo and the Holy Places* (facsimile vesion) (Jerusalem: Ariel, 1980).

33. This is particularly the case with the Greek Orthodox community, who have experienced serious tensions between clergy and laity for over a century. See Sotiris Roussos, "The Greek Orthodox Patriarchate and Community of Jerusalem," in *The Christian Heritage in the Holy Land,* ed. Anthony O'Mahoney, Goran Gunner, and Kevork Hintlian (London: Scorpion Cavendish, 1995); Anthony O'Mahoney, "Church, State, and the Christian Communities and the Holy Places of Palestine," in *Christians in the Holy Land,* ed. Michael Prior and William Taylor (London: World of Islam Festival Trust, 1994).

34. For a fuller exposition of this view, see Michael Dumper, "The Churches of Jerusalem in the Post-Oslo Period," *Journal of Palestine Studies* 122 31, no. 2 (Winter 2002): 51–65.

35. Zander, *Israel and the Holy Places of Christendom.* See also Oded Peri, *Christianity Under Islam in Jerusalem: The Question of the Holy Sites in Early Ottoman Times* (Leiden: Brill, 2001).

36. Ramon, *Christians and Christianity in Jerusalem.* See also Itamar Katz and Ruth Kark, "The Church and Landed Property: The Greek Orthodox Patriarchate of Jerusalem," *Middle Eastern Studies* 43, no. 3 (2007): 383–408.

37. One can compare this with 69 mosques and 1,198 synagogues. *Statistical Yearbook (1999),* table IX/2: Religious Institutions in Jerusalem, 1999. The explanatory notes to this data set say that these figures refer to institutions under the supervision of the Israeli Ministry of Religious Affairs. This may account for the improbably low number of mosques cited. Most of them will not be under the Israeli supervision.

38. A study on the Old City carried out by the Palestinian development agency, the Welfare Association, estimated that 12.4 percent of the properties in the Old City belonged to the Greek Orthodox Patriarchate, and between 6–7 percent to the Armenian Orthodox Patri-

archate. See Welfare Association, "Jerusalem, Heritage and Life: The Old City Revitalisa-tion Plan" (Jerusalem: Welfare Association, 2004), pp. 105–9.

39. Ramon, *Christians and Christianity*.

40. Conflict in Cities Interview with Amnon Ramon, researcher at the Jerusalem Institute for Israel Studies, February 4, 2011.

41. Tracking the Roman Catholic vote in the UN is a complex task and contingent upon which period and particular forum is being examined. The emergence of a "Roman Catho-lic bloc" can be traced mainly to the recognition of the Latin American states as members of the UN General Assembly. See Danilo Di Mauro, *The UN and the Arab-Israeli Conflict: American Hegemony and UN Intervention Since 1947* (Abingdon: Routledge, 2012). See also Paul Charles Merkley, *Christian Attitudes Towards the State of Israel* (Montreal: McGill-Queen's University Press, 2001), pp. 47–48, 140–42.

42. See, for example, United States Department of State, "Israel and the Occupied Territories," *International Religious Freedom Report* (July-December 2010), available online at www .state.gov/j/drl/rls/irf/2010_5/168266.htm.

43. For a further analysis of the St. John's Hospice incident, see Michael Dumper, "Christian-ity, Jerusalem, and Zionist Exclusivity: The St. John's Hospice Incident Reconsidered," in *Jerusalem Interrupted: Modernity and Colonial Transformation, 1917–the Present,* ed. Lena Jayyusi (London: Olive Branch, 2012).

44. See the following Web reports: "The Conflict in Jerusalem Between Orthodox Priests on the Position of the Patriarchate," *Mofakarat Al-Islam,* July 5, 2006, www.islammemo .cc/2006/07/05/8727.html; "Fleeing Greek Orthodox Treasurer Says Patriarch Irinuos Blessed, Signed the Deal," *IMEMC News—International Middle East Media Center,* March 30, 2005, www.imemc.org/index.php?obj_id=53&story_id=9858; "Arab Orthodox Conference Calls Patriarch Irinious I 'a Traitor,'" *IMEMC News—International Middle East Media Center,* April 7, 2005, www.imemc.org/index.php?obj_id=53&story_id=10136; "What Is Happening with the Orthodox Church," *Light in Galilee,* January 15, 2010, www .linga.org/christian-news-in-the-holy-land/article-1395.html. Subsequent to this contro-versy, Patriarch Theophilus has also been accused of selling property to Israeli ministries and is under investigation by the PNA.

45. Conflict in Cities, fieldwork, April 2010. See also Palestine Israel Ecumenical Forum, "Christians in the Holy Land Respond to Israeli Police Restrictions During Easter Celebrations," available online at www.oikoumene.org/en/programmes/public-witness -addressing-power-affirming-peace/churches-in-the-middle-east/pief/news-events/a/ browse/11/article/7313/christians-in-the-holy-la.html.

46. Moshe Dayan, *The Story of My Life* (Sphere: London, 1978), p. 390.

47. Interview, Shaykh Hassan Tahbub, May 2, 1989, cited in Michael Dumper, *Islam and Israel: Muslim Religious Endowments and the Jewish State* (Washington, DC: Institute for Pales-tine Studies, 1994), p. 160n29.

48. For further details, see my discussion, ibid., pp. 107–9.

49. Land ownership in the Old City confirms this sense of Israel being excluded. Only 19 per-cent of its land area is controlled by the Israeli state and its agencies, mostly expropriated

from Palestinian owners and the Waqf Administration. The rest of the property in the Old City is either waqf property, church property, or private Palestinian property. See Gilead Sher, Jonathan Gillis, and Amir Kadari, "The Legal Parameters of the Old City of Jerusalem Special Regime," Jerusalem Old City Project Special Report, University of Windsor (2005), p. 13. See also Michelle Oliel, "Property Rights and Ownership in the Old City of Jerusalem," Jerusalem Old City Project Special Report, University of Windsor (2006), p. 19. Both available online at www.uwindsor.ca/joci/commissioned-studies. From interviews I conducted during the mid-1980s the total of waqf property in the Old City, excluding the Haram area, can be estimated to be approximately between 45 and 50 percent. If you are including the Haram enclosure, which amounts to 17 percent of the Old City, I estimated that the grand total of waqf property in the Old City comes to approximately 67 percent. For further details, see Dumper, *Islam and Israel*, p. 106. A more recent survey carried out by the Old City of Jerusalem Revitalisation Programme of the Welfare Association is based on figures which suggest that 21.4 percent of residential houses were recorded as Islamic or Christian waqf, while another 24 percent were family waqfs. See Welfare Association, "Jerusalem: Heritage and Life: Old City Revitalization Plan," Welfare Association, Jerusalem and Ramallah (2004), p. 70 and pp. 105–6. An unpublished report by Ruth Lapidoth simply entitled "Old City Report" and cited in both Sher, Gillis, and Kadari, "The Legal Parameters of the Old City of Jerusalem Special Regime" and Oliel, "Property Rights and Ownership in the Old City of Jerusalem," p. 13 and p. 2, respectively, in supra, gives a figure of 24 percent of the Old City as Islamic waqf. However the citations do not say whether this includes the Haram enclosure or what proportion of the property in Palestinian private ownership is family waqf.

50. Aga Khan Award for Architecture, "Restoration of Al-Aqsa Mosque." Further details available online at www.akdn.org/architecture/project.asp?id=501.

51. *Idara al-awqaf al-islamiyya al-'ama, bayan:al-awqaf al-islamiyya fi al-daf al-gharbiyya, 1977–82* (Jerusalem: da'ira al-awqaf al-islamiyya), pp. 51–54, 60–63, 68–71, 74–78, 81–83, 97–91.

52. Interview with Adnan al-Husayni, March 31, 1987. Cited in Dumper, *Islam and Israel*, pp. 113–114. See also Dumper, *The Politics of Sacred Space*, pp. 4–5, where I also recount this story.

53. There is some evidence that these waqf schools are specifically being targeted by the Israeli municipality in order to weaken their role in the city. See UN-OCHA , *East Jerusalem: Key Humanitarian Concerns*, special focus (March 2011): pp. 85, 89, 91, available online at www .ochaopt.org/documents/ocha_opt_Jerusalem_FactSheet_December_2011_english.pdf.

54. Craig Larkin and Michael Dumper, "In Defence of Al-Aqsa: The Islamic Movement Inside Israel and Battle for Jerusalem," *Middle East Journal* 66, no. 1 (Winter 2012): 36.

55. See the Web site for the Welfare Association, available online at http://ocjrp.welfare -association.org/en/project/what-we-do/core-restoration-programmes/jerusalem-projects/ major-restoration-projects/islamic-museum.html.

56. See Dumper, *The Politics of Sacred Space*, pp. 78–82; Thomas Abowd, "The Moroccan Quarter: A History of the Present," *Jerusalem Quarterly File*, no. 7 (Winter 2000).

57. Michael Dumper, "Israeli Settlement in the Old City of Jerusalem," *Journal of Palestine Studies* 21 (Winter 1992): 32–53.

58. For further details on the radical settler movement, see Ian S. Lustick, *For the Land and for the Lord: Jewish Fundamentalism in Israel* (New York: Council of Foreign Relations, 1988); Gershom Gorenberg, *The Accidental Empire: Israel and the Birth of the Settlements, 1967–1977* (New York: Times, 2006).

59. The main groups during this period were Ataret Cohanim, Torat Cohanim, the Young Israel Movement, and the Yeshiva Birkat Avraham. They acquired property through another organization called Atara L'yoshna. For further details see Dumper, "Israeli Settlement in the Old City of Jerusalem," pp. 32–53.

60. This was known as the Klugman Commission, headed by a respected Israeli official, Haim Klugman. For further details see Margalit Meir, *Seizing Control of Space in East Jerusalem* (Jerusalem: Aliat Gag, 2010), p. 136ff. See also Dumper, *The Politics of Sacred Space*, pp. 58–67.

61. According to Israeli Ministry of Interior figures, the total number of Israelis residing in the Old City outside the Jewish quarter is 600. Cited in Meir, *Seizing Control of Space in East Jerusalem*, p. 58. The Welfare Association estimate for the year 2000 is 500 settlers. This figure is derived from subtracting its figure for the Jewish population residing in the Jewish Quarter (2,300) from its figure for the total Jewish population living in the Old City (2,800, itself derived from the Welfare Association's estimate that 1.7 percent of Israeli Jews living in East Jerusalem reside in the Old City); Welfare Association, "Jerusalem, Heritage and Life," p. 66. (Note a possible error in the Welfare Association calculations: 1.7 percent of Israeli Jewish settlers in East Jerusalem amounts to 2,810 people, but table 6 has this down as 3,800.) Note also that the Welfare Association defines, quite logically, all Israeli residents in the Old City as "settlers" and does not distinguish between those who have settled under government and municipal auspices and the radical groups I have delineated.

62. An extract of an application letter from a young couple to Atara L'yoshna wishing to participate in the *mitzva* (or good deed, religiously speaking) of settling in the Muslim quarters can be found in Dumper, *The Politics of Sacred Space*, p. 52.

63. Conflict in Cities, fieldwork, 2008–9. The cameras are numbered.

64. Welfare Association, "Jerusalem, Heritage and Life," pp. 66–68.

65. Conflict in Cities Interview, Dr Shadia Touqan, director, Technical Office of the Welfare Association Old City of Jerusalem Revitalisation Programme, March 18, 2012.

66. For more details, see Menachem Klein, *The Jerusalem Problem: The Struggle for Permanent Status* (Gainesville: University of Florida Press, 2003), pp. 55–56 and 116–18. An overview of settler activities in the Holy Basin area can be found in the reports by Ir Amim, such as "The Old City and the Historic Basin: Issues of Concern and Recent Developments"; see www.ir-amim.org.il/Eng/?CategoryID=271. See also Wendy Pullan and Max Gwiazda, "Jerusalem's Holy Basin: Who Needs It?" *Palestine-Israel Journal* 17, nos. 1–2 (2011): 172–79.

67. Wendy Pullan and Max Gwiazda, "The Biblical Present in Jerusalem's 'City of David,'" in *Memory, Culture and the Contemporary City: Building Sites*, ed. Andrew Webber, Uta

Staiger, and Henriette Steiner (London: Palgrave Macmillan, 2009). In 2008 approximately 380,000 people visited David's City (up from 25,000 in 2001). Contrast this, on one hand, to the 1.8 million who visited the Western Wall and, on the other hand, the Tower of David, a major Israeli state-run heritage site with biblical pretensions and fully developed museum, which only achieved 137,000 total visitors. The aim to make it one of Israel's most popular national historical parks is well within reach.

68. See the Ir Amim report, *Excavations and National Parks as Political Instruments*, available online at www.ir-amim.org.il/Eng/?CategoryID=269.

69. Michael Dumper and Wendy Pullan, "Jerusalem: The Cost of Failure," Chatham House Briefing Paper (London: Chatham House: The Royal Institute of International Affairs, February 2010), available online at www.chathamhouse.org.uk/publications/papers/view/-/id/835/.

70. For further details and an extensive discussion of these activities, see Dumper, *The Politics of Sacred Space*, pp. 86–93.

71. See Aga Khan Award for Architecture, 1986 Award Cycle, available online at www.akdn.org/architecture/project.asp?id=501.

72. The closure was opposed by certain members of the Austrian parent organization who provided funds to open up a clinic close by.

73. Naim Ateek, Cedar Duaybis, and Maurine Tobin, *The Forgotten Faithful: A Window Into the Life and Witness of Christians in the Holy Land* (Jerusalem: Sabeel Ecumenical Liberation Theology Center, 2007); Raymond Cohen, *Saving the Holy Sepulchre : How Rival Christians Came Together to Rescue Their Holiest Shrine* (New York: Oxford University Press, 2008).

74. See chapter 4 for a fuller discussion of PNA contributions to socioeconomic activities in East Jerusalem.

75. For the tortuous transition from effective Jordanian authority to that of the PNA in the appointment of the Mufti of Jerusalem, and also their respective roles in permanent status negotiations on the question of Jerusalem and the responsibility of the Waqf Administration, see Menachem Klein, *Jerusalem: The Contested City* (London: Hurst, 2001): pp. 176–82.

76. Old City of Jerusalem Revitalisation Programme, *Jerusalem: Heritage and Life: The Old City Revitalisation Plan* (Jerusalem: al-Sharq, 2004): p. 74. The Web site of the Old City of Jerusalem Revitalisation Programme is available online at http://ocjrp.welfare-association.org/en/section/what-we-do/core-restoration-programmes/jerusalem-projects/major-restoration-projects.

77. See Dumper, *The Politics of Sacred Space*, p.11 and 58ff for a fuller discussion of this issue. See also Old City of Jerusalem Revitalisation Programme, *Jerusalem: Heritage and Life*, pp. 106–10.

78. See objectives laid out in OCJRP, *Jerusalem: Heritage and Life*, p. 15.

79. See Aga Khan Award for Architecture, 1996 Award Cycle, available online at www.akdn.org/architecture/project.asp?id=2207.

80. For more details, see Jamil Dakwar, "The Islamic Movement Inside Israel: An Interview with Shaykh Ra'id Salah," *Journal of Palestinian Studies* 36, no. 2 (Winter 2007): 66–76. A

detailed analysis of the role of the Islamic movement in Jerualem since 2000 can be found in Larkin and Dumper, "In Defence of Al-Aqsa," pp. 31–52.

81. Larkin and Dumper, "In Defence of Al-Aqsa," pp. 35–36. See also Dan Diker, "The Expulsion of the Palestinian Authority from Jerusalem and the Temple Mount," *Jerusalem Centre for Public Affairs* 3, no. 51 (August 5, 2004): 1–9.

82. See Hillel Cohen, *The Rise and Fall of Arab Jerusalem, 1967–2008* (London: Routledge, 2010).

83. The restoration of the Marwani Halls can be viewed as a preemptive move by Palestinians to prevent Israeli settlers from tunneling under the Haram from the tunnels they had completed along the western wall of the Haram enclosure.

84. The role of UNESCO will be discussed more fully in the next chapter. On the Maghrabi Gate, see Michael Dumper and Craig Larkin, "The Politics of Heritage and the Limitations of International Agency in Divided Cities: The Role of UNESCO in Jerusalem's Old City," *Review of International Studies* 38, no. 1 (January 2012): 39–43. This new monitoring mechanism was proposed at the thirty-first session of the WHC in Christchurch, New Zealand, 2007, and immediately applied to the Mughrabi Gate controversy. The first Reinforced Monitoring Report was received in October 2007, and this has been followed by five others. The fifth report, in September 2008, recommended the continuation of this specific form of supervision, reporting back "at least every three months, until the 33rd session of the World Heritage Committee in 2009." See also Daniel Seidemann, "The Events Surrounding the Mugrabi Gate—2007: A Case Study," Jerusalem Old City Initiative, University of Windsor (June 2007), available online at http://cronus.uwindsor.ca/units/jerusalem/main.nsf/54ef3e94e5fe816e85256d6e0063d208/54709e03ea461c2f8525712400 54390b/$FILE/Mugrabi%20-%20FINAL%5B1%5D.pdf.

85. See Michael Dumper, "Jerusalem's Troublesome Sheikh," *Guardian*, October 7, 2009, available online at www.guardian.co.uk/commentisfree/2009/oct/07/jerusalem-sheik-raed-salah-islamic.

86. See figures cited in Larkin and Dumper, "In Defence of Al-Aqsa," p. 48*n*76.

87. See the Islamic Movement's Web site: www.islamic-aqsa.com/Web/pages/Details.aspx?ID=803.

88. I first explored this idea in Michael Dumper, "Security and the Holy Places in Jerusalem: An Israeli Policy of Incremental Control—'Hebronisation'?" in *Locating Urban Conflicts: Ethnicity, Nationalism, and the Everyday*, ed. Wendy Pullan and Brit Baillie-Warren (Basingstoke: Palgrave-Macmillan, 2013). See also Michael Dumper and Wendy Pullan "Jerusalem: The Cost of Failure," Chatham House Briefing Paper (London: Chatham House: The Royal Institute of International Affairs, February 2010), available online at www.chathamhouse.org.uk/publications/papers/view/-/id/835/.

89. Yitzhak Reiter, "Contest or Cohabitation in Shared Holy Places? The Cave of the Patriarchs and Samuel's Tomb," in *Confrontation and Co-existence in Holy Places: Religious, Political, and Legal Aspects in the Israeli-Palestinian Context*, ed. Marshall Breger, Yitzhak Reiter, and Leonard Hammer (London: Routledge, 2010).

90. For further details see Dumper, "'Hebronisation'?" in Pullan and Baillie-Warren, *Urban Conflicts*.
91. See chapter 2, note 36. See Jerusalem Institute for Israel Studies, *Jerusalem Statistical Yearbook (2011)*; further details are available online at http://jiis.org/.upload/yearbook/10_11/C/shnaton%20C0III.pdf. Note that these figures refer to the municipal borders established in 1967 and not only those areas inside the Separation Wall. For settler totals, see Foundation for Middle East Peace, *Settlements in East Jerusalem—General Stats*, available online at www.fmep.org/settlement_info/settlement-info-and-tables/stats-data/settlements-in-east-jerusalem.
92. The rabbinical ruling on Jews not entering the Haram al-Sharif/Temple Mount can be found in *Temple Mount Faithful et al v. Attorney General*, Israel Supreme Court sitting as the High Court of Justice, 4185/90, *Piskei Din* 47, no. 5 (1993): 221–28, cited in Yitzhak Reiter, "Jewish –Muslim *Modus Vivendi* at the Temple Mount/Haram al-Sharif since 1967," in *Jerusalem: A City and Its Future*, ed. Marshall J. Breger and Ora Ahimeir (Syracuse, NY: Syracuse University Press, 2002.), p. 273.
93. Yizhar Be'er, "Targeting the Temple Mount: A Current Look at Threats to the Temple Mount by Extremist and Messianic Groups" (Center for the Protection of Democracy in Israel—Keshev) January 2001, available online at www.keshev.org.il/images/stories/PDF/2001_temple_mount%20_full_text_eng.pdf. See also Jeremy Sharon, "Rabbis Warn Jews Against Going to Temple Mount," *Jerusalem Post*, March 6, 2012, available online at www.jpost.com/Jewish World/JewishNews/Article.aspx?id=260681.
94. Sufyan Abuzayda, "Continuity and Change in Israeli Policy Over Jerusalem Before and After the Establishment of the Israeli State" (PhD diss., University of Exeter, 2005). See also Amnon Ramon, "Delicate Balances at the Temple Mount, 1967–1999" in Breger and Ahimeir, *Jerusalem*.
95. See Edmund Sanders, "More Jews Praying on Site Also Sacred to Muslims," *Los Angeles Times*, October 27, 2012, available online at www.latimes.com/news/nationworld/world/la-fg-jerusalem-prayers-20121028,0,954464.story.

4. THE INTERNATIONAL COMMUNITY AND THE LIMITS OF SOVEREIGNTY

1. The "greenness" of the western areas is also due to many factors in addition to climatic ones, not least the acquisition of Palestinian land in 1948 and their afforestation by Israeli bodies in order to erase signs of demolished villages. See also Shaul Ephraim Cohen, *The Politics of Planting: Israeli-Palestinian Competition for Control of Land in the Jerusalem Periphery* (Chicago: Chicago University Press, 1993).
2. Noel Denholm-Young, "The Mappa Mundi of Richard of Haldingham at Hereford," *Speculum* 32, no. 2 (April 1957): 307–14.
3. The search was carried out between May 7 and 25, 2012, and made in the Any Language category. See the appendix. I also searched in six languages (English, French, Arabic, Russian, Farsi, and Chinese), but the totals exceeded the Any Language category. This high-

4. THE INTERNATIONAL COMMUNITY AND THE LIMITS OF SOVEREIGNTY

lights one of the vagaries of the search formulas of the Web, which often have repeat citations. It is also important to note that citations on the Web do not by definition mean that the Web site is a Web site on the city being searched. The citations will also pick up Web sites that simply have the city in the address and surnames, such as Jack London and Isaiah Berlin.

4. See my discussion on the definition of a holy city in chapter 3.

5. See the appendix for a breakdown of all the figures cited in this section.

6. See the appendix.

7. E-mail correspondence with Tim Llewelyn, former BBC correspondent covering the Middle East. June 18, 2012.

8. All foreign journalists working on the Palestine-Israel from Jerusalem have to be accredited by the Israeli Government Press Office.

9. See chapter 3n41.

10. See Shaher Awawdeh, "Changing Pan-Islamic Perspectives on Palestine: The Internal Dynamics of the Organisation of the Islamic Conference: 1991–2004" (PhD diss., University of Exeter, May 2006).

11. See Michael Burgoyne, *Mamluk Jerusalem: An Architectural Study* (London: World of Islam Festival Trust, 1987), p. 45; Abdul Aziz Duri, "Jerusalem in the Early Islamic Period," in *Jerusalem in History,* ed. Kamil J. al-'Asali (London: Scorpion, 1989), pp. 110–11.

12. See comments on the pilgrim trade and numbers arriving in the city by Constantine Volney, *Voyage en Syrie et en Egypte pendant les annees 1783, 1784 et 1785,* 1st ed. (Paris, 1787), republished with an introduction and notes by Jean Gaulmier (Paris, 1959), pp. 335–36, cited in Francis E. Peters, *Jerusalem: The Holy City in the Eyes of Chroniclers, Visitors, Pilgrims, and Prophets from the Days of Abraham to the Beginnings of Modern Times* (Princeton: Princeton University Press, 1985), pp. 552–53.

13. Mentioned in chapter 3.

14. One of the earliest waqfs in Jerusalem was the Pool of Silwan (Siloam) and its surrounding groves and gardens southwest of the Old City. According to the Muslim historian and geographer of the Middle Ages, Muqaddasi, this was dedicated by Caliph 'Uthman ibn Affan as an endowment for the poor of the city between 644–656 c.e. See Mohammad al-Muqaddasi, *Description of Syria Including Palestine,* trans. Guy Le Strange, Pilgrims Text Society 3 (New York: AMS, 1971), pp. 48–49.

15. Among those endowed buildings still standing are the Khanqah Salahiyya, endowed in 1189 c.e., now a mosque and residences. See Kamil Al-Asali, *Mu'ahida al-'ilm fi bayt al-maqdis* (Amman: Institutions of Learning in the Holy City, 1981), p. 330.

16. Excluding minarets, sabils, and one-room turbas, of the forty-one monumental buildings mentioned in Burgoyne's classic study of Mamluk Jerusalem, thirty-nine have waqf endowments. See Michael Burgoyne, *Mamluk Jerusalem: An Architectural Study* (London: World of Islam Festival Trust, 1987).

17. Uriel Heyd, *Ottoman Documents on Palestine, 1552–1615* (London: Oxford University Press, 1960), pp. 146–48.

18. See Ben Arieh, *Jerusalem in the Nineteenth Century: The Old City* (London: Palgrave Macmillan 1985), pp. 283–84; see also p. 360. A brief summary of the system can be found in Richard Nyrop, *Israel: A Country Study* (Washington, DC: American University, 1979), p. 66.

19. See the discussion in Alexander Scholch, "Jerusalem in the Nineteenth Century, 1831–1917," in *Jerusalem in History: 3000 BC to Present,* ed. Kamil al-Asali (London: Kegan Paul, 2002), p. 230f.

20. The standard work on the status quo is Lionel G. Cust, *The Status Quo and the Holy Places* (Jerusalem: Ariel, 1980). See also Saul P. Colbi, "The Christian Establishment in Jerusalem," in *Jerusalem: Problems and Prospects,* ed. Joel. L. Kraemer (New York: Praeger, 1980). See also Albert Rock, *The Status Quo in the Holy Places* (Jerusalem: Franciscan, 1989).

21. While external influence during the late Ottoman period was dominated by European states, we should not overlook either the U.S. involvement that resulted in the construction of the American Colony or that of Muslims from India.

22. See full titles in abbreviations.

23. See the Palestinian Academic Society for the Study of International Affairs, *Documents on Jerusalem* (Jerusalem: PASSIA, 1996), pp. 225–91. Excluding UNESCO resolutions, these include *Inter Alia Measures Taken by Israel to Change the Status of the City of Jerusalem*, GA Res. 2253 (ES-V), UNGAOR, 5th Emergency Special Session, Supp. No. 1, UN Doc. A/6798 (1967); *Measures Taken by Israel to Change the Status of the City of Jerusalem*, GA Res. 2254 (ES-V), UNGAOR, 5th Emergency Special Session, Supp. No. 1, UN Doc. A/6798 (1967); *The Situation in the Middle East*, GA Res. 35/207, UNGAOR, 35th session, UN Doc. A/RES/35/207 (1980); *Recent developments in Connection with Excavations in Eastern Jerusalem*, GA Res. 36/15, UNGAOR, 36th session, UN Doc. A/RES/36/15 (1981); *Question of Palestine*, GA Res 36/120, UNGAOR, 36th session, UN Doc A/RES/36/120 (1981); *The Situation in the Middle East*, GA Res. 37/123, UNGAOR, 37th session, UN Doc. A/RES/37/123 (1982); *Question of Palestine*, GA Res. 38/58, UNGAOR, 38th session, UN Doc. A/RES/38/58 (1983); *The Situation in the Middle East*, SC Res. 252, UNSCOR (1968); *The Situation in the Middle East*, SC Res. 258, UNSCOR (1968); *The Situation in the Middle East*, SC Res. 279, UNSCOR (1970); *The Situation in the Middle East*, SC Res. 298, UNSCOR (1971); *Territories Occupied by Israel*, SC Res. 452, UNSCOR (1979); *Territories Occupied by Israel*, SC Res. 465, UNSCOR (1980); *Territories Occupied by Israel*, SC Res. 476, UNSCOR (1980); *Territories Occupied by Israel*, SC Res. 478, UNSCOR (1980); *Territories Occupied by Israel*, SC Res. 672, UNSCOR (1990).

24. See chapter 1, fig. 1.6.

25. See chapter 1, fig. 1.7.

26. UNRWA was created by a UN General Assembly Resolution: *Assistance to Palestinian Refugees*, GA Res. 302(IV), UNGAOR, 4th session, UN Doc. A/Res/302(IV) (1949): para. 7.

27. Salim Tamari, *Jerusalem 1948: The Arab Neighbourhoods and Their Fate in the War* (Jerusalem: Institute of Jerusalem Studies 1999), pp. 6–7, 84.

28. Michael Dumper, *The Politics of Jerusalem Since 1967* (New York: Columbia University Press, 1997), p. 175.

29. Meron Benvenisti, *Jerusalem: The Torn City*, (Minneapolis: Israel Typeset and University of Minneapolis, 1976), p.43; Avi Plascov, *The Palestinian Refugees in Jordan, 1948–1957* (London: Frank Cass, 1981), p. 109.

30. Since 2003 the camp has been located on the Palestinian side of the separation barrier. See chapter 1, p. 00.

31. Cited in Terry Rempel, "Dispossession and Restitution in 1948 Jerusalem," in *Jerusalem 1948: The Arab Neighbourhoods and Their Fate in the War,* ed. Salim Tamari (Jerusalem: Institute of Jerusalem Studies, 1999), p. 84, table 9. See also pp. 6–7 for estimates of figures of Jerusalemites in West Bank (table 1) and related explanations.

32. See UNESCO Web site: www.unesco.org/new/en/.

33. UNESCO has a comprehensive framework of standard-setting instruments comprising seven conventions. These are *Protection and Promotion of the Diversity of Cultural Expressions* (2005), *Safeguarding of the Intangible Cultural Heritage* (2003), *Protection of the Underwater Cultural Heritage* (2001), *Protection of the World Cultural and Natural Heritage* (1972), *Prohibiting and Preventing the Illicit Import, Export and Transfer of Cultural Property* (1970), *Protection of Cultural Property in the Event of Armed Conflict* (1954), *Universal Copyright Convention* (1952, 1971). See Convention Concerning the Protection of the World Cultural and Natural Heritage, UNESCO Doc. 17/C/106, November 16, 1972. Articles 1 and 2 of the "World Heritage Convention" (1972) remain the preeminent guidelines on defining "Cultural heritage" and "Natural heritage." Definitions and interpretations of "World Heritage" are outlined in UNESCO's normative texts and standard procedures. See the 2005 operational guidelines for the Implementation of the World Heritage Convention (WHC.05/2) for a comprehensive overview.

34. The main partner organizations are the International Council on Monuments and Sites (ICOMOS) and International Centre for the Study of the Preservation and Restoration of Cultural Property (ICCROM). These are available online at www.icomos.org/index.php/en and www.iccrom.org/ respectively.

35. For a fuller exposition of the history of UNESCO's involvement in Jerusalem, see Michael Dumper and Craig Larkin, "The Politics of Heritage and the Limitations of International Agency in Divided Cities: The Role of UNESCO in Jerusalem's Old City," *Review of International Studies* 38, no. 1 (2012): 25–52. See also Simone Ricca, *Reinventing Jerusalem: Israel's Reconstruction of the Jewish Quarter After 1967* (London: I. B. Tauris 2007).

36. The Jerusalem case is not unique, but has been replicated in various contexts, such as China's controversial Sinification policies in Tibet and Cambodia's questionable strategy of inscribing Khmer Temples (Preah Vihear in July 2008 and Prasat Ta Moan Thom currently pending) along the much disputed Thai border. Robert Shepherd, "Unesco and the Politics of Cultural Heritage in Tibet," *Journal of Contemporary Asia* 36, no. 2 (2006): 243–57. For a more detailed account of Preah Vihear's official inscription as a Cambodian World Heritage site, see Peter Cuasay, "Borders on the Fantastic: Mimesis, Violence, and Landscape at the Temple of Preah Vihear," *Modern Asian Studies* 32, no. 4 (1998): 849–90. The

Preah Vihear temple was awarded to Cambodia by the International Court of Justice in the temple case in 1962; see www.icj-cij.org/docket/index.php?p1=3&p2=3&k=46&case=45 &code=ct&p3=4. Cambodia is currently seeking an interpretation of this judgment from the court; see www.icj-cij.org/docket/index.php?p1=3&p2=1&code=ct2&case=151&k=89. I would like to thank the anonymous reviewer for this ICJ information.

37. This periodization differs from an earlier one of four phases delineated in Dumper and Larkin, "The Politics of Heritage," pp. 25–52, which in turn was amended from Ricca, *Reinventing Jerusalem;* see his chapter 5.

38. Dumper and Larkin, "The Politics of Heritage," pp. 35–36.

39. David Brinn, "UNESCO Chief Pays a Visit—and a Compliment," *Jerusalem Post,* February 8, 2008. Assaf Uni, "UNESCO Chief: We Are Trying to Mediate Over Mughrabi Gate," *Haaretz,* February 2, 2008.

40. See Larry Derfner, "Rattling the Cage: UNESCO Is Right, Israel Is Wrong," *Jerusalem Post,* October 11, 2010.

41. UNESCO, "Jerusalem and the Implementation of 35 C/Resolution 49 and 185 Ex/Decision," Executive Board 186 EX/11, Item 11 of the Provisional Agenda, Paris, April 8, 2011, available online at http://unesdoc.unesco.org/images/0019/001919/191953e.pdf.

42. Ibid.

43. UNESCO, World Heritage Center, "Manual for Housing Maintenance and Rehabilitation," Action Plan for the Safeguarding of the Cultural Heritage of the Old City of Jerusalem, section 3:3 (2007), p. 2, available online at http://unesdoc.unesco.org/images/0015/001525/152539e.pdf.

44. UNESCO, "Jerusalem and the Implementation of 35 C/Resolution 49 and 185 Ex/Decision."

45. UNESCO, World Heritage Center, "Manual for Housing Maintenance and Rehabilitation," p. 2.

46. UNESCO, World Heritage Center, "Action Plan for the Safeguarding of the Cultural Heritage of the Old City of Jerusalem," project 13 (2007), pp. 118–25. WHC officials argue that these strictly political issues are not within its remit to solve and expectations that it should do so are ill grounded. In the words of the former UNESCO director general, Koichiro Matsuura, UNESCO "doesn't want to deal with political issues—we are duty-bound to preserve the authenticity of Jerusalem." Assaf Uni, "UNESCO Chief: We Are Trying to Mediate over Mughrabi Gate," *Haaretz,* Feburary 2, 2008.

47. For further details of the al-Marwani and Mamilla disputes, see Craig Larkin and Michael Dumper, "In Defence of Al-Aqsa: The Islamic Movement Inside Israel and the Battle for Jerusalem," *Middle East Journal* 66, no.1 (Winter 2012): 31–52.

48. See Etgar Lefkowitz, "Eastern Temple Wall in Danger of Collapse," *Jerusalem Post,* May 19, 2004.

49. The causes of the collapse are also the subject of much dispute. Some argue that it was caused by gradual erosion and an earthquake; others are convinced that it is a direct consequence of the Israeli renovation of the Western Wall plaza and destruction of the Mughrabi quarter in 1967. The Israel presented its proposals as "Preventive archaeology," see

Report of the Israeli National Commission for UNESCO, February 28, 2007, cited in Dumper and Larkin, "The Politics of Heritage," note 53. See also Daniel Seidemann, "The Events Surrounding the Mugrabi Gate—2007: A Case Study Jerusalem," June (2007), available online at www.uwindsor.ca/joci/system/files/Mugrabi%20-%20FINAL[1].pdf. A full copy of this report is in my possession.

50. The Jordanian government urged Israel to delay the project and offered to carry out a more modest reconstruction scheme, using the precedent set by its work previously at the southern wall of al-Aqsa. Israel declined. For the involvement of the Islamic movement, see Larkin and Dumper, "In Defence of Al-Aqsa," pp. 31–52.

51. UNESCO, Report of the Technical Mission to the Old City of Jerusalem (February 27 to March 2, 2007), March 12, 2007. A full copy is available online at www.unesco.org/bpi/pdf/jerusalem_report_en.pdf.

52. This was proposed at the thirty-first session of the WHC in Christchurch, New Zealand, 2007. The first Reinforced Monitoring Report was received in October 2007. The fifth report, in September 2008, recommended the continuation of this specific form of supervision, reporting back "at least every three months, until the 33rd session of the World Heritage Committee in 2009." See UNESCO, World Heritage Center, "World Heritage Site of the Old City of Jerusalem and Its Walls' State of Conservation of the Mughrabi Ascent: Fifth Reinforced Monitoring Report," September 2008.

53. Ibid., part II 2(9).

54. The only tool in UNESCO's armory is the threat of "delisting." For example, the decision by UNESCO to delist the Dresden Elbe Valley by the WHC, only the second site to have been removed from the World Heritage List, was taken after the construction of a four lane bridge in the heart of the designated heritage area, but it failed, nonetheless, to prevent the construction of the bridge. See "Dresden Is Deleted from UNESCO's World Heritage List," June 25, 2009, available online at http://whc.unesco.org/en/news/522/. Oman's Arabian Oryx Sanctuary was also delisted in 2007. See "Oman's Arabian Oryx Sanctuary: First Site Ever to Be Deleted from UNESCO's World Heritage List," June 28, 2007, available online at http://whc.unesco.org/en/news/362.

55. In the absence of progress in other areas of state building and compelling Israel to withdraw, the PNA appears to be adopting a proactive strategy of registering heritage sites and World Heritage Sites including several in Jerusalem; see George Hale, "The PA's Pitiable Strategy," Daily Beast, July 12, 2012, available online at www.thedailybeast.com/articles/2012/07/12/the-pa-s-pathetic-strategy.html.

56. Boycott, Divestment, and Sanctions (BDS) movement, "UNESCO Distances Itself from Israeli Government Youth Conference," November 18, 2011, available online at www.bdsmovement.net/2011/unesco-statement-8372#. The statement issued from the Ramallah office of UNESCO states "UNESCO also wishes to take this opportunity to reiterate that there has been no change in UNESCO's position on Jerusalem. In line with overall UN policy, East Jerusalem remains part of the occupied Palestinian territory, and the status of Jerusalem must be resolved in permanent status negotiations."

57. See Roberto Aliboni, George Joffe, and Tim Niblock, Security Challenges in the Mediterranean Region (London: Frank Cass, 1996). Werner Weidenfeld, Europe and the Middle East

(Gutersloh: Bertelsmann Foundation, 1995); Peter Ludlow, *Europe and the Mediterranean* (London: Brasseys, 1994). European relations with the Middle East and, in particular, with the Arab-Israeli conflict and peace negotiations are an emerging subdiscipline. Some key texts include Roland Dannreuther, "Europe and the Middle East: Towards a Substantive Role in the Peace Process?" Geneva Centre for Security Policy Occasional Paper Series 39 (2002). Alain Greilsammer, *Europe's Middle East Dilemma: The Quest for a Unified Stance* (Boulder: Westview, 1987): Barbara Roberson, *The Middle East and Europe: The Power Deficit* (New York: Routledge, 1998). Nazih Ayubi, *Distant Neighbours: The Political Economy of Relations between Europe and the Middle East/North Africa* (Reading: Ithaca, 1995). Sven Behrendt and Christian-Peter Hanelt, *Bound to Cooperate—Europe and the Middle East* (Gutersloh: Bertelsmann Stiftung, 2010); Dimitris Xenakis and Dimitris Chryssochoou, *The Emerging Euro-Mediterranean System* (Manchester: Manchester University Press, 2001); Charlotte Bretherton and John Vogler, *The European Union as Global Actor* (New York: Routledge, 2006); Steve Marsh and Hans Mackenstein, *The International Relations of the European Union* (London: Longman, 2004), see chapter 7. Roland Dannreuther, *EU Foreign and Security Policy: Towards a Neighbourhood Strategy* (New York: Routledge, 2004), see chapter 10. See also Michael Dumper, "The Return of Palestinian Refugees and Displaced Persons: The Evolution of a European Union Policy on the Middle East Peace Process," in *The Absorption of Palestinian Refugees,* ed. Rex Brynen and Roula El-Rifai (London: I. B. Tauris, 2006).

58. Dannreuther, *EU Foreign and Security Policy,* p. 3.

59. Joel Peters, *Pathways to Peace: The Multilateral Arab-Israeli Peace Talks* (London: Pinter, 1996).

60. EU foreign policy comprises at least two main strands: the Common Foreign and Security Policy (or CFSP), and the European Security and Defence Policy (or ESDP).

61. The EUSE undertook various small-scale initiatives aimed at building confidence between the parties in a number of areas, including refugees. For example, the establishment of a Refugee Task Force, chaired by Karen Roxman, a Swedish diplomat seconded to the EUSE office, was an attempt to draw in the expertise of the member countries and to coordinate their different agendas on the refugee issue. See Joel Peters, "Europe and the Arab-Israeli Peace Process: The Declaration of the European Council and Beyond," in Behrendt and Hanelt, *Bound to Cooperate*, pp. 159–60.

62. The EMP process (also known as the Barcelona process) included three programs: the political and security partnership, the economic and financial partnership, and the partnership in social, cultural, and human affairs. The process was designed to create a Mediterranean Free Trade Area (MEFTA) and to enhance the political security of the Mediterranean region.

63. Xenakis and Chryssochoou, *The Emerging Euro-Mediterranean System.*

64. The Berlin Declaration of 1999 was an important marker for the EU and distinguished its policies from that of the U.S. The declaration announced the EUs support for the creation of a Palestinian state as the best way of ensuring the security of Israel. In addition, it provided substantial aid, to the tune of $6 billion, and an equivalent amount in loans from the European Investment Bank, with the purpose of laying the infrastructure for such a state.

This was followed by an interim trade agreement between the EU and the Palestinian Authority that focused on liberalizing trade and contributing to the economic development of the West Bank and Gaza as part of the EMP process.

65. See for example the European Council, "Declaration on the Middle East," Annex 1, Madrid, June 27, 1989, p. 16–17, available online at www.ab.gov.tr/files/ardb/evt/1_avrupa_birligi/1_4 _zirveler_1985_sonrasi/1989_madrid_zirvesi_baskanlik_avrupa_topluluklari_en.pdf.

66. See Council of European Union Press Office, "Council Conclusions on the Middle East Peace Process," Brussels, December 8 2009, December 13, 2010, and May 14 2012. The press release of December 8, 2009, is available online at www.consilium.europa.eu/uedocs/cms _data/docs/pressdata/EN/foraff/111829.pdf. It states in paragraph 8: "The Council recalls that it has never recognised the annexation of East Jerusalem. If there is to be a genuine peace, a way must be found through negotiations to resolve the status of Jerusalem as the future capital of the two states."

67. EU Heads of Mission East Jerusalem Report, "Reinforcing the EU Policy on East Jerusalem," Annex 2, section A (2012), available online at www.scribd.com/doc/78665443/ EU-Heads-of-Mission-East-Jerusalem-Report-2012.

68. Ibid.

69. See Tal D. Eisenzweig, "The Jerusalem Light Rail Train: A Bumpy Ride in an Ethnically Polarized City" (Senior Thesis, Woodrow Wilson School of Public and International Affairs, 2012), p. 75.

70. See Nora Barrows-Friedman, "BDS Victory: French Transportation Giant Alstom Loses $10 billion Contract Due to BDS Pressure," *Electronic Intifada*, October 28, 2011, cited in Eisenzweig, "The Jerusalem Light Rail Train," p. 75*n*273.

71. The key texts that deal with the U.S. and its policies on Jerusalem are Stephen Adler, "The United States and the Jerusalem Issue," *Middle East Review* 17 (1985); Jody Boudeault and Yasser Salaam, "The Status of Jerusalem," Institute for Palestine Studies, U.S. Official Statement Series (Washington, DC: Institute for Palestine Studies, 1992); Yossi Feintuch, *U.S. Policy in Jerusalem* (New York: Greenwood, 1987); Donald Neff, "U.S. Policy on Jerusalem," *Journal of Palestine Studies* 23, no. 1 (1993): 20–45; Shlomo Slonim, "The United States and the Status of Jerusalem, 1947–1984," *Israel Law Review* 19 (1984): 179–252.

72. A popular joke in Palestine during the mid-1990s, when the peace process was beginning to stall, was that, in addition to Jerusalem, the White House was also Israeli-occupied territory.

73. For further details see Dumper, *The Politics of Jerusalem Since 1967*, p. 236.

74. This was in response to UNSC Resolution 478 which condemned the Basic Law as a violation of international law. Thirteen states—Bolivia, Chile, Colombia, Costa Rica, Dominican Republic, Ecuador, El Salvador, Guatemala, Haiti, the Netherlands, Panama, Uruguay, and Venezuela—all moved their embassies out of Jerusalem. This information is available online at http://domino.un.org/UNISPAL.NSF/b86613e7d92097880525672e007227a7/6de 6da8a650b4c3b852560df00663826?OpenDocument.

75. Text of the Helms Agreement and the Lease Agreement can be found in Anis F. Kassim, *The Palestine Yearbook of International Law V* (Brill: Leiden,1989), pp. 327–35.

76. The Senate adopted the measure by 93 votes to 5 and the House of Representatives by 374 votes to 37.

77. Jerusalem Embassy Act, 104th Congress, first session (1995). Full text available online at www.gpo.gov/fdsys/pkg/BILLS-104s1322es/pdf/BILLS-104s1322es.pdf.

78. The current policy continues to cause enormous difficulties for the U.S. in reconciling its position on the embassy with its strong support for Israel in all other matters. See Natasha Mozgovaya, "What's the Capital of Israel? Don't Ask the U.S. State Department," *Haaretz,* March 28, 2012. Available at www.haaretz.com/blogs/focus-u-s-a/what-s-the-capital-of-israel-don-t-ask-the-u-s-state-department-1.421341.

79. Walid Khalidi, "The Ownership of the U.S. Embassy Site in Jerusalem," *Journal of Palestine Studies* 29, no. 4 (Summer 2000): 80–101.

80. It may be obliged to go through with the construction of the facilities, but Congress does not have the constitutional authority to designate a premise as an embassy. This remains the prerogative of the executive. See the discussion in Geoffrey W. Watson, "The Jerusalem Embassy Act of 1995," *Catholic University of America Law Review* 45, no. 3 (1996): 837–50; Marshall J. Breger, "Jerusalem Gambit: How We Should Treat Jerusalem Is a Matter of U.S. Constitutional Law as Well as Middle Eastern Politics," *National Review,* October 23, 1995. "Congress cannot use the power of the purse to seize a power textually committed to the Executive alone. While Congress can probably appropriate money for the construction of a building in West Jerusalem (and create a financial penalty if no construction takes place) it cannot use the 'spending power' to order the Executive either in 1996 or 1999 to make that building an embassy rather than a consulate or cultural center. Nor can it order the President to recognize Israeli sovereignty over Jerusalem."

81. See chapters 1 and 3.

82. Marshall Breger estimates that approximately 15 percent of the municipality's budget can be derived from donor contributions. See Marshall Breger, "Understanding Jerusalem," *Middle East Quarterly* 4, no. 1 (March 1997). In August 2012 I carried out a Web search on major U.S. Jewish donors to Jerusalem and counted a grand total of approximately $632 million since 2006. These included $4.7 million by the Charles H. Revson Foundation over five years to the Jerusalem Institute for Israel Studies (www.revsonfoundation.org/programs_jpe_11.html); $25,000,000 in 2007 by the Adelson Family Foundation for the Yad Vasham Holocaust Research Centre in Jerusalem (www.adelsonfoundation.org/AFF/prf/VadVasham.pdf); $15,000,000 from the Robert H. Smith Family Foundation to the Hebrew University of Jerusalem (www.milliondollarlist.org/donors/robert-h-smith-family-foundation); $40,000,000 by the Gary Winnick Organization for the establishment of the Winnick Institute Jerusalem (www.slate.com/articles/life/the_slate60/features/2001/the_2000_slate_60_the_60_largest_american_charitable_contributions_of_2000/_7.html); $12,000,000 in 2009 from the Mandel Supporting Foundations for the Israel Museum, (http://ejewishphilanthropy.com/12m-mandel-gift-completes-israel-museum%E2%80%99s-100m-capital-campaign/); $75 million in 2007 from William and Karen Davidson toward the new in-patient tower at Hadassah Medical Center (www.milliondollarlist.org/search?q=jerusalem&submit=go); $28 million from the Society of

Major Donors toward the building of a new center for emergency medicine at the Hadassah Hospital (http://articles.sun-sentinel.com/2002-01-02/news/0112280337_1_lecture
-art-exhibit-hollywood-city-hall); and $50 million in 2011 from Arcadi Gaydamak toward
rescuing the failing Bikur Cholim Hospital in Jerusalem (www.israelnationalnews.com/
News/News.aspx/143288). These donations for charitable and cultural purposes are easily matched by those for more political purposes. For example, in 2012 supporters of the
Israeli settlers in East Jerusalem, Ira Rennert and Irving Moskowitz, contributed $25.4 mil-
lion toward the building of houses in East Jerusalem (www.jpost.com/LandedPages/Print
Article.aspx?id=150519), while in 2005 alone Farleigh International IT, Ovington World
Wide Ltd., Leston Holdings, Dwide Ltd., and Jacobsen contributed $9.5 million to the
Elad settler group (www.haaretz.com/print-edition/news/group-judaizing-east-jerusalem
-accused-of-withholding-donation-sources-1.233668); finally, the American Friends of
Ateret Cohanim donated $10 million to Ateret Cohanim (60 percent of its revenue) be-
tween 2002–2008 (www.pij.org/details.php?id=1280).

83. See chapter 2*nn*28 and 30. Nir Hasson, "Jerusalem Official: Areas East of the Fence Not
Part of the City," *Haaretz*, January 8, 2010, available online at www.haaretz.com/hasen/
spages/1141313.html. See also report by the *Xinhua News Agency* citing a report in the Israeli
daily *Ma'ariv:* "PNA De Facto Controls Jerusalem's Arab Neighborhoods," *Xinhua News
Agency*, November 10, 2010, available online at http://news.xinhuanet.com/english2010/
world/2010–11/09/c_13599001.htm.

84. In this respect Faisal Husseini was also seen as a potential challenger to the leadership of
PLO chair and president of the PNA, Yassir Arafat. The perceived threat to Arafat's position hampered Palestinian attempts to pursue a coherent strategy.

85. Israel has shown awareness of this strategy and, in addition to forbidding the PNA to operate in East Jerusalem, has closed down twenty-two Palestinian NGOs or quasi-NGOs
since 2002. They include, with date of closure in parentheses: 1. Orient House (August 10,
2001); 2. the Arab Chamber of Commerce and Industry (August 10, 2001); 3. the Palestinian Prisoners' Society (August 10, 2001); 4. the Jerusalem Institute for Planning (August 10,
2001); 5. the Department of Prisoners and Detainees (August 10, 2001); 6. the Department
of Social Services (August 10, 2001); 7. the Arab Studies Society (August 10, 2001); 8. the
Office for National Institutions (August 10, 2001); 9. the Department of Cartography and
Information Systems (August 10, 2001); 10. Small Businesses Development Center (February 8, 2002); 11. the Supreme Council of Tourism (February 8, 2002); 12. Land Research
Center (February 8, 2002); 13. General Union of Arab Chambers of Commerce, Agricul-
ture, and Industry (June 5, 2002); 14. the Jerusalem Multi-Sector Review Project (a branch
of the Arab Studies Society; 2002); 15. the Alumni Club Forum (April 4, 2004); 16. the
Welfare Association of Arab Women (April 4, 2004); 17. Friends of the Emirates Association (2004); 18. Iqra' Association (July 11, 2006): 19. the Association of Hospitality Chari-
ties (January 15, 2006); 20. Cultural Forum (February 4, 2008); 21. the Jerusalem Society for
Culture and Arab Heritage; 22. the Center for Muslim-Christian Brotherhood, cited in
Najat Hirbawi and David Helfand, "Palestinian Institutions in Jerusalem," *Palestine-Israel*

Journal of Politics, Economic and Culture 17, no.12 (2011), available online at www.pij.org/details.php?id=1306.

86. Successive interviews with former minister of Jerusalem, Hind Khoury, and Dr. Rami Nasrallah, the former adviser on Jerusalem affairs to former PNA prime minister Ahmad Qura'i, Jerusalem, 2008–11.

87. Released by the PNA's Office of the President, November 2010.

88. Arieh O'Sullivan, "Ailing Palestinian Hospital Awaits Cash Infusion," *Jerusalem Post,* May 23, 2012, available online at www.jpost.com/VideoArticles/Video/Article.aspx?ID=271090&R=R1.

89. Ministry of Education and Higher Education PowerPoint presentation sent to the author in March 2012 by Dima Samman, director general of Jerusalem Affairs Unit in MoEHE. Copy in my possession.

90. Further details can be found at Municipal Development and Lending Fund, Implemented MDLF project for Jerusalem Governorate 2009, 2010, 2011, Jerusalem (2012), available online at www.mdlf.org.ps/etemplate.php?id=148.

91. Details of funders and different projects are available on the council's Web site: phc-pal .org/english.php.

92. See Web site of al-Quds Committee (Bayt Mal Al Quds Asharif Agency): www.bmaq .org/projects.

93. See chapter 3 for further details of the work of the Welfare Association in the Old City, note 74. See also Dumper and Larkin, "The Politics of Heritage," *Review of International Studies* 38, no. 1 (2012): 29ff; and Michael Dumper, *The Politics of Sacred Space: The Old City of Jerusalem in the Middle East Conflict* (Boulder: Lynne Rienner, 2002).

94. Projects under OCJRP budget include Al-hilal Club ($222,266); Al-Madrassa Al-Jawhariya ($225,000); Spafford Children Centre ($682,000); Palestinian Counseling Center ($157,000); Community Center at Al-Quds University ($115,000); Islamic Museum ($338,500); Al-Madrassa al-Ashrafiya ($750,000); Al-Aqsa Library ($278,000); Madrassa al-Tushtumariyya ($230,000); Al-Madrassa al-Manjakiyya ($335,000); Coptic Youth Club ($140,600); Dar al-Aytam al-Islamiya ($3,500,000); OCJRP Technical Office ($158,000); Riyad al-Aqsa School ($133,200). The Web site of the Old City of Jerusalem Revitalisation Programme is ocjrp.welfare-association.org/en/section/what-we-do/core-restoration-programmes/jerusalem-projects/major-restoration-projects.

95. Figures derived from the Augusta Victoria Hospital Web site: www.avh.org/donors/donors.html; the Welfare Association Web site, welfare-association.org/en/content/view/334/109/; and the UNRWA Web site, www.unrwa.org/etemplate.php?id=889. One of the main problems in conducting such a survey of external funding sources is disentangling the various partnership agreements so that the same donations are not counted twice. In the case of the Islamic Development Bank, it is likely that the total exceeds the $5 million mentioned as not all donations were identified.

96. For further details, see the Faisal Husseini Foundation Web site: www.fhfpal.org/programs/fpc2_e.htm.

4. THE INTERNATIONAL COMMUNITY AND THE LIMITS OF SOVEREIGNTY

97. The program was launched in 2005. For further details, see www.fhfpal.org/programs/fpe_yth1e.htm.
98. Al-Quds Foundation for Medical Schools in Palestine, Web site, www.fqms.org/fund.html; Palestine Red Crescent Web site, www.rcsh-jerusalem.org/en/index.php?option=com_content&view=article&id=52&Itemid=54.
99. See chapter 2, p. 00. Also see UNOCHA, East Jerusalem: Key Humanitarian Concerns, Special Focus (March 2011), p. 85, available online at www.ochaopt.org/documents/ocha_opt_Jerusalem_FactSheet_December_2011_english.pdf; see also the Web site of the Waqf Administration, Directorate of Education in Jerusalem: www.jdoe.edu.ps/index.php?option=com_content&view=article&id=131:2011–01–15–18–19–56&catid=43:2010–11–30–20–56–57&Itemid=100.
100. For a fuller description of the restoration programs and other activities of the Waqf Administration in East Jerusalem, see Michael Dumper, *Islam and Israel: Muslim Religious Endowments and the Jewish State* (Washington, DC: Institute for Palestine Studies, 1997), p. 101ff, and *The Politics of Sacred Space*, p. 86ff.

5. JERUSALEM IN THE TWENTY-FIRST CENTURY

1. Clinton Heylin, *Can You Feel the Silence? Van Morrison: A New Biography* (Chicago: Chicago Review, 2003).
2. Ron E. Hassner, "'To Halve and to Hold': Conflicts Over Sacred Space and the Problem of Indivisibility," *Security Studies* 12, no.4 (2003): 27.
3. See Moshe Hirsch, Deborah Housen-Couriel, and Ruth Lapidoth, *Whither Jerusalem: Proposals and Positions Concerning the Future of Jerusalem* (The Hague: Martinus Nijhoff, 1995); see also Palestinian Academic Society for the Study of International Affairs, *Documents on Jerusalem* (Jerusalem: PASSIA, 1996), pp. 225–91; Moshe Amirav, *Jerusalem Syndrome: The Palestinian-Israeli Battle for the Holy City* (Eastbourne: Sussex Academic, 2009), pp. 144–45; Menachem Klein, *The Jerusalem Problem: The Struggle for Permanent Status* (Gainesville: University Press of Florida, 2003).
4. For a good analysis and typology of the peace proposals on Jerusalem, see Cecilia Albin, "Negotiating Indivisible Goods: The Case of Jerusalem," *Israel Journal of International Relations* 13 (1991): 45.
5. UN Trusteeship Council, Draft Statute for the City of Jerusalem, UN TSCOR, 2d Sess., UN Doc. T/118/Rev.2 (1948), pp. 19–27.
6. Cited in Shlomo Slonim, "The United States and the Status of Jerusalem, 1947–1984," *Israeli Law Review* 19, no. 179 (1984): 180. See also Michael Dumper, *The Politics of Jerusalem Since 1967* (New York: Columbia University Press, 1997), p. 254n29.
7. Walid Khalidi, "Thinking the Unthinkable: A Sovereign Palestinian State," *Foreign Affairs* 56 (1978): 705.
8. Sari Nusseibeh and Mark Heller, *No Trumpets, No Drums: A Two-State Settlement of the Israeli-Palestinian Conflict* (London: I. B. Tauris, 1991), pp. 114–24.

9. Moshe Amirav and Hannah Siniora, "Jerusalem: Resolving the Unresolvable," *International Spectator: Italian Journal of International Affairs* 27, no. 3 (1992).

10. Dore Gold, *Jerusalem in International Diplomacy: The Positions of the Principal Parties on the Jerusalem Question,* Jerusalem Center for Public Affairs, available online at www.jcpa.org/index.htm.

11. Adnan Abu Odeh, "Two Capitals in an Undivided Jerusalem," *Foreign Affairs* 71, no.2 (1992): 183.

12. See Jerusalem Old City Initiative, "Proposals for the Old City of Jerusalem," Department of Political Science, University of Windsor (2010). A copy of the final set of proposals is in my possession. While this set is not publicly available, further details on JOCI, including many of the documents that contributed to the final set of proposals, can be obtained from their Web site, available online at www.uwindsor.ca/jerusaleminitiative. An earlier version was entitled "The Jerusalem Old City Initiative Discussion Document: New Directions for Deliberation and Dialogue" (Munk Centre for International Studies, University of Toronto: MCIS Briefings, 2005). See http://webapp.mcis.utoronto.ca/resources/MCIS_Briefings/2005_December_Bell_etal_Jerusalem.pdf.

13. United Nations Information System on the Question of Palestine, "Abu Mazen-Beilen Plan" (October 31, 1995), available online at UNISPAL, http://domino.un.org/UNISPAL.nsf/3d14c9e5cdaa296d85256cbf005aa3eb/7ba18696d92a8b6a85256cd3005a6e48, article VI, nos. 11 and 12.

14. Shimon Shamir and Bruce Maddy-Weitzman, *The Camp David Summit—What Went Wrong?* (Brighton: Sussex Academic Press and Tel Aviv University, 2005).

15. William J. Clinton, "President Clinton's 'Parameters' for a Comprehensive Agreement Between Israelis and Palestinians," January 7, 2000, available online at UNISPAL, http://unispal.un.org/unispal.nsf/9a798adbf322aff38525617b006d88d7/d57afcdd6eb1445585256e37006655e4?OpenDocument&Highlight=0,clinton,parameters.

16. Akiva Eldar, "The 'Moratinos Document'—The Peace That Nearly Was at Taba," *Ha'aretz,* February 14, 2002.

17. Ehud Olmert, press conference of June 14, 2006, cited in Geoffrey Aronson, "Olmert Divides Jerusalem," Report on Israeli Settlement in the Occupied Territories (Washington, DC: FMEP, 2006), p. 6.

18. Ibid.

19. Galia Golan, "Israel's Positions on Jerusalem," *Palestine-Israel Journal of Politics, Economics and Culture* 17, nos. 1 and 2 (2011): 212–13.

20. Geneva Initiative, the Geneva Accord: A Model Israeli-Palestinian Peace Agreement (December 1, 2003), full text available online at www.geneva-accord.org/mainmenu/english.

21. Michael Bell et al., "The Jerusalem Old City Initiative Discussion Document: New Directions for Deliberation and Dialogue," 2005.

22. Geneva Initiative, the Geneva Accord, 2003. See note 20 for Web address.

23. See chapter 1: comments made by a group of architects and planners: "over time, Road 1 [Jerusalem's central north-south road, which connects Israeli settlements to the city] may

be more damaging than a wall. After all, in a few short years, the Berlin wall was obliterated and its path lost in many parts of the city; but road alignments are perhaps the most enduring of urban interventions," Wendy Pullan, P. Misselwitz, R. Nasrallah, H. Yacobi, "Jerusalem's Road 1," *City* 11, no. 2 (2007): 188.

24. For example, it is not clear from the drawings whether or not the border that is to run along the middle of Road 60, the main road leading out of Jerusalem northward, is designed to be impermeable. Consisting of a low barrier and a narrow ditch, hidden by green shrubs, presumably to soften the visual impact of a border in this central location, I cannot imagine it offering much deterrent to a determined infiltrator despite the electronic surveillance. See Geneva Initiative, "Annex 05, Jerusalem: Urban Challenges and Planning Proposals," p. 156–57, available online at www.geneva-accord.org/images/PDF/Jerusalem.pdf.

25. Ibid., p. 159.

26. Jerusalem Old City Initiative, "Proposals for the Old City of Jerusalem."

27. Ibid., p. 45.

28. These were John de Chastelain, former chief of the Canadian Defence Staff and the chief of the Northern Ireland Independent Commission of Decommissioning, and Roy Berlinquette, former deputy commissioner of the Royal Canadian Mounted Police and member of the Oversight Commission on Police Reform in Northern Ireland.

29. Jerusalem Old City Initiative, "Proposals for the Old City of Jerusalem," p. 77ff.

30. In a private discussion with John Bell, a member of the Windsor University core team, regarding my criticisms, he defended the "mini-municipality" approach (my phrase, not his) by saying that building up the authority and responsibilities of the OCA would counterbalance any undue influence that one side or the other would have in the Old City. This would probably curtail Israeli influence, as the dominant party, more than any Palestinian influence. Skype conversation, December 5, 2012.

31. Jerusalem Old City Initiative, "Proposals for the Old City of Jerusalem."

32. See the analysis by the PLO's chief negotiator and head of the PNA Negotiations Affairs Department, Dr. Sa'eb Eraqat, The Political Situation in Light of Developments with the U.S. Administration and Israeli Government and Hamas: Continued Coup d'etat: Recommendations and Options," leaked PLO internal memo, December 2009. Copy in author's possession.

33. See As'ad Ghanem, "The Bi-National State Solution," *Israel Studies* 14, no. 2 (Summer 2009): 120–33; Leila Farsakh, "Israel-Palestine: Time for a Bi-national State," *Electronic Intifada*, March 20 (2007), available online at electronicintifada.net/content/israel-palestine-time-bi-national-state/6821; Virginia Tilley, "From 'Jewish State and Arab State' to 'Israel and Palestine'? International Norms, Ethnocracy, and the Two-State Solution," *Arab World Geographer* 8, no. 3 (2005): 140–46; Tamar Hermann "The Bi-National Idea in Israel/Palestine: Past and Present," *Nation and Nationalism* 11, no. 3 (2005): 381–401; and Ali Abunimah, "Can Israel Escape a Binational Future?" *Electronic Intifada*, December 20, 2003, available online at electronicintifada.net/content/can-israel-escape-binational-future/4914. See also the contributions of Professor Ian Lustick and Dr. George Bisharat: Ian Lustick, "One State or Two? A Cruel Examination of the Two-States-Are-Impossible

Argument for a Single-State Palestine/The Land of Israel," pp. 279–96, and George Bisharat, "Maximizing Rights: The One-State Solution to the Palestinian-Israeli Conflict," pp. 297–329, in *International Law and the Peace Process*, ed. Susan Akram, Michael Dumper, Michael Lynk, and Iain Scobbie (London: Routledge, 2010).

34. For a broader discussion of the position of the Israeli right and the Palestinian Islamic movement, see Raja Halwani and Tomis Kapitan, *Israel, Palestine, One-State Solution: Philosophical Essays on Self-determination, Terrorism, and the One-State Solution* (Basingstoke: Palgrave Macmillan, 2008); Ehud Sprinzak, *The Ascendance of Israel's Radical Right* (Oxford: Oxford University Press, 1991); Oren Yiftachel, "Democracy or Ethnocracy? Territory and Settler Politics in Israel/Palestine," *Middle East Report* 207 (1999): 9–13; Alisa Peled, "Towards Autonomy? The Islamist Movement's Quest for Control of Islamic Institutions in Israel," *Middle East Journal* 55, no. 3 (Summer 2001): 378–98.

35. Salim Tamari, "The Dubious Lure of Binationalism," in *Palestinian-Israeli Impasse: Exploring Alternative Solutions to the Palestine-Israel Conflict*, ed. Mahdi Abdul Hadi (Jerusalem: PASSIA, 2005), pp. 67–72.

36. Shimon Shamir and Bruce Maddy-Weitzman, *The Camp David Summit—What Went Wrong? Americans, Israelis, and Palestinians Analyze the Failure of the Boldest Attempt Ever to Resolve the Palestinian–Israeli Conflict* (Brighton: Sussex Academic, 2005), p. 233.

37. See also Hermann, "The Bi-National Idea in Israel/Palestine," pp. 382–84.

38. As'ad Ghanem, "The Binational Solution to the Israeli-Palestinian Crisis: Conceptual Background and Contemporary Debate," in Abdul Hadi, *Palestinian-Israeli Impasse*, pp. 19–44.

39. As'ad Ghanem, "The Binational State Is a Desired Palestinian Project and Demand," *al-Majdal: Quarterly Magazine of Badil Resource Center for Palestinian Residency and Refugee Rights*, no. 28 (Winter 2005): 15–18.

40. For details of the numerous permutations of the Track 2 negotiations, see Menachem Klein, *The Jerusalem Problem: The Struggle for Permanent Status* (Gainesville: University of Florida Press, 2003).

41. See chapter 2, pp. 00–00.

42. See Gabriel Almond, "The Return to the State" and Eric Nordlinger, Theodore J. Lowi, and Sergio Fabbrini, "The Return to the State: Critiques," in *American Political Science Review* 82, no. 3 (1988): 853–901; Eric Nordlinger, *On the Autonomy of the Democratic State* (Cambridge: Harvard University Press, 1981); Ernest Haas, *Nationalism, Liberalism, and Progress* (Ithaca, NY: Cornell University Press, 1997).

43. Dankwart A. Rustow, "Transitions to Democracy: Towards a Dynamic Model," *Comparative Politics* 2, no.3 (1970): 2.

44. Ibid., p. 2. See also Michael Dumper, "Israel: Constraints on Consolidation," in *Democratization*, ed. David Potter, David Goldblatt, Margaret Kiloh, and Paul Lewis (London: Polity, 1996), pp. 1–20.

45. I explored some of these ideas in Michael Dumper, "A False Dichotomy? The Binationalism Debate and the Future of Divided Jerusalem," *International Affairs* 87, no. 3 (May 2011): 671–86.

46. Menachem Klein argues that the open city idea was initially an Israeli idea predicated on continuing Israeli control over both sides of the city. It was later taken up and amended by the Palestinians to promote greater political parity. See his "Jerusalem as an Open City," unpublished paper submitted to the London Track meetings hosted by the UK Foreign and Commonwealth Office, April 2001. Copy in my possession.

47. This definition and the following details are derived from Peter Marcuse, "Report on Jerusalem Municipal Issues," submitted to PLO Negotiations Support Unit, December 7, 2000. Copy in my possession. See also papers by Menachem Klein, Shai Javetz, Riyad Malki, Riad Dajani, and Elinoar Barzacchi submitted to the London Track meetings hosted by the UK Foreign and Commonwealth Office, April 2001, which explore and critique different aspects of this concept.

48. In June 2010 the Palestinian Non-Paper on Jerusalem spelled out in more detail its vision of an open city:

> Consequently, in the spirit of peaceful coexistence and cooperation, a joint development council, composed of an equal number of representatives from both sides will be established by the parties to oversee cooperation between Israel and Palestine in both parts of Jerusalem, including with respect to planning and zoning, water, waste water and the environment, roads and industrial zones. A central objective of such cooperation shall be to minimize practical impediments to the free movement and access of people, vehicles, services and goods arising from the existence of an international boundary running through the city. Notwithstanding this cooperation, each state shall enjoy full sovereignty over its respective part of Jerusalem.

> Jerusalem Non-Paper, June 2010, available online at www.nad-plo.org/userfiles/file/ Non-Peper/Jerusalem%20Non-Paper-%20Final%20%20June%202010.pdf.

49. Anthony Coon, "Urban Planning Implications of Jerusalem Open City," Negotiations Support Unit, Ramallah. Unpublished manuscript, October, 2001. Copy in my possession.

50. EUR-LEX, "Consolidated Version of the Treaty of the European Union," title 1, article 2, 1993, available online at http://eur-lex.europa.eu/en/treaties/dat/12002M/htm/C _2002325EN.000501.html.

51. For further details, see William Walters, "Mapping Schengenland: Denaturalising the Border," *Environment and Planning* D 20, no. 5 (2002): 564–80.

52. Council of the European Union, "Schengen Catalogue: Recommendations and Best Practices: Police Cooperation," Brussels, January 25, 2011, p. 13, available online at www.state watch.org/news/2011/feb/eu-council-schengen-catalogue-police-coop-15785-rev2–10.pdf.

53. See Didier Bigo, "When Two Become One: Internal and External Securitizations in Europe," in *International Relations Theory and the Politics of European Integration: Power, Security and Community*, ed. Morten Kelstrup and Michael Williams (London: Routledge, 2000), pp. 171–204.

54. An online complaints procedure has been introduced by Hamas in the Gaza Strip. See Yezid Sayigh, "'We Serve the People': Hamas Policing in Gaza," Crown Paper 5, Crown Center for Middle East Studies, Brandeis University, April 2011.

BIBLIOGRAPHY

Abowd, Thomas. "The Moroccan Quarter: A History of the Present." *Jerusalem Quarterly File*, no. 7 (Winter 2000).

Abu-Lughod, Janet, "Islamic City: Historical Myth, Islamic Essence, and Contemporary Relevance." *International Journal of Middle East Studies* 19 (1987): 155–76.

Abu-Lughod, Janet, "The Demographic Transformation of Palestine." In *The Transformation of Palestine* by Ibrahim Abu-Lughod, pp. 139–63. Evanston: Northwestern University Press, 1971.

Abu-Lughod. Janet. "Urbanisation in the Arab World and the International System." In *The Urban Transformation of the Developing World*, ed. Josef Gugler, pp. 185–208. Oxford: Oxford University Press, 1996.

Adler, S. "The United States and the Jerusalem Issue." *Middle East Review* 17, no. 4 (Summer 1985): 45–53.

Akram, Susan et al. *International Law and the Israeli-Palestinian Conflict: A Rights-Based Approach to Middle East Peace*. Abingdon: Routledge, 2011.

Akram, Susan, Michael Dumper, Michael Lynk, and Iain Scobbie. *International Law and the Peace Process*. London, Routledge, 2010.

Albin, Cecilia. "Negotiating Indivisible Goods: The Case of Jerusalem." *Israel Journal of International Relations* 13, (1991): 45–76.

Aliboni, Roberto, George Joffe, and Tim Niblock. *Security Challenges in the Mediterranean Region*. London, Frank Cass, 1996.

Almond, Gabriel. "The Return to the State." Eric Nordlinger, Theodore J. Lowi, and Sergio Fabbrini, "The Return to the State: Critiques." *American Political Science Review* 82, no. 3 (1988): 853–901.

Amirav, Moshe. *Jerusalem Syndrome: The Palestinian-Israeli Battle for the Holy City*. Eastbourne: Sussex Academic, 2009.

Amirav, Moshe, and Hannah Siniora. "Jerusalem: Resolving the Unresolvable." *International Spectator: Italian Journal of International Affairs* 27, no. 3 (1992).

Armstrong, Karen. *Jerusalem: One City, Three Faiths.* London: HarperCollins, 1996.

al-'Asali, Kamal. *Jerusalem in History.* London: Scorpion, 1989.

al-'Asali, Kamal. *Mu'ahida al-'ilm fi bayt al-maqdis.* Institutions of Learning in the Holy City. Amman, 1981.

Ateek, Naim, Cedar Duaybis, and Maurine Tobin. *The Forgotten Faithful: A Window Into the Life and Witness of Christians in the Holy Land.* Jerusalem: Sabeel Ecumenical Liberation Theology Center, 2007.

al-Barghuti, Mustafa. *Health and Segregation: The Impact of the Israeli Separation Wall on Access to Health Care Services.* Ramallah: Health Development, Information and Policy Institute, 2004.

Bechhofer, Yosef Gavriel. *The Contemporary Eruv: Eruvin in Modern Metropolitan Areas.* BookSurge, 2006.

Beilin, Yossi. *Touching Peace: From the Oslo Accord to a Final Agreement.* London: Weidenfeld and Nicolson, 1999.

Ben Arieh, Yehoshua. *Jerusalem in the Nineteenth Century: The Old City.* New York: St. Martin's, 1984.

Ben Arieh, Yehoshua. *Jerusalem in the Nineteenth Century: Emergence of the New City.* Jerusalem: Yad Izhak Ben-Zvi and New York: St. Martin's, 1989.

Benvenisti, Meron. *City of Stone: The Hidden History of Jerusalem.* Berkeley: University of California Press, 1996.

Benvenisti, Meron, and Uzi Benziman. *Jerusalem: The Torn City.* Minneapolis: Israel Typeset and the University of Minneapolis, 1976.

Bigo, Didier. "When Two Become One: Internal and External Securitizations in Europe." In *International Relations Theory and the Politics of European Integration: Power, Security and Community,* ed. Morten Kelstrup and Michael Williams, pp. 171–204. London: Routledge, 2000.

Bisharat, George. "Maximizing Rights: The One-State Solution to the Palestinian-Israeli Conflict." In *International Law and the Peace Process,* ed. Susan Akram, Michael Dumper, Michael Lynk, and Iain Scobbie, pp. 297–329. London, Routledge, 2010.

Blum, Yehuda Zvi. *The Juridical Status of Jerusalem.* Jerusalem: Hebrew University, 1974.

Blum, Yehuda Zvi. "The Missing Revisioner: Reflections on the Status of Judea and Samaria." *Israel Law Review* 3 (1968): 279–301.

Boal, Frederick, and Stephen Royle. *Enduring City: Belfast in the Twentieth Century.* Belfast: Blackstaff, 2007.

Boudreault, Jody, and Yasser Salaam. *The Status of Jerusalem.* IPS U.S. Official Statement Series. Washington, DC: Institute for Palestine Studies, 1992.

Bollens, Scott. *Cities, Nationalism, and Democratization.* New York: Routledge, 2007.

Bollens, Scott. *City and Soul in Divided Societies* London: Routledge, 2012.

Breger, Marshall J., and Ora Ahimeir *Jerusalem: A City and Its Future.* Syracuse: Syracuse University Press, 2002.

Brereton, Joel P. "Sacred Space." In *The Encyclopaedia of Religion,* ed. Mircea Eliade, pp. 526–35. New York: Macmillan, 1987.

BIBLIOGRAPHY

Bretherton, Charlotte, and John Vogler. *The European Union as Global Actor*. New York: Routledge, 2006.

Brown, Kenneth. *People of Sale: Tradition and Change in a Moroccan City, 1830–1930*. Manchester: Manchester University Press, 1976.

Brownlie, Ian. *Principles of Public International Law*. 4th ed. Oxford: Oxford University Press, 1990.

Bundy, Rodman. "Legal Approaches to the Question of Jerusalem." In *Jerusalem Today: What Future for the Peace Process?* ed. Ghada Karmi, pp. 45–000. Reading: Ithaca, 1996.

Burgoyne, Michael. *Mamluk Jerusalem: An Architectural Study*. London: World of Islam Festival Trust, 1987.

Calle, Sophie. *L'erouv de Jerusalem*. Arles Cedex: Actes Sud, 1996.

Cattan, Henry. *Jerusalem*. London: Croom Helm, 1981.

Cheshin, Amir, Bill Hutman, and Avi Melamed. *Separate and Unequal: The Inside Story of Israeli Rule in East Jerusalem*. Cambridge: Harvard University Press, 1999.

Clancy-Smith, Julia. *Rebel and Saint: Muslim Notables, Populist Protest, Colonial Encounters (Algeria and Tunisia, 1800–1904)*. Berkeley: University of California Press, 1997.

Cohen, Hillel. *The Rise and Fall of Arab Jerusalem: Palestinian Politics and the City Since 1967*. New York: Routledge, 2011.

Cohen, Raymond. *Saving the Holy Sepulchre: How Rival Christians Came Together to Rescue Their Holiest Shrine*. Oxford: Oxford University Press, 2008.

Cohen, Shaul. *The Politics of Planting: Israeli-Palestinian Competition for Control of Land in the Jerusalem Periphery*. Chicago: Chicago University Press, 1993.

Colbi, Saul P. "The Christian Establishment in Jerusalem." In *Jerusalem: Problems and Prospects*, ed. Joel L. Kraemer, pp. 153–77. New York: Praeger, 1980.

Cole, Juan. *Sacred Space and the Holy War: The Politics, Culture and History of Shi'ite Islam*. London: I. B. Tauris, 2002.

Corr, E., Joseph Ginat, and Shaul Gabbay. *The Search for Israeli-Arab Peace: Learning from the Past and Building Trust*. Brighton: Sussex Academic, 2007.

Cuasay, Peter. "Borders on the Fantastic: Mimesis, Violence, and Landscape at the Temple of Preah Vihear." *Modern Asian Studies* 32, no. 4 (1998): 849–90.

Cust, Lionel G. A. *The Status Quo and the Holy Places*. Facsimile version. Jerusalem: Ariel, 1980.

Dakwar, Jamil. "The Islamic Movement Inside Israel: An Interview with Shaykh Ra'id Salah." *Journal of Palestinian Studies* 36, no. 2 (Winter 2007): 66–76.

Dannreuther, Roland. "Europe and the Middle East: Towards a Substantive Role in the Peace Process?" Geneva Centre for Security Policy Occasional Paper Series 39 (2002).

Dayan, Moshe. *The Story of My Life*. Sphere: London, 1978.

Debray, Régis. *Éloge des frontières*. Paris: Gallimard, 2010.

Denholm-Young, Noel. "The Mappa Mundi of Richard of Haldingham at Hereford." *Speculum* 32, no. 2 (1957): 307–14.

Diker, Dan. "The Expulsion of the Palestinian Authority from Jerusalem and the Temple Mount." *Jerusalem Centre for Public Affairs* 3, no. 51, August 5, 2004.

Di Mauro, Danilo, *The UN and the Arab-Israeli Conflict: American Hegemony and UN Intervention Since 1947*. Abingdon: Routledge, 2012.

Dolphin, Ray. *The West Bank Wall: Unmaking Palestine*, pp. 129–30. London: Pluto, 2006.

Dumper, Michael. "A False Dichotomy? The Binationalism Debate and the Future of Divided Jerusalem." *International Affairs* 87, no. 3 (May 2011): 671–86.

Dumper, Michael. "Christianity, Jerusalem and Zionist Exclusivity: The St John's Hospice Incident Reconsidered." In *Jerusalem Interrupted: Modernity and Colonial Transformation, 1917–the Present,* ed. Lena Jayyusi. New York: Olive Branch, 2012.

Dumper, Michael. *Islam and Israel: Muslim Religious Endowments and the Jewish State.* Washington DC: Institute for Palestine Studies, 1997.

Dumper, Michael. "Israeli Settlement in the Old City of Jerusalem." *Journal of Palestine Studies* 21 (Winter 1992): 32–53.

Dumper, Michael. "Security and the Holy Places in Jerusalem: An Israeli Policy of Incremental Control—"Hebronisation"? In *Urban Conflicts: Nationalism, Ethnicity, and Religion,* ed. Wendy Pullan and Brit Baillie-Warren. London: Palgrave-Macmillan, 2013.

Dumper, Michael. "The Churches of Jerusalem in the Post-Oslo Period." *Journal of Palestine Studies* 31, no. 2 (Winter 2002): 51–65.

Dumper, Michael. *The Future of Palestinian Refugees*. Boulder: Lynne Reinner, 2007.

Dumper, Michael. *The Politics of Jerusalem Since 1967.* New York: Columbia University Press, 1997.

Dumper, Michael. *The Politics of Sacred Space: The Old City of Jerusalem in the Middle East Conflict.* Boulder: Lynne Rienner, 2002.

Dumper, Michael. "The Return of Palestinian Refugees and Displaced Persons: The Evolution of a European Union Policy on the Middle East Peace Process." In Rex Brynen and Roula Rifai, *The Absorption of Palestinian Refugees*. London: I. B. Tauris, 2006.

Dumper, Michael, and Craig Larkin "The Politics of Heritage and the Limitations of International Agency in Divided Cities: The Role of UNESCO in Jerusalem's Old City." *Review of International Studies* 38, no. 1 (January 2012): 25–52.

Duri, Abdul A. "Jerusalem in the Early Islamic Period." In *Jerusalem in History,* ed. Kamal al-'Asali, pp. 105–29. London: Scorpion, 1989.

Eickelman, Dale. "Is There an Islamic City? The Making of a Quarter in a Moroccan Town." *International Journal of Middle East Studies* 5 (1974): 274–94.

Febvre, Lucien. "Frontière: The Word and the Concept." In *A New Kind of History: From the Writings of Febvre,* ed. Peter Burke, pp. 208–18. London: Routledge and Kegan Paul, 1973.

Feintuch, Yossi. *U.S. Policy in Jerusalem.* New York: Greenwood, 1987.

Fenster, Tovi. *The Global City and the Holy City: Narratives on Knowledge, Planning and Diversity.* Harlow: Pearson Education, 2004.

Friedland, Roger, and Richard D. Hecht. *To Rule Jerusalem.* Berkeley: University of California Press, 2000.

Garfinkle. Adam. *Politics and Society in Modern Israel: Myths and Realities.* 2d ed. New York: Sharp, 2000.

Ghanem, As'ad, "The Binational Solution to the Israeli-Palestinian Crisis: Conceptual Background and Contemporary Debate." In *Palestinian-Israeli Impasse: Exploring Alternative*

Solutions to the Palestinian-Israeli Conflict, ed. Abdul-Hadi Mahdi, pp. 19–44. Jerusalem: PASSIA, 2005.

Ghanem, As'ad. "The Binational State Is a Desired Palestinian Project and Demand." *al-Majdal: Quarterly Magazine of Badil Resource Center for Palestinian Residency and Refugee Rights*, no. 28 (Winter 2005): 15–18.

Giacaman, George, and Dag Jorund Lønning. *After Oslo: New Realities, Old Problems*. London: Pluto, 1998.

Ginat, Joseph, and Edward Perkins. *The Palestinian Refugees Old Problems, New Solutions*. Brighton: Sussex Academy Press, 2001.

Golan, Galia. "Israel's Positions on Jerusalem." *Palestine-Israel Journal of Politics, Economics and Culture* 17, nos. 1 and 2 (2011).

Gold, Dore. *Jerusalem in International Diplomacy: The Positions of the Principal Parties on the Jerusalem Question*. Jerusalem Center for Public Affairs. www.jcpa.org/index.htm.

Goldscheider, Calvin. *Israel's Changing Society Population, Ethnicity, and Development*. 2d ed. Boulder: Westview, 2002.

Gorenberg, Gershon. *The Accidental Empire: Israel and the Birth of the Settlements, 1967–1977*. New York: Times/Henry Holt, 2006.

Guinn, David E. *Protecting Jerusalem's Holy Sites: A Strategy for Negotiating a Sacred Peace*. Cambridge: Cambridge University Press, 2006.

Haas, Ernest. *Nationalism, Liberalism, and Progress*. Ithaca: Cornell University Press, 1997.

Habib, Ibrahim. *A Wall in Its Midst: The Separation Barrier and Its Impact on the Right to Health and on Palestinian Hospitals in East Jerusalem*. Tel Aviv: Physicians for Human Rights, 2005.

al-Haj, Majid. *Education, Empowerment and Control: The Case of the Arabs in Israel*. Albany: State University of New York Press, 1995.

al-Haj, Majid, and Henry Rosenfeld. *Arab Local Government in Israel*. Boulder: Westview, 1990.

Halper, Jeff. "Jewish Ethnicity in Jerusalem." In *Jerusalem: City of the Ages*. ed. Alice Eckhardt, pp. 184–98. New York: University Press of America, 1987.

Halwani, Raja, and Tomis Kapitan. *Israel, Palestine, One-State solution: Philosophical Essays on Self-Determination, Terrorism, and the One-State Solution*. Basingstoke: Palgrave Macmillan, 2008.

Haneda, Masashi, and Toru Miura. *Islamic Urban Studies: Historical Review and Perspectives*. London: Kegan Paul International, 1994.

Harley, John B., and David Woodward. *The History of Cartography*, vol. 2: *Cartography in Prehistoric, Ancient, and Medieval Europe and the Mediterranean*. Chicago: University of Chicago Press, 1987.

Hassner, Ron. E. "'To Halve and to Hold': Conflicts Over Sacred Space and the Problem of Indivisibility." *Security Studies* 12, no. 4 (Summer 2003): 1–33.

Helton, Arthur. *The Price of Indifference: Refugees and Humanitarian Action in the New Century*. Oxford: Oxford University Press 2002.

Hepburn, Anthony. *Contested Cities in the Modern West*, Basingstoke: Palgrave Macmillan, 2004.

Hermann, Tamar. "The Bi-National Idea in Israel/Palestine: Past and Present." *Nation and Nationalism* 11, no. 3 (2005): 381–401.

Heyd, Uriel. *Ottoman Documents on Palestine, 1552–1615.* London: Oxford University Press, 1960.

Heylin, Clinton. *Can You Feel the Silence? Van Morrison: A New Biography.* Chicago: Chicago Review Press, 2003.

Hilal, Jamil. *Where Now for Palestine? The Demise of the Two-State Solution.* New York: Zed, 2007.

Hintlian, Kevork. *History of the Armenians in the Holy Land.* Jerusalem: Armenian Patriarchate, 1989.

Hirbawi, Najat, and David Helfand. "Palestinian Institutions in Jerusalem." *Palestine-Israel Journal of Politics, Economic and Culture* 17, no. 12 (2011).

Hirsch, Moshe, Deborah Housen-Couriel, and Ira Lapidus. *Whither Jerusalem: Proposals and Positions Concerning the Future of Jerusalem.* The Hague: Martinus Nijhoff, 1995.

Hirst, Paul. *Space and Power: Politics, War and Architecture.* Cambridge: Polity, 2005.

Hutman, Bill and Amir Cheshin. "Living Together and Apart in Jerusalem." In *Jerusalem: A City and Its Future,* ed. Marshall J. Breger and Ora Ahimeir, pp. 401–30. Syracuse: Syracuse University Press, 2002.

Hyman, Benjamin, Israel Kimhi, and Joseph Savitzky. *Jerusalem in Transition: Urban Growth and Change, 1970's and 1980's.* Jerusalem: Jerusalem Institute for Israel Studies, 1985.

Israeli, Raphael. *Jerusalem Divided: The Armistice Regime, 1947–1967.* London: Frank Cass, 2002.

Jefferis, Danielle. "Institutionalising Statelessness: The Revocation of Residency Rights of Palestinian in East Jerusalem." *International Journal of Refugee Law,* forthcoming.

Jiryis, Sabri. *The Arabs in Israel.* London: Monthly Review Press, 1976.

Jones, Emrys. *A Social Geography of Belfast.* London: Oxford University Press, 1960.

Kark, Ruth. *Jerusalem and Its Environs, Quarters, Neighborhoods, Villages, 1800–1948.* Detroit: Wayne State University Press, 2001.

Kark, Ruth. *Jerusalem Neighbourhoods: Planning and By-Laws (1855–1930).* Jerusalem: Magnes, 1991.

Kassim, Anis F. *The Palestine Yearbook of International Law,* pp. 327–35. Leiden: Brill, 1989.

Katz, Kimberly. *Jordanian Jerusalem Holy Places and National Spaces.* Gainesville: University Press of Florida, 2005.

Katz, Itamar, and Ruth Kark. "The Church and Landed Property: The Greek Orthodox Patriarchate of Jerusalem." *Middle Eastern Studies* 43, no. 3 (2007): 383–408.

Keely, Charles B. "The International Refugee Regime(s): The End of the Cold War Matters." *International Migration Review* 35, no. 1 (2001): 303–14.

Khalidi, Walid. "The Ownership of the U.S. Embassy Site in Jerusalem." *Journal of Palestine Studies* 39, no. 4 (Summer 2000).

Khalidi, Walid. *All That Remains: The Palestinian Villages Occupied and Depopulated by Israel in 1948.* Washington DC: Institute for Palestine Studies, 1992.

Kimhi, Israel. *A Socio-Economic Survey of Jerusalem, 1967–1975.* Jerusalem: Jerusalem Committee, 1978.

Kisaichi, Masatoshi. "Maghrib." In *Islamic Urban Studies: Historical Review and Perspectives,* ed. Masashi Haneda and Toru Miura, pp. 11–74. London: Kegan Paul International, 1994.

Klein, Menachem. *Jerusalem: The Contested City.* London: Hurst, 2001.

Klein, Menachem. *The Jerusalem Problem: The Struggle for Permanent Status*. Gainesville: University of Florida Press, 2003.

Kochler, Hans. *The Legal Aspects of the Palestine Problem with Special Regard to the Question of Jerusalem*. Vienna: Wilhelm Braumuller, 1981.

Koury, Stephanie. "Legal Strategies at the United Nations: A Comparative Look at Namibia, Western Sahara, and Palestine." In *International Law and the Israeli–Palestinian Conflict: A Rights-Based Approach to Middle East Peace*, ed. Susan Akram et al., pp. 147–62. Abingdon: Routledge, 2011.

Kyle, Keith, and Joel Peters. *Whither Israel: The Domestic Challenges*. London: Royal Institute for International Affairs, 1993.

Lauterpacht, Elihu. *Jerusalem and the Holy Places*. London: Anglo-Israel Association, 1968.

Lapidot, Ruth, and Moshe Hirsch. *The Jerusalem Question and Its Resolution: Selected Documents*. Dordrecht: Kluwer Academic, 1994.

Lapidot, Ruth. "Jerusalem: Some Legal Aspects." In *Jerusalem: A City and Its Future, ed.* Marshall J. Breger and Ora Ahimeir, pp. 61–90. Syracuse: Syracuse University Press, 2001.

Lapidus, Ira. *Muslim Cities in the Later Middle Ages*. Cambridge: Cambridge University Press, 1967.

Larkin, Craig and Michael Dumper. "In Defence of Al-Aqsa: The Islamic Movement Inside Israel and Battle for Jerusalem." *Middle East Journal* 66, no. 1 (Winter 2012): 31–52.

Le Strange, Guy. *Translation of Muqaddasi: Description of Syria Including Palestine*. Pilgrims Text Society 3. New York: AMS, 1971.

Litvak, Meir. *Shi'i Scholars of Nineteenth-Century Iraq: The 'Ulama' of Najaf and Karbala'*. Cambridge: Cambridge University Press, 1998.

Ludlow, Peter. *Europe and the Mediterranean*. London: Brasseys, 1994.

Lustick, Ian. *Arabs in the Jewish State: Israel's Control of a National Minority*. Austin: University of Texas Press, 1980.

Lustick, Ian. *For the Land and for the Lord: Jewish Fundamentalism in Israel*. New York: Council of Foreign Relations, 1988.

Lustick, Ian. "Has Israel Annexed Jerusalem?" *Middle East Policy* 5, no. 1 (1997): 34–45.

Lustick, Ian. "One State or Two? A Cruel Examination of the Two-States-Are-Impossible Argument for a Single-State Palestine/The Land of Israel." In *International Law and the Peace Process*, ed. Susan Akram, Michael Dumper, Michael Lynk, and Iain Scobbie, pp. 279–96. London: Routledge, 2010.

Lustick, Ian. "Reinventing Jerusalem." *Foreign Policy* 93 (Winter 1993): 41–59.

Lustick, Ian. "The Fetish of Jerusalem: A Hegemonic Analysis." In *Israel in Comparative Perspective*, ed. Michael N. Barnett, pp. 143–72. Albany: State University of New York Press, 1996.

Makovsky, David. *Making Peace with PLO: The Rabin Government's Road to the Oslo Accord*. Boulder: Westview, 1995.

Man, John. *Genghis Khan: Life, Death and Resurrection*. London: Transworld, 2005.

Mann, Barbara. *Space and Place in Jewish Studies*. New Jersey: Rutgers University Press, 2012.

Marcuse, Peter. "Not Chaos but Walls: Postmodernism and the Partitioned City." In *Post-modern Cities and Spaces*, ed. Sophie Watson and Katherine Gibson. Oxford: Blackwell, 1995.

Margalit, Meir. *Discrimination in the Heart of the Holy City*. Jerusalem: International Peace and Cooperation Centre, 2006.

Margalit, Meir. *Seizing Control of Space in East Jerusalem*. Tel Aviv: Sifrei Aliat Gag, 2010.

Mar'i, Sami. *Arab Education in Israel*. Syracuse: Syracuse University Press, 1978.

Medding, Peter. *The Founding of Israeli Democracy, 1948–67*. Oxford: Oxford University Press, 1990.

Merkley, Paul Charles. *Christian Attitudes Towards the State of Israel*. Montreal: McGill-Queen's University Press, 2001.

Misselwitz, Philip, and Tim Rieniets. *City of Collision: Jerusalem and the Principles of Conflict Urbanism*. Basel: Birkhäuser, 2006.

Murphy, Emma, and Clive Jones. *Israel: Challenges to Identity, Democracy and the State*. London: Routledge, 2002.

Nakash, Yitzhak. *The Shi'is of Iraq*. Princeton: Princeton University Press, 1994.

Nasrallah, Rami. "Transformations in Jerusalem: Where Are We Heading?" In *Divided Cities in Transition: Challenges Facing Jerusalem and Berlin*, ed. Michele Auga et al., pp. 205–25. Jerusalem: Friedrich Ebert Stifftung, 2005.

Neff, Donald. "U.S. Policy on Jerusalem." *Journal of Palestine Studies*, no. 89 (1993): 20–45.

Nimni, Ephraim. *The Challenges of Post-Zionism: Alternatives to Fundamentalist Politics in Israel*. London: Zed, 2003.

Nordlinger, Eric. *On the Autonomy of the Democratic State*. Cambridge: Harvard University Press, 1981.

Nyrop, Richard. *Israel: A Country Study*. Washington, DC: American University, 1979.

O'Mahoney, Anthony. "Church, State and the Christian Communities and the Holy Places of Palestine." In *Christians in the Holy Land*, ed. Michael Prior and William Taylor, pp. 160–214. London: World of Islam Festival Trust, 1994.

O'Mahoney, Anthony, Goran Gunner, and Kevork Hintlian. *The Christian Heritage in the Holy Land*. London: Scorpion Cavendish, 1995.

Owen, Roger. *State, Power, and Politics in the Making of the Modern Middle East*. London: I. B. Tauris, 2000.

Paasi, Annsi. "Boundaries as Social Processes: Territoriality in the World of Flows." *Geopolitics* 3, no. 1, Boundaries Territory and Postmodernity, special issue (1998): 69–88.

Papadakis, Yiannis. *Echoes from the Dead Zone: Across the Cyprus Divide*. London: I. B. Tauris, 2005.

Peled, Alisa. "The Crystallization of an Israeli Policy Towards Muslim and Christian Holy Places, 1948–1955." *Muslim World* 84, nos. 1–2 (January-April 1994).

Peled, Alisa Rubin. "Towards Autonomy? The Islamist Movement's Quest for Control of Islamic Institutions in Israel." *Middle East Journal* 55, no. 3 (Summer 2001): 378–98.

Peters, Francis E. *Jerusalem and Mecca: The Typology of the Holy City in the Near East*. New York: New York University Press, 1986.

Peters, Francis E. *Jerusalem: The Holy City in the Eyes of Chroniclers, Visitors, Pilgrims, and Prophets from the Days of Abraham to the Beginnings of Modern Times*. Princeton: Princeton University Press, 1985.

Peters, Joel. "Europe and the Arab-Israeli Peace Process: The Declaration of the European Council and Beyond." In *Bound to Cooperate: Europe and the Middle East,* ed. Sven Behrendt and Christian Hanelt. Gutersloh: Bertelsmann Foundation, 2000.

Peters, Joel. *Pathways to Peace: The Multilateral Arab-Israeli Peace Talks.* London: Pinter, 1996.

Peri, Oded. *Christianity Under Islam in Jerusalem: The Question of the Holy Sites in Early Ottoman Times.* Leiden: Brill, 2001.

Plascov, Avi. *The Palestinian Refugees in Jordan, 1948–1957.* London: Frank Cass, 1981.

Potter, David et al. *Democratization.* London: Polity, 1997.

Prior, Michael, and William Taylor. *Christians in the Holy Land.* London: World of Islam Festival Trust, 1994.

Pullan, Wendy, Phillip Misselwitz, Rami Nasrallah, and Haim Yacobi. "Jerusalem's Road 1." *City* 11 (2007): 176–98.

Pullan, Wendy, and Max Gwaizda. "Jerusalem's Holy Basin: Who Needs It?" *Palestine-Israel Journal* 17, nos. 1–2 (2011): 172–79.

Pullan, Wendy, and Max Gwaizda. "The Biblical Present in Jerusalem's 'City of David.'" In *Memory, Culture, and the Contemporary City: Building Sites,* ed. Andrew Webber, Uta Staiger, and Henriette Steiner, pp. 106–25. London: Palgrave Macmillan, 2009.

Reiter, Yitzhak, Marlen Eordegian, and Marwan Abu Khallaf. "Between Divine and Human: The Complexity of Holy Places in Jerusalem." In *Jerusalem: Points of Friction—and Beyond,* ed. Moshe Maoz and Sami Nusseibeh, pp. 95–153. The Hague: Kluwer Law International, 2000.

Rempel, Terry. "Dispossession and Restitution in 1948 Jerusalem." In *Jerusalem 1948: The Arab Neighbourhoods and Their Fate in the War,* ed. Salim Tamari, pp. 189–237. Jerusalem: Institute of Jerusalem Studies, 1999.

Rempel, Terry. "The Significance of Israel's Partial Annexation of East Jerusalem." *Middle East Journal* 51, no. 4 (1997): 520–34.

Ricca, S. *Reinventing Jerusalem: Israel's Reconstruction of the Jewish Quarter After 1967.* London: I. B. Tauris, 2007.

Rock, Albert. *The Status Quo in the Holy Places.* Jerusalem: Franciscan, 1989.

Romann, Michael, and Alex Weingrod. *Living Together Separately,* Princeton: Princeton University Press, 1991.

Rouhana, Nadim. *Palestinian Citizens in an Ethnic Jewish State: Conflict in Identities.* New Haven: Yale University Press, 1997.

Roussos, Sotiris. "The Greek Orthodox Patriarchate and Community of Jerusalem." In *The Christian Heritage in the Holy Land,* ed. Anthony O'Mahoney, Goran Gunner, and Kevork Hintlian, pp. 211–44. London: Scorpion Cavendish, 1995.

Rustow, Dankwart A. "Transitions to Democracy: Towards a Dynamic Model." *Comparative Politics* 2, no. 3 (1970): 337–63.

Savitch, Hank. "Anatomy of Urban Terror: Lessons from Jerusalem and Elsewhere." *Urban Studies* 42, no. 3 (2005): 361–95.

Savitch, Hank, and Yaakov Garb. "Terror, Barriers, and the Changing Topography of Jerusalem." *Journal of Planning Education and Research* 26, no. 2 (2006): 152–73.

Said, Edward. *The End of Peace Process: Oslo and After*. New York: Pantheon, 2000.

Schmelz, Uriel. *Modern Jerusalem's Demographic Evolution*. Jerusalem: Hebrew University of Jerusalem, 1987.

Scholch, Alexander. "Jerusalem in the Nineteenth Century, 1831–1917." In *Jerusalem in History: 3000 BC to the Present*, ed. Kamil al-Asali, pp. 228–48. London: Kegan Paul, 2002.

Segal, Rafi, Eyal Weizman, and David Tartakover. *A Civilian Occupation: The Politics of Israeli Architecture*. London: Verso, 2003.

Shamir, Shimon, and Bruce Maddy-Weitzman. *The Camp David Summit—What Went Wrong?* Brighton: Sussex Academic Press and Tel Aviv University, 2005.

Shepherd, Robert. "Unesco and the Politics of Cultural Heritage in Tibet." *Journal of Contemporary Asia* 36, no. 2 (2006): 243–57.

Shirlow, Peter, and Brendan Murtagh. *Belfast: Segregation, Violence and the City*. London: Pluto, 2006.

Slonim, Shlomo. "The United States and the Status of Jerusalem, 1947–1984." *Israel Law Review* 19 (1984): 179–252.

Sprinzak, Ehud. *The Ascendance of Israel's Radical Right*. Oxford: Oxford University Press, 1991.

Sprinzak, Ehud, and Larry Diamond. *Israeli Democracy Under Stress*. Boulder: Lynne Rienner, 1993.

Stone, Julius. *Israel and Palestine: Assault on the Law of Nations*. Baltimore: Johns Hopkins University Press, 1981.

Svensson, Isak. "Fighting with Faith: Religion and Conflict Resolution in Civil Wars." *Journal of Conflict Resolution* 51, no. 6 (2007): 930–49.

Swisher, Clayton. *The Truth About Camp David: The Untold Story About the Collapse of the Middle East Peace Process*. New York: Nation, 2004.

Talhami, Ghada. *Palestinian Refugees: Pawns to Political Actors*. New York: Nova Science, 2001.

Tamari, Salim. *Jerusalem 1948: The Arab Neighbourhoods and Their Fate in the War*. Jerusalem: Institute of Jerusalem Studies, 1999.

Tamari, Salim. *Return, Resettlement, Repatriation: The Future of Palestinian Refugees in the Peace Negotiations*, Washington, DC: Institute for Palestine Studies, 1996.

Tawil, Sobhi and Alexandra Harley. "Education and Identity-Based Conflict: Assessing Curriculum Policy for Social and Civic Reconstruction." In *Education, Conflict and Social Cohesion* 9, ed. UNESCO International Bureau of Education, no. 39, April 27, 2004.

Thomas, Mark. *Extreme Rambling: Walking Israel's Separation Barrier. For Fun*. London: Ebury, 2011.

Tilley, Virginia. *Beyond Occupation: Apartheid, Colonialism and International Law in the Occupied Palestinian Territories*. London: Pluto, 2012.

Tsimhoni, Daphne. *Christian Communities in Jerusalem and the West Bank Since 1948: An Historical, Social and Political Study*. Westport, CT: Praeger, 1993.

Waldron, Jeremy. "Settlement, Return, and the Supersession Thesis." *Theoretical Inquiries in Law* 5, no. 2 (July 2004): 237–59.

Waldron, Jeremy. "Superseding Historical Injustice." *Ethics* 103, no. 1 (October 1992): 4–28.

BIBLIOGRAPHY

Watson, Geoffrey W. "The Jerusalem Embassy Act of 1995." In *The Catholic University of America Law Review* 45, no. 3 (Spring 1996): 837–50.

Watson, Geoffrey W. *The Oslo Accords International Law and the Israeli-Palestinian Peace Agreement.* Oxford: Oxford University Press, 2000.

Watson, Sophie. "Symbolic Spaces of Difference: Contesting the Eruv in Barnet, London and Tenafly, New Jersey." *Environment and Planning D: Society and Space* 23 (2005): 597–643.

Weidenfeld, Werner. *Europe and the Middle East.* Gutersloh: Bertelsmann Foundation, 1995.

Weizman, Eyal. *Hollow Land: Israel's Architecture of Occupation.* London: Verso, 2007.

Weizman, Eyal. "The Subversion of Jerusalem's Sacred Vernaculars: Four New Planning Tools for a Holy Environment." In *The Next Jerusalem: Sharing the Divided City,* ed. Michael Sorkin, pp. 120–45. New York: Monacelli, 2002.

Xenakis, Dimitris, and Dimitris Chryssochoou. *The Emerging Euro-Mediterranean System.* Manchester: Manchester University Press, 2001.

Yarwood, John. *Rebuilding Mostar: Urban Reconstruction in a War Zone.* Liverpool: Liverpool University Press, 1999.

Yiftachel, Oren. "Democracy or Ethnocracy? Territory and Settler Politics in Israel/Palestine." *Middle East Report* 207 (1999): 9–13.

Yiftachel, Oren. "State Policies, Land Control, and an Ethnic Minority: The Arabs in the Galilee Region, Israel." *Society and Space* 9 (1991): 329–62.

Young, Gavin. *Iraq Land of Two Rivers.* London: Collins St. James Place, 1980.

Zander, Walter. *Israel and the Holy Places of Christendom.* London: Weidenfield and Nicolson, 1971.

WEB ARTICLES

Abukhater, Jalal. "Israel Censors Palestinian Textbooks in East Jerusalem." *Electronic Intifada,* October 25, 2011. http://electronicintifada.net/blog/jalal-abukhater/israel-censors-palestinian-textbooks-east-jerusalem.

Abunimah, Ali. "Can Israel Escape a Binational Future?" *Electronic Intifada,* December 20, 2003. http://electronicintifada.net/content/can-israel-escape-binational-future/4914.

Aga Khan Award for Architecture. "Restoration of Al-Aqsa Mosque." www.akdn.org/architecture/project.asp?id=501.

Asmahan, Masry-Herzalla, Razin Eran, and Choshen Maya. "Jerusalem as an Internal Migration Destination for Israeli-Palestinian Families." *Floersheimer Institute for Policy Studies,* Policy Studies 2011. www.fips.org.il/site/p_publications/item_en.asp?doc=&iss=&iid=852.

Badil Resource Centre for Refugees and Residency Rights. "Palestinians Boycott Israeli Municipal Elections in Jerusalem." www.badil.org/fr/ressources-en-francais/51-press-releases-1998/87-press32–98.

Badil Resource Centre for Refugees and Residency Rights. "The Municipality of Jerusalem Seeks Controlling the Palestinian Education System in the City." Civic Coalition for Defending the Palestinians' Rights in Jerusalem. Press release, n.d. www.badil.org/phocadownload/Press_Releases/2010–2015/THe%20Civic%20Coalition%20for%20Defending%20the%20Palestinians'%20Rights%20in%20Jerusalem_The%20Municipality%20of%20Jerusalem%20 seeks%20controlling%20the%20Palestinian%20Education%20System%20in%20the%20 City.pdf.

Be'er, Yizhar. "Targeting the Temple Mount: A Current Look at Threats to the Temple Mount by Extremist and Messianic Groups." Center for the Protection of Democracy in Israel— Keshev, January 2001. www.keshev.org.il/images/stories/PDF/2001_temple_mount%20_full _text_eng.pdf.

Boycott, Divestment, and Sanctions (BDS) Movement. "UNESCO Distances Itself from Israeli Government Youth Conference," November 18, 2011. www.bdsmovement.net/2011/unesco -statement-8372#.

Bush, Kenneth D., and Diana Saltarelli. "The Two Faces of Education in Ethnic Conflict." Florence: United Nations Children's Fund, Innocenti Research Centre, 2000. www.unicef-irc .org/publications/pdf/insight4.pdf.

Central Elections Commission for Palestine. "Voting Procedures for Jerusalem Residents PLC Elections 2006." www.elections.ps:90/template.aspx?id=266.

Council of Religious Institutions of the Holy Land. "Statement Condemning Desecration of St. Francis Convent." October 3, 2012. www.crihl.org/view/updates.

Council of the European Union. "Schengen Catalogue: Recommendations and Best Practices: Police Cooperation." Brussels, January 25, 2011. www.statewatch.org/news/2011/feb/eu -council-schengen-catalogue-police-coop-15785-rev2-10.pdf.

Dumper, Michael. *An Inter-religious Council for Jerusalem.* Madrid: Toledo International Centre for Peace (CITpax), 2011. www.toledopax.org/uploads/Religious%20Council%20of%20 Jerusalem.pdf.

Dumper, Michael. "Jerusalem's Troublesome Sheikh." *Guardian,* October 7, 2009. www.guardian. co.uk/commentisfree/2009/oct/07/jerusalem-sheik-raed-salah-islamic.

Dumper, Michael, and Wendy Pullan. "Jerusalem: The Cost of Failure." Chatham House Briefing Paper, Chatham House: The Royal Institute of International Affairs, February 2010. www.chathamhouse.org.uk/publications/papers/view/-/id/835/.

Eldar, Akiva. "Discrimination Is Flourishing in East Jerusalem." *Ha'aretz,* May 3, 2010. www .haaretz.com/print-edition/opinion/disrimination-is-fluorishing-in-east-jerusalem-1.287733.

Eldar, Akiva. "The 'Moratinos Document'—The Peace That Nearly Was at Taba." *Ha'aretz,* February 14, 2002.

EUR-LEX. "Consolidated Version of the Treaty of the European Union." Title 1, article 2, 1993. http://eur-lex.europa.eu/en/treaties/dat/12002M/htm/C_2002325EN.000501.html.

Farsakh, Leila. "Israel-Palestine: Time for a Bi-national State." *Electronic Intifada,* March 20, 2007. http://electronicintifada.net/content/israel-palestine-time-bi-national-state/6821.

Foundation for Middle East Peace. "Israeli Settlements in the Occupied Territories: A Guide." *Settlement Report* 12, no. 7 (2002). www.fmep.org/reports/special-reports/a-guide-to-israeli -settlements-in-the-occupied-territories/israeli-settlements-in-the-occupied-territories-a -guide.

Gedalyahu, Tzvi Ben. "Jerusalem Arabs View 'Eruv' as New Political Border." *Arutz Sheva,* October 8, 2010. www.israelnationalnews.com/News/News.aspx/139040.

Geneva Initiative. *The Geneva Accord: A Model Israeli-Palestinian Peace Agreement.* December 1, 2003. www.geneva-accord.org/mainmenu/english.

Geneva Initiative. *Annex 05: Jerusalem: Urban Challenges and Planning Proposals*, www.geneva -accord.org/images/PDF/Jerusalem.pdf.

Glass, Joseph, and Rassem Khamaisi. "Report on the Socio-Economic Conditions in the Old City of Jerusalem." Unpublished draft, the Jeruslem Project, Munk Centre for International Studies, University of Toronto, 2005. www.uwindsor.ca/joci/system/files/section1.pdf.

Greenberg, Joel. "Premier Palestinian Medical School Graduates Struggle to Work in Jerusa-lem." *Washington Post*, July 16, 2012. www.washingtonpost.com/world/middle_east/premier -palestinian-medical-school-graduates-struggle-to-work-in-jerusalem/2012/07/15/gJQAlzp DoW_story.html.

Hale, George. "The PA's Pitiable Strategy." *Daily Beast*, July 12, 2012. www.thedailybeast.com/ articles/2012/07/12/the-pa-s-pathetic-strategy.html.

Hasson, Nir. "Israel Sanctions East Jerusalem Family for Straddling Palestinian Border." *Ha'aretz*, September 27, 2011. www.haaretz.com/print-edition/news/israel-sanctions-east -jerusalem-family-forstraddling-palestinian-border-1.386897.

Hasson, Nir. "Jerusalem Official: Areas east of the fence not part of the city." *Ha'aretz*, January 8, 2010. www.haaretz.com/hasen/spages/1141313.html.

Hasson, Nir. "J'lem Police 'Waging War' on Secular Protests, Activists Say." *Ha'aretz*, February 23, 2010. www.haaretz.com/hasen/spages/1151398.html.

International Court of Justice. "Legal Consequences of the Construction of a Wall in the Oc-cupied Palestinian Territory, Advisory Opinion 2004," p. 136. www.icj-cij.org.

Ir Amim. "State of Affairs—Jerusalem 2008: Political Developments and Changes on the Ground." December 2008. http://eng.ir-amim.org.il/_Uploads/dbsAttachedFiles/Annual Report2008Eng(1).pdf.

International Court of Justice. "Legal Consequences of the Construction of a Wall in the Oc-cupied Palestinian Territory, Advisory Opinion of 9 July 2004." www.icjcij.org/docket/index .php?p1=3&p2=4&k=5a&case=131&code=mwp&p3=4.

Israeli Central Bureau of Statistics. Social Survey. www1.cbs.gov.il/reader/?MIval=cw_usr _view_SHTML&ID=576.

Jerusalem Institute for Israel Studies. *Jerusalem Statistical Yearbook*, 2011. http://jiis.org/.upload/ yearbook/10_11/C/shnaton%20C0111.pdf.

Jerusalem Institute for Israel Studies. "Sources of Population Growth in Jerusalem by Popula-tion Groups and Sub-Quarters." Table III//8, Jerusalem Statistical Yearbook, 2009. http://jiis .org/.upload/yearbook/10_11/C/shnaton%20C0111.pdf.

Kamel, Lorenzo. "Interview: A Day in the Life of a Jerusalem Refugee Camp Doctor." *+972Mag-azine.* December 28, 2011. http://972mag.com/interview-a-day-in-the-life-of-a-jerusalem -refugee-camp-doctor/31427/.

Khasan, Hilal. "Palestinian Resettlement in Lebanon: Behind the Debate." *Palestinian Refugee ResearchNET*, April 1994. www.arts.mcgill.ca/mepp/new_prrn/research/papers/khashan_9404 .htm.

Lein, Yehezkel, and Alon Cohen-Lifshitz. *Under the Guise of Security: Routing the Separation Barrier to Enable the Expansion of Israeli Settlements in the West Bank.* Bimkom and B'tselem, 2005. www.btselem.org/download/200512_under_the_guise_of_security_eng.pdf.

McCarthy, Rory. "Israel Is Annexing East Jerusalem Says EU." *Guardian,* March 7, 2009. www .guardian.co.uk/world/2009/mar/07/israelpalestine-eu-report-jerusalem.

"Most Jerusalemites Attend Haredi-Religious Schools." *Arutz Sheva,* May 25, 2009. www .israelnationalnews.com/News/Flash.aspx/165421#.T5VdWNkrLEE.

Oliel, Michelle. "Property Rights and Ownership in the Old City of Jerusalem." Jerusalem Old City Project Special Report, University of Windsor, 2006. www.uwindsor.ca/joci/ commissioned-studies.

Palestine Israel Ecumenical Forum, "Christians in the Holy Land Respond to Israeli Police Restrictions During Easter Celebrations." www.oikoumene.org/en/programmes/public -witness-addressing-power-affirming-peace/churches-in-the-middle-east/pief/news -events/a/browse/11/article/7313/christians-in-the-holy-la.html.

Palestinian Authority. *Pathway Toward a Palestinian Vision for 2005 and Beyond.* Palestinian National Authority Web site, 2001. www.pna.org.

Ramon, Amnon. *Christians and Christianity in Jerusalem.* Jerusalem: Jerusalem Institute for Israel Studies, 2011. Unpublished paper. http://jiis.org/?cmd=newse.444&act=read&id =780.

Sabel, R., "The International Court of Justice Decision on the Separation Barrier and the Green Line." 38 *Israel Law Review* 316 (2005).

Sanders, Edmund. "More Jews Praying on Site Also Sacred to Muslims." *Los Angeles Times,* October 27, 2012. www.latimes.com/news/nationworld/world/la-fg-jerusalem-prayers-20121028, 0,954464.story.

Seidemann, Daniel. "The Events Surrounding the Mugrabi Gate—2007: A Case Study." Jerusalem Old City Initiative, University of Windsor, June 2007. http://cronus.uwindsor.ca/units/ jerusalem/main.nsf/54ef3e94e5fe816e85256d6e0063d208/54709e03ea461c2f852571240054390b/ $FILE/Mugrabi%20-%20FINAL%5B1%5D.pdf.

Sharon, Jeremy. "Rabbis Warn Jews Against Going to Temple Mount." *Jerusalem Post,* March 6, 2012. www.jpost.com/Jewish World/JewishNews/Article.aspx?id=260681.

Shragai, Nadav. "Jerusalem, the Dangers of Division: An Alternative to Separation from the Arab Neighbourhoods." *Jerusalem Centre for Public Affairs,* n.d. www.jcpa.org/text/shragai_last2 .pdf.

Stein, Yael. "The Quiet Deportation: Revocation of Residency of East Jerusalem Palestinians." Joint report by HaMoked and B'Tselem (April 1997). www.hamoked.org/items/10200_eng .pdf.

The Association for Civil Rights in Israel. "The State of Human Rights in East Jerusalem 2009: Facts and Figures." May 2009. www.acri.org.il/en/2010/10/27/publications/.

The Association for Civil Rights in Israel and Ir Amim. *The East Jerusalem School System—Annual Status Report.* September 2011. www.ir-amim.org.il/Eng/?CategoryID=254.

UNESCO. "Dresden Is Deleted from UNESCO's World Heritage List." June 25, 2009. http:// whc.unesco.org/en/news/522/.

BIBLIOGRAPHY

UNESCO. "Jerusalem and the Implementation of 35 C/Resolution 49 and 185 Ex/Decision." Executive Board 186 EX/11, Item 11 of the Provisional Agenda, Paris, April 8, 2011. http://unesdoc.unesco.org/images/0019/001919/191953e.pdf.

UNESCO. "Oman's Arabian Oryx Sanctuary: First Site Ever to Be Deleted from UNESCO's World Heritage List." June 28, 2007. http://whc.unesco.org/en/news/362.

UNESCO. "Report of the Technical Mission to the Old City of Jerusalem." February 27–March 2, 2007. www.unesco.org/bpi/pdf/jerusalem_report_en.pdf.

UNESCO. World Heritage Centre, "Manual for Housing Maintenance and Rehabilitation, Action Plan for the Safeguarding of the Cultural Heritage of the Old City of Jerusalem," section 3:3 (2007). http://unesdoc.unesco.org/images/0015/001525/152539e.pdf.

UNGAOR. Ad Hoc Committee on Palestinian Question, "Future Government of Palestine." General Assembly Resolution A/RES/181(II), 2nd Sess. 1947. www.un.org/depts/dhl/resguide/r2.htm.

United Nations Convention on the Law of the Sea. Article 77, December 10, 1982. www.un.org/Depts/los/convention_agreements/convention_overview_convention.htm.

United States Department of State. "Israel and the Occupied Territories." *International Religious Freedom Report*, July-December 2010. www.state.gov/j/drl/rls/irf/2010_5/168266.htm.

UNOCHA. "East Jerusalem: Key Humanitarian Concerns" (March 2011). http://unispal.un.org/pdfs/OCHASpFocus_230311.pdf.

UNOCHA. "Special Focus: Barrier Update" (July 2011). www.ochaopt.org/documents/ocha_opt_barrier_update_july_2011_english.pdf.

UNOCHA. *Walled Horizons* (DVD). www.ochaopt.org/videos.aspx#.

UN Trusteeship Council. *Draft Statute for the City of Jerusalem*, UN TSCOR, 2d Sess., UN Doc. T/118/Rev.2 (1948), pp. 19–27.

Wilson, T. *Frontiers of Violence: Conflict and Identity in Ulster and Upper Silesia, 1918–1922.* Oxford: Oxford University Press, 2010.

Xinhua News Agency. "Jerusalem Mayor Intends to Contour City Border Along Security Barrier." *Xinhuanet,* December 23, 2011. http://news.xinhuanet.com/english/world/2011-12/23/c_131323390.htm.

OTHER REPORTS, STUDIES, VWW RESEARCH PAPERS

Abuzayda, Sufyan. "Continuity and Change in Israeli Policy Over Jerusalem Before and After the Establishment of the Israeli State." PhD diss., University of Exeter, 2005.

Abu-Lughod, Janet. "What Is Islamic About a City? Some Comparative Reflections." In *Urbanism in Islam: The Proceedings of the International Conference on Urbanism in Islam* 1. Tokyo, 1989.

Ahimeir, Ora. *Jerusalem—Aspects of Law.* Discussion paper no. 3. Jerusalem: Jerusalem Institute for Israel Studies, 1983.

Aronson, Geoffrey. "Olmert Divides Jerusalem." *Report on Israeli Settlement in the Occupied Territories.* Washington, DC: FMEP, 2006.

Assaf, Uni. "UNESCO Chief: We Are Trying to Mediate Over Mughrabi Gate." *Ha'aretz*, February 2, 2008.

Auga, Michele. "Divided Cities in Transition: Challenges Facing Jerusalem and Berlin." International Peace and Cooperation Center, 2005.

Awawdeh, Shaher. "Changing Pan-Islamic Perspectives on Palestine: The Internal Dynamics of the Organisation of the Islamic Conference, 1991–2004." PhD diss., University of Exeter, May 2006.

Be'er, Yizhar. *Targeting the Temple Mount: A Current Look at Threats to the Temple Mount by Extremist and Messianic Groups.* Center for the Protection of Democracy in Israel, Keshev, January 2001.

Brinn, David. "UNESCO Chief Pays a Visit—and a Compliment." *Jerusalem Post*, February 8, 2008.

Coon, Anthony. "Urban Planning Implications of Jerusalem Open City." Negotiations Support Unit, Ramallah. Unpublished MS, October, 2001.

Derfner, Larry. "Rattling the Cage: UNESCO Is Right, Israel Is Wrong." *Jerusalem Post*, October 11, 2010.

Eisenzweig, Tal D. "The Jerusalem Light Rail Train: A Bumpy Ride in an Ethnically Polarized City." Unpublished senior thesis presented to the Faculty of the Woodrow Wilson School of Public and International Affairs, April 3, 2012.

Friedman, Menachem. *The Haredi (Ultra-Othodox) Society: Sources, Trends and Processes.* Jerusalem: Jerusalem Institute for Israeli Studies, 1991.

Goldenberg, Suzanne. "The Street Was Covered with Blood and Bodies: The Dead and the Dying." *Guardian*, August 10, 2001.

Grunebaum, Gustave Von. "The Structure of the Muslim Town." *Memoir* 85. American Anthropological Association, 1955.

Hasson, Shlomo. *The Cultural Struggle Over Jerusalem.* Jerusalem: Floersheimer Institute for Policy Studies, 1996.

al-Haq, *Redrawing Occupied East Jerusalem.* Briefing paper, Ramallah, n.d.

Hutman, B. "Jerusalem Losing Best of Its Young People." *Jerusalem Post*, May 25, 1992.

Idara al-awqaf al-islamiyya al-'ama, bayan:al-awqaf al-islamiyya fi al-daf al-gharbiyya 1977–82. Jerusalem: Da'ira al-awqaf al-islamiyya, n.d.

International Crisis Group. "Squaring the Circle: Palestinian Security Reform Under Occupation." Middle East Report, no. 98, September 7, 2010.

International Peace and Cooperation Centre. *Jerusalem on the Map III.* Jerusalem: International Peace and Cooperation Centre, 2007.

Klein, Menachaem. "The Good and Bad News About Israel's 'Peace Index.'" *Ha'aretz*, May 23, 2012.

Koechler, Hans. *The Legal Aspects of the Palestine Problem with Special regard to the Question of Jerusalem.* Vienna: International Progress Organisation, 1981.

Laws of the State of Israel. Law and Administration Ordinance (Amendment No. 11) Law 5727/1967. *Laws of the State of Israel* 21 (1966/67): 75.

Laws of the State of Israel. Municipalities Ordinance (Amendment No. 6) Law, 5727/1967. *Laws of the State of Israel* 21 (1966/67): 75–76.

Laws of the State of Israel. Article 4, Legal and Administrative Matters (Regulation) Law (Consolidated Version), 5730–1970. *Laws of the State of Israel* 24 (1968/70): 144–283.

Lefkowitz, Etgar. "Eastern Temple Wall in Danger of Collapse." *Jerusalem Post,* May 19, 2004.

Maya, Choshen, and Israel Kimhi. "Migration to and from Jerusalem." *Jerusalem Institute for Israel Studies,* 1991.

Molaroni, Elena. Report of the Third Committee. "Right of Peoples to Self-determination: Draft Resolution III." The Right of the Palestinian People to Self-determination in UNGAOR. 61st Sess., UN Doc. A/61/442, 2006.

Old City of Jerusalem Revitalisation Programme. *Jerusalem: Heritage and Life: The Old City Revitalisation Plan.* Jerusalem: al-Sharq, 2004.

Palestinian Academic Society for the Study of International Affairs. *Documents on Jerusalem.* Jerusalem: PASSIA, 1996.

Palestinian Authority. *Palestinian Development Plan 1999–2003.* Ramallah, Palestinian Authority, 1999.

Palestinian Liberation Organization, Negotiations Affairs Department. *Israel's Wall.* Ramallah: Palestinian Liberation Organization, 2004.

Palestinian Liberation Organization Department of Refugee Affairs, *Comments on the Report "Prospects for Absorption of Returning Refugees in the West Bank and the Gaza Strip."* Ramallah: Palestinian Liberation Organization Department of Refugee Affairs, 2000.

Ramon, Amnon. "The Christian Element and the Jerusalem Question." *Background Papers for Policy Papers,* no. 4. Unofficially translated by the Society of St. Ives. Jerusalem: Jerusalem Institute for Israel Affairs, 1996.

Rempel, Terry. "The UN Relief and Works Agency (UNRWA) and a Durable Solution for Palestinian Refugees." Badil Information and Discussion Brief, no. 6 (2000).

Sabella, Bernard. "Palestinian Christians: Realities and Hopes." Unpublished MA, 1998, n.p.

Sayigh, Yezid. "Policing the People, Building the State: Authoritarian Transformation in the West Bank and Gaza." *Carnegie Middle East Center,* Carnegie Papers, February 2011.

Sayigh, Yezid. "'We Serve the People': Hamas Policing in Gaza." *Crown Center for Middle East Studies,* Crown Paper 5, Brandeis University, April 2011.

Tanmiya. "Schools in Jerusalem." *Quarterly Newsletter of Welfare Association* 73 (2006).

The Times Concise Atlas of the World. New York: Times, 2000.

Tsardanidis, Charalambos, and Asteris Huliaras. "Prospects for Absorption of Returning Refugees in the West Bank and the Gaza Strip." Unpublished MS. Athens: Institute of International Economic Relations, 1999.

UNGAOR. "Illegal Israeli Actions in Occupied East Jerusalem and the Rest of the Occupied Palestinian Territory." *General Assembly Resolution ES-10/13,* 10th Emergency Session, UN Doc. A/RES/ES/10–13, 2003.

UNGAOR. *Report of the Special Committee to Investigate Israeli Practices Affecting the Human Rights of the Palestinian People and Other Arabs of the Occupied Territories: Note by the Secretary-General.* 61st Sess., UN Doc. A/61/500, 2006.

BIBLIOGRAPHY

Welfare Association. "Jerusalem: Heritage and Life: The Old City Revitalisation Plan," pp. 105–9. Jerusalem: Welfare Association, 2004.

OTHER WEB SITES

Conseil international des monuments et des sites. www.icomos.org/index.php/en.

Council of Religious Institutions of the Holy Land. www.crihl.org.

International Centre for the Study of the Preservation and Restoration of Cultural Property. www.iccrom.org/.

Ir Amim. www.ir-amim.org.il/Eng/?CategoryID=271.

Old City Jerusalem Revitalisation Programme. http://ocjrp.welfare-association.org/en/project/what-we-do/core-restoration-programmes/jerusalem-projects/major-restoration-projects/islamic-museum.html.

Palestinian National Authority. www.pna.org.

UNESCO. www.unesco.org/new/en/.

UNISPAL. http://unispal.un.org/unispal.nsf/udc.htm.

INDEX

Abbas, Mahmud (Abu Mazen), 193

ABC (network), 155

Abdullah bin Hussein (school), 77

Absentee property, 65, 130–31

Absentee Property Law, 65

Absorptions, laws of, 277n20

Abu Dis (village), 26–27, 49, 77

Abu Mazen, *see* Abbas, Mahmud

Abu Mazen–Beilin Plan, 193

Abu Odeh, Adnan, 192, 197

Abu Sitta, Salman, 161

Abu Zahriya, 29

Acre, Israel, 2, 66, 78, 118

ACRI, *see* Association for Civil Rights in Israel

Advisory Opinion, OCJ, 52, 60

Aga Khan Award for Islamic Architecture, 120, 132, 135

Agence France Presse, 154

Aggression, walls of, 15

Ahimeir, Ora, 3

Alstrom, 176

American Academy of Arts, 63

Amirav, Moshe, 93, 95

Amman, 48, 111, 195

Anglicans, 112

Anglo-Irish peace agreement, 190

Annapolis summit, 12, 195

"Annex 04, Multinational Presence in al-Haram al-Sharif/Temple Mount Compound" (Geneva Initiative), 203

"Annex 05, Urban Challenges and Planning Proposals" (Geneva Initiative), 201, 202, 203

Annexation, 50, 118; East Jerusalem and, 60–66; hegemony of, 277n18

ANPRS, *see* Automatic number plate reading systems

Anti-Semitism, 215

Anti-Zionism, 62, 278n31

Aqabat al-Suwana (village), 47

Al-Aqsa Mosque, 8, 40, 97–98, 121, 185; March of Flags and, 138; Muslim community and, 117; renovation of, 120, 132

Al-Aqsa Museum, 144

Arab Spring, 214

Arafat, Yasser, 20, 22, 191, 193–94, 200, 300n84

Architectural Heritage Preservation Institute, 166

Architecture, 1, 89

'Ard al-Samar (village), 47

Area A, 21–22

Area B, 21

Area C, 21

Ari, Ben Michael, 144

Ariel (settlement bloc), 39

Armenian Catholic Church, 112

Armenian Orthodox Church, 112–13, 285n38

Armenian Quarter, 98, 133

Armistice Lines (1949), 6, 42, 45–48, 51, 161, 268n8; colonization and, 59; as educational border, 74; Jordan and, 45–46, 63; open city and, 194; reinstatement of, 275n7; Seam Zone and, 27; separation barrier and, 21–25, 27, 38, 219; sovereignty and, 223; territorial exchanges and, 52

Arnona (municipal tax), 28

Ascension, service of, 114

Ashkenazi Jews, 108

Associated Press, 154

Association for Civil Rights in Israel (ACRI), 79

Atara L'yoshna, 288n59

Ataret Cohanim, 288n59

At-Tur, *see* Mount of Olives

Augusta Victoria Hospital, 34, 184

Austrian Hospice Hospital, 133

Automatic number plate reading systems (ANPRS), 227

Autonomous zones, 105

'Ayn Karim (village), 47, 106

Al-Azariyya (village), 49, 132

Bab al-Silsilah (Chain Gate), 122

Bagrut (Israeli matriculation), 76

Ballot receptacles, 71

Banksy (graffiti artist), 34

Barak, Ehud, 22, 144, 193, 215

Barakat, Nir, 279n52

Barcelona process, 297n62

Barkan, Nir, 110

Barricade walls, 15

Basic Law (1980), 64, 174, 178

BBC, 154–55

Beilin, Yossi, 193, 200

Beirut, Lebanon, 8, 56, 58, 101, 186, 234; internal borders in, 88; Web sites on, 148, 150, 153

Beit Hanina (village), 31, 49, 132

Beit Jalah, 87

Belfast, Ireland, 8, 56–57, 186, 188, 190, 234; Catholic Republican enclaves, 57, 84; civil rights movement in, 84; Conflict in Cities project and, 4; housing in, 84; internal borders in, 88; Web sites on, 147–48, 153

Bell, John, 304n30

Benvenisti, Meron, 2, 46, 49

Berko, Reuven, 72

Berlin Declaration (1999), 297n64

Berlinquette, Roy, 304n28

Berlin Wall, 18, 214

Bethlehem, West Bank, 23, 36, 49, 77, 87

Bevingrad, 59

Big Three, 112–13

Bilal ibn Rabah Mosque, 165

Binational model, 214–22

Al-Birah, West Bank, 49

Bir Nabala, West Bank, 27, 29

Bollens, Scott, 14

Bombing, of Sbarro Pizzeria, 19–20, 23

Bonaparte, Napoleon, 2

Borders, 6–7, 12, 88, 203; disaggregation of, 16; of education, 6, 74; *eruv*, 105–6, 106, 107, 108–9, 111, 283n17; fluid, 233; functional, 93; globalization and, 15–16; invisible, 14; of Jerusalem, 39–53, 42, 50; visible, 10, 14; *see also* Hard borders; Scattered borders; Soft borders

Boycotts, of elections, 67, 72–73, 74

Breger, Marshall, 3, 299n82

British and French League of Nation Mandates, 170

British Mandate period (1922–1948), 5–6, 41–44, 47, 58

Brussels, Belgium, 8, 147, 150, 154, 186

B'Tselem (NGO), 90

Butcher's Row, *see* Suq al-Lahamiin

Cambodia, 294*n*36

Cambridge University, 4

Camp David summit (2000), 9, 12, 22, 190–95, 215; collapse of, 144; partial integration and, 217; territorial exchanges and, 274*n*83

Canadian Department of Foreign Affairs and International Trade, 197

Capitulation treaties, 158

Catholic Church, 112; *see also* Roman Catholic Church

Cave of the Patriarchs, 139, 144

CBS (network), 155

CCTV, *see* Closed-circuit television cameras

CEC, *see* Central Electoral Commission

Celebration of the Holy Fire, 114, 116

Cemeteries, 2

Center for Research and Information, 192

Center for Restoration of Islamic Manuscripts, 166

Central authority, 228

Central Electoral Commission (CEC), 70, 71

Centre for Jerusalem Studies, 81

CFSP, *see* Common Foreign and Security Policy

Chaim, Hafetz, 124

Chain Gate, *see* Bab al-Silsilah

Channel Four (news network), 155

Checkpoints, 6, 24, 36, *142*

Cheshin, Amir, 93

China, 155, 294*n*36

Christianity, 62, 99, 132; community of, 111–16; diaspora organizations and, 9; fundamentalist churches, 181; holy sites of, 2, 7, 114–15, 158–59; population and, 133, 284*n*28; *see also* *specific churches and denominations*

Christian Quarter, 125, 133

Christmas, 114

Church of the Holy Sepulchre, 2, 40, 112, 114, 158, 231

Church of the Nativity, 158

Citizenship, 26, 90–91

City of Collision (Misselwitz and Rieniets), 3

City of David (theme park), 129–30, 145

City of London Corporation, 105

Clan-based protection groups, 28–29

Clerical hierarchy, 17, 100

Clinton, Bill, 22, 190, 193

Clinton parameters, 108, 129, 194–95

Closed-circuit television cameras (CCTV), 126, 141

CNN (news network), 155

Cohanim (priests), 124

Cohen, Hillel, 77, 278*n*39

Cold war, 171

Colonization, 22, 131; Armistice Lines and, 59; of land and property, 53; policy of, 85

Commerce, 26

Commercial crime, 229

Commodification, of Islam, 137

Common Foreign and Security Policy (CFSP), 297*n*60

Community: Christian, 111–16; Jewish, 21, 105–11; Muslim, 116–22; *see also* International community

Conflict in Cities and the Contested State, 4–5, 15, 32, 147, 186, 234

Congress, 299*n*80

Control points, 226

Coon, Antony, 227

Cooperation, 217–18, 224

Coordination, 230

Coptic Catholics, 112

Coptic Orthodox Catholics, 112

Corpus separatum, 45, 47, 160, 177–78, 191

Council of Higher Education, 80–81

Council of Religious Institutions of the Holy Land, 102

Crime, 229

Croat-Serb-Bosniak federation, 8
Culture, 66–96, 233; education and, 74–82; elections in East Jerusalem and, 67–74, 70; structure and infrastructure, 82–96
Cust, L. G. A., 112
"Cyprus Avenue" (Morrison), 188

Dayan, Moshe, 117
"Days Like This" (Morrison), 188
Dead Sea, 146
Debray, Régis, 1
de Chastelain, John, 304n28
Declaration of Israeli Independence, 177
Declaration of Principles, 69
Delisting, 296n54
Denominations, 112–13
Department of Archaeology, 120
Department of Foreign Affairs and International Trade, 197
Department of Islamic Archaeology, 120
Department of the Revival of Tradition and the Islamic Sciences, 121
Diaspora organizations, 9
Dickens, Charles, 41
Disputed territory, 35
Divided cities, 187–88, 234
Dolphin, Ray, 34
Dome of the Rock, 40, 97, 116–17, 121, 185, 236
Donor contributions, 299n82
Draft Statute for Jerusalem, 191
Dresden Elbe Valley, 296n54
Dumper, Michael, 3, 11, 177
Dur al-hadith, 121
Dur al-qur'an, 121

Easter, 114, 116, 231
East Jerusalem, 5, 20, 47, 52, 59, 65, 118–19, 175–77; annexation and, 60–66; as disputed territory, 35; education in, 6, 74–82; elections in, 67–74, 70; EU in, 173; Islamic movement in, 137; Israeli settlers in, 143; JOCI and, 212; Orthodox Judaism in, 110;

Palestinians in, 24, 30, 33–36, 46, 111, 122, 185; PNA in, 133, 181–83; residency rights in, 26; Seam Zone and, 27; structure and infrastructure, 82–96; UNESCO and, 170; Waqf Administration in, 132, 184; see also Israeli occupation (1967)
EC, see European Community
Economic and Social Research Council, 4
Economic development, 224
Education, 60, 121, 279n42, 279n52; activities for, 100; borders of, 6, 74; in East Jerusalem, 6, 74–82; parallel system of, 16; segregation in, 6, 75, 78; separation barrier and, 33
Educational Bookshop, 277n24
El-Ad (settler group), 130
Eldad, Arieh, 144
Election Law (1995), 69
Elections, 60, 110; in East Jerusalem, 67–74, 70
Electricity distribution network, 92
Electronic media, 154
Éloge des frontières (Debray), 1
EMP, see Euro-Mediterranean Partnership
Enclaves, 11, 56–60, 89, 104, 226, 235; annexation and, 60–65; Catholic Republican, 57, 84; as controlled zones, 92; corpus separatum, 45, 47, 160, 177–78, 191; education and, 74–75, 77, 79–81; elections and, 69; identity and culture of, 66, 68–69, 73–74; Israeli occupation and, 16; as prisons, 17; Protestant Unionist, 57, 84; religious, 104–22; residential, 84
Engineering and Maintenance Department, 119
Eruv border, 105–6, 106, 107, 108–9, 111, 283n17
ESDP, see European Security and Defence Policy
Ethiopian Copts, 112
Ethnic cleansing, 235
Ethnic lines, 8
Ethnopolitical groups, 57
Etz Hayim, 167
EU, see European Union

EU-Israel Association Agreement, 176

Euro-Mediterranean Partnership (EMP), 172, 297*n*62

European Commission, 166

European Community (EC), 171, 173

European Security and Defence Policy (ESDP), 172, 297*n*60

European Union (EU), 9, 105, 156; Heads of Mission Report, 12, 174, 176, 276*n*10; international community and, 170–76; in Mostar, 234; Municipal Council and, 68; partial integration model of, 217; Schengen Agreement of, 16, 227–29

Evangelicals, 112

External factors, 9

Extremism, 102

Facebook, 150, *151, 152, 153*

Fada' il al-quds (merits of Jerusalem), 157

Fadlallah, Ayatollah, *88*

Faisal Husseini Foundation, 81, 184

Fatah, 198, 213

Federal arrangements, 105

Finance Office, 119

First Temple period, 164

Flexibility of urban form, 14

Fluid borders, 233

Foreign policy, 155, 171, 173–74, 297*n*60

Fox (network), 155

Fragmentation, 203

French Hill, 31

Functional borders, *93*

Functional interconnectedness, 217, 218

Functional internationalization, 192

Fungibility, 103

Galilee, Israel, 31, 39, 50, 63, 219

Garden of Gethsemane, 2, 114

Gaza Strip, 20–22, 38, 68, 218–19; as disputed territory, 35; education in, 75–76; PNA and, 268n2; refugees in, 13; Resolution 242 and, 201; settler movement in, 123

General Assembly, UN, 35, 45, 160, 172, 191

Geneva Initiative (Geneva Accords), 196–97, 199, 200–205, *204*, 223, 226

Geula (suburb), 109

Ghanem, As'ad, 216

Gilo (settlement), 87, 106

Giv'at Ze'ev (settlement), 6, 24

Glebe land, 100

Global City Index, 147

Globalization, 15–16

Global public discourse, 154

Golan Heights, 218

Goldstein, Baruch, 140

Google, 148

Governance Working Group (JOCI), 208

Great Powers, 158, 170

Greek Catholics, 112

Greek Leventis Foundation, 167

Greek Orthodox Church, 112, 115–16, 128, 159, 285*n*33, 285*n*38

Green Line (1949), *see* Armistice Lines

Guevara, Che, 34

Gulf War, 171

Gush Emunim (activist movement), 130

Gush Etzion (settlement), 6, 24, 39, 201

Hadassah Hospital, 47, 106

Hadawi, Sami, 43, 273*n*66

Haifa, Israel, 118

Al-Hakawati Theatre, 277*n*24

Halukka, 158

Hamas, 19–20, 22, 72, 198, 213; in Gaza Strip, 38; Islamic Jihad and, 36

HaMoked (NGO), 90

Al-Haram al-Ibrahim, 165

Haram al-Sharif, 2, 97, 202, 206, 231, 282*n*12; Muslim community and, 116–17; PNA in, 136; restoration projects in, 120, 185; settler movement in, 143–44; sovereignty in, 193–95, 200, 203; UNESCO in, 165–69; Waqf Administration in, 132

Hard borders, 16, 18, 19–53, 225; borders of
 Jerusalem and, 39–53, *42*, *50*; separation
 barrier as, 23–39; visible, 10, 14
Har Homa (settlement), *86*, 87, *87*, 106
Hashemite Madrasati Initiative, 81
"Has Israel Annexed Jerusalem?" (Lustick), 3
Hasmonean era, 157
Hassner, Ron, 103, 190
Heads of Mission Reports (EU), 12, 174, 176,
 276*n*10; Annex 2, 175
Health care, 34
Hebrew Ark of the Covenant, 282*n*12
Hebrew University, 46
Hebron, Palestine, 11, 104, 139, *140*, 143, 145
Hebronization, of Jerusalem, 138–45
Hebron Protocol, 139
Hegemony of annexation, 277*n*18
Heller, Mark, 192
Helms Amendment, 178
Hereford Mappa Mundi, 147
Heritage, 136, 163, 168
Heritage sites, 7
Herod's Temple, 40
High Court, 79
High Holy Days, 231
Hirsch, Moshe, 190
Hirst, Paul, 14
Hizbollah, *88*
Hoda al-Islam, 121
Holy Basin, 129, *130*, 194, 196, 206
Holy of the Holies, 143–44, 282*n*12
Holy sites, 7–8, 11, 197, 222, 229; activities in,
 100; of Christianity, 2, 7, 114–15, 158–59;
 defining, 202; extraterritorialization of,
 192; fluid borders and, 233; functional
 internationalization of, 191; Geneva Initia-
 tive and, 200, 202–3; Hebronization of
 Jerusalem and, 139; of Islam, 2, 40; Israeli
 settlers and, 122–31; JOCI and, 205, 208,
 211–12; Jordan and, 46; in Old City, 2, 96,
 99, 104, 196, 203; open city and, 223, 231–32;
 see also specific sites

Holy Sites Police Unit (HSPU), 231–32
Hot list, 227
Housen-Couriel, Deborah, 190
Housing, 133–34; segregation of, 8, 16, 83–84;
 shortages of, 30–31
Housing Ministry, 90
HSPU, *see* Holy Sites Police Unit
Hugo, Victor, 41
Human Rights Council, 176
Husseini, Faisal, 121, 136, 181–82, 300*n*84
Hutman, Bill, 93

Al-Ibrahimi Mosque, 139–41, *142*, 144
Ibrahimiya College, 70
ICCROM, *see* International Centre for the
 Study of the Preservation and Restoration
 of Cultural Property
ICJ, *see* International Court of Justice
ICOMOS, *see* International Council on
 Monuments and Sites
Identity, 66–96, 220, 233; cards, 26, 28–29, 34;
 education and, 74–82; elections in East
 Jerusalem and, 67–74, *70*; religious activi-
 ties and, 102; structure and infrastructure,
 82–96
Imam 'Ali, 99
Immigration, 83, 284*n*30
Impunity, 143
Indivisibility: of holy places, 103; problem of, 8
Indyk, Martin, 215
Infrastructure, 82–96
Institute of Islamic Archaeology, 81
Intelligence-led policing, 230
Internal walls, 16
International Centre for the Study of the
 Preservation and Restoration of Cultural
 Property (ICCROM), 294*n*34
International Committee of the Red Cross,
 161
International community, 146–56; EU and,
 170–76; international interest and, 156–59;
 joint sovereignty and, 160–70; other actors

of, 180–85; separation barrier and, 34–35;
U.S. and, 176–80
International Council on Monuments and
Sites (ICOMOS), 294*n*34
International Court of Justice (ICJ), 35, 52, 60
International interest, antecedents of, 156–59
International zone, 191
Internet, 155; *see also* Web sites
intractability, of disputes, 104
Invisible borders, 14
Ir Amim (NGO), 79
Irish Troubles, 84
Iron Age period, 164
Isaac Hall (Hebron), 140
Islam, 99, 122; commodification of, 137;
community of, 116–22; holy sites of, 2, 40;
Muslim Quarter, 123, 125–26, 128; studies
of, 100; Sufism, 100
Islamic Development Bank, 9, 183–84
Islamic Jihad, 36
Islamic movement, 136–38, 168–69
Islamic Museum, 166
Islamic resistance, 132–38
Islamization, 136–37
Israeli Antiquities Authority, 7, 120, 131
Israeli High Court of Justice, 24, 79
Israeli Jerusalem Municipality, 7
Israeli Ministry for Religious Affairs, 117
Israeli Ministry of Defense, 23, 118, 139
Israeli Ministry of Education, 74
Israeli Ministry of Foreign Affairs, 34, 178
Israeli Ministry of Interior, 91, 118, 288*n*61
Israeli National Insurance Institute, 26
Israeli occupation (1967), 5, 16–18, 48, 92, 104,
117; annexation and, 60–61, 64; education
and, 76; elections after, 67, 69; enclaving
and, 16; *eruv* border and, 108; EU and,
173; permanent residency and, 26; physi-
cal structure of, 86; resistance to, 132–38;
Resolution 242 and, 51; separation barrier
and, 34; UN and, 160
Israeli settlers, 122–31

Israeli state, 104–22; Christian communities
and, 111–16; Jewish communities and,
105–11; Muslim community and, 116–22
Israeli Supreme Court, 24
Israel Lands Administration, 125, 131
Israel Nature and Public Parks Protection
Authority, 130
Israel Palestinian Center for Research and
Information, 192
Israel Parks Authority, 131
ITN (news network), 155

Jabal al-Mukabbir (suburb), 86
Jado, Fuad, 29
Jaffa, Israel, 2, 66, 118
Jericho, West Bank, 78
Jerusalem : A City and Its Future (Breger and
Ahimeir), 3
Jerusalem Center for Public Affairs, 20
Jerusalem Embassy Act, 178
Jerusalem Institute for Israel Studies, 3, 114,
284*n*24
Jerusalem Light Rail Train project, 176
Jerusalem Old City Initiative (JOCI), 12, 193,
199, 205–12, 223, 225
Jerusalem Periphery District, 270*n*31
Jerusalem: The Contested City (Klein), 3
Jewish National Fund, 7, 125
Jewish Quarter, 98, 110, 200, 202, 210, 273*n*66;
Israeli settlers in, 122, 126; reconstruction
of, 3, 135, 166
Jewish Temple, 124
Jiryis, Sabri, 277*n*20
JOCI, *see* Jerusalem Old City Initiative
Joint sovereignty, 160–70
Jordan, 47–48, 64–65, 161; armistice agree-
ments and, 45–46, 63; matriculation in,
76–77; PLO and, 132; refugees in, 13; Waqf
Administration and, 133–34; West Bank
and, 268*n*8, 274*n*82
Jordanian Custodian of Enemy Property,
161

Jordanian Ministry of Waqfs and Religious
Affairs, 184
Jordanian-Palestinian curriculum, 6, 77–78
Judaism, 99, 180, 221; anti-Semitism, 215;
community of, 21, 105–11; diaspora organizations and, 9; education and, 75, 77; nationalism, 62; Orthodox, 31, 68, 98, 109–10;
population and, 46; residential zones, 61;
separation barrier and, 31; settlers, 42; *see
also* Jewish Quarter

Kaaba, 55
Khalidi, Walid, 191
Khan, Genghis, 282*n*12
Khanqah Salahiyya, 292*n*15
Khmer Temples, 294*n*36
Khomeini, Ayatollah, *88*
Kibbutzim (Jewish-only collective), 61
Kirkuk, Iraq, 8, 84
Kiryat Arba (settlement), 139
Kiryat Yovel (suburb), 109
Klein, Menachem, 3, 4, 16, 73, 306*n*46
Klugman Commission, 128, 288*n*60
Knesset, 64, 114, 178, 195
Kollek, Teddy, 20, 62, 93, 95

Land, 276*n*15; colonization of, 53; Glebe, 100;
no-man's land, 45, *46*; ownership of, 43, *44*,
286*n*49
Lands Administration, 131
Lapidoth, Ruth, 190–91
Law and Administration Ordinance Law, 65
Laws of absorption, 277*n*20
Lease Agreement (1989), 178
Legitimacy, 209
Light Rail Train project, 176
Light touch model, 209–10
Likud Party, 93, 123, 132
Linguistic lines, 8
List of World Heritage Sites in Danger, 165
Local council, *see Majlis*

Lupiansky, Uri, 110
Lustick, Ian, 3, 50, 63–65, 277*n*18
Lutherans, 112
Lydda, Israel, 66

Maale Adumim (settlement), 6, 24, 201
Maastricht Treaty, 171
Madrasa al-Kilaniyya, 167
Madrasa al-Muzhuriyya, 120
Madrasa Manjakiyya, 119
Madras Tankiziyya, 123
Madrid conference, 171–72
Magen David Adom, 29
Magharib quarter, 122, 165
Maghrabi Gate, 136; *see also* Mughrabi Gate
Ascent
Majlis (local council), 41
Al Makassed Hospital, 182
Makassed Islamic Charitable Hospital, 184
Malha (suburb), 106
Malley, Robert, 215
Ma'muniyyeh Intermediate School, 76
Mandela, Nelson, 18, 214
Mandelbaum Gate, 48
Manhattan, New York, 56
Manual for Housing Maintenance and Reha-
bilitation, 167
March of Flags, 138
Marcuse, Peter, 15
Mar Elias monastery, 114
Margalit, Meir, 94
Mar-Haim, Amos, 31
Maronites, 112
Marwani Halls, 290*n*83
Mashriq, 170
Al-Masri, Izzidine, 20, 23
Matriculation, 77
Mea She'arim (suburb), 48, 55, 105, 109, 159
Mecca, 55, 99, 100, 157
Media, 154–55
Medieval maps, 146–47

Mediterranean, 146

MENA, *see* Middle East and North Africa

Merits of Jerusalem, *see Fada' il al-quds*

Metropolitan ring, 85

Mevaseret Zion (suburb), 6

Middle East and North Africa (MENA), 170

Middle East studies, 100

Military coercion, 204

Miller, Aaron, 215

Mini-municipality model, 209, 211, 304*n*30

Misselwitz, Philipp, 3

Mitchell summit, 12

Mitzpayim (Jewish-only "look-out post"), 61

Mizrahi Jews, 108

Mobile frontier, 105

Money changers, 65, 277*n*21

Montreal, Canada, 8

Morrison, Van, 188, 190

Moshavim (Jewish-only collective), 61

Mostar, Bosnia and Herzegovina, 8, 56, 101, 186, 188, *189*; enclaving in, 58; EU in, 234; housing in, 84; internal borders in, *88*; Web sites on, 148, 153

Mount of Olives (At-Tur), 1–2, 129, 200, 235; settlements in, 85–86; tourism and, 114; view of Old City from, *17*

Mughrabi Gate Ascent, 168–69, 290*n*84

Multifaith plurality, 101

Municipal budget, 281*n*77; allocations of, 67, 92, *94*, 94–95; donor contributions and, 299*n*82

Municipal Council, 67–68, 78, 94, 110

Municipal Development and Lending Fund, 183

Municipal schools, 77–78

Municipal tax, *see Arnona*

Muqaddasi, 292*n*14

Al-Muqassed Hospital, 34

Musallem, Sami, 3

Museum of Tolerance, 168

Muslim community, 116–22

Muslim Quarter, 123, 125–26, 128

Nablus, West Bank, 78, 143

Napoleon Bonaparte, 2

Nationalism, 44, 61; education and, 82; Israeli, 82, 124; Jewish, 62; Palestinian, 8, 71, 76, 113, 198–99, 215

National Parks Authority, 7

Native Americans, 220

Nature and Public Parks Protection Authority, 130

NBC (network), 155

Negotiations Support Unit (PLO), 227

Neighborhood councils, 192

Netanyahu, Benjamin, 133

Neve Ya'akov (settlement), 31, 49

New City, 43, 48, 58, 84, 111, 159

News agencies, 154

NGOs, *see* Nongovernmental organizations

Nicosia, Cyprus, 8, 101, 186, 234

No-go areas, 15, 57–58

Nomadic societies, 282*n*12

No-man's land, 45, *46*

Non-fungibility, of holy places, 103

Nongovernmental organizations (NGOs), 9, 33, 79, 90–91, 134, 166

Nonpaper agreement, 193

Northern Irish peace movement, 188, 207

Norway, 172

NPR (network), 155

Nuseibeh, Sari, 192

OCA, *see* Old City Administration

Occupied cities, 187

Occupied Palestinian Territories (OPTs), 21–22, 26, 92, 176, 268*n*2; education in, 78, 81; elections in, 67

OCJRP, *see* Old City of Jerusalem Revitalisation Programme

Office of the Custodian of Absentee Property, 130–31

Office of the Presidency, 182

OIC, *see* Organization of Islamic Conferences

"Old and New Walls in Jerusalem" (Klein), 16

Old City, 5–6, *46*, 48, 66, 97–98, *140*, 195, 203, 204; Action Plan for, 166; architectural styles in, 1; bombings in, 22; Christian churches in, 114; Christian population in, 133; extraterritorialization of, 192; holy sites in, 2, 96, 99, 104, 196, 203; housing and renovation in, 134; Israeli settlers in, 123–26, *126*, *127*, 128–31; Jews in, 43, 45, 139; Jordan and, 46; Muslim community in, 118–22; Palestinians in, 143; refugees in, 48, 161; settlements in, 85; sovereignty in, 13; view from Mount of Olives, *17*; Welfare Association projects in, 134–35, *135*; World Heritage List and, 9, 165; *see also* Jerusalem Old City Initiative; Jewish Quarter; Muslim Quarter

Old City Administration (OCA), 206–7, 211

Old City of Jerusalem Revitalisation Programme (OCJRP), 135, 184

Olmert, Ehud, 95, 195

One-state model, 215–16

Open city, 223–24, 226, 231, 306*n*46

OPTs, *see* Occupied Palestinian Territories

Organization of Islamic Conferences (OIC), 155

Orient House, 71, 133

Orthodox Judaism, 31, 68, 98, 109–10

Oslo Accords (1993), 3, 13, 21, 77, 145, 221, 268*n*2; binational model and, 214; dual capital and, 193; Israeli settlers and, 124–25; PLC and, 69; PNA and, 133; Resolution 242 and, 51

Ottoman Empire, 39, 41, 158–59, 170, 293*n*21

Pahang River, 54

Pakistan, 274*n*82

Palestine Housing Council, 183

Palestine Liberation Organization (PLO), 11, 21–22, 71–73, 224; Hebron Protocol and, 139; Jordan and, 132; Negotiations Support Unit, 227; Orient House and, 20; separation barrier and, 34–35; Venice Declaration and, 171; in West Bank, 268*n*2

Palestine Red Crescent Maternity Hospital, 184

Palestinian Academic Society for the Study of International Affairs, 277*n*24

Palestinian Election Law (1995), 69

Palestinianization, 31

Palestinian Legislative Council (PLC), 69–70, 73

Palestinian Ministry of Education, 77

Palestinian Ministry of Education and Higher Education, 121, 182

Palestinian Musrara, 129

Palestinian Nakba (1948), 78

Palestinian National Administration, 132

Palestinian National Authority (PNA), 21, 136, 181–83, 198–99; bombing of, 20; Christian communities and, 113, 115–16; education and, 77–78; in Gaza Strip, 268*n*2; Hamas and, 22; nationalism and, 76; NGOs and, 134; Oslo Accords and, 133

Palestinian National Development Plan for 2011–2013, 182

Palestinian Red Crescent Society, 29

Palestinian resistance, 132–38

Palestinian Strategic Multi-Sector Development Plan for East Jerusalem, 182

Palestinian Supreme Muslim Council, 123

Parent-teacher associations, 78

Parks Authority, 131

Partial integration, 217

Partition Plan, UN, 45, 50–51, 63, 160

Past practice, 202

PBS (network), 155

Peace-keeping operation, 204

Peace negotiations, 12, 22, 34, 59–60, 94, 124, 190–96, 198; agreement and, 222–36; binational model and, 214–22; Geneva Initiative and, 196–97, 199, 200–205, 204, 223, 226; JOCI, 205–12; prospects and, 212–36

Permanent residency, 26, 63, 90–91

Peters, Francis, 100

Pisgat Ze'ev (settlement), 31, 36, 106, 201

PLC, see Palestinian Legislative Council

PLO, see Palestine Liberation Organization

Plurality, multifaith, 101

PNA, see Palestinian National Authority

Police, 28, 207, 229–32, 270n31

The Politics of Jerusalem Since 1967 (Dumper), 3, 177

The Politics of Sacred Space (Dumper), 11

Pool of Silwan, 292n14

Power: balance of, 213, 216; secular, 10; soft, 198; supply of, 92

Primary sources, 2–3

Princess Basma Center for Disabled Children, 184

Prison walls, 15

Private schools, 77

Private spaces, 131

Problem of indivisibility, 8

Property, 136–37; absentee, 65, 130–31; of Christian churches, 114; colonization of, 53; ownership of, 83

Protection groups, clan-based, 28–29

Protestants, 112, 190

Protestant Unionist enclaves, 57, 84

Public Law 104–105, U.S., 178

Pullan, Wendy, 4

Qalandya, West Bank, 28, 36, 161

Qalqiliya, West Bank, 23, 36

Al-Quds ("the holy"), 5

Al-Quds Committee of the Organization of the Islamic Conferences, 183

Al-Quds University, 80–81, 192, 280n58

Queen's University, 188

Rabbo, Yasser Abed, 200

Rabin, Yitzhak, 23

Rabinovich, Itamar, 215

Rabinowitch, Avraham, 93

Rachel's Tomb, 165

A-Ram (village), 26–27, 49

Ramadan, 231

Ramallah, West Bank, 33, 36, 77, 143, 162

Ramle, Israel, 66

Ramot (settlement), 105–6

Ras al-'Amud (village), 31, 47, 86, 114, 129

Rashidiyyeh School, 77

Recognised but unofficial schools, 79

Reconstruction and renovation, 125, 183–84; of al-Aqsa Mosque, 120, 132; of Jewish Quarter, 3, 135, 166; of Mostar, 8, 58; by Waqf Administration, 132; by Welfare Association, 129, 134–35, 135

Red Crescent Society, 29

Red lines, 232

Refugees, 13, 199, 219; education and, 77; in Old City, 48, 161; Oslo Accords and, 21; Shu'fat (refugee camp), 28, 31, 47, 77; warehousing and, 91–92

Refugee Task Force, 297n61

Regional Economic Development Working Group, 171

Reinforced monitoring mechanism, 12, 169

Reinforced Monitoring Report, 290n84, 296n52

"Reinventing Jerusalem" (Lustick), 3

Reiter, Yitzhak, 139

Religious enclaves, 104–22; Christian communities and, 111–16; Jewish communities and, 105–11; Muslim community and, 116–22

Religious lines, 8

Religious reclamation, 7

Religious sites, *see* Holy sites

Renovation, *see* Reconstruction and renovation

Resacralization, 7, 10

Residency rights, 26

Residential segregation, 8, 16, 83–84

Resistance, 132–38

Resolution 181 (Security Council), 174, 191

Resolution 242 (Security Council), 51, 161, 174, 194–96, 201, 208

Resolution 478 (Security Council), 298*n*74

Reunification, 275*n*6

Reuters (news agency), 154

Ricca, Simone, 3

Rieniets, Tim, 3

Rieter, Yitzhak, 3

Road system, 32–33, 83

Roberts, David, 123

Roman, Michael, 3

Roman Catholic Church, 112, 115, 190, 286*n*41

Roman period, 164

Roxman, Karen, 297*n*61

Russian immigrants, 284*n*30

Russian Orthodox Church, 115, 159

Rustow, Dankwort, 220–21

Sabbath, 109; *see also* Shabbat

Sadat, Anwar, 191

Sainz, Xavier, 18

Salah, Shaykh Ra'id, 136–37

Salah ed-Din, 157

Sarajevo, Bosnia and Herzegovina, 8

Saturation surveillance, 126

Sbarro Pizzeria, bombing of, 19–20, 23

Scattered borders, 14, 97–145; Hebronization of Jerusalem and, 138–45; holy places and, 122–31; Islamic resistance, 132–38; Israeli settlers and, 122–31; Israeli state and, 104–22; Palestinian resistance, 132–38; religious enclaves, 104–22

Scattered sovereignty, 192

Schengen Agreement, 16, 227–29

Schengen Information System (SIS), 228

Schneller, Otniel, 195

School of Architecture, Cambridge University, 4

School of Humanities, 81

School systems, 284*n*24

Scopus, Zion, 46, 48, 105

Seam Zone, 27

Secondary sources, 2–3

Second Intifada, 195

Second Temple period, 164

Second World War, 155

Sects, 112–13

Secular power, 10

Secular protests, 109

Security concerns, 222–29

Security Council, UN, 61, 160, 172, 210; Resolution 181 of, 174, 191; Resolution 242 of, 51, 161, 174, 194–96, 201, 208; Resolution 478 of, 298*n*74

Security framework, 207

Security zone, 224–25

Segregation: in education, 6, 75, 78; residential, 8, 16, 83–84

Seidemann, Danny, 36

Separation barrier (the Wall), 4–7, 10, 23–39, 85, 267*n*16; Armistice Lines and, 21–25, 27, 38, 219; benefits of, 35–36; education and, 33; housing shortages and, 30–31; as iconic monument, 35; identity cards and, 26, 28–29; international community and, 34–35; Jewish population and, 31; map of, 25; residency rights and, 26; roads and, 32–33; Seam Zone and, 27; "Through the Drainage Pipe" (mural), 37; West Bank and, 23–24, 26–28, 217, 219

Sephardi Jews, 108

Services, provision of, 92–95

Serviis (shared taxis), 33

Shabbat, 105–6; *see also* Sabbath

Shared taxis, *see Serviis*

Shari'a College, 121

Shari'a law, 117

Sharon, Ariel, 20, 195

Shaykh Jarrah (suburb), 48, 85, 129, 162, 273n66

Shaykh Sa'ad (suburb), 26

Sheltering walls, 15

Sher, Gilead, 215

Shu'fat (refugee camp), 28, 31, 47, 77

Silwan (village), 47, 85, 98, 114, 273n66; Pool of
    Silwan, 292n14; refugees in, 77

Sinai Peninsula, 218

Sinification policies, 294n36

Siniora, Hanna, 67

SIS, see Schengen Information System

Sky (news network), 155

Social networks, 151

Social welfare, 138, 161

Soft borders, 14, 16–18, 54–96, 225; annexation
    and, 60–66; identity and culture, 66–96

Soft power, 198

Solomonic era, 157

Sovereignty, 59, 68–70, 155–56, 180, 208–9;
    Armistice Lines and, 223; in Haram al-
    Sharif, 193–95, 200, 203; joint, 160–70; Old
    City and, 13; scattered, 192; state, 7, 11, 14,
    105; UNESCO and, 162

Soviet Union, 171, 173, 214

Stalin, Joseph, 155

Stari Most (bridge), 188

State Department, U.S., 178

State sovereignty, 7, 11, 14, 105

Status quo, 61, 232

The Status Quo in the Holy Places (Cust), 112–13

St. John's Hospice, 115, 128

St. John's Ophthalmic Hospital, 34, 184

St. John the Baptist Church, 167

St. Joseph Hospital, 184

Street of Chains, see Tariq Bab al-Silsilah

Structure, 82–96

Suez Canal, 159, 171

Sufism, 100

Suleiman the Lawgiver, 40

Supreme Muslim Council, 123

Suq al-Lahamiin (Butcher's Row), 66

Suq al-Qattanin, 167–68

Sur Bahir (village), 87

Surveillance, 126, 131

Svensson, Isak, 103

Syria, 13, 41, 161

Syrian Catholics, 112

Syrian Orthodox Catholics, 112

Taba summit, 12, 194, 197, 200, 217

Tahan River, 54

Tahbub, Shaykh Hassan, 118, 136

Talmudic law, 105–6

Tariq Bab al-Silsilah (the Street of Chains),
    122–23

Tawjiihi (Jordanian matriculation), 76–77

Tel Aviv, Israel, 24, 43, 109, 177–78, 180

Tembeling River, 54

Temple Mount, 2, 124, 143, 194–95, 206,
    282n12

Territorial exchanges, 52, 210, 223, 274n83

Terrorist attacks, 19–20, 36

Theophilus (patriarch), 116

Third Party, 192

Thomas, Mark, 34

"Through the Drainage Pipe" (mural), 37

Tibet, 294n36

Tomb of the Patriarchs, 165

Torat Cohanim, 288n59

The Torn City (Benvenisti), 2

Tourism, 114, 130

Track 2 discussions, 8, 217, 225

Treaty of Amsterdam, 227

The Triangle, 39, 50, 63, 136, 219, 271n39

Truce Supervision Organization, UN, 45, 160

Trusteeship Council, UN, 45

Tulkarm, West Bank, 23, 78

Tunnel network, 130

Two-state plus model, 222

UfM, see Union for the Mediterranean

UK Economic and Social Research Council, 4

Umm al-Fahm, Israel, 136

UN, *see* United Nations

UNESCO, 9, 121, 156, 162–70, 294*n*33; Action Plan, 166–67; Geneva Initiative and, 200; map of projects by, *167*; reinforced monitoring mechanism of, 137

UNHCR, *see* United Nations High Commissioner for Refugees

Unilateralism, 218–19

Union for the Mediterranean (UfM), 172

United Kingdom, 274*n*82

United Nations (UN), 3, 9, 11, 25, 44, 155–56, 191, 234; General Assembly, 35, 45, 160, 172, 191; joint sovereignty and, 160–61; Partition Plan, 45, 50–51, 63, 160; Roman Catholics and, 115; Truce Supervision Organization, 45, 160; Trusteeship Council, 45; *see also* Security Council

United Nations High Commissioner for Refugees (UNHCR), 91

United Nations Relief and Works Agency (UNRWA), 77–78, 156, 161–62, 184

United States (U.S.), 9, 11, 71, 156, 197, 234; EU and, 173; international community and, 176–80; PNA and, 21; Soviet Union and, 171

University of Windsor, 193, 206

UNOCHA, 24, 27–29

UNRWA, *see* United Nations Relief and Works Agency

Urban Conservation, 163

Urban functionality, 14

Urban settlements, 99

Urban walls, 15

U.S., *see* United States

'Uthman III (sultan), 159

Valley of the Cross, 114

Vandalism, 109

Vatican, 112

Venice Declaration (1980), 171

Veolia, 176

Vested interests, 105

Via Dolorosa, 125

Visible borders, 10, 14

Volney, Constantine, 157

Voter turnout, 71–72

Wadi Joz (suburb), 86

Wailing Wall, 40, 122, 200, 202–3, 206, 231–32

Waldron, Jeremy, 276*n*12

The Wall, *see* Separation barrier

Wall Opinion, 35

Waqf Administration, 132–34, 140, 168, 184, 287*n*53; Muslim community and, 117–21; schools and, 77–78, 80

Waqf Directorate of Education, 78

Warehousing, 91–92

War of 1948, 181

War of 1967, 160

Waters, Roger, 34

Web sites, 147–51, *149*, *150*

Weingrod, Alex, 3

Weizman, Eyal, 105

Welfare, social, 138, 161

Welfare Association, 128–29, 183, 285*n*38, 288*n*61; Architectural Heritage Preservation Institute and, 166; in Haram al-Sharif, 132; in Old City, 134–35, *135*

West Bank, 6, 20–22, 49, 68, 165; annexation and, 60, 64; as disputed territory, 35; education in, 75–76; Jordan and, 268*n*8, 274*n*82; PLO in, 268*n*2; refugees in, 13; Resolution 242 and, 51, 201; separation barrier and, 23–24, 26–28, 217, 219; settler movement in, 123, 130; *see also specific cities and villages*

Western Wall Foundation, 145

West Jerusalem, 6, 47–48, 109–10, 174, 226; bombing in, 19–20, 23; Jewish residential areas in, 273*n*66; Orthodox Judaism in, 110; Partition Plan and, 45; separation barrier and, 24; UNRWA and, 162; Zionists and, 84, 95

West Malaysia, 54

Windsor University, 193, 206

The Wire (TV series), 83

Women's College, 81

World Bank, 183

World Council of Churches, 156

World Heritage Center, 137, 163, 165, 169

World Heritage List, 9, 165, 169, 296n54

World news agencies, 154

World War II, 155

World Wide Web, 147–51, *149, 150*

Yerushalayim ("abode of peace"), 5

Yeshiva Birkat Avraham, 288n59

Young Israel Movement, 288n59

Yugoslavia, 8

Zionism, 53, 86, 96, 111, 134, 159, 215, 218–21, 233; annexation and, 61–62; anti-Zionism, 62, 278n31; East Jerusalem and, 75; international community and, 180–81; Oslo Accords and, 21; PNA and, 198; radical, 131; West Jerusalem and, 84, 95

Zoning policies, 86, 89